The Transition from Communism to the European Union

The Transition from Communism to the European Union

Restructuring Romanian Industry and Agriculture since 1990

David Turnock

Emeritus Professor of Geography,
University of Leicester

Edward Elgar
Cheltenham, UK • Northampton, MA, USA

Published by
Edward Elgar Publishing Limited
The Lypiatts
15 Lansdown Road
Cheltenham
Glos GL50 2JA
UK

Edward Elgar Publishing, Inc.
William Pratt House
9 Dewey Court
Northampton
Massachusetts 01060
USA

A catalogue record for this book
is available from the British Library

Library of Congress Control Number: 2008935943

PEFC/16-33-111
CATG-PEFC-052
www.pefc.org

ISBN 978 1 84064 046 5

Printed and bound in Great Britain by MPG Books Ltd, Bodmin, Cornwall

Contents

Abbreviations

bln	billion
dwt	tonnes deadweight
GW	gigawatt
h	hour
ha	hectare
j.v.	joint venture
km	kilometre
m	meter
MW	megawatt
MWh	megawatt hour
mln	million
n.a.	not available
pc	per capita
ptp	per thousand of the population
sq. km	square kilometre
t	tonne
tln	trillion
toe	tonnes oil equivalent
yoy	year on year
yr	year
AEC	Atomic Energy Company of Canada
APFO	Association of Private Forest Owners
APMSH	State Holdings Privatisation/ Management Agency (APAPS)
ARSA	Agency for Recovering State Assets (AVAS)
ASA	Agriculture Sector Adjustment
ATM	Automatic Teller Machine
AVC	Astra Wagon Works (Passenger)
BA	Banca Agricolă = Agricultural Bank (Raiffeisen)
BASF	Badische Analin und Soda Fabrik
BB	Broad Band
BBAG	Brau Beteilungs Aktiengesellschaft
BOOT	Build-Own-Operate-Transfer
BOT	Build-Operate-Transfer
BPO	Business-Process-Outsourcing

BR	Banca Românească
BT	Banca Transilvania
BTT	Youth Travel Agency
BTC	Baku-Tbilisi-Ceyhan Pipeline
Candu	Canadian Deuterium Uranium
CAP	Cooperative Farm
CC	County Council
CCCF	Railway Construction Company
CCHBC	Coca-Cola Hellenic Bottling Company
C&C	Cash & Carry
CCI	Chamber of Commerce & Industry
CCIA	Chamber of Commerce Industry & Agriculture
CCINA	Chamber of Commerce, Industry, Navigation & Agriculture
CDF	Comprehensive Development Framework (World Bank)
CDMA	Code Division Multiple Access
CEE	Central & Eastern Europe (including FSU)
CEFTA	Central European Free Trade Organisation
CFR	Căilor Ferate Romane (Romanian Railways)
CIS	Confederation of Independent States
CoE	Council of Europe
COST	Special Steel Works Târgovişte
CP	Conservative Party: PC (formerly Humanist Party: PU)
CTF	Compania de Transport Feroviar
CUASC	Council of State and Cooperative Farms
DAMA	Demand Assignment Multiple Access
DCR	Democratic Convention of Romania (CDR)
DECT	Digital Enhanced Cordless Telecommunications
DMHI	Daewoo Mangalia Heavy Industries
DP	Democratic Party: PD (now Liberal Democratic Party: PD-L)
DTA	Direct to Home
DUHR	Democratic Union of Hungarians of Romania (UDMR)
EADS	European Aeronautic Defence & Space System
EBRD	European Bank for Regional Development
ECE	East Central Europe
ECECs	East Central European Countries
EGR	European Goldfields Romania
EIB	European Investment Bank
EMBO	Employee-Management Buy-Out
ENGO	Environmental NGO

EU	European Union
FAO	Food & Agriculture Organisation
FDI	Foreign Direct Investment
FIC	Foreign Investors' Council
FMCG	Fast-Moving Consumer Goods
FME	Functional Market Economy
FPSME	Foundation for the Privatisation of SMEs
FSU	Former Soviet Union
FTPD	Fund for Tourism Promotion & Development
GEC	General Electric Company
GECC	General Electric Capital Corporation
GDP	Gross Domestic Product
GFR	Romanian Railway Group
GM	General Motors
GRP	Greater Romania Party (PRM)
GSM	Global System of Mobile Communications
IAR	Romanian Aviation Industry
IAS	Intreprinderi Agricole de Stat (state farms)
IBRD	International Bank for Reconstruction & Development
ICA	Inter-Country Adoption
ICC	International Criminal Court
IFC	International Finance Corporation
IFI	International Financial Institutions
IMF	International Monetary Fund
IMGB	Heavy Machine Works Bucharest
IRMV	Institute of Road Motor Vehicles
ISDN	Integrated Services Digital Network
ISO	International Standards Organisation
ISP	Internet Service Provider
ISPA	Instrument for Structural Policies for Pre-Accession Aid
IT	Information Technology
ITC	Information Technology & Communications
JBIC	Japanese Bank for International Cooperation
JIT	Just in Time
JTA	Justice & Truth Alliance
KPO	Knowledge-Process-Outsourcing
LD	Linz-Donawitz Furnace
LDP	Liberal Democratic Party: PD-L (formerly PD)
LFA	Less-Favoured Area

LNM	Lakshmi Niwas Mittal (Galați steelworks owner)
LPG	Liquid Petroleum Gas
MAN	Maschinenbau Augsburg-Nürnberg
MHPP	Micro Hydro Power Plant
MIG	Minimum Income Guarantee
MIT	Moody International Trading
MLSP	Ministry of Labour & Social Protection (MMPS)
MLT	Michailides Leaf Tobacco
MTS	Machine Tractor Station (SMT)
MPWTH	Ministry of Public Works Transport & Housing
MWFEP	Ministry of Waters Forests & Environml.Protection (MAPPE)
NAAC	National Agency for Agricultural Consultation (ANCA)
NACR	National Authority for Communications Regulation (ANRC)
NAE	National Agency for Employment (ANE)
NAP	National Agency for Privatisation (ANP)
NARET	National Assoc. for Rural & Ecological Tourism ('Antrec')
NAT	National Agency for Tourism (ANT)
NATO	North Atlantic Treaty Organisation
NBR	National Bank of Romania (BNR)
NDA	National Dwellings Agency (AND)
NFA	National Forest Administration (ANP/'Romsilva')
NGN	Next Generation Network
NGO	Non-Governmental Organisation
NLIC	National Land Improvement Company (CNAP)
NLP	National Liberal Party (PNL)
NP	National Park
NPA	National Privatisation Agency (ANP)
NPARD	National Plan for Agriculture & Rural Development
NPC	National Pitcoal Company ('Huilei Petroşani')
NPCDP	National Peasants' Christian Democrat Party: PNTCD
NSF	National Salvation Front (FSN)
NTFP	Non-Timber Forest Products
NTO	National Tourist Office ('ONT Carpați')
NWC	National Water Company (CNA)
OACT	Office of Authorisation & Control for Tourism
OECD	Organisation for Economic Cooperation & Development
OJT	County Tourist Office
ONLC	Oltenia National Lignite Company ('Lignit')
OSCE	Organisation for Security & Cooperation in Europe

OTE	Greek Telecom
Phare	Poland-Hungary: Actions for Economic Reconstruction
PCC	Precision Castparts Corporation
PCDP	Popular Christian Democrat Party: PPCD (now NPCDP)
PFI	Publicly Funded Investment
PPPt	Public-Private Partnership
PPPy	Purchasing Power Parity
PR	Posta Romană
PRNU	Party of Romanian National Unity (PUNR)
PSAL	Public Sector Adjustment Loan
PSD	Party of Social Democracy
PSDR	Party of Social Democracy of Romania (PSDR)
PVC	Polyvinyl Chloride
RABE	Romanian Association of Building Entrepreneurs
RAFI	Romanian Agency for Foreign Investment (ARIS)
RAIF	Romanian-American Investments Fund
RCB	Romanian Commercial Bank (BCR)
RCS	Romanian Cable Systems
RBR	Risk Bonus Reduction
R&D	Research & Development
RDA	Regional Development Agency (ADR)
RDB	Romanian Development Bank (BRD)
RDS	Romanian Data Systems
RERP	Regional Environmental Reconstruction Programme
PET	Polyethylene Terephtalate
RICOP	Industrial Restructuring & Professional Reconversion Progm.
RO	Autonomous National Company ('regie autonome')
ROL	Romanian Lei (the new 'heavy lei' = 10,000 old lei)
Ro-La	Rollende Landstrasse (for container transport)
Romag	Romanian Heavy Water Administration
RSB	Romanian Savings Bank (CEC)
RT	Romtelecom
RTV	Romania Television (TVR)
SAAF	Societatea de Administratare Active Feroviare
SAPARD	Special Action Programme for Agriculture & Rural Develpt.
SCR	Serviciile Comerciale Romane (Romanian Comm.Services)
SECI	South East Europe Cooperation Initiative
SEE	South East Europe
SEECs	South East European Countries

SEECI	South East Europe Cooperation Initiative
SIF	State Investment Fund
SMEs	Small & Medium-Sized Enterprises
SNCFR	State Railway (Societatea Naţională a Cailor Ferate Române)
SOE	State-Owned Enterprise
SOF	State Ownership Fund
SPAR	Societatea Proiectului Agricol Român
SUV	Sport Utility Vehicle
TB	Tuberculosis
TIW	Telesystem International Wireless
TLEA	Turism Litoral Employers' Association
TNC	Trans-National Company
TPO	Tourist Promotion Office
TR	Romanian Tobacco (Tutun Românesc)
TRACECA	Transport Central Europe-Central Asia
TV	Television
UCMR	Machine-Building Works, Reşiţa
UCTE	Union for the Coordination of the Transport of Energy
UEA	Underground Economic Activity
UK	United Kingdom
UN	United Nations
UNCTAD	United Nations Conference on Trade & Development
UNECE	United Nations Economic Commission for Europe
UNESCO	United Nations Educational Scientific & Cultural Organisatn.
USA	United States of America
USAID	United States Agency for International Development
USTDA	United States Trade & Development Agency
VAT	Value Added Tax
VFR	Visiting Friends & Relatives
WLL	Wireless Local Loop
WMD	Weapons of Mass Destruction
WTO	World Trade Organization
WTmO	World Tourism Organization
ZTE	Zhongxing Telecommunications Equipment Corporation
3G	Third Generation (telecomms)

Preface

This book has been compiled somewhat painfully over virtually a whole decade after it became clear that economic restructuring was going to be a radical and traumatic exercise. Following the sudden and unexpected revolution in December 1989, when Ceauşescu's seemingly iron grip was released by spontaneous defiance in Timişoara and Bucharest, it seemed that the Salvation Front intended to proceed very much with 'business as usual'. History seemed set to repeat itself with the new president (Ion Iliescu) taking a conservative approach by winning popularity for cancelling the most hated laws of old regime while refusing to 'sell the country' to foreign investors and relying on the Jiu Valley miners to intervene in Bucharest against more radical reforms championed politically by the first post-communist prime minister Petre Roman. Although Iliescu stayed in power until the beginning of 1997 – and then regained office in 2001 for a further four years – he was eventually forced to concede that a 'third way' between the capitalism of a neoliberal EU and the orthodox communism of the pre-Gorbachev era was impossible. And while reform was extremely tentative in the early years – justified by the Romanians' desire for 'peace and quiet' after their buffeting by Ceauşescu's excesses (increasingly aberrational in the 1980s) – the direction of change eventually became unmistakable.

Uneasy compromise was swept away in the elections of December 1997 and while the resulting centre-right coalition suffered greatly from inexperience, factional struggles and a hostile environment (both within the Romanian establishment and the wider world of the Balkans and CIS) it made overdue changes and committed Romania unambiguously to the EU project that was sufficiently compelling by 2001 to command the support of the erstwhile conservatives of the Party of Social Democracy (PSD) who were now returned to power. And it was doubly fortunate that the unexpected defeat of Adrian Năstase (prime minister during 2001/4) in the presidential election run-off at the hands of the charismatic centrist Traian Băsescu (leader of the Democratic Party: a coalition partner during 1997/2000 and heir to the Roman reformist politics of the Salvation Front era) should then inspire a realignment of finely-balanced parliamentary forces and deny PSD a further term of office, along with the likely persistence of corruption with which the Năstase premiership had been justifiably tainted. Instead the centrist government of Popescu Tăriceanu did enough to raise standards in public life (with vigorous attention to the criminal justice system) and stimulate the economy (continuously in growth since 2000) to satisfy critics in Brussels to clear the way for EU accession in January 2007.

This book was conceived as an in-depth review of a radical reform project that emerged out of the early years of ambivalence and uncertainty to follow a 'road' every bit as rough and unpredictable as the country's basic transport system is regularly (though somewhat unfairly) portrayed. Setbacks have been frequent and quite bitter in the case of the initial denial of NATO membership in 1997 after the government had staked 'everything' to achieve a favourable outcome. Dealings with the IMF have produced a sort of 'merry go round' where the desired facilities have been compromised by failure to meet the stringent conditions required (although one programme was successfully concluded in 2001). However the Romanian electorate, while certainly polarised between the strongly rural and conservative east and a progressive urban middle class prominent in Bucharest and the Transylvanian metropoles, has not moved far from the centre ground despite the negative campaigning of the nationalist parties while government had avoided major economic crises comparable with the Bulgarian 'melt-down' of 1997.

It is a happy coincidence that publication of this book should broadly coincide with EU membership that may be seen as a fitting conclusion to a specific 'transition' phase. This was certainly not intended at the outset but has arisen from the time taken to collect and digest material built up from notes and impressions related to my basic research (geared to various rural and historical themes which have of course demanded a great deal of my time in themselves). From 1997 until 2003 I have followed the Romanian Business Journal and since then I have made increasing use of the Internet including daily briefings from 'Evenimentul Zilei', 'Ziarul Financiar' and the Foreign Investors' Council. Each chapter has necessarily evolved as successive phases of consolidation and reassessments to keep pace with the unceasing flow of current affairs. And when the length of the book became too great for Edward Elgar to contemplate it was necessary to separate out much of the contextual material, published separately by Ashgate in 2007 as a companion volume with a broader economic history focus with the title 'Aspects of Independent Romania's Economic History with Particular Reference to Transition for EU Accession', while chapters on various aspects of the tertiary sector have also been removed to provide the basis for a future project. This radical restructuring took a lot of time during 2005–7 although I feel there is a positive outcome in avoiding overlaps and creating works of conventional length that have their complementary interests. This work therefore covers the 'nuts and bolts' of restructuring, with a focus on selected industrial sectors along with energy and agriculture, as opposed to longer-term historical perspectives of the Ashgate volume, including some coverage of the vastly enlarged service industries. Especially with these latest 'twists' in mind I would like to express my thanks to the publishing staff (Edward Elgar, Alex Minton, Jenny Wilcox and Elizabeth Clack) for their patience and understanding.

By way of a few practical details I should acknowledge that I have not set out to reference every detail noted in the proverbial 'thousand and one' media notes from which the book has been built up and citations generally refer to the substantive literature on which the bibliography is based. Furthermore the references to EU 'Country Reports' – annual reviews (often highly critical) of Romania's progress in meeting the conditions required for accession – are available on the Internet <www.europa.eu.int/comm/enlargement/index/htm> and are not included in the bibliography. Other matters concern first, the introduction of the new 'heavy' leu or ROL (each worth 10,000 of the old) which came fully into force in 2007 after a transition period. All lei values relate to the new currency unless stated otherwise. Second, Ceauşescu's tinkering with placenames by adding the Roman names to two cities – producing Cluj-Napoca and Drobeta-Turnu Severin – is acknowledged in the first mention of these places in each chapter but is not repeated throughout. Third, Romanian names for organisations e.g. ministries, agencies and NGOs are anglicised along with the names of businesses (e.g. the leading banks) that are frequently used (with the Romanian names or acronyms in brackets in the list of abbreviations). But the names (or acronyms) of other businesses are given in Romanian with some English translation. And fourth, for the sake of simplicity the present Yugoslav successor states (including Kosovo and Montenegro) are used retrospectively for the whole post-communist period: hence the references throughout to Serbia rather than the (smaller) Yugoslavia or Serbia & Montenegro. Finally, all $ references relate to US dollars.

I am greatly indebted to people who have helped in various ways with the project, notably many friends in Romania including Ioan Ianoş and Dan Platon for statistical data and the late Nicolae Muică for some elusive pieces of literature. My sincere thanks also go to Ruth Pollington for drawing all the maps (some of them produced specially for this publication). And finally I must express great appreciation for the patience and support of my wife Marion who has made numerous contributions, most of all through preparation of the camera-ready copy for this book after other arrangements failed to materialise.

David Turnock, June 2008

1. The Political Context: A Chronological Review

Romania's transition has been difficult on account of the radical approaches taken under communism and the absence of any significant reform before the revolution. A period of calm reflection was certainly needed but tension quickly emerged between conservatives, striving to defend their privileged positions and seeking only an escape from the worst excesses of the communist programme, and reformers keen to embrace the European project. Government has alternated between the relatively conservative (initially neo-communist) centre-left administrations of 1990–96 and 2001–4 (running in parallel with the two phases of the Iliescu presidency) and their radically reformist counterparts of 1997–2000 and 2005 onwards – the first under President Emil Constantinescu and the second under President Traian Băsescu. It is not just a question of ideas and approaches, for the conservative phases have been marred by corruption linked with elements of the former communist *nomenklatura*, while the reformist governments have been less tainted by corruption but have nevertheless struggled without conspicuous success to censure previous wrongdoing. A concluding note therefore considers the progress made by Romanian democracy in the light of the alternation between what some see as corrupt centre-left governments and more enlightened democratic, reformist centre-right coalitions, despite the eventual consensus over EU accession.

GOVERNMENT AND CIVIL SOCIETY

The First Iliescu Presidency, 1990–96

The revolution – seen not only as a spontaneous uprising but also as an internal communist coup – occurred very suddenly after demonstrations in Timişoara in December 1989 when Hungarians and Romanians combined to oppose the expulsion of a Hungarian priest, Lászlo Tőkés, to a rural parish. Siani-Davis (2005) rejects the myths of an all-powerful Securitate (albeit subordinate to Ceauşescu and not the government) and credits the 'anonymous masses' of the factories and football grounds for the decisive actions across the country after the Hungarian Reformed Church unwittingly provided the catalyst. Distracted to some extent by a state visit to Iran, President Ceauşescu lost the initiative when he was heckled on his return at a party rally in Bucharest some days later.

Instead of supporting the communist authorities, the army arrested and executed the Ceauşescus (although on the orders of the provisional government) as they fled Bucharest in the direction of Sibiu. In the ensuing chaos – giving rise to largely unpremeditated violence – former communists led by Ion Iliescu moved quickly to dominate the National Salvation Front (NSF) and thereby generated speculation – that still remains unsubstantiated – that regime change had been prepared (possibly with some external assistance) by disillusioned communist elements. The provisional government disbanded the communist party, repealed the most unpopular of Ceauşescu's laws and abandoned the highly controversial 'sistematizare'programme for rural settlement, while the general state of instability (rather than any alleged Securitate rearguard action) ensured that the transition would be tarnished by civil and social unrest; for, apart from Yugoslavia, Romania was the only country in the bloc where the collapse of communism led to violence. Iliescu then exploited the 1989–90 power vacuum within the fragile emerging civil society when the intellectuals – as 'privileged tools of the state [standing] aloof from the grievances of the peasants and workers' (Carey 2004b, p.586) and lacking any credibility through dissidence or 'samizdat' (underground literature) – could in no way claim to have been safeguarding the conscience of the nation.

The Salvation Front and the Constitution

The NSF successfully turned itself into a political party to shelter former communists (including the Securitate) and policy was driven by their vested interests in evading responsibility for past excesses – by keeping a firm grip on security files and indeed the whole judicial system – and claiming a disproportionate share of the fruits of economic restructuring and privatisation. Meanwhile, although the army supported an initially diverse non-Securitate coalition in December 1989 it acceded to a weak position in the new order compared with the intelligence agencies emerging out of the former Securitate. The bureaucracy saw Iliescu as a potential protector (Mungiu 1996, p.349), while the party also gathered an effective constituency among the managers and workers of the state sector who had most to fear from the introduction of market reforms. This ensured that an end to central planning and toleration of private enterprise would go hand in hand with state subventions for state-owned enterprises (SOEs) and a very gradual dismantling of price controls that prevented a 'level playing field' for all forms of business.

Reform followed a conventional pattern: a parliamentary republic and a new constitution (approved by parliament and endorsed by referendum in 1991) providing for a bicameral parliament with a Senate (140 seats) and Chamber of Deputies (345) elected from 41 multi-member constituencies. There remain problems of overlap between the two chambers and also between the offices of president and prime minister. However, the 'mimicking' of western institutions went along with a powerful commitment to continued central control by a regime widely seen as neo-communist (Dăianu 2001). The NSF was confirmed in power by the 1990 elections, thanks to firm control of rural areas in Moldavia and Wallachia. There was some intimidation, with the aid of state television, in consequence of which 'voting for the NSF appeared as the only alternative to a slide into anarchy' (Tismaneanu 1993, p.341). The new government sought stability after the trauma of the later Ceauşescu years, marked by the most severe austerity combined with extravagant and socially disruptive public works. But it seemed as though Ceauşescu's heavy-handed suppression of any reformist tendencies made for 'a stricter trade-off between moral credibility and experience for the post-1989 nascent political elite' with gradual replacement of top communists in a distinctly 'belated replica of the negotiated transition which Hungary witnessed several years earlier' (Pop-Eleches 1999, p.147). There was certainly an initial preference for a populist–authoritarian approach rather than the western/EU agenda for civil society and sustainable development. King Mihai, living in exile, made a visit over Easter 1992 but had no early impact: the government was anxious to keep him at arm's length while other parties were nervous about compromising their commitment to the republic.

Gradualism. Romania was faced with a 'quintuple transition: building from scratch political, civil and economic societies; developing an autonomous – yet accountable – state bureaucracy and all the while constraining these aforementioned areas through the development of the rule of law and an independent judicial system to enforce the equal rights of Romania's citizenry' (Carey and Eisterhold 2004, p.4). But the result was a transition marked economically and socially by extreme 'gradualism'. Political life was 'dominated by politicians who were socialised by the Communist Youth Organisation, in which convictions were overshadowed by the desire for personal enrichment and advancement, creating an ideal political culture of patrimonialism, personalism and corruption' (Carey 2004, p.580). Only from such an extreme vantage point could elderly liberal octogenarians with pre-war political records be castigated as being 'out of touch' for advocating a constitutional and accountable form of government. President Iliescu has been portrayed as a man who despised his tyrannical predecessor yet saw no need for urgent economic reform or the adoption of liberal western-style democratic values. He commended himself well through modesty and a certain degree of affability along with resilience, although he was ambivalent towards the USA and preferred a secret treaty with Moscow in 1991 pledging resistance to any alliance detrimental to the USSR. But with the state guiding the transformation process, the absence of an enlightened, reform-oriented faction within the party made for 'a lack of political credibility at the highest levels' (Jackson 1995, p.576). Hence the crypto-communist regime of 1990–91 and the eventual split between the president and Prime Minister Petru Roman in 1991, after a long period of struggle between conservative and progressive movements (Beck 1991b, 1993).

Struggle for Democracy. As early as May–June 1990, anti-government elements were camped in University Square to express 'disgust with the still repressive and exclusive Romanian politics' (Duran 2000, p.21) and demand liberal democracy and the removal of apparatchiks. Iliescu demonstrated his authoritarian credentials by dismissing the protesters as 'golani' (hooligans) and thereby echoed one of Ceauşescu's jibes. The sit-in then ended with the arrival of Jiu Valley miners in June. This was the first of a series of such interventions that continued with the removal of the Roman government in 1991 (replaced by Theodor Stolojan) and the subsequent break-up of the Iliescu–Roman alliance – the heart of the NSF – after the 1992 local elections precipitated a separation into 'soft-liners' (forming the new Democratic Party: DP) and 'hard-liners' who formed a Democratic National Salvation Front in 1992 and then merged with four smaller leftist parties to form the Party of Social Democracy of Romania (PSDR). After his removal Roman initially continued to lead the NSF's reformist wing and was confident enough to promise late in 1991 that no former communist party activist would be adopted by the party for the 1992 parliamentary election. But after a poor showing in the preceding local elections (when the NSF vote fell from 65 to 33 per cent, retaining support in rural areas while the opposition took the cities) he evidently concluded that a separate party was needed to project his platform of economic liberalisation if not political pluralism. Indeed, even Iliescu was forced into political manoeuvres to divert the wrath of the miners appalled at the sudden collapse in the party's fortunes. Meanwhile, some Transylvanian Romanians, alarmed at the accommodations being made to the Hungarian minority, had formed a 'homeland' movement ('Vatra Românească') that quickly gave rise to a nationalist Party of Romanian National Unity (PRNU) in 1992. Reflecting a traditional dichotomy of 'autochthonists' and 'westernisers' (Iordache and Trencsenyi 2003), 'protochronism' – projecting the originality of Romanian culture as a justification for isolationism (supported by many Orthodox priests) – was set up in opposition to synchronism and the 'spirit of Europe' (Marga 1993, p.21).

Such an outlook was a hangover from communism to excuse dictatorship and economic failure on the grounds that Romania's destiny ran counter to socialist integration. The Greater Romania Party (GRP), supported by a successful newspaper and the conservative wing of the NSF, also argued for protection by an interventionist system to support a centralised economy (through subsidies and social benefits) and counter perceived risks of subversion on the part of some ethnic minorities and neighbouring governments. In 1992, the protochronism of Ilie Bădescu and the 'Movement for Romania' seemed reminiscent of the Legionary/Iron Guard Movement of the 1930s and equivalent to the 'propaganda mythology of Ceauşescu's providential role in the country's history' (Tismaneanu and Pavel 1994, p.405). At a time when the NSF was making 'promises everywhere', nationalism had to be exploited as a cover for economic failures. Snyder and Vachudova (1997) placed Romania in a group with Bulgaria and Slovakia where – in the absence of dissident groups – former communists could launch nationalist attacks on large ethnic minorities to establish legitimacy and consolidate support during difficult economic times. As vicious circles poisoned political debate further, 'ethnic minorities [were] further radicalised and populations misinformed about the causes of economic pain' (ibid p.32). The support of the nationalist parties (and the small Socialist Labour Party) was needed to sustain the government under Nicolae Văcăroiu, with no prior political affiliations, after the 1992 elections when PSDR suffered a sharp setback, partly a reflection of concern over the prominence of former communists. The nationalists were against significant privatisation involving foreign capital, as well as concessions to the ethnic minorities, so reformist pressures were contained. However, Gallagher (1995, p.131) argues that if the government had fallen there would have been advantages for PSDR arising from a weak government by the opposition while the tarnishing of Iliescu's international reputation (through courting the nationalists) would have been avoided. However, there was no formal pact of co-operation until 1995 (though some diplomatic posts were received and three PRNU members joined the government in 1994) but the alliance was short-lived because the PRNU was thrown out of government later in 1995 when the leader (Gheorghe Funar) launched a vicious attack on Iliescu for negotiations with Hungary (leading to the 1996 treaty) while the GRP was rejected after its leader (Corneliu Vadim Tudor) accused Iliescu of assassinating Ceauşescu in cold blood.

Political Parties

The NSF, and later the PSDR, was flanked on the centre-right by the Democratic Convention of Romania (DCR), formed in 1991 to consolidate the opposition at a time of increasing austerity. The grouping came to include two historic parties which quickly reformed after 1989: the National Liberal Party (NLP), traditionally representing business interests, and the National Peasants' Christian Democrat Party (NPCDP) which had a base in rural areas but also attracted urban dwellers. The DCR drew strong support from the towns (especially Bucharest, Transylvanian cities such as Braşov and Timişoara in Banat) with its programme of market reform. It was ideologically close to the ethnically-based Democratic Union of Hungarians in Romania (DUHR), although any formal alliance was constrained by the sensitive nature of politics involving ethnic groups until the treaty of friendship was signed with Hungary in 1996. The DCR sought a blueprint for a radically new society: hence there were major disputes with government 'concerning privatization, the pace of economic reforms and the attitude towards foreign capital' as components of a reform policy requiring wholesale renewal of bureaucratic and political elites (Dăianu 2002, p.95). Although the DCR gained 20.9 per cent of the votes in 1992 (after its constituent parties had managed only 4.6 per cent in 1990), it is widely believed that Iliescu stayed in power through a rigged election in 1992 – and hence the reference to 'endangered democracy' at this time, although there could have been a 'violent polarisation' (Carey 2004, p.565) if the DCR had taken over before Iliescu began a belated 'tilt to the west'. But Gallagher (2005, p.108) says 'it was calamitous for Romania that in the first two elections in 1990 and 1992 a clear majority showed that they vastly preferred such a guided democracy in which a new élite heavily drawn from the former intelligence services and other privileged groups were able to ignore or undermine the law'.

Foreign Policy

There was some progress in foreign affairs as Romania qualified for assistance from the EBRD, formed in 1991 to finance development in CEE after communism, including encouragement of private sector investors. Over the years Romania has been a major beneficiary along with Poland and Russia: at the end of 2003 €2.4bn was committed to Romania and €7.5bn was mobilised in PPPt projects. Romania joined the Council of Europe (CoE) in 1993 and also signed an agreement with EFTA and won MFN status in the USA. Romania was also part of OSCE (which replaced the CSCE of 1972 in 1994) with a High Commissioner for National Minorities in The Hague (identifying ethnic tensions); an Office for Democratic Institutions and Human Rights in Warsaw (promoting human rights and monitoring elections); and an Office of the Representative for Freedom of the Media in Vienna (freedom for broadcasting, journalism and access to information). In 1996 Romania joined the Central European Initiative (originally a 'quadrilateral' comprising Austria, Hungary, Italy and Yugoslavia) to improve regional co-operation between Western Europe and the former communist bloc with assistance for infrastructure and commercial development projects. Also in 1996, Romania was included in a Southeast Europe Co-operative Initiative (co-operating with UNECE and OSCE) instigated by the USA to encourage regional co-operation through cross-boundary solutions to shared economic and environmental problems – a catalyst in bringing countries together. Finally, in 1997 Romania joined CEFTA, launched five years earlier by the Czech Republic, Hungary, Poland and Slovakia to counteract Comecon's demise with the gradual introduction of a free trade area as a step towards European integration.

Election Prospects

It seemed that PSDR had a good chance of further re-election in 1996 in view of its astute reading of the public mood of extreme caution over the DCR's more radical approach to reform and its restricted access to the media. But the economic situation became very difficult. After the recession years of 1990–2 there was growth and diminishing inflation from 1993 before strains arose through a rapid increase in external debt and the need to finance trade deficits. Reform momentum was lost through expensive price controls (retained until 1997) and an overvalued exchange rate that sucked in imports while constraining exports. Investment stayed low and the country remained burdened by a poor economic infrastructure, while industry depended too heavily on imported raw materials and offered exports that tended to be low in terms of added value. The government then engineered an economic boom in 1995 when heavy borrowing (capitalising on the low debt levels of the early 1990s) was followed by inflation, devaluation and industrial slowdown as investment funds dried up. The energy crisis of the 1995–96 winter further reduced foreign exchange earnings at a time when reserves were too low to provide a cushion: even so, imports were restricted to 70 per cent of the oil and electricity needed and petrol stations were forced to close. A decree in July 1996 required some companies to sell foreign exchange earnings to the National Bank at the official exchange rate and so create a fund enabling Romfirim (oil), Renel (electricity and primary fuels) and Romgaz (gas) to pay for import contracts. Around 100 companies (mostly SOEs including Sidex Galați, Alro Slatina, ARO Câmpulung and Dacia Mioveni – the core of the PSDR 'sympathetic business plutocracy') were then guaranteed energy in return for compliance. Inflation meant that the value of the monthly minimum wage fell to $30 compared with $35 in 1993.

Economic Problems. Meanwhile agriculture was in difficulties at just the wrong time, with a poor harvest in 1996 reflecting a difficult planting season and delayed provision of a 1.1bln.lei credit (in any case destined largely for the state farms) until spring 1996. Private farmers were reluctant to sell cereals to the National Agency for Agricultural Produce because the prices did not cover production costs: indeed the only sales came from farms that had taken out state-subsidised loans obliging them to sell part of their output. Private speculators hoped to make money when the bakeries ran out of flour with inadequate foreign exchange to finance imports. Further problems in agriculture arose through corruption, with Comcereal managers in Oltenia accused of illegal grain speculation. An increase in bread prices embarrassed the PRNU agriculture minister Valeria Tăbară after part of the 1995 cereal stock (0.73mln.t of wheat and 0.19mln.t of maize) had been exported. The government's position was also weakened by scandal when PSDR was found to have links with the state-owned foreign trade bank Bancorex, whose funds were misused to make unsecured loans. Police evidence suggested that Bancorex credits financed large purchases of fuel on international markets, with several different firms set up to provide cover for business linked with sanctions-busting to help Yugoslavia.

Scandals that also arose over the bankrupted Credit Bank, the collapse of Dacia Felix Bank (the first post-1989 private bank) and the investment fund FMOA were not linked directly with the governing party, but Iliescu's bland confidence in the banking system seemed highly irresponsible, and the regime was tarnished by its record of economic mismanagement. A former Dacia Felix vice-president, M. H. Hossu, was charged with years of insider dealing along with S. Mureşan, once the country's 'richest man'. There were also investigations into the affairs of G. Păunescu, who acquired a major shareholding in Bankcoop by dubious means: panic-stricken investors began a run on a bank that had been in trouble for a couple of years. The demise of Mureşan and Păunescu brought an end to the fraudulent plutocracy that sprouted during the years 1992–96. The writing was on the wall after the summer of 1996 when the DCR and Petre Roman's Union of Social Democrats (USD) – later the Democratic Party (DP) – did particularly well in local elections while PSDR failed to win control of any large city apart from Galaţi. A notable success was the CDR–USD alliance in the second round of voting for the office of general mayor of Bucharest when the DCR candidate Victor Ciorbea topped the poll.

Civil Society. Despite a nominally free press after 1989, the democratic opposition was hardly assisted by the rudimentary state of Romanian journalism in the early 1990s: described as 'a mixture of polemics, rumour, and half-accurate, incomplete and biased information' (Gross 2004, pp.195–6): it was at best pre-professional and highly politicised, with little attempt at objectivity. Although the DCR gradually increased its effectiveness in media terms, its newspapers were difficult to find in the rural areas, allegedly because of the action of the National Office for Press Distribution (subordinate to the Ministry of Posts and Telecommunications). The PSDR government certainly had reservations about media freedom and the end of the state TV monopoly – starting in 1992 when SOTI was able to transmit for one hour, late in the evening, from the official TV headquarters – was tolerated (presumably) in the hope that party supporters would control the private channels; although this did not apply in the case of all 53 private stations operating by 1996, including the BBC World Service. It was revealing to hear PSDR senators complaining in a debate just after their 1996 election defeat that the party had made a big mistake in tolerating a free press, since the daily *Evenimentul Zilei* had been particularly effective in exposing corruption. Even so, independent media continued to be excluded from the countryside by the state distribution system.

Gender Issues. Initially after 1989 women seemed to disappear from political life and decision-making structures, partly owing to the revival of traditional, rural patriarchal values after 1989. Feminist demands were met 'top-down' under communism so feminist values had 'never really been acknowledged and internalized by citizens' (Carey and Eisterhold 2004, p.14). There was little recovery until 1996 when a Department for Women's Rights and Family-Oriented Policies was established in the Ministry of Labour and Social Protection. It was also noted how women became 'victims of social disintegration and related effects such as addiction to alcohol, crime and violence' (Ionete and Dinculescu 2000, p.81). Women suffered particular hardship under conditions of poverty by reducing their own consumption in the interests of other family members while struggling to make ends meet and suffering domestic violence through increasing addiction to alcohol. Women were also disadvantaged by reliance on traditional methods of contraception and the lack of education concerning alternatives. There was an excessive level of abortion, equivalent to 6.1 terminations per live birth in Bucharest in 1990 and 3.1 nationally: the average Romanian woman was having three to four abortions during her lifetime (compared with less than one in the west), contributing massively to the high maternal death rate, since half the cases were due to abortion).

Church Affairs. Social reform was hardly assisted by the privileged position of the Orthodox Church, prone to religious, sexual and ethnic intolerance: opposing Protestant evangelism and decriminalisation of homosexuality (Ramet 2004, p.289). Only in 1996 was the criminal code amended to remove the prescription of prison terms of up to five years for any homosexual relationship as the price of CoE membership. And further liberalisation was inhibited by the politicisation of the Orthodox Church, while the attitude to the Uniate (Greek Catholic) Church – allowed to reconstitute itself in 1990 – was less than generous considering the abusive way in which the merger of the two denominations had taken place under communism. Over property disputes – enabling Uniates to regain only about 150 out of over 250 churches previously theirs – the Orthodox Church often behaved as the aggrieved party since legalisation did not prescribe restitution and instead relied on pressure for a voluntary surrender (ibid p.287). At the same time, relations with local authorities were 'far from perfect' reflecting 'an unsympathetic but legally correct attitude towards religious questions' (Luxmoore 1997, p.89).

The Unions. Outlawed in 1940 and then neutralised under the umbrella of the communist 'Uniunea Generală a Sindicatelor din România' (apart from strikes in the Jiu Valley in 1977 and protests in Braşov in 1987), free trade unions re-formed immediately after 1989 along the lines of a 'vigorous pluralism' (Bush 2004, p.422). Strike action was called against price rises late in 1990 leading to major government concessions on wages; and while labour mobility was impeded by housing shortages, legislation during 1990–91 set legal standards for collective bargaining, codified the rights and obligations of employers and employees, set a minimum wage and provided for unemployment: all reflecting productive union relations with the Stolojan government. In return, the major union confederations did not support the miners in their violent interventions against meaningful reform (especially the contraction of the former communist industrial establishment), although without genuine tripartite negotiations since there were no 'significant employer associations independent of government' (ibid p.426). Social dialogue developed under the Văcăroiu government, with EU pressure and Phare assistance (from 1993) encouraging bipartite and tripartite relations and the emergence of employer organisations (though many represented state enterprises). And a political realignment balanced elements supporting the Văcăroiu government with others aligned with the DCR (notably Victor Ciorbea's Confederation of Democratic Trade Unions).

Crime. Levels were low (especially violent crime and crime against property), although petty theft in the large towns hit foreigners while cyber-crime became a growing problem. There was a lack of serious organised crime – limited to drugs, prostitution and trafficking in humans, forms that did not threaten normal private business (though money laundering also occurred). But there were many dubious financial practices, notably the Caritas pyramid investment that started in Braşov in 1992 and transferred to Cluj-Napoca later in the year. Attractive to the less well-educated with only modest funds to invest at a time of high inflation and unattractive bank interest rates, it was linked with money laundering and suspected of acting as a conduit for PRNU funding; attracting some 30 per cent of the population's savings by the end of 1993 followed by total collapse the following year. Investors made an eightfold return in three months, but only as a result of new capital investment (rather than real profits earned in commerce) but the scheme was unsustainable because the supply of funds could not rise exponentially for ever, leaving the early investors rich and later ones bankrupt. Yet in 1993 Cluj was seen as 'a new El Dorado' when up to 4.0mln people invested around $1.0bln despite government warnings.

Corruption became an issue when Iliescu and other political leaders defended their positions through patronage and tolerated the rent-seeking behaviour of bureaucrats. The prominence of informal networks carried over from communism served to undermine democratic development. An element of coercion was also present since there were 'no visible moves to dismantle the old Romanian secret police apparatus' (Duran 2000, p.20). While hardly practising an extreme form of 'sultanism' – whereby a dictator 'masters an entire state and society with near-total control' (Sellin 2004, p.117) – the early governments showed signs of 'patrimonialism', with administration as Iliescu's personal instrument 'subordinating the legislative and judicial branches of government to an extra-constitutional dominance of a personal and partisan nature' (ibid., p.122). This meant a fusion of political and economic power since state enterprise directors had been drawn into the ranks of PSDR and acted as an oligarchy. At the same time the ideological polarisation evident in parliament created a power vacuum that made it necessary for Iliescu (and also his successor) to rely on executive decrees. CoE monitoring of human rights prior to 1997 led to censure over the handling of local government, for during 1992–96 133 mayors (all but 35 being independent or from opposition parties) were removed by prefects for not implementing government policy.

The Constantinescu Presidency 1997–2000

Dissatisfied with low living standards, corruption and uncertainty, the electorate turned to the DCR's vigorous reform programme – including a radical start through a 'Contract for the First 200 Days' – that paved the way for a new governing coalition. Considered ideologically out of touch in 1992, when the neo-communist 'third way' was being widely proclaimed by the centre-left, the new programme was attractive to workers, entrepreneurs and the unemployed. Meanwhile there was a school of thought in the mid-1990s favouring a younger president: someone not involved with the former regime who might act against corruption and accelerate restructuring. The DCR's presidential candidate (the academic Emil Constantinescu: well-prepared by National Peasants' Christian Democrat Party (NPCDP) leader Corneliu Coposu and running against Iliescu for the second time) was certainly effective in promoting his own programmes for educational reform ('Contract with the Young'), cultural transformation and a convincing anti-corruption agenda for moral leadership, including a resolution of ethnic tensions following the treaty with Hungary entered into during the last months of the outgoing government. Constantinescu also highlighted corruption and illegality as a major problem. He wanted Romania to join 'a world of law and order' as the only guarantee of a better life. In the end PSDR did not resort to rigging since it was 'too risky to rely on double-digit rates of ballot nullifications to stay in power' (Carey 2004, p.602) and it seemed that a change of government at the end of 1996 possibly rescued Romania from 'an abyss of corruption, clientelistic networks or a Bulgarian crisis' (Craiutu 2004, p.6).

A Coalition of Coalitions

However, the DCR (itself a group of separate parties) could take power only in alliance with the DP and the DUHR; so the new government faced the task of working in coalition when each individual party leader sought to make an impact. Moreover, the parties were under strain as their established memberships were assailed by a flood of new opportunists including Securitate elements attracted to the parties in power, 'seeking employment and contractual patronage, subsidies and world-class salaries for cronies' (Carey 2004, p.580). Post-communist oligarchs such as Dinu Patriciu were able to 'shunt aside' old-time members of the NLP, while the death of Copoşu (a lawyer and former political prisoner) in 1995 curtailed efforts to control infiltration into the NPCDP by agents under 45 years of age. The DP was in the ambivalent position of being a junior coalition member while having ample experience of government through its origins within FSN. Hence the party tended to act as both a governing and an opposition force, with ministers working to personal and party agendas that made for compromise and inconsistency in government action as a whole. DP ambivalence was evident over the privatisation of state farms announced in 1997 to avoid escalating losses; for in 1998 Roman chose to back an influential NLP member (ideologically wedded to state ownership) wishing to maintain state interest in pig and chicken farms for reasons of food security! Again, while going slow on privatisation through DP control of some important economic ministries, Roman was ready enough to harry the government over its performance in other departments (for example, in 1999) along with the opposition PSDR. Nevertheless, while there seems to have been surprising ineptitude in planning a cohesive reform movement (Gallagher 2005, p.176), the 'coalition of coalitions' was delicate in the extreme, with a lack of will to compromise as each party sustained its own brand of clientelism and ideological rhetoric that threatened at times to make the country ungovernable. Even at the outset the DCR had no agreed plan for government and did not communicate effectively with its own supporters or the population at large. Lack of effective partnership between government and presidency was also an issue.

Tensions over Reform. Nevertheless, after the lost years of the early 1990s, the new government felt obliged to reform quickly 'with their backs to the wall': pressed by the global financial institutions and by western governments while constrained by the danger of social unrest. Some 480 laws were passed during 1997–98, the same number as in the first five years of transition. Further progress was made with land-restitution legislation in 2000 to raise the ceilings laid down by the NSF from 10 to 50ha (arable equivalent) for agricultural land and 1.0 to 10ha for woodland. At the same time, integration ('synchronism') became central to foreign policy: western-style liberalism and pluralism was no longer seen as alien to indigenous traditions. The drive for European integration accelerated under a national programme for the adoption of the 'acquis communautaire' and a much stronger regional component was injected into government with the introduction of eight large regions (appropriate for EU statistical purposes) with regional development agencies (RDAs) – subordinate to the national body – including representatives of local government, especially from the counties that remained the highest-level local authorities (see Figure 1.1). Price controls ended in 1997, with a surge of inflation, while exchange was liberalised and the leu depreciated. Bankruptcy legislation was streamlined and privatisation accelerated. Nevertheless, the momentum of reform stalled in late

1997, leading to a coalition crisis at the turn of the year. Unhappy with Ciorbea's reform programme, the DP left the government at the beginning of 1998 and supported his minority government meanwhile until he was eventually forced to resign (ostensibly by the Senate's failure to approve use of Hungarian in local government: a measure opposed by some coalition members). Ciorbea's background with the Democratic Confederation of Free Trade Unionists (supporting the DCR) clashed with its rival 'Frația' that inclined to the left. Also, Roman's DP disliked the technocrats brought in by Ciorbea in 1997 (such as finance minister Daniel Dăianu) – preferring the strict allocation of jobs according to electoral strength – as well as the early privatisations that brought no benefits to DP supporters. Meanwhile the restoration of citizenship to the former King Mihai in 1997 was a decision long overdue.

But there were also factions within the NPCDP since Radu Vasile stood close to the DP and enjoyed good relations with the opposition while finding it difficult to work with the 'moralistic, unbending Ciorbea' (Sellin 2004, p.126). Indeed, Vasile undermined Ciorbea with his own party faction and was then propelled into his place to start another round of 'stop-go transformation'. However a further factional revolt occurred when Vasile refused to heed party directives and warnings from the party president, Ion Diaconescu. Vasile in turn resented the president's attempts to influence cabinet decisions (and also sought to remove Diaconescu from his chair) but was himself removed from power in 1999 having lost the confidence of the party: Constantinescu orchestrated mass resignations of NPCDP ministers, followed by a presidential decree (a questionable procedure that caused a minor split in the party and ended its Senate majority). A new premier had to be found outside the party and the technocrat Mugur Isărescu (National Bank governor) was now accepted as an independent to mitigate partisan attacks. He proved very effective and his appointment coincided with great optimism over EU accession and negotiations that included a medium-term development strategy for 2000–2006.

Economic Pressures. In the economic sphere the government was immediately concerned to avoid the melt-down taking place in Bulgaria. In January 1997 it met with the World Bank, IMF and EU/EBRD, thereby emphasising its desire for immediate reform. There was also embarrassment at finding that the previous government had run down National Bank foreign reserves to below $700mln at the end of 1996 in pursuit of higher consumption. Later DCR reforms boosted reserves so that a major crisis was avoided in 1999 (when repayment of large external debts of over $3.0bln became due) by 'a remarkable fiscal and balance of payments adjustment', halving the current account deficit from eight to four per cent (Dăianu 2002, p.96). In view of this important 'success', on top of the unsustainable boom orchestrated by their predecessors, it was hardly surprising that economic expansion ceased. But the government was never forgiven for three years of negative growth (–16 per cent during 1997–9) to finish the decade at only 74 per cent of the 1989 level (80 per cent in the case of GDP per capita). There was a modest turnaround only in 2000 by Isărescu's competent management, but this was too little too late, especially in view of further bad news through the National Investment Fund crash when 13,200 investors suffered losses of 2.5mln.lei after it transpired that the manager, I.M. Vlas, had signed 28 fictitious reports on the fund's value. In the course of subsequent legal proceedings since 2003, Vlas admitted guilt and asked for 20 years in jail. In view of policy inconsistencies it was 'beyond doubt that the economic programme could have been better put together to diminish costs' (Dăianu 2002 p.96). Unemployment led to deprivation and poverty that intensified opposition to restructuring from the PSDR and the nationalist parties.

Privatisation Prospects were undermined when the initial 1996–7 surge in foreign interest was forced into reverse by recession – also by low credit ratings reflecting high perceived political risk, as well as instability in the Balkans and the CIS. There was some transformation to place autonomous state companies on a more commercial basis in 1998 while the restructuring of Renel and SNCFR (the national electricity and railway companies) checked mounting deficits. But the EU 'Country Report' on Romania in 1999 (p.24) concluded that 'as the experience between 1990 and 1996 showed, the failure to restructure or close down large public loss-making industrial companies and banks has constantly threatened the gains achieved in terms of macroeconomic stabilization'. It is possible that significant privatisation was prevented by the same self-interest as was evident among the PSDR with elements in the DP looking for personal gain. There was also inevitable sniping from the opposition, which saw privatisation as a distraction from short-term welfare issues. Meanwhile, the fastest growth occurred in underground economic activity (UEA), covering legal and illegal activities (construction work, and drug trafficking and prostitution respectively). UEA sustained the equivalent of 5.4mln full-time jobs in the economy in 1998, with many people working simultaneously in the formal and underground economies.

Mining and 'Mineriada'. The position was not yet hopeless, as the DCR won the local elections in Bucharest in 1998. Yet supported to some extent by the opposition, much industrial unrest (including large street demonstrations) occurred in March 1999 and violent protest in Braşov by 'Roman' truck workers over the non-payment of wage increases led to government compromises. Furthermore, reorganisation of the mining industry was started in 1998 to reduce the losses of the state coalmining companies based in Petroşani and Ploieşti and the metalliferous ore producing companies in Baia Mare and Deva. Austerity measures were essential in view of debt repayments due in 1999 while further IMF loans were conditional on slimming down loss-making state industries. Redundancies attracted generous severance payments, made in the unrealistic expectation that money would be invested in small businesses. Also, there were incentives for job creation in the relevant 'less-favoured areas' (LFAs) but this still provoked violence from Jiu Valley miners who launched their final two assaults on Bucharest in January and February 1999. The first (actually the fifth 'mineriada') was linked with a strike in the Jiu Valley in pursuit of large pay rises and $10,000 redundancy settlements. 15,000 marchers set out for Bucharest and were eventually halted near Râmnicu Vâlcea (having advanced some 100kms from Petroşani) after an appalling failure by the interior ministry precipitated government approval of limited pay increases while miners accepted responsibility for two threatened mines that were kept open for a time.

The second march was triggered by the conviction (*in absentia*) by the Supreme Court of the miners' leader Miron Cozma ('the black prince') for his part in earlier actions against the state in 1991. His sentence of 18 years triggered a march of 3,000–4,000 miners that ended at Stoeneşti (Vâlcea county) with the arrest of Cozma and 500 followers. The expedition was ill-conceived since Cozma would probably have been safe from arrest in his bastion of Petroşani; while the government's victory against the 'black army' was important in demonstrating its authority in the eyes of the IMF and foreign investors. The miners would have created more damage had the opposition not behaved with restraint in order to prevent a descent into anarchy. But even so the demonstrations inflicted enormous damage in terms of public opinion since the political class as a whole was now seen as one of the country's problems. Although perhaps a somewhat perverse attitude, reflecting the continued lack of a clear consensus at the grass-roots, it certainly underlined the necessity for the very gradual incremental change so deplored internationally: any approval by the international community was of little concern to domestic opinion pre-occupied by economic pressure, reinforced by substantial debt repayments of $2.8bln at the end of 1998 and $3.2bln a year later. Many thought life had been better under Ceauşescu, and the PSDR was now clearly overtaking the DCR in poll ratings. Meanwhile, advocates of faster change were demoralised by the coalition's failure and went abroad permanently, while many others found ways – not all legal – of finding temporary work as a way out of poverty.

Foreign Affairs also contributed to the government's demise. While negotiations for EU and NATO membership were certainly popular, the support for NATO over the Kosovo crisis in 1999 was not. The bombing of Serbia seemed unjustified to many who had been brought up to see Belgrade as a close ally in the later communist years (whereas the country was altogether more detached from the problems of the Albanian minority). Moreover, Romania's support gained only scant reward from NATO, and Gallagher (2005, pp.217–18) argued that compensation should have been negotiated for economic losses that were to arise from closure of the Danube; also needed were better lending terms from the IMF, concessions for Romanians to work abroad, and humanitarian assistance for the Serbs. Constantinescu was therefore disappointed when no invitation to join NATO was forthcoming (indeed it was still three years away). The Stability Pact for Southeastern Europe was launched in 1999 as a 'second Marshall Plan' for long-term development to restore peace and stability in the Balkans (with a focus on infrastructure for the first funding conference in 2000) but the level of resourcing was quite poor. However, support for NATO in Kosovo did help over negotiations for accession to the EU in 1999 that launched the Isărescu premiership. Meanwhile, the Organisation of the Black Sea Economic Co-operation was set up in 1999 to expand economic co-operation, with a co-ordination centre in Ankara, a business council in Istanbul, a Project Promotion Fund for regional development, and the Black Sea Trade and Development Bank to finance joint regional projects. And during a delayed papal visit in 1999, the Catholics' property dispute with the Orthodox church was still sensitive enough to prevent the Pope going to Transylvania.

Other Projects. There were, however, various ways in which useful initiative was shown, but without reaping any reward in terms of public opinion. There was a need for decentralisation to empower regions and minorities – thereby reducing tensions in an area where Romania felt isolated through its Latin foundation within Slav territory. This process was started by regional development measures involving the creation of seven large regions – groups of counties which remained the top-tier units of governments (complementing the towns and communes) – each with a population some two to three million and coordination through a regional development organisation based in one of the county towns. There were also changes in local government finance in order to reduce dependence on central government allocations and encourage an entrepreneurial approach through the promotion of businesses that would be subject to substantial local taxation. And, although there was no major breakthrough in building a public service-oriented bureaucracy, there was legislation on security for senior civil servants in 1999. Meanwhile, 'strengthening the independence of the judiciary also proved to be an impossible task' (Craiutu 2004, p.6) given a lack of enthusiasm for the anti-corruption drive since most judges understandably feared a return of the PDSR; yet the matter was clearly seen as central to any reform agenda. And although there was no significant tilt towards monarchism, the ex-King Mihai was given a role in pressing Romania's case for NATO membership and gained lifetime access to his old Elisabeta and Săvârşin palaces. Finally, in 1999 Constantinescu started work on a new tax regime through, although the new fiscal code (covering 80 per cent of fiscal provisions, omitting some 20 special state revenues) did not emerge until 2004. The aim was to consolidate separate laws – over income tax (for residents and non-residents), profits tax, excise tax, local taxes and VAT – and introduce the concept of taxing capital gains. Profits tax was eventually set at 25 per cent: high for the region but with allowance for deductible expenses.

Civil Society
A Commission for Equal Opportunities was established 1997. And an Economic and Social Council was created in 1997 to accompany structural reforms, stabilise social consensus and support dialogue between the social partners and government. But despite the need for more on equality of opportunity for people with mental and physical disabilities – and likewise over religious freedom and gender issues – it did not live up to expectations and was often ignored by government and further compromised by unrealistic deadlines for the evaluation of proposed legislation. Work on a draft Labour Code in 1999 under the labour and social protection minister Alexandru Athanasiu replaced its communist-era predecessor and incorporated ILO and EU standards. But 'formal mechanisms for tripartite decision making [were not] transformed into stable cooperative relationships among union, employer and government representatives' (Carey and Eisterhold 2004, p.19). Moreover, labour relations were not good during the period 1996–2000 as a whole because with government 'under constant pressure from international lending agencies to cut state expenditures it had little margin to accommodate labour's economic demands' (Bush 2004, p.432). However, women became better integrated into business and company management: the case of Oriflame cosmetics (a foreign firm's subsidiary) was widely mentioned at the time; meanwhile the army started recruitment of women while the banks and the stock exchange included women in management positions. New organisations included an Association for the Promotion of Women in Romania and a Coalition of Women's Business Associations. NGOs grew to exceed 17,000 (Pralong 2004) but too many were seen as 'collaborationist' – often quasi profit-seeking companies – rather than self-funded grassroots organisations pressing from the bottom upwards. Again, many were relying heavily on salaried employees rather than volunteers. USAID provided funding for NGOs in Braşov, Miercurea Ciuc, Alexandria and Slobozia concerned with common actions for community development.

The Media did well enough over the quality of transmission and coverage: it was sufficiently pluralist for the 'open-minded reader [to] obtain a general sense of Romania's politics by reading several newspapers' (Carey and Eisterhold 2004, p.10). As a result of the growth of television programmes, cinema attendances slumped catastrophically from some 30mln in 1990 to barely 2.0mln in 2005 with halls in use down from 420 to just 39, though it remains to be seen whether privatisation of the film distribution company (Dadef) and the partial disposal of assets will lead to a turnaround. Film companies meanwhile were also in the doldrums, with Anima and Rofilm in debt, though not Sahia. However, expectations after 1996 that state control over national TV would be lifted (after manipulation and 'triumphalism' under Iliescu), that the role of the media would be redefined along western lines with an independent TV station to compete with RTV – also that the 1996 penal code (providing for prison sentences for journalists guilty of defamation and insult) would be reconsidered – were all largely disappointed. Close links between the RTV leadership and both the presidency at Cotroceni palace and the government at Piața Victoriei continued, while RTV's financial situation remained precarious. Imprisonment of journalists continued, particularly in the countryside at the instigation of local authorities (though the courts did not use the defamation law as a political tool), and two proposed laws to strengthen media protection and improve access to information did not make progress. With politicians worried about the 'terror' of the press, slow reform reflected to a degree the behaviour of some journalists who remained 'highly opinionated [and] published unverifiable, incomplete and even fictitious articles which were often sensationalized, trivialized and corrupted by personal, political or financial exigencies' (Gross 2004, p.205). Journalism remained 'a dubious blend of advocacy, communication and reporting mixed with rumour in the guise of news' with little concern for verification (ibid., p.205). So there were arrests of journalists during the Constantinescu presidency and some intelligence agency intimidation of newspapers, while attempts to professionalise journalism through ethical norms were frustrated. However, the private 'Antena 1' TV channel was a significant innovation; owned by Dan Voiculescu of the Humanist (now Conservative) Party along with other media outlets. As regards religious affairs, a joint commission was set up in 2000 to look into disputes between the Orthodox and Greek-Catholic churches; the latter having taken over 144 churches and built 150 new ones.

Corruption was a priority but the Constantinescu administration could not deliver in any convincing way. Half-heartedness over dealing with Securitate files within the government in 1997 prevented effective legislation to regulate access after some prominent coalition advocates of reform were discredited by revelations of their past. Likewise, when Constantinescu set up a National Council of Action Against Corruption and Organised Crime, Roman did not go along with this and there were also prominent figures in DCR who did not welcome the initiative either. The president made no attempt to transform the Supreme Council of National Defence (co-ordinating nine intelligence agencies) and quickly retreated from the DCR position that elements of the communist nomenklatura should not hold public office in a young democracy. Ciorbea even had to sack V. Stan – the head of the Department of Control and Anti-Corruption – when the DP threatened to withdraw support after Stan uncovered an abuse whereby state-owned houses were being given to prominent figures including some from DP! Constantinescu 'appeared to have grudgingly accepted that this was an unavoidable feature of the post-communist system; one which could not be reformed without causing the kind of political instability which might lead the regime to collapse' (Hall 2004, p.221). But the ultimate blow to the anti-corruption drive was a large cigarette-smuggling incident in 1998 involving a military figure providing Constantinescu's personal security; whereupon the president's approval rating immediately fell sharply. Very little corruption was uncovered in government, although the NLP justice minister Valeriu Stoica gave some business to his family law firm and the NPCDP mayor of Bucharest's Fourth Sector was arrested on corruption charges in 2000 (although Traian Băsescu of the DP was still able to win the office of general mayor for the whole city). But this record of clean government seemed to count for nothing in view of the coalition's indecision combined with 'squabbling over the spoils of patronage' (Carey 2004, p.603) and failure to confront entrenched communist networks. Given the public's respect for 'strong' leadership, Constantinescu's admission that the old Securitate had undermined his presidency merely underlined a public image of a weak and ineffectual leader, propelled by the DCR engine but unable to cleanse the civil service. Popular support for the president collapsed, despite the lack of any hint of corruption on his part, and he felt unable to contest the election at the end of 2000.

The Second Iliescu Presidency

A return to centre-left government was inevitable. The winners of 1996 lost 'pathetically' in 2000, after a period of indecisive reform with falling living standards and an increase in poverty. Disillusionment and alienation resulted in a lower election turnout: 66.5 per cent compared with 71.0 per cent in 1996. Appealing disproportionately to older people, women and village or small town residents, PSD, as the former PSDR was now known, also picked up more votes in Transylvanian cities. The GRP made a late surge, appealing to younger voters (especially students) – despite their elderly parliamentarians and predominantly male leadership – and winning 23 per cent of their votes from people who had previously supported the DCR and another 17 per cent from former PSDR voters. But the party did not build in former areas of strength such as northern Moldavia: with only a small stable vote, it may have gained from the novelty of 'new' media coverage for their charismatic leader (C.V. Tudor), especially on the private TV channel 'Antena 1', in contrast to the other nationalist party (PRNU) that performed relatively poorly. It was understandable that the party would do well in view of the split in the rival nationalist party in 1997 (provoking a shift to the GRP made by the influential Cluj politician Gheorghe Funar the following year). Through the promise of action over poverty, injustice and insecurity, it offered a vision to unemployed youth and to older people with nostalgia for the state paternalism of the past. But it was curious that the party polled particularly well, with over 40 per cent in several Transylvanian counties (Alba, Arad, Caraş-Severin, Maramureş, Sălaj and Sibiu) and also Gorj in Oltenia and Tulcea in Dobrogea: perhaps there were particularly heavy transfers from DCR and PRNU in areas where Iliescu and the PSDR were relatively unpopular. One specific factor was the controversial Hungarian external passport scheme that threatened to attract Romanians with some Hungarian ancestry and so raised the spectre of a weakened Romanian stake in Transylvania. The GRP's isolationist and chauvinistic programme could have caused havoc, but fortunately the party secured merely a protest vote and in the presidential run-off moderates chose to turn out in numbers to back Iliescu as the 'wise statesman' – the old communist sympathetic to poorer people suffering hunger and cold – against Tudor's extreme populist stance. And there was some reassurance to the middle class because in loyal opposition Iliescu had signalled that he (also) could deliver on arrangements with the EU while his support for the reformist premier Adrian Năstase suggested that the party had 'engaged in some democratic learning while in opposition' (Carey 2004, p.603).

The Parties

All the former coalition parties suffered in the election for their failure to co-operate more effectively. The DCR broke up and while the DP and NLP secured enough votes to cross the five per cent threshold and get back into parliament there was disaster for the NPCDP through its alliance with smaller parties in a revamped 'DCR 2000' that, with only 5.3 per cent of the vote, failed to cross the higher (10 per cent) threshold required for coalitions. As the largest party in the old DCR, the NPCDP was now made the principal scapegoat for its failures, but it was also seen as 'ideologically ossified' (following the death of Coposu in 1995) by a rift between communist-era opportunists and older generation members who nevertheless competed for patronage. It seemed that a great mistake had been made by Diaconescu in breaking with the more dynamic, modern and ideologically-coherent NLP, but at the time this was justified by the susceptibility of some NLP elements to intimidation by the GRP and more especially by inclinations towards the left through a 'Social Liberal' Initiative in 1999 that eroded the NPCDP's confidence in NLP commitment to the DCR project. Damage also arose from Constantinescu's pull-out from the presidential contest: a hasty decision, apparently arising from the scale of corruption and the mafia system behind it, but a reckless one, in the opinion of Gallagher (1995, p.264), since Tudor took over the anti-corruption mantle – despite welcoming Securitate members at the same time – while Isărescu, who became the NPCDP's presidential candidate, gained only a tenth of the vote in the first round. With Constantinescu on board, the new DCR might well have crossed the threshold for parliamentary access. Instead the question was now one of how far the NPCDP could regroup under Andrei Marga (rector of the Babeş-Bolyai University in Cluj) to provide an alternative in 2005–8, for although the party retained part of its historic 'aura' the post-communist electorate showed little nostalgia or respect for the politics of pre-1948. But Marga resigned within a few months – and 'further undermined the credibility of intellectuals who wished to play a progressive role in politics' (ibid. p.318). Rivalry between Ciorbea and Vasile Lupu was resolved in the former's favour but with little improvement in the party's ratings. Constantinescu meanwhile disappeared into obscurity as leader of a minor party called 'People's Action' in 2003.

Continuity for the Economy

Despite Iliescu's speeches in 2000 that identified privatisation as anti-Romanian and preached hostility towards the IMF and the World Bank – suggesting that a return to centre-left government might reverse the reforms so painfully enacted over the previous four years and bring the European project into question – the minority PSD government of 2001–4 (with 46 per cent of parliamentary seats) provided a period of stability with significant reform, including a reorganisation in 2003 to cut the number of ministries from 23 to 14. There were tensions between modernisers and others close to the GRP, sceptical of the west and the market economy, but the new government adopted a European programme for accession in 2007, while Iliescu himself fell into line with a visit to the USA in 2002 where he conceded his mistake in thinking that western identity could be combined with a reformed socialist system. Surprisingly, much of the centre-right domestic agenda was also taken over, with consistent commitment to reform and a more radical privatisation strategy – a major success being the sale of the Galaţi steelworks (accounting for five per cent of GDP) to the Anglo-Indian consortium LNM/ISPAT in 2001. The indigenous sector of the economy was not very strong and there was heavy dependence on FDI and remittances from abroad (mainly from Italy and Spain) while export growth was heavily dependent on textiles and footwear – with little added value – and very sensitive to wage competition. But a possible refugee influx from a poverty-stricken Moldova did not occur (migrant workers found opportunities elsewhere) and the country was able to build on the positive growth trajectory bequeathed by Isărescu: perhaps this made it easier to undertake difficult structural reforms against the interests of some of the party's supporters, especially when money coming in from Brussels was 'sufficient to facilitate the enrichment of a *nomenklatura* already attuned under communism to the benefits of western business' (Carey 2004, p.603) and ready to retreat further from an eastern political culture. Internal demand became the engine for growth but the balance of payments deficit rose to 6.5 per cent in 2003 (reflecting delays in restructuring), and heavy arrears reflecting continuing soft budget constraints.

A European Agenda

There was also a reconciliation with the DUHR who agreed to formal co-operation, as a result of which they became involved in patronage. The PSD's former chauvinist attitude was abandoned in favour of a law in 2001 on minority language use in local government areas where a minority accounted for a fifth or more of population The NLP also offered co-operation in return for constitutional reform over the roles of the two houses of parliament. Changes in 2003 brought the 1991 constitution into harmony with the EU with more emphasis on human rights, property rights and provision for judicial review (though still without a clear separation of powers between government and judiciary). Progress was made in approximating to Brussels's directives. Criminalisation of same-sex relations ceased in 2002 and a low and falling level of crime was noted (against both persons and property), although attention was still required to reform the prison system, with Phare and budget funding to address issues of overcrowding, underage offenders and the rights of inmates. There were good marks for child protection, including action taken to control trafficking in adopted babies (starting with a one-year ban on the adoption of Romanian children in 2001, later extended to 2003 and then made permanent in 2004 after minor concessions), although concern remained over trafficking in children for begging and stealing as well as women and girls for sex. The 2003 'Country Report' also included criticisms over consistency in the judicial system as well as concern over the independence enjoyed by the National Council for Combating Discrimination. Some 1,300 tenured civil servants were dismissed despite depoliticisation of the state service, while restitution included property fund shares for some properties abusively seized during 1945–89.

Monarchy

There was even reconciliation with the monarchy. King Carol II's remains were brought back to Romania in 2003 and buried at Curtea de Argeş in a move commended by Năstase as 'another sign of our reconciliation with ourselves and our past'. Meanwhile, Iliescu normalised relations with King Mihai in 2001 when the former monarch gained an income and a role in society. Furthermore, the property restitution law of 2001 (concerned with land, forest, real estate and production facilities) returned 300,000 properties abusively seized by the communists and granted shares in a property fund for other claims that could not be met (although this was opposed by former owners' associations, arguing that this procedure would not secure adequate recompense from a 'proprietatea' fund capitalised with €3.9bln drawn from 114 state companies and part of the RCB privatisation proceeds. However, the legislation enabled Mihai to ask that his rights be acknowledged for Peleş Castle (currently a museum administered by the Ministry of Culture and Cults), Pelişor Villa, the Economat Hotel Complex and Knights House Villa, along with plots of land in Azuga, Buşteni,

Predeal and Sinaia. Other royal claims came from descendants of Princess Ileana (Bran Castle); also the Corvin family (at Hunedoara), the Ghika and Sturdza families (valuable urban land and other land at Bicaz flooded by the lake), and the Bragadiru family with extensive property claims in Bucharest – valued at over €400mln in 2005 – that have only been met to a symbolic extent. In 2004 the government reached a political settlement with Mihai whereby he would receive €30mln compensation for the Sinaia plots, although this deal first languished with a Senate commission (given public disquiet when it was disclosed that 42 paintings left the country with Mihai when he abdicated) and has now been refused as unconstitutional. However, Bran Castle has been restored to the Habsburg family and major land claims are being processed.

Civil Society

A shift in union support to the PSD in 2000 led to a tripartite social pact in 2001, with a new labour code agreed in 2002 and presented to parliament in 2003. A deal with the unions also improved workplace safety, sought to reduce the grey economy, stopped managerial appointments to SOEs on the basis of political connections and promised new job creation to keep unemployment below 10 per cent. For their part, the unions accepted that wage rises should be linked with productivity. However, Bush (2004, p.436) argued that despite progress towards a successful corporatism, 'the culture and expertise necessary to support genuine tripartite relations, especially in the private sector, has yet to mature'. In 2003 the US-based NGO Freedom House reported that Romania was the only EU candidate country where the media were not completely free. Carey and Eisterhold (2004, p.10) concluded that 'a truly professional and independent media' was still compromised by political and economic subordination while coverage of political events was 'highly partisan and ideologically driven', with opposition politicians routinely discredited for alleged links with western or Russian intelligence: even Iliescu was blamed for an insufficiently nationalistic stance over Moldova (attributed to his Soviet and Russian links). But the national public broadcasting monopoly was eroded by private CATV networks (often compromised through ownership by people with PSD connections), although the national RTV leadership seemed encouraged to believe that it had a political mandate. State television – including TVR1, TVR Continental, TV2 (for youth) and the quality cultural channel – could certainly try to justify licence fees through better programmes and improve on its fourth-place news rating after ProTV (owned by US Central Europe Media Enterprises and run by Adrian Sirbu, a former prime-ministerial adviser of the early 1990s: this station attracts much of the advertising revenue while showing some partiality towards the PSD during a period of indebtedness). Other competition has come from the Voiculescu family's 'Antena 1' and 'Realitate TV' that started in 2001 and was relaunched in 2004 as a higher-quality provider. And

SBS Broadcasting built a platform in a growing market by gaining 86 per cent of Prima TV (established in 1997) as well as control of two FM radio stations – Kiss and Star – set up in 2003.

Press. Berry (2004, p.175) noted a failure to build 'an adequate communications system that aids the democratic process'. The number of independent media sources in general was limited, while freedom of expression remained compromised through protection of the authorities from slander. However, 'insult' was decriminalised and the possibility of a prison sentence for slander was removed (a restrictive press law prescribing jail sentences for the defamation of public officials was passed by parliament but shelved), although journalists were still harassed and could face violence from officials embarrassed by their questions, especially in PSD strongholds. Newspapers reporting abuses were liable to be harassed by tax inspectors looking for minor fiscal irregularities for which they could be heavily fined. The issue of press freedom also concerned abuse through government pressure on Romanian publishers to tone down opposition, and a decision that SOEs should restrict advertising to pro-government media, with Năstase's office directly allocating advertising contracts. But questions also arose over foreign-owned papers and magazines since owners needed to get involved with governments to prevent the expansion of their interests being blocked by the competition council. In 2003 'independent-minded' journalists working for BBC Romania were sacked (and others then resigned in protest), with the result that a more pliant team emerged. In 2004 P.M. Băcanu, the editor of *România Liberă* (imprisoned under Ceauşescu), was removed by the owner, Westdeutsche Allgemeine (WAZ).

There was the disturbing case of the newspaper *Evenimentul Zilei* (*EZ*) – established in 1992, with the 4,000th edition published in February 2005, and described as the 'flagship of a shrinking band of independent newspapers' – that was sold in 2004 by Bertelsmann (Germany) to Ringier, a Swiss publisher and one of the large media conglomerates in ECE, controlling over 40 papers and magazines in the Czech Republic, Hungary, Serbia, Slovakia and Romania (Berry 2004). The new owner needed to get involved with the government to ensure approval for the takeover (after the company experienced difficulty with regulatory authorities in Hungary), and the editor, Cornel Nistorescu, left when it seemed that Ringier wanted to tone down *EZ*'s criticism of government and perhaps move closer to the PSD before the 2004 elections. Then the new editor, Dan Tuturica, was 'exiled' to Bacău after the elections (despite demonstrations and resignations and falling circulation) after the paper had reported on state assets acquired by PSD members, the fraudulent appropriation of EU funds, and most incredibly (on 24 November 2004) a transcript of a PSD strategy meeting openly discussing the derailing of the justice system and election rigging! Not surprisingly, the authorities sought to purchase and destroy as much of this edition as possible, although it was normal for each of the paper's 100,000 copies to pass through the hands of six readers each day! Fortunately *EZ* seems not to have been too badly compromised, although its radical approach was complemented by 'pillars of corruption' in the form of low-circulation papers supporting the PSD and financed by government advertising. However, while the NGO Media Monitoring Agency reported continuing bias, especially during 2001–4, little action was taken apart from changing the membership of statutory boards, since government always likes to have influential supporters.

Corruption. The PSD attracted radically different judgements on this matter. To some it was a legitimate party of social democracy, competent at running the economy with a ruling oligarchy that was no more than 'par for the course' in Europe, and with Iliescu as a man of stature in world affairs with enough sensitivity to avoid flaunting his personal wealth. But despite an anti-corruption law in 2003 and another on ethics in 2004, others saw the party as hopelessly corrupt: a 'mafia' involving extended families combining government with private business interests. It was basically a question of whether the patronage and corruption was moderate or excessive, and whether it was acceptable in the context of a relatively cohesive and effective government. Certainly most Romanians thought that government became more dishonest during this time and much was made of Năstase's power base among county barons – such as Dan Lilion Gogoncea (Galați), Constantin Ivanovici (Ilfov), Nicolae Mişchie (Gorj), Marian Oprişan (Vrancea) and Dumitru Sechelariu (Bacău) who managed PSD strongholds with easy access to state and EU funds – as well as substantial business interests in industry and agriculture. In some cases wealth was openly displayed to a remarkable degree, as in the case of Sechelariu who, as mayor of Bacău, invited thousands of guests to a birthday party in medieval style. Yet at the same time many supporters, like the Moldavian peasants voting for PSD 'like a gaggle of geese being taken to market', still believed in the party's wish to protect them and appreciated the small favours extended to them at the polling stations.

The Băsescu Presidency 2005–8

In the 2004 elections there was a presumption of further PSD success with the Hungarians and Humanists in tow and the latter apparently exposed to absorption – not least on the basis of its economic strength, with the Humanist leader Dan Voiculescu championing small entrepreneurs. Tudor's GRP also angled for an alliance with the PSD (albeit ruled out by the latter) by conceding – over the highly sensitive matter of wartime persecution of Jews – that the Antonescu regime was responsible for the deaths of some 400,000 Jews during 1941–44. He also promised a pilgrimage to Auschwitz to show that the party was no longer xenophobic and anti-Semitic. Opposition came from the Justice and Truth Alliance (JTA), formed in 2003 by the DP and the NLP (after the latter had merged the previous year with Melescanu's Alliance for Romania – comprising left-wing elements with some Securitate connections) to confront the PSD's ruling oligarchy of 'barons' who were making corruption a state institution. The alliance was already in a strong position, through support from the well-educated younger generation in the cities – giving the JTA 36 per cent of the mayoral positions in the local elections of 2004, compared with 28 per cent for the PSD (down from 65 per cent!) – when a more radical tone was adopted following the withdrawal of the NLP's candidate (Stolojan) from the presidential contest, apparently because of ill-health, and his replacement by the DP leader Traian Băsescu who was already general mayor of Bucharest and much more highly critical of the PSD ascendancy. A 16 per cent flat tax rate was offered (after the PSD had previously settled for a non-progressive tax of 23 per cent and a promise to 'reduce fiscality'). But there was much emphasis on personalities in preference to discussion of policy alternatives. Meanwhile the presidential election initially showed all the signs of a victory for Năstase, well known as the outgoing prime minister, although the campaigns made much use of TV and international political consultants, with little campaigning outside main cities, a strategy that seemed to reflect a fear of the voters. But there was all-out war when the charismatic Băsescu called for a 'fissure in the PSD bunker [to] prevent the globalisation of corruption within Romania's borders'. He was helped by *Evenimentul Zilei* appeals to Banat and Transylvanian voters in Braşov, Cluj, Sibiu and Timişoara not to be put off by Băsescu's 'Balkan/southern ways', his uninhibited comments on taboo subjects and his 'irregular' dress sense.

Corruption

This played a large part in the election. PSD economic control reflected the party's successful privatisation of the Securitate and communist party and the scandal of EU money accessed by local barons, with the Oltenian counties a particular case (although in Bacău mayor Sechelariu was accused of distributing SAPARD money for construction work to firms run by his family). The Minister for European Integration, Hildegard-Carola Puwak, was exposed by allegations that €150,000 of EU infrastructure funding had been channelled into family firms and she stepped down in a cosmetic exercise to improve the climate for the 2003 EU 'Country Report'. But there were many other allegations that are worth itemising to illustrate the wide range of dubious activities that contributed to the corruption scandal. Viorel Matei was criticised for apparently using his position as former head of the Senate farming committee, with contacts at the State Domain Agency and Timiş county, to help Italian investors to buy arable land in Timiş and hold it in fallow for the price to rise while receiving subsidies for not cultivating anything. There were also allegations that the prefect's position in Iaşi might be traded for cash on the basis of scope for enrichment through involvement with local administration and business. Contracting irregularities frequently arose. As Gorj county council chairman, Nicolae Mişchie was accused of awarding building projects to ARC (Târgu Cărbuneşti) and paying illegal bonuses in return for refurbishment of the council's guest house, while Constanţa town hall was accused of a lack of transparency in the development of a shopping mall at Tăbăcarie Park.

There was also an evident lack of transparency in the allocation of lucrative road contracts for snow clearance to firm run by prominent PSD members Costel Caşuneanu and the 'road king' Dorinel Umbrărescu. The same problem occurred over the supply of computers by Siveco under a $96mln Ministry of Education contract awarded without tender (as part of a computer-based education programme) on which subsequent re-negotiation by the new government saved $26.5mln. PSD elements were also thought to have profited handsomely from the flood of European funding through favours to family firms. In addition to €150,000 of business that forced Puwak's resignation, some $4.0bln of publicly funded investment (PFI) contracts were granted without the open tendering required by the EU: €2.5bln to Bechtel (USA) for the Braşov–Cluj–Oradea–Borş motorway (now well-advanced in its western sector); €1.0bln to the European Aeronautical Defence and Space (EADS) Company of Germany for border security and €0.48bln to Vinci (France) – criticised as 'a most severe break' from European laws on public acquisitions that could affect EU co-financing of future infrastructure projects. There were also complaints from the Danish Embassy over the disqualification of the Danish–Romanian consortium Daploma–Romsys from the competition for a ten-year, €78mln contract by the National Sanitary Veterinary and Food Standards Authority (subordinate to the prime minister) for a short-term IT and animal-identification system that went to a favoured company, IQ Management.

Other cases involved gross extravagance at public expense. Ion Dumitru, the head of Romsilva (promoted from the Dâmboviţa sylviculture department after organising hunting parties attended by premier Năstase) ran up expenses of almost 7.5mln.lei for pistols, bullets and hunting outfits. The director of the railway infrastructure company (convicted by the National Anti-Corruption Prosecutor's Office of trading on his office) established a 1,500-sq.m luxury restaurant called 'Zero Platform' in the basement of the transport building during 2002–3, leaving huge unpaid bills of 750mln.lei owing to suppliers and requiring a monthly rent of $40,000 for viability. The vice-president of the Romanian International Bank was charged with granting 51mln.lei in illegal credits to favoured companies. Other cases also involved companies. An 'iron mafia' operated a scam at Hunedoara through stealing scrap from the SOE 'Siderurgica' and selling it back through teams in touch with each other by mobile phones (presumably to avoid the police); while the scrap-collecting companies such as Ecosid, buying legally at 0.6lei/kg and selling for at least 1.4, were in the hands of people connected with both the Siderurgica company and the local PSD. Massive fraud was also alleged at the privatised Rafo oil refinery in Bacău county through false accounting and government co-operation in converting debts into shares. It was subsequently revealed by the National Agency for Fiscal Administration that some 0.8bln.lei was being 'well kept in fiscal paradises' with little chance of recovery. Private petrol stations in Constanţa were linked to the theft of 100,000t of oil products from the pipeline system. Other matters concerned corrupt dealings by the state-owned BCR at Novaci (Gorj) with local business, and special treatment for PSD tycoons over hunting areas: while Culiţă Ţărâţă was favoured in the Great Island of Brăila, a more outrageous case emerged with regard to the banker Ion Tiriac at Balc near Oradea – a hunting property leased for ten years to his Zimbrul company (claiming an investment of €1.34mln) without a transparent auction. Given Năstase's close connections with the affluent hunting fraternity, a high-profile wild boar shoot in late December 2004, attended by an international gathering of businessmen, may well have influenced the second round of the presidential election as the story broke. Certainly, in Hunedoara PSD supporters attributed their party's defeat to corruption and 'a mocking of leftist policy' as well as the 'clumsy elitism of the baron hunt' at Balc when 100 wild boar were shot.

Excesses by the PSD continued right up to election day, with JTA claims of fraud at some 4,000 of the 17,600 polling stations, including handouts of money to voters and electoral tourism by PSD 'caravans': some 300,000 invalid votes were allegedly credited to the PSD, with an overall fraud level estimated at 3–5 per cent; so, whereas PSD and their allies obtained 36.6 per cent of the votes for the Chamber of Deputies and 37.1 per cent for the Senate (virtually the same as in 2000) the JTA won 31.3 and 31.8 per cent respectively – more than doubling their shares of 14.5 and 15.5 per cent in 2000 mainly at the expense of the GRP with 12.9 and 13.6 per cent respectively (down from their high point of 19.5 and 21.0 per cent in 2000, despite a propaganda outlet through Cosmos TV. For the GRP (now renamed the Greater Romania Popular Party), Tudor's presidential ambitions also appeared to be limited by Năstase's strong claim to replace the unavailable Iliescu (after two full terms his further election was barred). On the other hand the NPCDP was still in a state of oblivion despite being controversially (and temporarily) renamed the Popular Christian Democrat Party (PCDP) – removing the 'peasant' tag, to the disgust of older members, in a bid to attract an increasingly urban-based constituency of younger people subjected to an suburbanising or 'mahalagizare' process by communist education. Although ably led at the time by Gheorghe Ciuhandu, mayor of Timişoara (the most prestigious local government office still held by a member of the party) and a presidential hopeful, centre-right voters clearly preferred the

JTA as the best way of frustrating the PSD, although Ciuhandu responded to Băsescu's appeal to voters in Timişoara not to spread the centre-right vote with his own appeal to Bucharesters to support the Christian Democrat project. The NPCDP has since merged with the small Romanian Reconstruction Union and may be joined by a Romanian Civic Forum that seeks full property restoration.

Lurch to the Centre-Right.

The big surprise was Băsescu's victory over Năstase in the second round of voting for the presidency by 5.12mln votes (51.2 per cent) to 4.88mln, with a remarkable turnaround in Gorj county (usually a PSD stronghold), where 53 per cent voted for Băsescu. He won over most of Tudor's supporters after accusing Năstase of treason for pledging autonomy for Szeklers – but evidently without eroding DUHR support! He also won some three-quarters of the votes cast abroad (attracting the many votes that had gone to Ciuhandu in the first round). Although the president may appoint a prime minister at will, it was initially assumed that Băsescu would 'cohabit' with Năstase as premier and would thus enjoy the advantage of not having to provide a protective umbrella for a mediocre or corrupt government. The PSD tried to encourage this by proposing a broad alliance, but this was rejected by the JTA, aiming to clear out corruption. But Băsescu went boldly for a minority JTA government under the NLP's Călin Popescu-Tăriceanu (on the grounds that the JTA had one more seat than the PSD). Although some 'remarkable horse-trading' was required to attract the support not only of the DUHR but also of the Humanist (now Conservative) Party (CP), already pledged to the PSD, as well as a National Democratic Bloc that detached itself from the GRP, Băsescu's decision was all the easier in view of Iliescu's blunder in providing a pardon for the imprisoned miners' leader Miron Cozma, on condition that he stayed away from Bucharest and Petroşani for five years. Iliescu also pardoned 44 others, including many guilty of corruption, and also the Timiş militia deputy leader who had put down the 1989 demonstration in Timişoara. Iliescu revoked his decision after widespread protest (even from within the PSD) including a US comment that the pardon was 'surprising and alarming' (considering that Iliescu had previously demoted judges involved in the Cozma trial). However, the damage had already been done, with the newspaper 'Evenimentul Zilei' sensing a sinister move to intimidate and 'sanction the destruction of democracy'. The incident also helped to propel the DUHR into supporting the JTA in parliament. Iliescu's lack of judgement amounted to a massive personal setback after he had started 2004 with the blessing of a highly supportive biography by an influential American historian and used his patronage to attract former opponents (even a new generation of intellectuals). But he lost his party position as the new PSD leader (Mircea Geoană) made desperate efforts to project a new image.

The shift to the centre-right fitted the wider trend in ECE with the need for a new focus on identity after the technocratic work on restructuring. But in order to succeed the JTA had to be efficient as well as clean after the clientelism of the PSD. In fact, political stability was often questioned after the DCR experience, and the government seemed unlikely to last the full term; but the IMF standby agreement – due to run to mid-2006 – and prospective EU accession have been disciplining factors. Băsescu favoured early elections because of the risk of incoherence due to dependence on elements outside the JTA. He regarded cooperation with the Humanists – now Conservatives (CP) – as immoral; rewarded as it was by administrative posts as state secretaries and sub-prefects. Commentators saw little future in the arrangement because of the inevitability of a showdown between the prime minister and CP leader Dan Voiculescu. However the CP senator Gheorghe Copos (representing Piteşti, the base of much of the manufacturing by his Ana Group) became a deputy prime minister with responsibility for investment. On the other hand, Valeriu Stoica failed to fuse the two alliance parties into a single centre-right party during 2004–5. But although the tension between the NLP and DP soured relations badly, the minority NLP government stayed in power until the 2008 elections.

Cleaning the Stable. Given the prospect of EU accession in 2007 (now achieved), there was a strong reform momentum within a cabinet packed with young western-educated reformers, partly to compensate for what was not done in 2004 for electoral reasons. An emergency decree brought in a 16 per cent rate for income and profit tax (the income tax rate was previously 20–40 per cent), in the hope of improving revenue collection (with larger penalties for evasion), boosting growth (with saving, investment and innovation) and limiting the budget deficit to 1.5 per cent through reduced public spending – although the current account deficit was expected to rise to 6.5 per cent. Băsescu was very keen on an anti-corruption agenda (included in the national defence strategy since mafia structures could hire assassins abroad) that will root out pervasive PSD networks. Following an early meeting with the National Defence Supreme Council, he asserted that five major threats to national security were: bad governance linked with corruption; international terrorism; totalitarian regimes supporting terrorism; WMD proliferation; and crisis situations (including frozen conflicts) in Romania's vicinity. European countries have been asked to help with the investigation of corporate fraud. With Securitate files leaving 'a constant threat of political blackmail hanging over politicians in the parliament' (Carey and Eisterhold 2004, p.22), he wanted them transferred to a national council for examination. He also wished to remove political influence from state institutions including justice, the police and the prosecutor general's office. Other ideas included a crime and terrorism investigation department within the public order ministry; and the subordination of intelligence to the presidency as a politically neutral institution. Scathing criticism was heaped on the interior ministry for allowing corruption in the police force and for failing to decentralise the police on a community basis, while the new justice minister Monica Macovei criticised the politicisation of the justice system, in particular the Supreme Council of the Magistrature's election of persons with a tarnished public image to the offices of secretary and deputy secretary. Magistrates are now checked against security files to see whether they were informers and still have connection with the security services that could lead to justice being dispensed in two ways. Băsescu allowed the police, prosecution (especially the Anti-Corruption Prosecutor's Office which had clearly under-performed) and judges six months to start producing results over corruption otherwise he will go to parliament for legislation to replace them all! The results have not been substantial but it is clear that prosecutors are now more proactive.

There were early dismissals for irregularities at the Agency for State Domains – also at the top of the police force and in state radio and TV. Former ministers have had their immunity removed (and so became accountable for corruption) and further protection will be lost by the removal of slander from the penal code. Some decisions made by the previous government were scrutinised: for example, the €1.0bln EADS contract for software, radars, helicopters and naval vessels was renegotiated on the grounds that it duplicated programmes already financed by the EU for border security (with the threat of cancellation if changes could not be made to take care of overlaps with Phare projects that duplicated expenses of €400mln). Checks were also made in the counties where some officials (including the DP president of Buzău County Council) had wrongly used public money to buy cars. New regulations on advertising by the state organisations were drawn up to prevent political bias. Tighter border controls were signalled by the removal of the head of border security for inadequate activity over security and criminality. However, Băsescu himself raised some eyebrows when he appointed as national security adviser reserve general C. Dejeratu who was a controversial figure in the 1989 events.

Coalition Strains occurred in the JTA reminiscent of the DCR era. But tension also occurred between president and prime minister. Băsescu's desire for the press and TV to be free of party political interference was resisted by the NLP, which found itself joining forces with GRP and PSD (highlighting the need for a full party merger between the two alliance parties, although this is very unpopular at the local level where the DP has perceived business links with the PSD). But a greater storm erupted when the judicial reforms essential for EU accession were rejected by the Constitutional Court. The appointment of magistrates to tackle corruption first requires the removal of the PSD's 'pervasive influence' through the officials installed by the PSD government to select magistrates, although the reforms also provide for mandatory retirement of judges and competition for judicial appointments. This seemed to underline the case for new elections later in 2005 in the expectation of a clear JTA majority (though hardly the two-thirds required to pass this key legislation without which EU accession would be highly unlikely). But in July 2005 the premier went back on his decision to resign (on the grounds of the flood relief crisis that was eroding his initially high ratings) and was promptly rebuked by Băsescu who accused him of bowing to interest groups that wanted him to stay on. The president's suspicions were aroused by hasty liberalisation of the energy market, illegal dealings in Petrom shares allocated to company employees, and corruption in the health service where hospital directors are difficult to remove.

However, Băsescu's hyper-sensitivity over mafia groups operating in the area of transport as well as energy and health suggested an element of mischief-making (recalling his campaign for Ciorbea's resignation in 1998). Băsescu probably overstated the case since Tăriceanu's controversial meetings were non-political contacts with close friends, but the president enjoyed 50–60 per cent approval ratings, especially after resolving a hostage crisis in Iraq: captured Romanian journalists were freed in May 2005 (thanks to action by the Romanian security services, Iraqi police and coalition forces) after agreeing to make a visit to Iraq organised and financed by two businessmen of Arab origin (one linked with the PSD, which merely added to that party's problems). However the government remained popular with the great benefit of a continuing economic boom. Meanwhile sideshows were provided by an unfortunate 'war' to remove parliamentary chairmen (Năstase and Văcăroiu) in favour of JTA appointees, while the Brussels connection attracted anti-European sentiments from the PSD – and the GRP, where Tudor was able to make something of a comeback as a magnet for those seeking an escape into nostalgia. Moreover there was an opportunistic (though enigmatic) political movement launched by the alluring Gheorghe Becali who currently embodies the Romanian dream as owner of Steaua football club with an estimated wealth of €400mln. He runs a New Generation Party and a TV channel, though promises are few apart from the cancellation of debts to the electricity company for the poor families of one Bucharest suburb. And as the NPCDP waited in the wings with its then-leader (Ciuhandu) active on the European stage, controversially supported by the independent parliamentarian Ioan Talpeş who was once one of Iliescu's advisors, former premier Stolojan (expelled from the NLP) talks of a new centre-right grouping that could involve the DP (renamed the Liberal Democratic Party: PD-L) and even the NPCDP.

Political alliances suffered the additional strain of more searching scrutiny by state prosecutors who upset not only the PSD 'barons' but Voiculescu's party, through their scrutiny of Copos; and even the Liberals, given the pressure on Dinu Patriciu and his Rompetrol company (for which it was convenient to hold the president responsible), who might have thought at one stage of a merger with the CP, stimulated by the attraction of Voiculescu's own TV channel. With the threat of 'proper cleansing' through 'justice à la Macovei', there were certainly questions over what the revolution was delivering. In 2005 it seemed that the PSD might be gaining by doing nothing while the electorate was 'switched off' by deepening tensions between president and premier so reminiscent of 1996–2000 (despite the fact that reforms needed by Romania to become a rule-of-law state with a functioning market economy were passed at this time). Băsescu's discrimination between support for his old DP and friction with the NLP drove down the latter's ratings and encouraged some prominent Liberals to stop demonising the official opposition. But obligations now in force requiring those in public life to declare their sources of wealth (including the assets of spouses) have now placed Năstase under renewed pressure through property dealing in the highly desirable Corbeanca area of Bucharest, to which some highly implausible under-valuations have been attached. There was further strain when the coalition parties joined different groups in Strasbourg.

Yet over three years the alliance managed to advance political/economic reform and secure EU accession – while also presiding over a 40 per cent growth in incomes and 8.0 per cent economic growth in 2006. An expansionist fiscal policy continued through 2008, despite the global credit crunch and rapidly growing budgetary and current account deficits. But a full union between the two parties was always impossible, since both seek the limelight (as they did during 1997–2000) and DP ministers eventually resigned as part of a process of political fragmentation that has seen the minority Liberal government strengthening links with the PSD opposition (with an unlikely liaison that secured a parliamentary majority in 2007 to dismiss the president). Parliament was also able to vote to remove justice minister Macovei whose efforts to curb corruption were not always appreciated by politicians rarely over-anxious to have their wealth scrutinised. This incident, which followed on from a special parliamentary session performing a symbolic burial of communism in the presence of King Mihai and foreign visitors including V.Havel and L.Wałęsa, was not altogether unrelated to the predicament of former economy minister Codrut Sereş who has been charged with leaking classified information to foreign companies. Meanwhile foreign affairs highlighted the Brussels dimension and the strain imposed on eastern relationships as the new EU frontier becomes a reality. Despite Romanian support for Moldova's claim to membership and Bucharest's good intentions over visas and passports, the steady ebb of population away from Voronin's communist state has attracted a fiery denunciation from Chişinău on the state of Moldavians in Romania where the North East is clearly the poorest region. As this book goes to press new alliances for the 2008 election have yet to crystallise. After strong growth both president and prime minister will be difficult to dislodge, but the DP is very popular while PSD has regained much of its former credibility.

CULTURAL CHANGE OR CONTINUITY?

The situation is – as ever – delicately poised because in spite of the spontaneity of the 1989 revolution there was no constructive dialogue and no effective progressive force to check the anti-democratic impulses (nationalist and xenophobic) within the NSF, thereby enabling the political elite and the economic oligarchy to support and overlap. At the same time outside support has not always been well directed, with excessive pressure from the IMF over budget deficits at the end of the 1990s that brought higher taxes that were extremely damaging for fledgling SMEs; while the EU seemed blissfully unaware of the mounting corruption of the Năstase government during 2001–4. A political culture prone to patrimonialism, nepotism and excessive personalisation seems an obstacle to substantive – as opposed to procedural – democracy and invites complicity over cosmetic transformations. So, while substantial progress has been made since 1989, with peaceful transfers of power after the elections of 1996, 2000 and 2004, the other side of the coin is the gap that remains between Romania – and the SEECs as a whole – and the more mature democracies of Western Europe. This is partly a matter of 'institutional thickness' and capacity. The democratisation process has not been adequately decentralised to intermediate levels of government, grassroots partnerships between local governments and NGOs are hardly evident, and lack of confidence in state institutions and political parties is reflected in declining electoral participation. A major issue involves corruption or, to put it more mildly, a failure to cope with the discipline of transparency. For Gallagher (2005) Romania's whole independent existence has been tarnished by the perverted democracy of the old Liberal Party, the monarcho-fascist Carol II, the communist regime and now the PSD while the search for higher standards of government spearheaded by Iuliu Maniu in the 1930s, Ion Antonescu during the Second World War and Victor Ciorbea in 1997–98 was blocked by depression, war and coalition instability. But this seems too simple, given the recent experiences of political dependence and neo-serfdom that place a premium on strong leadership and personal ties so well expressed in the PCR (communist party) network of 'pile' (friends), 'cunoştinţe' (acquaintances) and 'relaţii' (connections)! The leaderships that are grounded in the masses will tend to the most corrupt because, as *Evenimentul Zilei* put it on 20 September 2005, 'bastards will always win because the poor education of the electorate will always be their ally' in villages and small towns: gladly surrendering votes in return for charity and free music. Certainly PSD elements are thought to have profited handsomely from the flood of European funding through favours to family firms: notably the business allocated by a former European integration minister (Puwak) and large payments from some $4.0bln of publicly funded investment (PFI) granted without open tendering.

Rather than leave the corruption of the past in peace, PSD county barons are being investigated: Mişchie in Gorj has been accused of evading customs on two imported Italian cars because his company qualified for an investor's certificate (carrying exemption for such payments) through registration in Mătăsari commune (with LFA fiscal status), although it emerged that the business address was an empty apartment! In another PSD stronghold – Vrancea – a case of embezzlement and misappropriation was tabled in respect of 2.3mln. lei spent on fixed tenders and preferential contracts for roadwork. Meanwhile the Vrancea CC leader, Marian Oprişan, was charged with abuse of office, forgery and misappropriation of funds. The present PSD leader, Mircea Geoană wants to eliminate corrupt members, including county barons, and admits that his party will not be fit to govern again until this has been done. Meanwhile, parties looking more towards westernised middle-class elements can afford to be more European, yet there are family and interest feuds in counties where the staffs of all the large parties are recruited (justifying the model of larger regions with serious budgets and multiple prerogatives) and with opportunistic transfers from the communist ranks it is possible in all parties for corrupt members to climb to the top of the lists. Meanwhile, it is noticeable how easily public opinion is offended by the perceived weakness of coalitions that lack the coherence of leadership fortified by networks of patronage because the party machines are in conflict, however minimal the ideological differences. The Popescu Tăriceanu government inevitably repeated some of the mistakes of its DCR predecessor while the prime minister himself lost some credibility for appearing insufficiently decisive when faced with the serial flood disasters of 2005. However, he appears comfortable at the moment and his less committed allies declined to rock the boat in the run up to EU accession.

Corruption becomes a disease which quickly spreads to the foreign business community where it can easily threaten the conventional logic of 'best practice' when two-thirds of foreigners on temporary stay visas (46,800 at the start of 2005) need to resort to bribery in order to get extensions. Spurious claims can easily be made, as in the case of Peter Fallenius who was tried in Sweden in 2005 for retaining $5,000 of a historic debt repayment of $120mln he secured from the Romanian government (largely owed to the electrical engineering company ABB). Fallenius argued that a bribe had been paid to Bucharest general mayor Viorel Lis to secure the contract for the city's Nord power station – a claim that Lis vehemently denied. A more recent case concerns Rompetrol, which was privatised in 1993 and fell under the control of NLP tycoon Dinu Patriciu in 1998, while an American minority stake was acquired by the private equity fund 'International Equity Partners' belonging to G. P.Stephenson, who sold it on to a European investor when he started working for Rompetrol full-time in 2002 (with a personal interest in the company worth $100mln on paper). The company has been successful in modernising

Petromidia refinery (after Rompetrol acquired the government's stake for some $50mln in 2001): it has traded on the stock exchange since 2004 with a market value of some $500mln and aimed to have 300 filling stations by the end of 2005. But opponents of the company have started a smear campaign claiming tax evasion over the refinery takeover, including vitriolic press comment orchestrated by interests associated with another refinery (Rafo Oneşti) that Patriciu refused to take over. The case attracted international attention seeking greater transparency in the way that investigations are instigated. Clearly the press is capable of behaving unscrupulously through manipulation by blackmail, an art practised by individuals with a Securitate background with a capacity to destroy reputations if payments and favours are not granted. The most prominent figures in government are at risk, which helps to explain why even reformist administrations can be reluctant to grant all the press freedoms that the EU requires.

Corruption remained a key issue for EU accession into 2006 since the EU could not condone a political climate with rampant corruption and parties unable to clean their own back yards. The 2005 'Country Report' indicated profound dissatisfaction (especially over high-level corruption), with the failure of the state prosecutors to convict anyone in a prominent position. There are certainly 'dinosaurs' in the justice system, which explains why magistrates in their fifties (with 25 years' service) have been encouraged, since 2005, to retire on pensions higher than their salaries. However, it is easy to forget how far things have moved, because the present resistance to corruption charges is reminiscent of the stubborn defensive attitude of SOEs to any limitation of their absolute rights to milk the state through profligate management using their monopoly role for leverage during 1997–2000. So it is difficult to see how it will be possible for a future justice minister to help herself to the handsome salary of a retiring magistrate, as retiring justice minister Rodica Stănoiu was able to do before leaving office in 2005. Ten years on from his death in 1995, Corneliu Coposu is still a powerful force through his 'moral benchmark' that is being gradually translated into reality with the guarantee of private property under the constitution achieved in 2003; not to mention reconciliation with King Mihai, clean (or at least cleaner) elections and a historic achievement of both NATO and EU membership accompanied by an economic boom that could not have been contemplated a decade ago. Despite continued public scepticism, political outlooks are no longer so solidly grounded in the communist experiences now that most of the past 'wrongs' have been addressed (although much property restitution has still to be completed) and instead there is much more of a consensus on the desirability of maintaining economic progress and observing European standards of accountability.

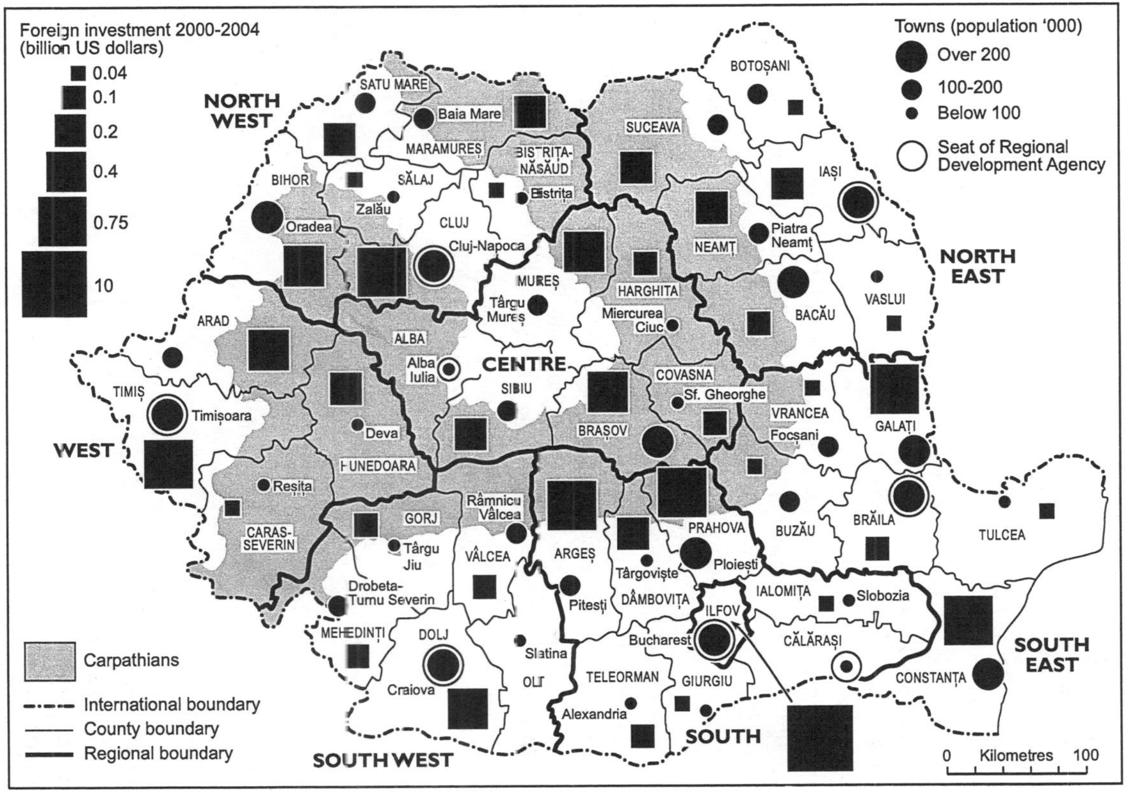

Figure 1.1 Romania's Regions and Counties Source: Statistical Yearbooks

2. Economic Restructuring, Investment and the Labour Market

This chapter looks at the restructuring process with particular reference to privatisation and foreign investment. Restructuring was absolutely essential in order to transfer responsibility for economic management from the state to private enterprise, given that the revolution reflected the state's inability to cope combined with a popular desire for decentralisation and a focus on wealth creation. However, a concern for social security – and the long-term survival of a substantial industrial establishment – has meant that the state can divest itself of responsibility only gradually, and the process has been highly contentious politically, especially during the 1990s. The climate for foreign investment is a critical matter given Romania's initial failure to realise its full potential in attracting participation by leading companies worldwide. The labour market has certainly been a great asset, although unemployment has been drastically reduced through emigration, both temporary and permanent, while the quality of the workforce is affected by the standards of the education and health services which are both examined at some length. Overall, restructuring has made great progress, but the failure to balance the run-down in centrally planned industrial production – inevitable in the context of the demise of central planning throughout the former Soviet bloc – with new opportunities in the global market economy resulted in a serious poverty problem, gradually eased by renewed growth since 2000. Many country people still have low incomes but the main problem is now one of maintaining growth at a time of almost full employment with wage increases no longer tied to productivity but instead reflecting scarcity in urban growth areas as well as convergence since 2007.

TRANSITION AND RESTRUCTURING

The difficult transition is well summarised by annual growth and inflation rates (Table 2.1). Given the depth of recession, growth averaged out at –1.0 per cent per annum during 1990–2002 compared with +1.5 per cent for 'first wave' EU accession states, while inflation since 1995 averaged 54 per cent per annum until 2002 compared with only 11 per cent for the first wave. For ordinary people this translated into reduced levels of employment and real wages, making for a serious poverty problem (Mete et al. 2003, p.3). Salaried

Table 2.1: *Basic economic indicators 1985–2005*

Year	A	B	C	D	E	F	G	H	I	J	K	L	M	N	O
1985	0.07	0.03	5.9	0.4	n.a.	n.a.	62.7	15.0	n.a.	n.a.	12.2	10.4	6.6	n.a.	n.a.
1990	0.08	0.04	-5.6	50.1	18.8	-2.9	40.5	21.8	n.a.	0.4	5.9	9.1	1.2	#	n.a.
1991	0.16	0.07	-12.9	174.5	19.6	1.2	37.9	18.9	40	0.4	4.3	5.4	2.1	0.01	3.0
1992	0.60	0.26	-8.8	210.9	22.0	-13.9	38.3	19.0	77	0.2	4.4	5.8	3.2	0.03	8.4
1993	2.00	0.88	1.5	256.1	1.3	12.4	33.8	21.0	94	1.0	4.9	6.0	4.2	0.08	10.4
1994	4.98	2.19	3.9	136.8	4.6	3.0	35.6	19.8	341	2.1	6.2	6.6	5.5	0.17	10.9
1995	7.21	3.18	7.1	32.3	9.4	4.9	32.9	19.9	419	1.7	7.9	9.5	6.7	0.20	9.5
1996	10.89	4.78	4.1	38.3	9.9	-3.1	33.2	19.2	263	2.1	8.1	10.6	9.2	0.31	6.6
1997	25.29	11.22	-6.6	154.8	7.4	1.4	30.9	17.9	1215	3.8	8.4	10.4	10.4	0.72	8.9
1998	37.25	16.55	-7.3	59.0	17.3	-7.6	30.2	14.4	2031	2.9	8.3	11.8	9.5	0.89	10.4
1999	*35.6	5.53	-1.2	45.9	8.0	4.7	24.8	13.3	1041	2.7	8.5	10.4	9.1	1.53	11.8
2000	*37.1	5.79	2.1	45.6	6.6	-15.8	25.2	11.1	1037	3.9	10.4	12.0	10.5	2.17	10.5
2001	*40.2	6.22	5.7	34.5	8.5	-1.0	27.6	13.4	1157	5.4	11.4	14.4	11.5	2.91	8.8
2002	*45.8	6.71	5.0	22.5	6.0	2.0	28.1	11.4	1141	7.2	13.9	16.5	14.7	3.31	8.1
2003	*57.0	7.15	4.9	15.3	1.0	5.0	25.0	11.6	1946	9.0	17.6	22.2	20.6	3.32	7.4
2004	*70.3	7.66	8.3	11.9	5.3	22.2	24.7	12.4	5183	12.7	25.5	32.6	24.5	3.26	6.3
2005	n.a.	8.28	4.1	8.9	4.0	1.9	21.5	8.5	5213	n.a.	30.2	38.8	28.6	3.05	5.9

Notes: A GDP bln.new lei (*$bln); B GDP pc (PPPy); C GDP percentage change y-y; D Change in consumer prices y-y; E Annual growth in industrial production per cent; F Annual growth in agricultural production per cent; G Industry share of GDP per cent; H Agriculture share of GDP per cent; I FDI in $mln but €mln from 2003 (RAFI) - total FDI stock in €bln: 10.1 (2003); 15.0 (2004); 20.1(2005); J Foreign currency/gold reserves $bln; K Exports $bln; L Imports $bln; M Foreign debt per cent GDP; N dollar exchange in new lei = 10.000 old lei (# below 0.1); O Unemployment rate per cent.

Sources: Statistical Yearbooks and Economist Intelligence Unit.

employment declined by a quarter and hit the 56–65 age group very badly as the proportion in employment fell from 22 to five per cent (while 83 per cent were retired); this compared with a decline from 70 to 44 per cent for the 46–55 group (with 26 per cent retired, while others were forced into a 'waiting retirement' strategy based on informal activities). At the same time there has been a sharp change in economic structure evident in terms of both GDP and employment. There was, meanwhile, substantial change in the employment structure by economic branches, with a sharp decline in mining and manufacturing during 1989–95 (from 35.3 to 25.0 per cent) and in construction, transport and community services (29.2 to 24.2 per cent), while gains occurred in utilities, finance and trade (up from 7.4 to 13.2 per cent) and in agriculture, as the 'employer of last resort' (27.9 to 37.5 per cent) (Dăianu et al. 2001). This clearly cannot be a sustainable distribution with agriculture (along with forestry) contributing only 14.7 per cent of GDP in 2004 compared with 37.6 per cent for industry and 48.7 per cent for services.

Depression and Inflation

All transition states experienced an initial depression – with de-industrialisation and a growth of employment in agriculture for reasons of subsistence – prior to a resumption of growth. But this 'J curve' syndrome operated in an extreme fashion in Romania and – partly because of a politically engineered boom in 1995–96 and poor management of the resulting crisis in 1997 when net investments were barely half the 1989 level – generated a second cycle of decline characterised by a deteriorating business environment with limited home demand, reduced international competitiveness, capital shortage and widening inequality. Romania's problems in opening up to a global economy under market conditions were bound to be challenging because of an inadequate infrastructure, including financial reserves and professional resources (CNPCS 1998, pp.19–22). But they were arguably made worse by the excesses of the Ceauşescu era through (a) excessive growth, unrelated to consumer demand and world prices, that made the country extremely vulnerable to a sudden opening up to world market trends and prices, and (b) the pressurising and pauperisation of the population during the 1980s in a highly irrational drive to maximise exports and pay off foreign debts. Ceauşescu's constant harassment of the population encouraged early transitional governments (often dismissed as 'neo-communist' because of their ultra-cautious approach to restructuring) to seek popularity on the basis of nationalism when reform should have been given higher priority from the start. Lack of political will to reform in the early years – along with constrained institutional and governance capacity – was widely blamed for poor economic performance and deteriorating social conditions.

High inflation made for great economic uncertainty. Although public works were reduced to limit inflation and prepare for currency convertibility, national income fell through reduced domestic output (caused partly by a lack of credit), while the burden of providing social services was increased by unemployment. Subsidies to limit unemployment in the SOEs and the printing of more money to stave off poverty both fuelled inflation – a form of welfare that avoided open-ended commitments, but also eroded international confidence and the value of savings. Each state had to regulate the process in its own way, according to the economic indicators, public opinion and the ideological preferences of governing coalitions. But the key elements summarised in this paragraph played a part in each national scenario. For Romania high taxes and poor regulation encouraged an underground 'black' economy accounting for some 6.7 per cent of GDP in 1992 but an estimated 20–40 per cent in 2000 when tax revenue should have been 70 per cent higher than was actually achieved. Complex regulations, including licensing and administrative procedures, were also blamed for a situation in which the most important part of the underground economy was under-reported value added. But the problem was also a consequence of poverty because 1.2mln Romanians worked unrecorded for some 1,600 separate employers at the turn of the millennium and this hit social security revenues as well as income tax. Such illegality was most common in textiles and footwear as well as service industries, but professional people were often paid a proportion of their fees in cash while many factory workers did farm work at weekends. There were also major smuggling rackets involving alcohol, cigarettes, coffee and cheap clothing, controlled by Arab, Chinese and Turkish traders. With rapid growth – outperforming the formal economy by many times – this problem needed an urgent solution to bring the budget into balance. But only in 2005 did a new government address the matter with a flat tax of 16 per cent and a promise to bring down social security deductions that constitute a heavy 'payroll tax'. Such was the scenario severely limiting government investment in SOEs over and above the obligation to support losses that was short-sightedly taken on board in the early corporatisation process.

Trade

Control of trade and prices collapsed so that goods could be readily imported to meet deficits. But liberalisation created serious difficulties because exporters could not easily switch to new markets – through lack of experience and inappropriate specifications for their products – when orders from the other formerly planned economies dried up. Dislocation of Romania's commerce was all the greater because of the 'shock' of German unification, meaning that East Germany started trading in (formerly West German) Deutsche Marks. Furthermore, the collapse of the Soviet Union brought many long-standing exchanges to an abrupt conclusion, while civil war in Yugoslavia led to a UN trade embargo against Serbia, another of Romania's important trading partners. New trade relations developed gradually with the EU and other countries, but production fell sharply in the meantime. Table 2.1 shows some narrowing of the trade gap during the early 1990s but the situation remains difficult because of the great propensity to import (especially when Romanian products are inferior), while export markets are highly competitive and the advantage of low labour costs is lost as soon as quality is compromised. Machinery and metallurgical products are prominent exports, although imports in this category are higher, whereas clothing, textiles and footwear are in surplus (but are also heavily dependent on outsourcing by West European firms that could easily transfer business to lower-wage economies). It has been suggested that too much trade was switched to western countries (highly competitive markets constrained by slow growth) and that more interest should be taken in the CIS, Middle East and Latin America. Commercial dealings with Arab states (boosted already by timber exports in the hands of Arab-owned companies) are not yet commensurate with the general level of the Arab activity in Romania: – businessmen from Egypt, Jordan, Lebanon and Syria active in real estate, tourism and restaurants; also young Arab students higher education sector. Fortunately there are institutions that can help: the Romanian Export Trade Centre promotes investment and exports along with Eximbank (Romania's Bank for Exports and Imports). But there may be a case for reduced tax on export business.

New Institutions

A modernised National Bank was critical in setting the stage for privatisation and much of the success has rested with the governor, Mugur Isărescu, first appointed from the Washington embassy in 1990 and confirmed in 1991, 1998 and again in 2004 after a spell as prime minister during 1999–2000. Faced with an almost total exhaustion of foreign exchange reserves and precious metals (following the Ceauşescu years) and the surge in post-1989 imports, he was able to restore the situation (to €10bln of reserves in 2005) and press for a tight monetary policy in 1991, damping what 'might otherwise have been an uncontrollable rush of resources towards scarce goods and services pushing inflation even higher' (Isărescu 1992, p.153). Despite inflation (enabling poorly performing companies to conceal their inefficiency) and delays in reaching agreement with the IMF, Romania gained an international credit rating that allowed a return to international capital markets in 1995 when a $150mln loan was arranged by Citibank to improve foreign currency reserves. There was also progress in supervising commercial banks, although this did not prevent a number of failures such as the scandal at Bancorex (Romanian Bank for External Commerce) involving loans to the regime's clients. In 1999, 70 per cent of its loans were non-performing, and Bancorex accounted for half of the total losses of $4.1bln arising from such loans in the entire banking sector during 1992–2004 (of which little more than a tenth was ever recovered). Banca Agricolă was undermined by the corruption of state farm managers, while Columna Bank, Dacia Felix Bank and the International Bank of Religion also found themselves in difficulty. Meanwhile the Bucharest Stock Exchange (BSE) was re-created in 1995 and the RASDAQ securities market (an electronic network for registering over-the-counter share sales) was established in 1996 following understanding with the USA over the Romanian Capital Market Development project to back up mass privatisation by offering a regulated environment for secondary trading. The two institutions merged in 2004 to unify capital markets with a daily trading value of $15–20mln. There has been a rapid growth of capitalisation to meet the target of 40 per cent of GDP: from €2.6bln in 2002 to €14.2bln in September 2005 (compared with €4.5bln in Bulgaria, €30.3bln in the Czech Republic, €30.8bln in Hungary and €69.2bln in Poland).

Restructuring State-Owned Enterprises (SOEs)

Throughout the region governments were navigating in uncharted waters but, despite deeply-entrenched vested interests, restructuring **was** widely seen as essential in order to reduce the state's commitments, overcome the inefficiency inherent in communism and create a well-functioning market economy (FME) on EU lines that is now seen as the goal of transition throughout the region. In the early 1990s there was some ambivalence on this issue, especially when the economic networks inherited from communism retained their political influence. While some transition states were keen to implement market-driven 'neo-liberal' policies to create a self-regulated market that would reduce the need for government co-ordination and prevent any chance of a return to authoritarian central planning, Romania's neo-communist government saw no immediate need to relinquish control and took action only slowly, partly so as to maintain and expand client networks within the business community. Experience revealed that while excessive resources might go into supporting loss-making SOEs – partly by tolerating huge payment arrears (42 per cent of GDP at the end of 1999) – the state could not single-handedly finance their modernisation with the new technology essential for long-term profitability. And as the economic case for restructuring has become clearer – with new investment by private enterprise in modernisation to achieve more efficient and higher-quality production, albeit combined with heavy redundancies – the political significance has increased, with restructuring now a critical barometer of progress in transition in the eyes of the EU, foreign investors and global financial institutions.

Transition states have found it difficult to finance improvements to SOEs beyond what any enterprise profits might support. Hence any initial goal of long-term viability under state ownership has usually given way (with declining competitiveness and employment) to a search for foreign buyers prepared to take over the daunting responsibilities. Romania's State Ownership Fund (SOF) can certainly claim some successes: it helped Electroprecizia Săcele to diversify into electrical sub-units for Daewoo 'Cielo' cars manufactured in Craiova with prototype starter and alternator units tested prior to being put into mass production. The Dacia car factory at Piteşti-Colibaşi (now Mioveni) was able to launch a new model thanks to SOF funding, while the Câmpulung 'Land Rover' builder ARO was able to update its engines and improve export prospects in collaboration with Austria. Of course, the state had to identify strategic industries and determine priorities over the targeting of its limited investment capability: hence, the neo-liberal approach has always been balanced by a pragmatic 'neo-statist' conception of change driven from the centre by a technocratic 'transformative' model imposed by decree or (more likely) a 'developmental' model of selective intervention to help certain firms solve their quality and productivity problems arising through changing circumstances. However, the neo-statist approach was handicapped in the early years by lack of experience in running a market economy that needed coherent policies for growth and resources to sustain them. Meanwhile, Romania's need was all the greater because not only had the Soviet Union broken traditional ties with the West (in favour of bloc co-ordination that initially involved heavy reparation demands), but Ceauşescu subsequently reacted against the foreign borrowings of the 1970s by repaying all debts in the following decade. Furthermore, the revolution saw the collapse of state revenues pending a new fiscal system (complicated by the growth of an underground economy), while government spending immediately had an inflationary effect as wages stimulated demand that attracted foreign goods.

Privatisation

This was a critical matter widely advocated as a high priority by international financial institutions (IFIs) so that resources could be allocated according to market forces and risk placed on a commercial basis – making for economic growth in the shortest time – with balanced budgets and a strong currency. But despite the merits over the long-term, there was always a risk of short-term crisis through lack of information (e.g. on the potential of enterprises on offer) and heavy redundancy through initial downsizing. The IMF tended to argue for a long-term strategic view while governments were all too aware of the short-term implications of change and doubted the capacity of private business to make up for jobs lost in the public sector. The general perception across the region was that IMF delegations sought only basic indicators for financial plans and took little account of the costs of transformation or the long-term potentials. Experience has shown that it is extremely difficult to design a privatisation process that will work to the political advantage of the government promulgating it, particularly where large enterprises in the state sector are concerned. Hence the marked tendency in transition states to equivocate and delay the sales of assets that might evoke political controversy, while using newly corporatised state firms as a source of patronage, and leaving more extensive 'reviews' of privatisation programmes to the next government.

Privatisation is also a comfortable way out of a political predicament in the context of financial difficulties and the need for harder budget constraints, while privatisation is viewed from the outside as an integral part of comprehensive systemic change and a barometer of commitment to reform. Privatisation can be achieved through purchases involving all economic actors, including foreign companies, but there is a school of thought that would restrict foreign penetration in favour of share allocations to citizens ('voucher privatisation') or special deals – typically lacking transparency – that favour an enterprise workforce (EMBO) or elements in the former *nomenklatura* seeking transformation into a capitalist oligarchy. The first option should bring the best returns, though it may require prior downsizing of the work-force and the hiving-off of sections separate from the core business such as services (catering, transport and maintenance). But if the business environment for 'foreign direct investment' (FDI) is poor, perhaps because of political instability, cheap labour offers the option of staying with old technology, especially where there is strong union resistance to redundancy (perhaps with the help of some j.v. capital). However, while this strategy protects jobs in the short term it can offer only a temporary respite because highly capitalised high-productivity enterprises are crucial for economic competitiveness in the long term. The process also involves choices over its scale: a 'critical mass' of private sector activity is desirable but the ultimate extent of the state sector is a factor and the market value of state assets may be problematic regarding the technical level, pollution hazards and property rights.

Privatisation by EMBO (usually on extremely favourable terms) was initially popular, along with transfers facilitated in part by free allocations of shares to citizens; although on this basis new owners typically found themselves unable to finance modernisation of their factories. Indeed, such were 'the political intricacies of Romania's post-socialist transition' (Stoica 2004, p.271) that power networks from the communist past re-profiled ex-cadres as 'born-again capitalists' using the organisational experience, education and network resources gained in communism's 'second economy'. Hence privatisation and the freedom for private enterprise created an economic elite of 3–5,000 businessmen favoured, above all, by the PSD, although other parties have 'their' businessmen. These include the NLP with Dinu Patriciu of Rompetrol as well as Gheorghe Copos (originally of PSD, but now prominent in the CP) who built up the diverse 'Ana Grup', beginning in 1990 with a confectionery business and a chain of shops, before diversifying into TV assembly in the following year. In

1996 he gained a majority holding in the Piteşti electric motor company IMEP (producing units for industrial use and household appliances since 1967 and renamed Ana-IMEP in 2003) and his interests in tourism gave rise to Ana Tours (1997) and Ana Teleferic (1999). He also has a transport company 'Ana Trans International' and runs the charitable 'Ana Foundation' as well as Bucharest's 'Rapid' football club. For a time he was a deputy prime minister in the Popescu Tăriceanu government with responsibility for foreign investment. A flexible and pragmatic approach in building profitability can also be seen in the case of Eurohouse that started in Piatra Neamţ in 1993 before changing its name to 'Serviciile Comerciale Române' the following year. A small partnership began in commerce (through a 'non-stop' supermarket in Buhuşi in 1994), while expanding into tourism (renting out rooms in the Dochia chalet at the Ceahlău mountain resort of Durău during 1994–96) and then into sporting tourism. But it went on to find a niche in commercial centres in 1995–97 – renting out warehouse space to small businesses in various Romanian towns, with stock market dealing on its Paşcani and Roman premises an innovation in 1998.

During the recession at the end of the 1990s SCR had money to invest in privatisation bids, with the first successes in 1999 over Contactoare (Buzău) – started in 1975 to produce electric motors, transformers and switchboards – and Sinterom (Cluj-Napoca) – which originated as the 'Triumf' chemical works in 1936 before turning to spark plugs in 1955 followed by ignition devices and sintered products. Acquisitions followed with Uzuc (Ploieşti) – chemical equipment – in 2002; Chimcomplex (Borzeşti) and Iaşitex (Iaşi) in 2003 – when the new owners received the award for Romanian Investor of the Year; followed in 2004 by Caromet (Caransebeş) and Novatex (Piteşti) – renamed Novatextile Bumbac (NTB) – and Someş (Dej). The process was assisted by subsidiary companies in Cluj (A1 Impex) and Ploieşti (A2 Impex) – the former selling car parts. The number of employees grew strongly from 15 in 1994 to 738 in 1999 and 6,500 in 2004. The factories in this wide-ranging portfolio are now managed in groups: Automotive (Contactoare and Sinterom), Cellulose & Paper (Someş), Chemicals (Chimcomplex), Industrial Equipment (Caramet and Uzuc), and Light Industry (Iaşitex and NTB). Indeed, for diversity SCR rivals some foreign investment groups such as Andrei Siminel's New Century Holdings (acting for Broadhurst Investments, Lindsell Enterprises and Ivington Enterprises) that have injected some $200mln into Romanian companies since 1995 – including, in the case of Broadhurst, interests in Vel Pitar bakery as well as several electrical equipment producers (Imsat, Electoparataj, Electrotehnica, Imsat and Umeb), all of which apply modern management concepts. By contrast, land restitution involved only tiny subsistence holdings, and, while some farm 'barons' emerged later by leasing state farm land, individual farming on small units is hardly a viable entrepreneurial strategy to accelerate economic growth (Chirca and Teşliuc 1999, p.27).

Small and Medium Sized Enterprises (SMEs)

Table 2.2: *Enterprises (th) by size-groups 1996–2005*

Year	Total	Industry*				Commerce				Other Services			
		A	B	C	D	A	B	C	D	A	B	C	D
1996	312.1	32.5	72.3	16.3	6.2	226.0	95.7	3.6	0.6	53.5	86.2	8.8	3.7
1997	315.8	36.4	71.4	17.6	6.4	226.1	85.2	4.2	0.6	54.2	84.9	9.9	4.0
1998	318.4	39.3	71.1	18.0	6.7	222.0	93.3	6.0	0.6	57.0	84.7	10.3	3.9
1999	318.7	41.5	72.3	18.1	7.4	217.4	94.3	5.1	0.6	59.8	84.9	10.5	3.8
2000	308.1	42.2	68.0	20.4	8.2	202.8	93.3	6.0	0.6	58.7	84.0	12.3	2.4
2001	311.3	43.5	67.1	20.8	8.9	192.6	92.7	6.6	0.7	75.2	85.1	10.9	3.4
2002	315.1	47.3	68.0	20.2	8.8	177.7	92.4	6.8	0.7	90.2	87.0	9.7	2.8
2003	349.1	51.8	69.4	19.5	8.4	179.3	91.5	7.6	0.8	118.0	89.0	8.3	2.3
2004	394.5	56.4	70.9	18.7	7.9	191.2	92.1	7.1	0.8	146.9	90.4	7.3	2.0
2005	433.0	59.1	71.4	18.9	7.6	200.4	91.9	7.3	0.8	173.5	90.8	7.2	1.7

Notes: A Total; B 0–9 employees; C 10–49 employees; D 50–500 employees (balance 500 plus) * includes extractive industries and electricity-gas-water
Source: Statistical Yearbooks: Table 15.3

Over the years perhaps the greatest efforts in job creation by the government – and external organisations – have gone into the formation of SMEs widely seen as a good indicator of progress in building a market economy, since they provide services essential for larger businesses – and for society as a whole – and cumulatively generate jobs on a scale that is significant in reducing the unemployment caused by restructuring. Thus, the US Commerce Department would advocate SMEs to drive economic growth after the American experience in creating two-thirds of all jobs and generating half of GDP in this way. In Romania, where there was much negative opinion regarding private investment in the early transition years, SMEs (falling overwhelmingly into the private sector) helped to inspire some confidence in a market economy. Managed by young people with vocational training, they were also seen as an appropriate vehicle for the introduction of new technologies encouraged by the R&D ministry and co-ordinated by the National Agency of Science, Technology and Innovation striving to prevent the country becoming a 'technological colony'. However, SMEs must be carefully nurtured through a national strategy that will also represent them in local power structures. Potential entrepreneurs need to learn business and management skills in a relatively sheltered environment, perhaps with a stimulative fiscal regime. Space constraints prevent further detail on this important policy issue that is assessed through each government's contribution in the author's parallel work (Turnock 2007, pp.93–126), while original contributions are available from Allen (1996), Ianoş (2000), Popescu (1993) and Rusu (2001). Table 2.2 shows significant growth in new enterprises during 2003-5 after several years of stagnation, including decline between 1999 and 2000. However figures are not available before 1996 and hence the surge in commerce in the early 1990s cannot be shown. Instead some consolidation is evident in commerce as the smaller units have declined with the growth of large stores. The total number of commercial units fell from 226,000 in 1996 to 200,400 in 2005 but the percentage with ten or more employees doubled from 4.2 to 8.1 per cent. Meantime total numbers increased substantially in industry and very rapidly (by more than three times) in other services, with enterprises in the latter category only 26,900 behind those in commerce by 2005.

FOREIGN DIRECT INVESTMENT

Limited domestic resources made FDI essential for generating a 'virtuous circle' in Romanian politics (Jolly and Kettanek 1999) through privatisation, and also the establishment of countless numbers of new enterprises needed for a successful economy through new technologies for competitive exports. This was all the more important while domestic savings were low and Romanian banks were not widely trusted as long as inadequate regulation meant there was a danger of running down reserves, not to mention misuse of funds linked with political networking. Hence, domestic capital was generally sufficient only for small commercial units (and often in these cases entrepreneurs might rely on contributions from relatives abroad rather than accept the high interest charges levied by the banks). Isărescu (1992, p.159) also stressed the importance of FDI for innovative production methods, managerial skills and know-how – the capacity for dynamism and change that is part of the mentality of a private company as opposed to one that is state-owned (or even privatised in some cases) – that can spill over to benefit domestic enterprises. Management is not so aggressive as it is in many Romanian-owned businesses and it appreciates the importance of good information and relations. Advisers of New Century Holdings advocate Six Sigma Quality Management (for the ISO9000 standard) to change the culture from control and orders to include a customer focus and improved productivity over product and service quality. Thus companies privatised through FDI rapidly show efficiency gains through a better strategy and an improved financial situation. They also offer technologies relevant for growth (such as up-to-date industrial and export structures). But decision making may be transferred abroad and FDI distinguishes carefully between regions and countries. On the other hand, countries attracting FDI may find disproportionate levels of investment going to capital cities, and production may be only lightly embedded in terms of local networks and interdependent facilities (hence the portrayal of some foreign-owned factories as 'cathedrals in the desert'). However, embeddedness will normally extend to dependence on local labour, services and infrastructure (reflected in wages, taxes and patronage of local suppliers), not to mention sub-contracting arrangements that may benefit locally-owned SMEs and 'bridgeheads' for the upgrading of local skills in both manufacturing and non-manufacturing. Companies may gradually increase their participation, so that, for example, Unilever now produces detergent in Ploieşti, margarine in Târgu Mureş and Knorr foods at Otopeni, while running a regional office in Bucharest (all now grouped together in Ploieşti).

Investment Modes

These are not restricted to the outright acquisition of specific enterprises. A j.v. may facilitate penetration by foreign capital and technology without the necessity for privatisation or high-productivity greenfield ventures, allowing the possibility of gradual SOE restructuring without the acceptance of massive job losses over a short period (especially if it can be supplemented by capital from other sources such as the firm's own profits, the SOF or banks). Good examples are the massive Daewoo Heavy Industries (DHI) investment of $156mln in Rodae Automobile at the former Oltcit factory in Craiova; the Siemens involvement in Elcaro of Slatina, a producer of electric cables, which enabled the factory to start exporting after technological updating; and the Stimin project in Oradea involving a $21mln injection by Stima Engineering (Italy) for the local Înfraţirea company. Romanian shipbuilding has benefited from partnerships with foreign ship owners, resulting in export opportunities, especially to Belgium, Germany and Norway: most orders relate to ship bodies exported for fitting-out overseas since Romania does not yet produce enough high-quality equipment. Brăila shipyard has built Arctic trawlers for Norway using the German 'Westfalia' type of engine. DHI have again been involved to the extent of $53mln at the Mangalia shipyard while Posada (Curtea de Argeş) has a j.v. with Gantner Electronics of Austria, producing security cards with imbedded electronic chips. IAR (Braşov) has a cooperation agreement with Franco-German Eurocopter (Aerospatiale and Daimler-Benz Aerospace) for the assembly of Ecureuil helicopters, while at one stage McDonnell-Douglas contemplated a deal with Avioane (Craiova) for components and sub-assemblies to help pay for the supply of American aircraft to the Romanian airline Tarom. Other deals include the food industry – $13.2mln by Kraft-Jacobs-Suchard in

Braşov and \$12.6mln by Brau und Brune International (Germany) in Pitber (Piteşti) – and also construction through the \$15.3mln investment by Bouygues (France) in the Bucharest World Trade Centre linked with housing for expatriates at the nearby 'sat franceză' (French village).

Investment banks and funds may acquire stakes in Romanian enterprises. Thus, the US SigmaBleyzer company's South Eastern Growth Fund makes \$1–10mln investments (possibly up to \$40mln) in Romanian and Bulgarian companies (through offices in Bucharest and Sofia) since these countries provide the best long-term investment opportunities. Also the Bulgarian–American and Romanian–American Enterprise Funds are acquiring a substantial portfolio, with a joint interest in a Balkan Accession Fund with €75mln capital to make €8mln cash injections in Romanian and Bulgarian businesses. Majority interests have been acquired in Policolor of Bucharest (Romania's largest manufacturer of lacquers, dyestuffs and industrial coating) and Orgachim (Ruse), the largest equivalent company in Bulgaria. The two enterprises have now been brought together through Whitebeams Holdings; making for an enlarged combined product portfolio, with the aim of joint marketing through a unitary sales network. Reference has already been made to the US company New Century Holdings controlling the \$200mln Broadhurst Fund – now supplemented by a further \$275mln to extend the profile embracing financial services, consumer goods and the food industry. And Advent International (USA) has made a \$40mln purchase to boost sales by the Cluj-Napoca drug company Terapia (number five in Romania, with sales in Romania and also Russia and Ukraine) and enable it to challenge the top four firms in this business – in descending order Pfizer (USA), Novartis (Switzerland), GlaxoSmithKline (UK) and Sicomed (Bucharest) – before selling on to the strategic investor Ranbaxy.

FDI Performance

A liberal foreign investment law in 1991 was followed by the 'Daewoo Law' of 1994, designed expressly to attract a hard-bargaining company through tax exemptions until 2001: 100 per cent foreign ownership of businesses is allowed, along with repatriation of profits, tax holidays and exemptions from customs duties. But ambivalence over restructuring prevented explicit political acknowledgement of FDI's crucial role, let alone stimulative procedures and an attractive business environment. The Romanian Development Agency (RDA) recognised a succession of investment waves. SMEs arrived in 1990–91, followed in 1991–94 by investment in large-scale projects by trans-national enterprises (TNEs) such as ABB, Alcatel and Siemens. Western 'storehouse industries' (such as Coca-Cola and its network of bottling plants, Colgate-Palmolive and McDonalds) met internal demand but without commensurate effort to develop production for export. 'Coca-Colonisation' brought in

$150mln during 1990–95, while traditional industries had to cope with imports of confectionery, soft drinks, textiles, plastics and construction materials. Hydrocarbon exploration was opened up in 1990 through production-sharing agreements. UK Enterprise Oil found gas in the Black Sea while Shell drilled for gas in Transylvania beneath a salt layer at depths of 1,500m (beyond the capacity of Romgaz, operating in shallower fields). Amoco also prospected onshore. From 1995 strategic investments were made by TNEs, encouraged by an improved international environment.

With a total of $10.3bln over 14 years since 1989 ($486pc) FDI has been generally below par, compared with $33.6bln in Hungary ($3,364pc) and strong performances in the Czech Republic and Poland as well. In 1995 and 1997 FDI failed to reach $500mln, although there was a surge to $2.1bln in 1998 before disillusionment with the DCR government was reinforced by the Asian–Russian crisis. Since 2000 FDI has increased considerably, aided by pressure on western firms to reduce operational costs by moving production offshore. In 2001 the government received 58 requests (totalling $400mln) from foreign and Romanian investors – outside banking, finance or insurance – seeking the benefits being offered for large investments of over one million dollars, thereby exerting a 'significant impact' in the context of the economic infrastructure: the incentive is referred to further below. Early major investments in this category (exceeding $10mln) concerned Kronospan (Cyprus) for a greenfield wood-processing venture, Pilkington (UK) for float glass, Cartiera di Pisa (Italy) partnering Romanian firms in the pulp and paper industry, and Fergat (Italy) for mechanical engineering. Others included Edemir (Turkey) for Târgovişte steelworks (COST), ACE Automobile Group (Spain) for car parts, and Selgros (Germany) for supermarkets. In the first half of 2005, 46 such investments were made, mostly in Bucharest-Ilfov: 25 greenfield and 21 brownfield.

A level of some $1.0bln of FDI was maintained during 2000–2, rising to $1.8bln in 2003 and a record €4.1bln in 2004, boosted by the Petrom privatisation at the end of the year that lifted the total substantially beyond the €2.2bln achieved during the first 11 months. Among the ECECs, only Poland did better than Romania for FDI in 2004, with €4.9bln. Indeed, the Romanian Agency for Foreign Investment (RAFI) thought that the 2004 level might have been some 20 per cent better if greenfield projects had gathered greater momentum following a succession of high profile privatisations. However, the improvement is being maintained, with a total of €5.20bln invested during 2005 (albeit with €3.75bln for RCB alone). Investment is now being boosted by the end of the state's monopoly on public utilities but this will only be a major influence for the next few years, and over the longer term much greater emphasis will have to come from greenfield investments if the country's potential is to be realised. RAFI will therefore push greenfield sites in future, targeting appropriate countries and economic objectives. They will also seek to improve the business environment and offer technical assistance (Guran-Nica 2002). After €9.1bln of FDI in 2006 a slight fall to €7.1bln occurred in 2007, though this was still much better than the €5.3bln average previously forecast.

National Rankings for Foreign Investors

Up to 2003, The Netherlands (including Netherlands Antilles) was in the top place by a huge margin: 23.7 per cent of the total, against 10.3 per cent for France and 8.5 per cent for Germany; followed by the USA (6.8 per cent), Italy (6.0 per cent) and Austria (5.7 per cent) (Table 2.3). However, in 2004 although all these countries remained prominent, Austria took the lead (19.3 per cent) followed by France (8.2 per cent), UK including the Virgin Islands (7.5 per cent), The Netherlands (4.2 per cent), Germany (3.8 per cent) and the USA (3.3). Individual years obviously show substantial differences according to the companies that happen to make the key investments: in 2004, €765mln was invested by ÖMV (Austria) and €196mln by Renault (France), followed by €145mln from Inquam (UK/Virgin Islands), €117mln by Rompetrol and Heidelberg (The Netherlands), €98mln by Sinara Holdings and Kaufland (Germany), €83mln by IFC and Florida Shipping (USA), and €48mln by Robank (Hungary). In the first half of 2005, The Netherlands, Austria, France, Germany and the USA were in the lead. There are also big differences between the rankings for total capital invested and the number of companies involved. For the period up to 2003, The Netherlands, France, Germany, the USA and Italy contributed 55.3 per cent of the capital but only 34.8 per cent of companies. Italy was in the lead for companies with 14.6 per cent, followed by Germany (11.3 per cent), Turkey (8.9 per cent), China (8.4 per cent) and Syria (5.4 per cent): the last three held much lower positions of ninth, 17th and 20th in terms of total capital invested. The top five in this latter category contributed 48.6 per cent of the companies but only 20.2 per cent of capital. While the average Dutch company invested $1.40mln, the value fell to $48,350 for Turkey and $12,667 for China. In 2004, Italy was again in the lead with 26.9 per cent followed by Germany (11.6 per cent) and Hungary (6.4 per cent), although the picture is limited by the restriction of the data to the top ten countries in terms of total investment. Of the top 100 foreign companies in 2002, The Netherlands held 24, Germany and USA 11 each, France nine, Austria eight, Switzerland six (though data is not available), Cyprus, Greece and UK five each, Hungary four, Italy three, South Korea and Turkey two each and one each for Canada, Japan, Luxembourg, Spain and Sweden (Table 2.4). 56 of the top 100 firms fell to industry and construction, followed by 18 for services and tourism, 17 for retailing and wholesaling, eight for transport and telecommunications and one for agriculture. The current profile (2003–6), highlighting recent investment, features a new generation of companies but with a broadly similar spread in terms of countries and sectors.

Table 2.3: *Foreign Direct Investment: leading countries 1991–2005*

1991–2003						2004–2005					
Rank/Country		Capital $mln	%	Companies Number	%	Rank/Country		Capital €mln	%	Companies Number	%
1	Netherlands	2458	23.7	1752	1.8	1	Netherlands	2927.6	24.3	2571	4.3
2	France	1068	10.3	3150	3.2	2	Austria	2605.7	21.6	4003	6.8
3	Germany	880	8.5	10954	11.3	3	France	1582.4	13.1	4562	7.7
4	USA	704	6.8	3800	3.9	4	Germany	1416.3	11.8	14080	23.8
5	Italy	625	6.0	14157	14.6	5	UK	841.5	7.0	2513	4.3
6	Austria	595	5.7	2785	2.9	6	Italy	821.7	6.8	21480	36.3
7	Cyprus	505	4.9	1144	1.2	7	USA	794.2	6.6	4812	8.2
8	UK	497	4.8	1848	1.9	8	Cyprus	551.8	4.6	1913	3.2
9	Turkey	419	4.0	8666	8.9	9	Greece	505.4	4.2	3164	5.4
10	Greece	318	3.1	2555	2.6	n.a.	n.a.	n.a.	n.a.	n.a.	n.a.
11	Switzerland	308	3.0	1252	1.3	n.a.	n.a.	n.a.	n.a.	n.a.	n.a.
12	Hungary	265	2.5	4329	4.5	n.a.	n.a.	n.a.	n.a.	n.a.	n.a.
13	S. Korea	218	2.1	82	0.1	n.a.	n.a.	n.a.	n.a.	n.a.	n.a.
14	Luxembourg	197	1.9	218	0.2	n.a.	n.a.	n.a.	n.a.	n.a.	n.a.
15	Spain	157	1.5	629	0.6	n.a.	n.a.	n.a.	n.a.	n.a.	n.a.
16	Sweden	109	1.0	782	0.8	n.a.	n.a.	n.a.	n.a.	n.a.	n.a.
17	China	104	1.0	8210	8.4	n.a.	n.a.	n.a.	n.a.	n.a.	n.a.
18	Belgium	65	0.6	1165	1.2	n.a.	n.a.	n.a.	n.a.	n.a.	n.a.
19	Portugal	63	0.6	92	0.1	n.a.	n.a.	n.a.	n.a.	n.a.	n.a.
20	Syria	63	0.6	5259	5.4	n.a.	n.a.	n.a.	n.a.	n.a.	n.a.

Notes: Netherlands includes Netherlands Antilles; USA includes Marshall Islands and UK includes the Virgin Islands. In the 1991–2003 table percentages relate the total investment in all companies; for the 2004–5 table they concern the top nine countries only: hence the latter sum to 100 per cent and the former to 75.9 per cent only.
Source: Arisinvest website.

Table 2.4: *Foreign Direct Investment: largest companies and investments*

	Rank/Country	Details of the five largest companies in the 'Top 100' including the name, position in rank order (according to investment value) and line of business (1999-2002)
1	Netherlands#	24: Ispat Sidex 3e; Rompetrol Rafinare 4d; Mobifon 5g, Petrotel Lukoil 19d; Unilever South Central Europe 20c
2	Germany	11: Reşiţa (Sinara Handel) 26e; Kaufland 28c; INA Schaeffler 31j; Continental 40j; Rommert Entsorgung (Recycling) 63I
3	USA#	11: Colgate-Palmolive 10h; Banca Comercială (IFC) 30a; Optinova Romania (Osman Trading) 32c; Salonul Auto Victoria 36i; Citibank 45a
4	France	9: Auto Dacia (Renault) 2j; Hiproma (Bearbull) 7c; Orange14g; Lafarge 48b; Apa Nova (Comp.Générale des Eaux) 58I
5	Austria	8: Petrom (ÖMV) 1d; Raiffeisen 8a; Brau-Union (Brau Immobilien) 22f; ÖMV Mineraloil 24d; Billa (Eurobilla) 50c
6	Cyprus	5: Romtelecom (OTE International) 13g; TV Rom International (Zareba Holdings) 33c; Kronospan 34b; Moara Loulis Romania Flour Mills (Loulis International Foods) 86f
7	Greece	5: Piraeus Bank 51a; Egnatia Bank 65a; Alpha Bank 70a; Poarta (Pantechniki) 74i; Intrarom (Intracom) 89g
8	UK#	5: Telemobil (Inquam Romania) 6g; Shell Romania (Shell Overseas) 15d; Rafinarea Astra Romană (Kreyton) 80d; Aviva Asigurari de Viaţa (CU) 83a; Europharm (Wellcome) 84h
Rank/Country		Large investments of over €5.0mln (excluding privatisation deals) listed in ascending order: company details: name, investment (€mln), line of business, location in Romania (* denotes other locations as well) and number of employees anticipated (2003-6)
1	Germany	9: Weidmüller 5.0g (Baia Mare 200); Willy Kreutz 8.0g (Timişoara 100); Schlemmer 10.0j (Satu Mare 80); Marquardt Schaltsysteme 23.0j (Sibiu 200); Ruwel 80.0g (Cluj-Napoca 700); Real International Holding 105.0c (Bucharest* 105.0); INA Schaeffler 180.0e (Braşov 1,200); Tengelmann 200c (Bucharest* 3,000); Selgros 250.0c (Bucharest* 4.800)

2	France	7: Air Liquide 10.0d (Călăraşi 20); Michelin 25.0 (Zalău 350); Saint-Gobain Isover 35.0b (Ploieşti 220); Hiproma (Bearbull) 50.0c (Bucharest/Iaşi 200); SNR Roulements 60.0j (Sibiu 1,000); Saint-Gobain 120.0 (Călăraşi 200); Renault 226.0j (Piteşti 650)
3	Austria	6: Zumtobel 5.0g (Arad 100); FB&C Handels-Romply 17.0k (Călăraşi 400); Wienerberger 20.0b (Gura Ocniţei 80); Umwelttechnic 35.0b (Corbenii Mari/Timişoara 800); Egger 210k (Suceava 700); Holzindustrie Schweighofer 210.0k (Sebeş/Suceava 820)
4	USA	5: Microsoft Emea 13.1n (Bucharest 750); Johnson Controls 16.6j (Ploieşti 800); Monsanto Corporation 23.0m (Sineşti 20); Hewlett Packard 50.0n (Bucharest 1,200); General Electric 80.0n (Bucharest 170)
5	Japan	4: Sol-Plus 5.0h (Timişoara 125); YKK 10.0l (Bucharest 100); Makata 25.0e (Braneşti 300); Yazaki 44.0j (Arad/Ploieşti 2,400)
6	Spain	4: Manufactura Moderna di Metales 5.0j (Turda 260); Caucho 6.0j (Sibiu 200); Bamesa-Arcelor 30.0j (Topoloveni 120); Graells & Llonch 300.0p (Prejmer 1,000)
7	India	2: Wimpro 5.0q (Bucharest 400); Liberty Commodities 10.0e (Călăraşi 150)
8	Portugal	2: Biomart Martifer 25.0d/m (Lehliu Gara 250); Coindu 30.0j (Curtici 300)
9	Others	7: Switzerland: Greenfiber 6.0h (Buzău 100); Netherlands: Medisystem 7.50 (Bucharest 200); Belgium: UCO Textiles 15.0l (Giurgiu 200); Poland: 16.0f (Vălenii de Munte 300); Tunisia: Coficab 25.0j (Arad 200); Turkey: Anchor Mall 50.0c (Bucharest 2,300); Canada: Celestica 84.0g (Braşov 1,000)

Notes: # Includes offshore. Other top 100 companies fall to Hungary (4), Italy (3), South Korea and Turkey (2), Canada, Japan, Luxembourg, Spain and Sweden (1). Classification for business activities: (a) banking and insurance; (b) building materials, wood processing and construction; (c) wholesale, retail and restaurants; (d) energy; (e) metals and engineering; (f) food and drink; (g) telecoms with telecoms equipment and electronics; (h) chemicals/ petrochemicals, pharmaceuticals and toiletries; (i) business property management and water treatment; (j) automotive; (k) wood processing/furniture;

(l) textiles; (m) agriculture; (n) computer services and technical support; (o) medical services; (p) industrial parks; (q) call centres. For the Top 100 companies the leading sectors were (a) – 15; (c) – 12; (d) – 12; (e) – 12; (f) – 10; (g) – 9; (h) – 7; and (j) – 6

Source: Arisinvest website

Some shifts can be seen in that Italy has become more prominent, as Romania's first commercial partner for the past five years (accounting for 24.1 per cent of Romania's foreign trade by end of 2002). Austria has also become more important, with particular strength in banks (HVB/Bank Austria Creditanstalt and Raiffeisen, followed in 2005 with Erste's winning bid of €3.75bln for RCB); also energy (ÖMV and Vatech); wood processing (Schweighofer), construction (Strabag); building materials (Wienerberger, Bramac Baumit and Rehau Polymer) and food and drink (Brau Union). Germany is also taking a stronger interest (notably through car component firms), in recognition of cultural and spiritual assets and generally good employer:labour relations, after years of relatively modest activity gave rise to rumours of a Franco-German deal allocating Romania to the French sphere while German investors were thought to be concentrating on the Baltic States, the Czech Republic, Hungary, Poland, Slovenia and Croatia. Năstase's visit to Germany in 2002 brought forth references to a 'strategic partnership' that might secure more German banking activity and greater interest in Romanian exports to balance trade. Meanwhile oil is an interest of The Netherlands, while Netherlands Antilles is the base of LNM Holdings that bought the Sidex and Siderurgica steel companies. French investors are prominent in consumer goods and retailing, although there is a perception that French firms are not maintaining their earlier profile despite some conspicuous projects by Auto Chassis, Michelin, Piroux, Saint–Gobain and others; Americans are into information technology, pharmaceuticals and cosmetics. Some 54 per cent of all FDI has gone into industry and 41 per cent to retailing and wholesaling, transport and other services, and the remainder to agriculture, construction and tourism. As regards the 535 'significant' investments of over $1.0mln made during 2001–6 (total value $6.61bln of which the foreign investment component was $4.75bln), $1.48bln came from The Netherlands (22.3 per cent); $0.72bln from Austria (10.9); $0.63bln from Germany (9.6); and $0.51bln from France (7.7).

Regional Trends for Foreign Investment

These continue to be highly uneven, with concentration on Bucharest and a handful of other urban centres. Western cities are among the most dynamic in the country, notably the Timişoara–Arad axis with powerful CCIA support (including initiatives such as Arad Expo), while Cluj-Napoca has now recovered from its association with the Caritas pyramid investment scandal. As regards the 535 'significant' investments 298 were located in Bucharest-Ilfov ($4.01bln of which $2.97 came from foreign sources); 81 in the Central region ($0.97/0.66) and 40 in the South ($.061/0.48). The core of the much-vaunted reliable and responsive West region (where Timişoara gained a reputation for delivering authorisations in three days) became saturated, so that investors moving across Transylvania to county towns in Wallachia and Moldavia e.g. Saint-Gobain at Călăraşi and Pirelli–Continental at Slatina, while Iaşi is now an attractive outpost. To try and achieve a wider spread, RAFI/Arisinvest built a database of 350 locations compiled through contacts with local authorities (but it cannot be accessed through the Internet). Finally it should not be overlooked that Romanian firms are making some investments abroad: Flamingo computer shops; ÖMV stations in Bulgaria, Montenegro and Serbia (as well as Romania) transferred to Petrom for €234mln; Rompetrol acquisition of Dyneff stations in France; and most recently Cuprom (owners of the Baia Mare and Zalău copper smelters) have made a winning bid of $400mln for the Serbian copper complex of RTB Bor (with $150mln to be invested in modernisation over 15–20 years.

The Climate for Investment

In the early 1990s, Romania's run-down economy seemed to have obvious productive potential in all sectors but especially in industry (with a highly developed infrastructure including oil and petrochemicals) and services. It offered the second-largest internal market in the region after Poland (over 20mln population, although with low spending capacity initially and only slowly rising absorption). Romania also occupies a geostrategic zone favourable to the development of commercial and processing flows between Western Europe, the Black Sea region, the Middle East, and Central and Eastern Asia: this area offers 200mln customers within 1,000 km, competitive transit costs with extensive maritime and river navigations, with the port of Constanţa and the Black Sea–North Sea route. Romania is also a convenient regional co-ordinating centre: in the case of General Electric, which has offices in Bucharest, 12 countries from Slovenia to Cyprus are covered, while Unilever products are sold from the South Central Europe headquarters in Bucharest to Albania, Bosnia & Hercegovina, Bulgaria, Macedonia, Moldova and Serbia. South Korean investment in the car industry appreciated Romania's gateway function for the Balkans, if not for Europe generally. Geo-Strategies (concerned with digital mapping, GIS, surveying and image processing) successfully exported the 'Cambridge Phenomenon' to Romania in the mid-1990s as a springboard for CEE and then the Middle East. On the other hand, other countries can offer similar advantages and so, with market decline, Colgate–Palmolive closed production in Bucharest in 1999 because it was cheaper to supply goods from Turkey, although some jobs were transferred to Braşov, where company production continues. Romania offers cheap labour that is also well trained with technical and IT skills (though some investors find Romanian workers 'superficial' in lacking strategic thinking, motivation and experience), while Italy claims affinities through language and the 'Latin spirit'.

However, Romania does not score so well on labour legislation and training, infrastructure, especially transport and telecoms (though mobile telecoms are well developed), and the persistence of obsolete and polluting technologies, while diaspora Romanians refer to the high cost of building materials that are imported with customs charges. The Foreign Investors' Council (FIC), founded 1997, has noted a generally slow rate of change but also highlighted the need for coherent, understandable and practical laws (with improved communication between economic and political actors); a more visible fight against corruption and the underground economy (though crime is not a major problem); confidence in property titles, with more viable mortgage and insurance systems; a culture of success, with a stronger spirit of entrepreneurship and a growing SME sector; and less bureaucracy. Business authorisation takes twice the time needed in Poland or Slovakia and particular frustration arises from complex, inconsistent and unstable fiscality – highlighted by the sudden withdrawal of incentives in 1999 (admittedly under IMF pressure) – that raises investors' margin of incertitude above the critical level. The UNDP has considered Romania's fiscal regime unstable – through frequent new laws and emergency ordinances – and there is widespread unease over the inadequate institutional capacity to implement and enforce legislation, which results in inconsistent tax collection involving favours for domestic companies. This makes for unfair competition from heavily-subsidised SOEs (and some private companies whose debts have been cancelled) and reinforces a perception that local oligarchic interests 'make foreign investors feel as though they are unwelcome competitors to their claims for market share' (Bacon 2004, p.386). Certainly, xenophobia over redundancies can make greenfield projects preferable despite the costs and delays. Protests over redundancies at the agricultural machinery factory Semănătoarea (Bucharest) blocked a proposed New Holland investment of \$50mln; some time later with the plant in the grip of bankruptcy, more realistic expectations on the part of the work force subsequently enabled a local buyer to invest only \$1.2mln initially. Corruption in the judiciary has made contract enforcement problematic, while corporate governance issues arise over protection for shareholders and international accounting and auditing standards.

Improvement since 2000 has followed a return to economic growth with falling inflation that, in the context of continuing political stability, has resulted in improved investment ratings. The economy is also more diversified and competitive. There is an improved industrial infrastructure and banking system as well as advanced state enterprise restructuring. Privatisation by FDI has accelerated through government realism over the value of assets. Most of the money that foreign firms are prepared to pay is in the form of guaranteed investment rather than payment for the assets as such. When 51 per cent of the equity in the Mangalia '2 Mai' shipyard was sold to DHI for \$51mln, the deal really amounted to \$20mln in cash plus Korean components for local assembly using Romanian labour. Legal and bureaucratic barriers have been modified. Contradictory tax regulations have been removed while in 2001, as already noted, government elaborated a law promoting direct investments with significant impact in economy. By exceeding $1.0mln they would contribute to the development and updating of the economic infrastructure and create new jobs, thereby earning exemption from customs taxes for technological equipment, postponement of VAT on imported goods until the start of production, fiscal deduction of 20 per cent of investment value and accelerated depreciation and other fiscal benefits – provided that investment is maintained for ten years. Excessive bureaucracy is also limited by a 'one stop' office for authorising firms making investments of at least a million dollars, while other procedures – e.g. work permits and building permits – have been simplified.

The Romanian Agency for Foreign Investment (RAFI)

RAFI was created in 2002 by the Năstase government to provide information and deal with blockages, although it has no offices abroad. The RAFI website, <www.arisinvest.ro>, also refers to investment legislation based on free non-discriminatory access to markets and sectors, the presence of international banks, diplomatic relations with 176 countries, free trade agreements through EU, EFTA and CEFTA and arrangements with other individual states (Bosnia & Hercegovina, Israel, Macedonia, Moldova and Turkey) and preferential trade regimes with Russia, Belarus and Kazakhstan. Also, the FME status was granted by the USA at the beginning of 2003 (following the restoration of MFN status) and has also been conceded by the EU. Impending EU accession is the key to the business environment since risk will be reduced (however, while Spain and Portugal experienced a surge of investment after joining, Austria and Greece did not). ECE may share the former experience since investment is already substantial, although with free trade it will be easier to supply home markets from outside and more investment might relate to export potential (especially newly privatised companies). Much depends on how quickly the risk bonus wears off: low and high 'risk bonus reduction' scenarios for Romania tend to show quite wide variations, in contrast to assessments for the Czech Republic in 2000, for example. However, Romania has become more attractive and services have improved considerably. Not only are there organisations to assist investors from particular countries (supplementing what embassies can offer), such as the American Chamber of Commerce in Romania with over 200 members, but Romania now has a cluster of firms providing sophisticated business support.

Gecis Global, 40 per cent owned by General Electric (USA), invested €80mln in a 4,000sq.m centre for finance, accounting, insurance and logistics services in northern Bucharest's Iride Business Park in 2005, with employment set to rise from an initial 170 to 1,500 and the floor space doubled in size.

Hewlett-Packard also have a new business processing and outsourcing centre for financial and accounting services in view of the growing demand for financial and accounting services (for which their Polish office is fully used), while international law firms are setting up, such as Schoenherr Rechtsanwalte and Wolf Theiss from Austria. The 19 business consultants on the RAFI website include the American Global Business Group with consultants with western and eastern backgrounds to help investors cope with a 'maze of mercurial legislation' and a 'Byzantine mentality', while the German business consultants TMG Stuttgart have opened an office in Sibiu. There is also growth in public relations companies and in business and management training through Achieve Global Romania. Good business practice is also encouraged by the J.M.Juran awards for quality in industry, after the Juran Foundation was set up in 1998 by the CCI and other organisations with Phare assistance. Romania is successfully competing with Bulgaria and the Czech Republic over IT outsourcing in the region, and significantly Wipro (India), a leading exporter of IT solutions, has set up an R&D Centre for the European market.

The present situation suggests that Romania is doing well enough as an outpost of EU expansion offering stability, high margins, moderate taxation and a competitive work force, combined with an agreeable social life. Yet at the time of writing it is evident that, as several high-profile projects by Calsonic Kansei, Elco Brandts, MAN and Montupet have been lost to the competition, investors still have some serious reservations. Cumbersome bankruptcy and liquidation procedures are hardly effective in fostering competition and preventing debt accumulation. There is a lack of legal capacity for effective contract enforcement, while local authorities tend to be very variable – broadly on a regional basis with some cases of 'rock-like indifference' to the needs and concerns of potential investors. Incentives are not over-generous (although tax levels have fallen) and there was enough instability to maintain some uncertainty over EU accession in 2007 (and improve the prospects for capital investment grants). Technological upgrading of an existing enterprise may well be more expensive than greenfield investment, given the sensitivity over job cuts – hence Landini-Laverda and INA-FAG decided not to buy Tractorul and Rulmenţul Braşov respectively but set up new facilities in Buzău and Braşov instead (Dăianu 2004, p.405). It can also be difficult getting land when up to 30 owners may be involved over a large plot; also, the high cost of land, especially with infrastructure lacking (the public utilities can be as expensive as the factory building), encourages the use of old rehabilitated spaces, although relatively few are on offer. Meanwhile industrial parks did not immediately attract the number of companies expected at the beginning of the new millennium. Salaries in the local currency rose dramatically with inflation to retain only 60 per cent of the 1990 value at the end of 2000, with industry and administration doing a little better (some 65 per cent) and commerce and construction around 55 per cent, followed by health and tourism (42 per cent) and education (37 per cent) (Ciupagea 2002a, p.195). Hence, while the Euro equivalent of the legal minimum monthly wage (€67 per month in 2003) was well above Ukraine (€30) and Russia (€12) it was minuscule compared with the top EU levels of Luxembourg (€1,369) and The Netherlands (€1,249). Competitiveness then declined slightly to 2005 to €72 (€219 at PPPy), just below Bulgaria €77 (€232), with Latvia – €116 (€283), the lowest for an EU member state – compared with Luxembourg €1,467 (€1,293) and The Netherlands €1,265 (€1,202). As in other SEECs, low value-added industries are prominent and more export-oriented, greenfield FDI is needed. The minimum investment of €50,000 is high by comparison with €15,000 in the Czech Republic and Hungary.

Culture-Changing FDI

Some FDI has had a major impact in shaping the business, especially a succession of key investments and their managers made during 1990–2004. Those from the first Iliescu presidency would certainly include Marian Alecu, who managed McDonalds Restaurants in Bucharest in 1995. Having influenced 'civilisation' in the capital, Alecu went on to coordinate for Bulgaria, Macedonia, Moldova, Montenegro, Serbia and Slovenia. Then Ion Tiriac got involved in banking and insurance before providing the catalyst for the first Metro store at Otopeni in 1996, a project worth $700mln that has now grown into a network of over 20 units; while Andrei Siminel provides a third illustration as general manager of the New Century Holdings active investment group (already referred to) injecting $200mln into Romanian companies from 1995 and introducing modern management concepts in each one. For the Constantinescu presidency the list would have to be headed by François Fourmont, general manager of Dacia Renault that reached the ultimate success with the launch of the new 'Logan' model in 2004: Mioveni has become the largest production centre of the Renault-Nissan alliance with a new gearbox factory to come on-stream. Supporting initiatives would introduce Dirk Serbruyns, chairing ING Romania, for the arrival of ING Asigurări in 1997 (now with some 70 branches and 2,500 consultants) introduced a strong foreign element after a competitive insurance industry returned in 1992 with companies like Agras, Ardaf and Romania Assurance International. A further example would involve both Mobifon (Connex – now Vodafone) – with Ted Lattimore as president – and Mobilrom (Orange) – with Richard Moat as general manager. These companies took out 900Mhz licences at the same time and jointly launched a mobile communications revolution with mobile banking, roaming and email.

During Iliescu's third term Banca Agricolă (BA) was successfully privatised by Raiffeisen (Austria) in 2001 – with Steven von Groningen at the helm as vice-president in 2001 and president in 2002 – to realise a profit of €4.6mln in 2003 when Raiffeisen came in third behind RCB and RDB and ahead of the RSB: the only one of the top four to raise its share thanks to the growth of consumer loans. Meanwhile Lakshmi Mittal (worth $25bln in 2001) brought Sidex Galaţi into the Mittal Steel empire and president Wolfgang Rüttenstorfer of ÖMV launched the giant vertically-integrated oil company Petrom towards expansion in CEE through a $1.6bln privatisation of Petrom. Trimming the worforce of over 50,000 – against the 6,000 others that ÖMV employ across the region – has hardly begun, but the company moved quickly to allow its prices to fluctuate with international trends that eased relations with its competitors considerably. Interesting ÖMV previously took an interest in Rompetrol, diversified by Liberal politician Dinu Patriciu from a small service company in 1996 into a fully-integrated oil company with particular success over the turnaround at the Petromidia refinery after 2001: modernising for the export of EU fuels after two failed attempts by the government to privatise a moribund installation weakened by a currency crisis that inhibited regular imports of crude, while provoking huge debts and layoffs.

Privatisation Scandals

There have been a number of troubled privatisations that have attracted media attention, but probably none more than the Rafo oil refinery at Oneşti in Bacău county with a capacity of 3.5mln.t. of fuels and products. As an SOE, it failed in 1999 when deliveries could not be paid for, but 2,600 workers were kept on while it worked at a very low level in the hope of finding a buyer. Losses piled up – for it needed to process 250,000t crude per month for profitability – but, although it was located away from other refineries and the main oil pipelines, it attained quality standards and was well-placed to sell to Moldova. Neither Petrom nor Rompetrol was interested (though some refining of diesel oil was subsequently done for Petrom) but after two years of closure the refinery was privatised in 2001 by the agency responsible for state assets (APMSH) in favour of one of the PSD government's leading clients in Bacău county, Corneliu Iacobov, whose Imperial Oil (linked in a j.v. with Canyon Servicos of Portugal) obtained massive support from the government (including tax relief), not to mention the seven-year period allowed for payment of the transaction value of $81mln. The point seems to be that through fraudulent payments the company accumulated large debts variously estimated at 1.6bln.lei (owed to the finance ministry, the customs collection in Iaşi and ARSA) but well over 2.0bln if debts accruing to the associated Carom rubber company and money owed to Petrom are taken into account. The state then cancelled this debt – effectively doubling the favours shown at the time of privatisation – by transferring it into shares in the new company Balkan Petroleum (linked with Central European Petroleum that was an interest of V.F.Timis of Roşia Montană fame), which took over the refinery from Iacobov's company in 2004 and also sought to buy out the interest of Portuguese Canyon Services and small investors, with the intention of investing $200mln. Some of the debt was allegedly diverted into PSD election funds in 2004 through a maze of companies under the cover of excessive payments for goods that treated scrap as new parts. The government was criticised during the election for giving direct help to a PSD client company to stop it from going bankrupt (in defiance of the bankruptcy laws). Iacobov was later charged with tax evasion, money laundering and embezzlement; while the new government has tried to recoup money owed by Rafo by sequestering Iacobov's company and property assets (conservatively estimated at $10mln in 2005) and also those of his former partner in oil affairs (and former Rafo manager) O.Tender, with his Timişoara-based business empire (Tender Grup) valued at some $170mln in 2005, including oil companies that had previously done business with Rafo. Proceedings continue and could include many others with responsibility as directors or administrators. PSD highlighted the JTA government's links with Rompetrol and the Petromidia refinery and Patriciu was assailed by apparently unfounded accusations rejected in court.

Another complex scenario concerns the Reşiţa metallurgical works, that was renationalised after Noble Ventures (USA) missed the privatisation payments due at the end of both 2001 and 2002. Confusion arose over the responsibilities of the company and the government since the deal was quickly overtaken by a new government in 2001. It was also compromised by falling steel prices and union objections to 50 further job cuts in a bid to reduce costs. In other cases foreign owners have clearly behaved badly. The Tepro tube mill in Iaşi was privatised in favour of the Czech company Żelezarny Veseli in 1997 but over the following year Tepro was reduced to bankruptcy by the Czechs who wanted to remove a rival from the market. A Czech agent, F. Priplata, was implicated in the assassination of the union leader V. Sahleanu in 2001, leading to an appeal against a 14-year prison sentence (after Năstase had allegedly tried to get the justice minister to find a way of letting him leave the country quietly). And the neglect of the SOF and government in 1999 enabled the Greek investment in Romtelecom to be partially recouped through higher charges raised under the pretext of currency devaluation (although the rise was double what would have been necessary on this account).

Another scandal involving a deal with Greece that was first investigated in 1993 involved huge losses to the state of over 1.1bln lei through the sale of 14 ships (initially 16 but two were rejected because of their dilapidated condition) from the Petromin fleet. Indeed, the restructuring of the merchant fleet has been a particularly troubled affair, with the scandal of effective abandonment of unseaworthy vessels (and their crews) in foreign ports in 1995. Although a private repairing company got a $118mln Bancorex loan, it was later

Table 2.5: *Employment and Production Value by sector 1995–2005*

Year	A	B	C	D	E	F	G	H	I	J
Waged Employment th										
1995	503	2615	443	775	516	262	130	326	427	6160
1996	442	2586	431	696	495	254	125	335	432	5939
1997	357	2443	387	731	462	218	130	321	423	5597
1998	316	2272	378	748	440	240	134	311	414	5369
1999	244	1991	309	670	374	236	141	283	415	4761
2000	199	1873	316	652	370	248	148	305	407	4623
2001	191	1901	309	652	358	249	143	304	403	4619
2002	162	1891	300	638	348	277	147	313	390	4568
2003	155	1848	325	669	344	288	152	313	390	4591
2004	145	1741	323	687	319	297	155	306	381	4469
2005	147	1672	348	767	319	317	167	321	381	4559
All Employment th										
1995	3265	2714	479	988	556	395	130	333	437	9493
1996	3320	2741	475	888	547	328	125	337	441	9379
1997	3384	2450	439	932	505	272	130	315	426	9023
1998	3349	2317	391	933	461	319	134	317	426	8813
1999	3466	2054	338	856	405	307	141	277	429	8420
2000	3575	2004	353	869	419	345	147	341	421	8629
2001	3502	2017	340	883	401	350	143	347	422	8563
2002	3015	2122	366	950	401	385	148	358	415	8329
2003	2888	2059	396	1011	402	427	155	359	420	8306
2004	2638	2052	419	1071	404	465	159	367	430	8238
2005	2678	1973	463	1171	418	476	173	370	430	8390

GDP bln.new lei with a change in methodology in 1995									
1995	1.43	2.37	0.48	0.76	0.56	0.70	0.27	0.13	0.19	6.66
1996	2.09	3.62	0.71	1.27	0.98	0.91	0.34	0.21	0.28	10.19
1997	4.55	7.81	1.32	2.88	2.27	3.02	0.68	0.37	0.52	23.28
1998	5.38	9.82	1.92	5.04	3.55	4.91	1.28	0.82	1.00	33.15
1999	7.28	13.53	2.74	7.46	5.43	7.91	1.83	1.08	1.63	48.05
2000	8.90	21.95	3.93	10.14	8.04	11.67	3.46	1.58	2.33	71.13
2001	15.62	32.30	6.23	13.12	11.66	17.96	4.25	1.81	3.11	104.28
2002	17.31	42.61	8.79	16.27	14.67	24.66	5.80	2.98	4.21	135.62
2003	22.85	49.49	11.48	20.54	19.31	28.28	12.82	4.61	6.02	175.40
2004	30.58	60.79	14.65	26.93	24.15	36.13	12.73	5.99	8.02	219.98
2005	24.39	69.35	18.29	35.13	29.58	42.46	17.69	7.37	9.93	254.39

Notes: A Agriculture Forestry and Fishing; B Industry; C Construction; D Commerce and Hotels; E Transport and Post; F Banking and Property Services; G Administration; H Health; I Education; J Total

Source: Statistical Yearbooks: Tables 3.9, 3.11 and 11.1

Table 2.6: *Indices of Gross Domestic Product 1991–2005*

Year	A	B	C	D	E	F	G	H	I	J	K
1991	0.08	88.2	87.7	87.2	80.6	74.5	91.2	99.7	98.2	116.5	98.0
1992	0.21	80.3	76.3	75.2	76.1	67.5	87.6	139.3	117.0	115.6	95.2
1993	0.59	83.0	86.7	76.0	94.9	62.7	90.0	140.0	114.7	119.6	97.3
1994	1.86	86.5	89.2	78.6	120.8	64.8	90.7	142.3	122.4	120.0	106.2
1995	4.60	92.4	93.4	83.0	128.9	77.0	92.2	144.3	136.0	124.2	109.1
1996	6.66	96.0	89.5	88.7	129.9	82.5	98.0	123.7	156.3	136.6	119.4
1997	23.28	89.0	88.3	81.6	104.9	74.9	88.7	95.8	145.6	123.8	105.2
1998	33.46	84.2	79.1	77.3	100.2	80.6	79.9	97.6	145.5	123.0	121.7
1999	48.05	99.5	103.3	98.5	97.7	101.2	96.8	100.6	103.8	103.7	81.0
2000	71.13	101.7	84.6	104.3	103.9	103.2	101.3	102.7	111.1	108.5	89.3
2001	104.28	108.5	108.3	108.9	115.4	104.9	105.0	135.6	123.0	105.6	75.2
2002	135.62	114.0	101.1	114.4	124.2	108.8	110.4	146.0	133.6	110.0	93.8
2003	168.17	119.7	106.4	119.4	132.9	125.5	119.7	136.4	136.6	111.1	89.2
2004	219.98	129.9	126.2	127.3	145.1	143.4	133.0	176.6	147.7	116.3	91.6
2005	254.39	134.5	104.2	130.3	159.3	167.0	143.9	187.8	157.3	117.7	91.9

Notes: For 1991-8 the figures relate to 1990 = 100; for 1999-2005 they relate to 1998 = 100.
A Gross value added (bln.new lei); B All sectors; C Agriculture and Forestry; D Industry; E Construction; F Trade; G Transport and Communications; H Financial Services; I Real Estate; J Education; K Health.
Source: Statistical Yearbooks: Tables 11.1 and 11.2.

alleged in 2000 by the then transport minister T. Băsescu (now the president) that the owners had taken the loan but failed to get the work done, with some senior members of Constanța port administration implicated. Other cases have shown preferences for domestic over foreign investors. Akmaya (Turkey) was interested in updating the Petromidia refinery but the deal was undermined by tensions between the main coalition partners, motivated by the NLP's apparent desire to replace the Turkish company with a capitalist ready to play a key role in the exploitation and trading of Caspian oil: this turned out to be Dinu Patriciu who had already acquired Rompetrol. Shen (1997, p.155) reported that Marriott placed the highest bid for the Intercontinental Hotel in 1995 'but lost to a local consortium bidding less'. This was no isolated phenomenon, given the low valuation for Vitopomicola of Sâmbureşti (Olt county) in order to fix a tender to the benefit of the employee association over a foreign company. Finally, although not a true privatisation, the hazards of doing business with a corrupt government are well illustrated by the experience of EDF Services with a 20-year agreement in 1992 to run duty-free shops at three international airports (and on board Tarom flights) that was abusively curtailed in 2002 after the company refused to pay a bribe of $2.5mln to ensure its continuation at a time when a relative of the prime minister ran the state airline.

THE LABOUR MARKET

The communist policy of stimulating a high birthrate has left the country with a large working population that was heavily underemployed in the 1990s. Table 2.5 examines the major economic sectors to reveal a substantial discrepancy between the occupied and the waged populations: very striking in agriculture but also evident in commerce and financial and property services, where many are self-employed. In the case of agriculture as the residual employer, this is further highlighted by a low GDP value. Table 2.6 is also instructive in this context in showing below-average GDP growth, while industry is in line with the average, and the more dynamic tertiary activities are way above (financial services, real estate and construction). However, for the future, the situation is again difficult given the combination of emigration and a demographic slide into natural decrease. The total population fell from 22.8mln in 1992 to 21.7mln in 2002 with further decline expected to 2020. Life expectancy remains fairly static but fertility has fallen to about 1.3 (below the level of replacement) while the population is ageing, especially in rural areas: the 0–14 cohort (19.9 per cent of the population in 1996) but will fall below 14.0 per cent in 2020, while the people over 67 will rise from 12.2 to 15.4 per cent. There is heavy out-migration on top of negative natural increase: after averaging +3.1 per thousand during 1989–91, successive three-year periods produced figures of –0.3 (1992–94), –2.0 (1995–97), –1.3 (1998–2000), –2.3 (2001–2) and –2.1 (2003–5).

Furthermore, Romania gives the outside world the impression that it cannot look after a declining number of live births (369.5 per thousand in 1989, falling to 212.5 in 2003). The problem of abandoned children inherited from the last years of communism – 'solved' through the expansion of orphanages that so shocked western public opinion after 1989 when the appalling inadequacy of state care was revealed – was eased through adoption by foreigners. There were some 30,000 inter-country adoptions (ICAs) of Romanian children during 1990–2001, usually involving payment of up to $30,000 (often arranged through American websites, with much of the money going to middlemen rather than Romanian social services). It is therefore alleged that ICA does not help Romanian services, while poor families were encouraged to part with children 'as if' they were orphans. Despite attempts at regulation in 1997, criticism by the European Parliament rapporteur Baroness Nicholson over corruption and trafficking (selling children who were then liable to suffer mistreatment) brought about a ban in 2001, modified in 2004 when grandparents living abroad were allowed to adopt and a campaign was launched at home to encourage fostering. There were still 1,500 street children in 2003 (400 in Bucharest), while UNICEF estimated that 4,000 children are still being abandoned in maternity and pediatric wards each year at a time when there were only 1,000 adoptions within Romania. In addition to some 10,000 in private placement there are 33,000 children in institutions (based on a conservative estimate in 2005) and some have to remain institutionalised after reaching the age of 18 because they have nowhere to go and local authorities have no money to support them. However, Romania has a good record of family-based care and the political 'battle' over ICA has moved on to Moldova, Russia and Ukraine.

Meanwhile, there has been some degradation of human resources through health problems – including a serious HIV-AIDS epidemic (see below) – and stress related to unemployment and poverty. In this situation the unemployed need new skills: hence the Phare human capital promotion programme, under the ministries of European Integration and of Labour & Social Solidarity, aimed at integrating the unemployed through training and placement to meet the changing demands of the labour market (difficult to implement because of insufficient trained people and competent institutions). Also, an Agency of Employment and Vocational Training was established in 1998 to promote vocational education in connection with Phare programmes. Yet there is a wider mentality challenge away from the passivity – appropriate to an atmosphere of repression, fear and complacency – to a disposition to take financial risks that place a premium on the adaptability of the young. There are strong regional differences: unemployment is less than three per cent in the western border counties of Bihor, Satu Mare and Timiş while it exceeds ten per cent in Braşov,

Hunedoara and Vaslui; but internal labour mobility is constrained by housing shortages. But labour is much more widely available in the towns than in the countryside owing to striking differences in the age structure: while the urban population was 1.14 times the rural population in 2003, the figures were 2.03 for young people below 15, 2.42 for the 15–24 cohort, 2.28 for those aged 25–34, 1.19 for those 35–59, and 0.72 for the over-sixties.

Regional Trends

It is appropriate at this juncture to refer to regional variations in the context of the eight 'development' regions created in 2000 to conform to EU statistical requirements (Figure 2.1) (Crețan et al. 2005). These regions represent groups of counties (still the highest-order local authorities) with a reasonably similar population of some two million (with the North East and South substantially larger at 3.7mln and 3.4mln respectively in 2003) (Table 2.7). The regions, overall, are by no means similar in profile, with the North East clearly the weakest as Bucharest–Ilfov is the strongest, but there are some important cases of underdevelopment within each region (apart from Bucharest–Ilfov) and various programmes have been introduced to address these problems. Apart from the free zones established (mainly at the ports) after 1991 and a number of ad hoc regional programmes in 1996 to stimulate growth on the basis of fiscal incentives, with some public investment in infrastructure (Apuseni, Danube Delta and the counties of Botoşani, Giurgiu and Vrancea), the main programmes for regional industrial restructuring evolved from the late 1990s with the Programme of Industrial Restructuring and Professional Reconversion (RICOP), followed by the selection of clusters of towns with financial support for new SMEs: one of several stimuli previously offered to less-favoured mining areas (Borcoş and Vîrdol 2002; Popescu et al. 2003). In terms of labour, regional contrasts are still highlighted by the variations in unemployment, FDI and sectoral imbalances, with agriculture over-represented in the North East with relatively poor opportunities in the industrial and service sectors. So, although Young (2001, p.240) argues that the need for transparency after 1989 brought greater equality in treatment by government, there was also a 'continual gradual divergence in economic activity', as also noted by Heller (2002). Less-developed regions continued to stagnate while the more developed 'through their strong industrial base and diversified structure [were] better suited to the challenges posed by the process of industrial restructuring' (ibid. p.252). These variations seem to have induced increasing inter-regional migration in recent years: for example with the Transylvanian cities have attracted construction workers from Moldavia to projects like the Bechtel motorway contract for the whole section through Transylvania from Braşov to Târgu Mureş, Cluj and Oradea, with intense activity in the western part beyond Câmpia Turzii with low

Table 2.7: *Regional Profiles: various years 1992–2003*

Criterion	Rom	Buc	Cen	NE	NW	S	SE	SW	W
Population 1992 (mln)	22.81	2.35	2.70	3.75	2.91	3.56	2.96	2.46	2.11
Population 2003(mln)	21.73	2.21	2.54	3.74	2.74	3.36	2.86	2.33	1.95
Urban pop'n (percent)#	53.4	88.8	59.2	40.8	51.2	40.7	55.2	45.3	61.7
Fertility#	378	288	383	460	385	378	375	365	339
Natural increase (th)#	-2.5	-3.1	-1.1	0.0	-2.4	-4.2	-2.0	-4.2	-4.0
Infant mortality#	16.7	10.4	15.1	20.1	14.2	19.3	18.2	15.1	15.6
Employment (th.pop)*	385	368	403	366	412	372	370	396	406
Empl: agriculture(percent)*	41.4	6.6	34.0	51.2	45.9	48.6	44.7	51.2	35.9
Empl: industry (percent)*	23.2	27.3	30.7	19.1	22.2	22.8	20.6	19.3	26.7
Empl: services (percent)*	35.4	66.1	35.3	29.7	31.9	28.6	34.7	29.5	37.4
Unemployment rate @	8.8	4.7	8.5	11.8	7.8	8.2	9.9	9.1	8.2
GNP p.c. (bln.new lei)+	3.97	7.95	4.24	2.87	3.72	3.21	3.51	3.32	4.24
FDI ($p.c.) 1990–2000	127	604	91	17	82	54	35	83	114
Industrial wages (new lei)#	487	517	445	427	434	502	521	581	517
Monthly spending (ditto)#	279	350	290	256	297	253	275	256	281
Living space (sq.m)#	14.1	15.7	14.7	12.5	14.5	13.7	13.6	14.0	15.0
Piped water*	54.9	52.5	52.9	47.7	69.1	48.3	74.0	38.2	61.4
Hospital beds (th.popn)#	6.5	10.5	7.1	5.7	7.2	4.8	5.5	5.8	7.3
Rural poverty (percent)<>	n.a.	33.0	37.3	43.6	33.0	33.4	41.9	35.2	34.8

Notes: *1995–7; <>2000; # 2003; +1998–2002 average; [] 1998–2003 average; @1991–2003 average. Fertility: live births/th.women; Infant mortality: deaths under one year/th.live births; FDI: cumulative figure for investments exceeding $1.0mln only; Industrial wages: per month; Monthly spending: household average; Piped water and sewerage: percentage of localities served; Rural poverty: households. **Source:** Statistical Yearbooks

Table 2.8: *Migration 1990–2000 by Regions*

Region	Year	Migration th A	B	C	D	Region	Year	Migration th A	B	C	D
Bucharest	1990	n.a.	26.49	5.05	145.01	South	2000	3.01	23.26	8.45	10.45
	1995	2.56	26.96	10.79	13.89		All	13.64	100.99	112.60	38.81
	2000	2.58	13.23	10.63	9.12	South East	1990	21.46	77.79	39.35	32.93
	All	5.13	66.68	26.48	168.02		1995	5.65	25.38	10.20	9.97
Centre	1990	10.15	37.82	19.54	41.29		2000	4.47	18.60	8.54	8.00
	1995	7.29	18.09	7.77	8.49		All	31.58	121.76	58.09	50.90
	2000	3.78	16.53	7.31	7.30	South West	1990	10.07	48.94	37.00	9.09
	All	21.22	72.44	34.62	57.08		1995	5.14	24.39	6.55	6.45
North East	1990	10.70	46.68	98.10	9.39		2000	4.82	20.43	5.08	5.67
	1995	6.74	31.16	14.69	9.93		All	20.03	93.76	48.63	21.21
	2000	6.57	27.05	11.16	9.75	West	1990	12.16	43.96	11.72	63.01
	All	24.01	104.90	123.95	29.07		1995	2.83	15.27	7.46	11.29
NorthWest	1990	8.25	39.01	24.53	9.45		2000	2.63	13.66	8.89	6.94
	1995	4.61	22.90	6.49	4.87		All	17.62	72.89	28.08	81.25
	2000	3.62	16.75	5.41	4.33	Total	1990	79.88	710.83	327.33	327.33
	All	16.48	78.66	36.43	18.65		1995	38.36	171.53	76.07	76.07
South	1990	7.09	49.74	92.05	17.18		2000	31.48	149.51	63.52	63.52
	1995	3.54	27.99	12.10	11.18		All	149.72	1031.87	466.92	466.92

Notes: A: Within counties; B: Between counties within regions; C Between regions: coming in; D Ditto: going out

Source: Demographic statistics kindly made available by Ioan Ianoş

unemployment – due to a surge of investment in industry and commerce which has made Cluj a 'hot new prospect' with a vibrant economy boosted by Nokia (Finland) making mobile phones and Emerson (USA) with electric motors; not to mention the IT&C sector which has recently involved Evaluserve (India) developing in the Business-Process-Outsourcing (BPO) field. Paradoxically the migration statistics for the 1990s show a pattern almost exactly the inverse.

Internal Migration

Taking the three years (with 1995–96 averaged out) there were 1.65mln cases of migration across administrative boundaries: 0.15mln within counties, 1.04mln between counties within regions and 0.47mln between regions. But 1.12m cases related to 1990 alone – at the onset of depression causing heavy redundancies that forced many workers to return home – with 0.53mln for the other two years put together (Table 2.8). However, when the 28 inter-regional flows (combining the two directions) are examined, eight are below 5,000 (5.9 per cent), six 5–10,000 (8.6 per cent), five 10–20,000 (14.8 per cent), eight 20–50,000 (49.1 per cent) plus one of almost 100,000 (21.2 per cent). The largest movement concerns Bucharest and the surrounding South region while the other substantial interactions connect Bucharest with the North East and South East, the Centre with the North East, the West with the North East and South West and the South East with the South. These flows, with the majority moving from the first-name region to the second (to the extent shown in Table 2.9), reflect the inverse of the main migrations under communism, with the Northeast as the great exporter of labour (mainly to Transylvania but also to Bucharest), while the relatively low rate of natural increase in the West induced particularly heavy migration that also included the North West and the South West. Thus, a third of the interactions account for 70.3 per cent of the total inter-regional migrants.

More moderate flows extend from the West to the Centre and from the Centre to the South East, with a quite evenly balanced exchange between the Centre and North West; also to be noted is migration from Bucharest and the South to the South West (another significant exporter under communism). The figures also show that the movements became more balanced later in the decade, and the few cases where the majority switched to the other direction indicate some return to a traditional pattern, such as that from the South into Bucharest in 1990; also from the South West to the West and slightly more from the North East and South West to Bucharest. This trend is likely to grow with greater awareness of migration abroad (which affects all regions) and may be influenced in the future by effective regional measures in the North East through stronger leadership (for example, from the regional CCI created in Iaşi in 2002 combined with an effective sector strategy to overcome the disparate local systems and the improved transport infrastructure expected for Euro-Corridor

Nine. Another interesting trend evident from the annual data for movements between urban and rural areas is that for the seven years 1990–96 there was a net annual transfer from rural to urban of 44,600 (total 312,000) whereas for the next seven years (1997–2003) there was a reverse annual flow of 22,900 (total

Table 2.9: *Migration between regions 1990–2000*

Regions	1990		1995–6		2000		All	
	A	B	A	B	A	B	A	B
B-S	78.35	98	11.44	56	9.24	43	99.03	88
B-NE	30.55	98	4.00	57	2.89	49	37.44	90
W-NE	24.79	93	4.94	65	4.11	53	33.84	84
C-NE	22.88	93	4.55	56	4.24	51	31.67	82
S E-NE	20.40	85	4.05	93	5.73	53	30.18	80
B-SE	20.93	94	4.22	68	3.21	57	28.36	85
W-NW	18.33	88	4.81	67	3.87	68	27.01	82
W-SW	13.54	80	3.71	50	3.21	43	20.46	68
SE-S	12.52	58	4.36	49	3.57	46	0.45	54
B-SW	12.75	96	2.52	59	2.05	49	17.32	85
W-C	9.06	79	2.55	59	2.22	57	13.83	72
NW-C	7.32	82	3.20	48	2.87	51	13.39	51
C-SE	9.33	71	2.07	50	1.80	49	13.20	65
S-SW	6.83	71	2.53	48	1.94	50	11.30	62
C-SW	6.38	86	1.50	56	1.36	54	9.24	76
S-NE	4.76	76	2.34	64	2.01	62	9.11	70
W-SE	3.91	79	1.20	55	0.90	53	6.01	71
S E-SW	3.59	71	1.15	49	0.86	46	5.60	62
C-S	2.74	67	1.37	51	1.14	54	5.25	60
B-C	2.97	81	1.08	40	0.98	43	5.03	65
W-S	2.94	76	0.81	56	0.71	46	4.46	67
NW-NE	2.14	68	1.10	58	0.96	61	4.20	64
SW-NE	2.01	68	1.12	67	0.97	59	4.10	66
B-NW	2.33	84	0.85	61	0.60	43	3.78	73
B-W	2.18	74	0.72	51	0.77	30	3.67	60
Total	323.53	82	72.19	58	62.21	51	457.93	74

Notes: A Total migration (th) both directions; B Percentage of the migration attributable to the predominant flow (from the first-named region to the second). The discrepancy between the total 457.93 in the penultimate column and the total of 499.92 in Table 2.7 arises from omission of the three smallest inter-regional exchanges (with no figure larger than 2,000)

Source: Demographic statistics kindly made available by Ioan Ianoş

160,000): people returning to the villages for retirement now outnumber the young leaving for the towns (in great numbers in 1991–92 because earlier moves were then being officialised) (Grigoraş 2001; Popa-Bota and Uiga 1999).

Emigration

Many younger people are moving abroad permanently, which accounts for the declining population of Romania – both urban and rural – since the revolution (Ianoş and Nica-Guran 1997). Some 78,300 persons emigrated to the USA during 1989–2002, although EU states – especially Germany, Italy and Spain – are also targeted. 14,000 Romanian IT specialists left in 2000, leading President Iliescu to raise the issue of 'intellectual property' the following year, in view of the attraction of higher wages for young people, trained at the country's 51 higher education institutions, whose departure left a deficit at home. The export of about a fifth of the doctors who qualify each year in Romania (700–800 out of 3,500) is partly a reflection of the difficulty of finding jobs at home (complicated in some instances by a lack of transparency in the recruitment process), although it leaves shortages, especially in Moldavia and Wallachia. However, accurate numbers are difficult to establish, for while border police say that 2.5mln Romanians have left the country and not returned they cannot all be assumed to be working temporarily in Europe. Research by Constantin et al. (2004) suggest that the emigration rate fell from two per thousand in the mid-1990s to one in 1999 and 0.6 in 2003 when some 10,000 people were involved (40 per cent from Bucharest and the four developed counties of Braşov, Cluj, Mureş and Timiş; ethnic and religious minorities disproportionately affected). But it seems to have accelerated again in 2007.

Meanwhile, those who sought temporary work and left their families at home in the early transition years often had to operate illegally by evading frontier controls or resorting to bribery. Some organised work has been available abroad for many years. Temporary work has been available in Germany for 50,000 Romanians who have received work permits each year since 1991, usually allowing three months' work out of a year, with strong demand in agriculture, construction, hotels and catering and the health service. Luxembourg offered reciprocal training of higher education graduates in 2001 while Portugal offered Romanians the right to work in unlimited numbers in 2002. However, a favourite destination is now Spain where picking strawberries and citrus fruit attracts many people (even with higher education qualifications) given the earnings of €600 per month compared with as little as €100 at home in 2005. Some 4,000 jobs are arranged by the Spanish government working with the Romanian Labour Migration Office that maintains a database, but the term 'strawberry picker' is used pejoratively for the infinitely larger numbers who have made their own way and taken up a wide range employments, in many cases on a permanent basis. Travel to the EU eased significantly in 2002 with visa-free entry to the Schengen zone, although travellers needed a return travel ticket, insurance, an invitation or tourist voucher and a substantial sum of money: €500 plus €100 per day – €3,000 for a month.

Since such a figure amounted to a year's average salary and was plainly unrealistic, it was common for travellers to lie about the intended length of their visit, or in the case of a return ticket to change the date once abroad, assuming it was not the intention to stay on – while the Romanian border police were often bribed to accept a 'wad of notes'. On top of the illegalities from previous years, when Romanians had to smuggle themselves into the EU, this produced a situation involving some 2.0mln Romanians residing illegally in Italy, Spain, France, Germany, UK, Ireland and Hungary, some 6,000 of whom were convicted by the courts for various irregularities. A further attempt to resolve the situation was made in 2005 when the money required was reduced to €30 (€20 for the less-rich Schengen states), while the Romanian border authorities looked more carefully into invitations and hotel bookings, even for day trippers to Hungary – an unfortunate procedure since accommodation can invariably be secured 'on the spot' more cheaply than through advance reservations made in Romania. Transport costs are minimised by coach travel and the services of the new Romanian low-cost airline Blue Air.

EU accession in 2007 eased the 'humiliation' for Romanian travellers when only minimal identification was required. There appear to be opportunities for all with Slovakia – imposing no restrictions on Romanian workers, along with the Baltic States, Cyprus, Czech Republic, Poland and Slovenia – seeking Romanian shepherds for €400/month plus food and accommodation. On the other hand, it could take at least two years and possibly as many as seven to get freedom to work as several member states have imposed restrictions in order to focus on sectors where shortages exist. Ireland and UK are allowing non-qualified workers in agriculture and the food industry only, but evidently it is easy to obtain a UK Construction Industry Scheme Card and operate on a self-employed basis while a mere course enrollment allows 'students' to work part-time. And Romanians are getting jobs in Ireland below the minimum wage – causing political debate on the grounds that the Irish government is not protecting the labour market. Meanwhile a two-year transition applies in Denmark, Greece, The Netherlands and Spain. Estimates of the total number of temporary workers (legal and illegal) varies from as few as 0.4mln to some far higher figures from reputable organisations dealing with the period 2003–5: 0.85mln by the labour ministry, 0.90mln by the Centre for Urban and Regional Sociology and 1.8-2.0mln by the International Organisation for Migration (which must be quite realistic for the 2008 situation), while the balance between legal and black market workers ranges between parity and 1:6! Annual remittances of $2–3bln represent a substantial addition to the $6b total for domestic earnings in 2002: hence the migrants make a massive contribution to help solve the problem of poverty among the elderly, for whom state provision is quite inadequate (the Romanian authorities would also like migrants to pay into social security 'welfare contracts' through consulates abroad). While some resent being driven to beg for work, it is becoming a fact of life, for instance for the 60,000 'strănieri' (workers abroad) in Neamţ county, who go home for the principal holidays and return to work with plum brandy ('ţuică') and salami ('cârnat'). Indeed many have prospered abroad like Nely Bratu who went to Spain as a chambermaid soon after the revolution and now runs her own property business in Castellon city. Of course there is a major benefit to Romania from cash sent home: estimated at €2.0bln from Spain alone (about a quarter of all wage income). However, the economic benefits have to be set against the problems for the families when men work away from home, the victims of trafficking for prostitution (following EU visa liberalisation) and the men who commit crime or encounter violence.

Italy is one of most popular destinations, with estimates between 75,000 and an astounding 1.06mln Romanians present: the latter figure would be equivalent to 37.2 per cent of all migrants in Italy, followed by 20.1 per cent for Moroccans and 16.1 per cent for Albanians. The largest groups are in Rome, Milan and then Veneto, which is facing a demographic crisis through ageing – hence the future for local industry would seem to start with the integration of migrant labour: some 4,200 Romanians in 1999 rising to 5,400 in 2000 when Veneto got an additional quota of 3,000 labour permits for Romanian immigration. The success of this process is leading Veneto enterprises to locate in Romania (moving plant or developing subcontracting relations) even though Veneto SMEs have limited knowledge of international operations and suffer problems of access to international finance. 'The complementarity may be positive for Romania if it helps in building local development and economic integration with the EU' (Stocchiero 2002, p.38) – that is, out-migration balanced by trade and FDI – with skill delocalisation a dynamic factor in remote locations through export of the Veneto Industrial District model: investing in Timiş in training workers and creating new infrastructures 'realizing a critical mass sufficient in augmenting contractual power in relation to local institutions' (ibid. p.41). Padua University has a research programme with Vasile Goldis University (Arad) on enterprise and governance networks to see how Veneto SMEs are stimulating local development: for example, how far can Veneto's cultural values and organisational capacities create a hybrid social capital involving cultural, political, economic and social relations? Italian FDI in Romania was only 11.1bln lire in 1995 but rose to 59.4bln in 1999 (generating 150,000 direct jobs and 500,000 indirectly). Unindustria Treviso (an association of industrial enterprises in Treviso province) says that 9,500 Italian enterprises (1,800 from Treviso province) were registered with Romanian CCIs by 2002: 3,780 in

Bucharest and 1,000 in Arad-Timişoara – with a clear complementarity between migration, trade and FDI in the latter. The same group started an annual conference in Timişoara in 2001 seeking public support for improved infrastructure, technology and industry parks and reduced bureaucracy. Meanwhile Treviso and Padua provinces are launching institutional and twinning agreements with Arad and Timişoara counties, with a focus on governance measures to improve economic and social relations (including migration management: housing, social services, training, quota planning). The Italian Ethical Bank, with headquarters in Veneto, is interested in financial schemes linked with SME internationalisation that could involve Romanian migrants returning home to help implement investments in small businesses linked with this region.

Immigration from Africa and Asia

This provides some demographic compensation, although the number of emigrants from Romania was exceeded only in 2001. In most cases these people are heading for Western Europe and hence the accommodation for refugees at Arad and Otopeni is linked with the flow of refugees, which increased in number from 315 in 1991 to 1,537 in 1999 (mostly from Afghanistan, Bangladesh, Congo, Iran, Iraq and Zaire). But there is a steady trickle of Africans, Chinese, 'Indians' and Kurds arriving through the formerly open border with Moldova or the border with Bulgaria – accompanied by guides ('snakeheads') of Bulgarian or Moldavian origin; and, while some move on into Hungary and others are detected and returned to their countries of origin, a proportion are able to settle illegally. Others arrive with the encouragement of agreements to abolish visas or bilateral agreements for education, and also the ease with which small businesses can be set up (or operated illegally), trading in cheap, poor-quality goods of Chinese, Indian, Middle Eastern or Turkish origin, matching the low spending power of the population. A business may also be a cheap way to get a residence permit. Dumbrăveanu-Andone and Dumitrache (1997) estimated the immigrant population at 170,000, including over 2,500 granted asylum or temporary protection and up to 80,000 illegal immigrants. Arabs establish small trading businesses, supermarkets, restaurants and fast-food outlets; generally trading legally (perhaps with some black market currency dealings), dealing fairly with customers and generating jobs for Romanians as bakers, drivers or shop assistants. They have integrated well, built up relationships and shown most interest in staying permanently; thereby attracting most tolerance from Romanians.

Many of the 25,000 registered Chinese immigrants are into commerce (bulk buying and selling, restaurants and shops), although they tend to live in isolation and employ only Chinese, with little intention of staying and little effort to integrate. However, there is no conflict with Romanians and any crime seems to remain within the Chinese community. Indians set up small trading businesses but keep a certain distance in relationships, for Romania is rarely their intended destination. Africans are much less involved in economic activity and are shown less tolerance by Romanians. However, there seems to be no proper monitoring and few organisations concern themselves with the immigrant population (although there is an International Organisation for Migrants and an NGO – Sirdo – that studies and represents the Arab community). Some 640 long-stay visa applications were approved for business reasons in 2004 (which, of course, does not concern citizens of EU countries, USA, Japan or other countries with which special arrangements are in force); 337 of the applications were from Chinese people, 182 Turkish and 106 from Middle Eastern states; the remainder came from India, Pakistan, Vietnam, Russia, Ukraine and African states. Meanwhile research suggested a substantial influx of population after accession with Romania as part of the EU's eastern border. The average of 24 variants adopted for a research project produced a figure of 60,000 immigrants per annum (Constantin et al. 2004).

There is now every prospect that the shortage of labour (especially skilled construction/clothing industry workers) will boost the numbers of foreign workers in Romania – 5,000 in 2006 (27 per cent Turks, 15 per cent Chinese, 14 per cent Moldovans) – to as many as 300,000 by 2015, with more emphasis on Bangladesh, Sri Lanka and Ukraine. A good example is the Daewoo shipbuilding business in Mangalia – with an order book of 32 ships (worth $2.50bln) for completion by 2011 – where there are some 400 foreign workers, mainly Chinese, Moldovans and Vietnamese. Accommodation is available at the nearby resort of Venus (where two hotels are being converted) and apartments built for workers to buy. In conclusion, there is always the option of maximising recruitment of the young, the handicapped and minorities (especially Roma) with more resources for training. With wages of €1.5–2.0/hr for building workers compared with 14 in Germany, few of Romania's 2.0mln workers abroad seemed likely to return – quite apart from money, the lack of corruption and 'bureaucracy' is appreciated – but the situation is changing as wage rates increase.

HEALTH AND EDUCATION

Romania's 'human development index' (reflecting living conditions) is below that of the northern countries of the region and equates with its Balkan and CIS neighbours (UNDP 1998). Education and health are crucial elements in enabling people to escape from poverty, since 'a large majority of children coming from poor households become the poor of the future' (Mete et al. 2003, p.*v*). High school and higher education really makes a difference in access to employment, although more basic education is important in avoiding 'consumption poverty' that arises when households fail to allocate resources to 'complementary inputs such as teaching materials or medicines' (C.Tesliuc et al. 2003, p.10). State programmes are under-financed and so it is common to see charitable efforts focused on these matters, as shown by the USAID Corporate Social Responsibility Program that encourages business to contribute to community projects. Thus, Energico equipped a Bucharest kindergarten with a new heating system, while Montaj Carpaţi restored the rural school of Pucheni Mari and Sofwin endowed schools and universities with IT programmes. On the health front, actions in 2002 included Mol minibuses to help disabled children travel to health and educational units, while Kraft-Jacobs-Suchard are disseminating information about children's nutrition (recognising that much disease is connected directly or indirectly with nourishment) and Kraft Foods have refurbished a number of children's hospitals in Botoşani, Piteşti and Sibiu.

Education

Romania has built some 300 new schools since 1989 and the renewal of old buildings continues with EIB finance in 2003 through a €131mln loan for 25 years for a six-year programme to rehabilitate, rebuild or upgrade 1,400 state schools and other buildings in the education system. Overall from 1980 to 2001 the mean number of years' schooling for students aged 15 increased from 7.8 to 9.5 years; while capacity increased by 50 per cent and school personnel by 72 per cent – although the school population has declined by 20 per cent. Spending has crept up from 3.5 per cent of GDP in the 1990s to 4.0 in 2000, reflecting the decision taken to extend compulsory education from eight to ten years, taken in 1997 and scheduled for introduction in 2004 (although there are problems in rural areas through pupils having to walk to school in the towns for the additional years). There was even a desire in 2001 to opt for 12 years to keep up with trends in Europe, but many think this cannot be implemented given the high drop-out level (affecting a quarter of pupils after eight years) due to poverty and lack of interest. Secondary education reached 90 per cent of the relevant cohort in 1990 but only 70 per cent in 1999. Some 40 per cent of the poor aged 15–24 are missing out on high school education (only a tenth for the non-poor) and the proportion has risen to over half for the rural poor, though the consequences may not be as great as in urban areas in terms of a rising share of unskilled labour among the young (Mete et al. 2003, p.*iii*). Poor families find it difficult to maintain school attendance with three or more children, even with minimum income guarantee (and there may also be differences in the quality of schooling between poor households and others). Hence government help has increased since 2000 to increase participation by children from poor and migrant families. Moreover the quality of education in the countryside is to be improved through $3.0mln to finance education courses – for 3,000 teachers at seven universities for 1.5 years – provided they then teach for at least four years in a rural area. A generous computer-acquisition programme has been implemented, albeit with allegations of corruption over the handling of contracts by the Năstase government. But more money is getting through to schools after a revamp of financial arrangements in 2005. Even so, teachers' salaries are low and many leave, especially when faced with high travel costs to rural schools still lacking basic amenities (Mete et al. 2003).

Higher Education and Research

Meanwhile, there has been a boom in higher education, affecting only 8.0 per cent of the cohort in 1990 but over 27 per cent in 2001, with the acceptance of fee-paying students especially after 1998. Enrolment has increased from 193,000 to 621,000 since 1989 while teachers have doubled. Of course, this improvement will take time to work through the whole workforce where the average education level remains relatively low (with less than a tenth having tertiary education in 2000). There has also been a remarkable explosion of private universities – with about 20 accredited – so that most county towns now have universities or faculties, with Alba Iulia, Arad, Târgovişte and Târgu Jiu among the centres that have acquired new facilities since 1989. However, private universities tend to concentrate on the cheaper courses and are largely staffed by part-timers – commuting from old university centres such as Bucharest, Cluj, Craiova, Iaşi and Timişoara – with courses copying the state sector. Of particular note was the initiative by the American International School in 1999 (accredited by New England Association of Schools and Colleges and the European Council of International Schools) in setting up a new university campus in Bucharest to provide for students from poor families; the building was undertaken by Ilbau of Austria. Teaching staff have doubled while resourcing per student has halved, with negative implications for IT (though it reflects a shift from technical subjects to economics, humanities, law and social sciences).

Even so, there seems to be an emphasis on mass provision of information rather than development of individual skills, and Gallagher (2005, p.341) offers a scathing criticism that covers not only poor funding but old-fashioned teaching methods, authoritarian professors and ineffective student organisations. More measured criticism of the so-called 'failure factories' would highlight the extremely rapid increase in the proportion of the school population going on to post-secondary institutions (from 10 to 35 per cent during 1990–2005, almost to the West European level thanks to the 'open door' policy) and a failure to gear university income to the quality of the finished product, in addition to the arrival of students with inadequate skills from the schools. Although some academics with foreign doctorates may feel marginalised, there is now more consideration of research quality as the basis for promotion (after former education minister M.Miclea had to resign in 2005 for advocating publications in international peer-reviewed journals as the key criterion). Meanwhile, there are innovations in distance learning through connections established by the Academy of Economic Studies in Bucharest with Buzău, Constanţa, Deva, Iaşi, Târgovişte, Slatina, Slobozia and Tulcea (1999). A restructuring of courses in 2005 will offer a three-year 'licence degree' in broader fields than previously available, with masters' courses and doctorates to follow. Meanwhile, in 2004 the places available exceeded the number of high school graduates, marking the start of a consolidation process and a decrease in the stake held by private universities. Finally, it is important to mention that Romania has a poor R&D record, with 80 per cent being undertaken in the public sector. Research workers comprised 1.6 per thousand persons in 1991 but 1.1 in 2002, while much of the infrastructure was plainly outdated and the human capital was deteriorating. There are some successes, however, such as the Rolling Mill Design Institute IPROLAM (privatised in 2000), which was holding on to its market by broadening its services.

Health

Life expectancy of 67.6 years for men and 74.9 for women in 2000–2 shows a small advance over the 1990 levels (66.6 and 73.1 years respectively) but this is low by European standards and reflects poor health. 'Stress leads to psycho-social disorders, unhealthy lifestyles, such as smoking and excessive alcohol consumption and increased suicidal behaviour linked with daily difficulties and the uncertainty about the future' (Phillips 1998, p.101; see also Matei 2003). But the problem goes much deeper (Dumitrache and Armas 1998, 2000). Women suffer from a relatively high maternal mortality rate (half due to complications arising from abortions) of 83.6 per 100,000 in 1990 and 41.8 in 1999: the highest rate in Europe – with 1.0mln in 1990 and 0.25mln in 2002 – six times the rate in Hungary and Poland. The average Romanian woman has three or four abortions in her lifetime (compared with less than one in the west) that makes women's health 'precarious'. However, the ratio of 3.1 abortions for each live birth (but 6:1 in Bucharest) – that is 866,900 abortions and 275,300 births – was reduced to 2 : 1 by the end of the decade. And in 2004 the number of live births exceeded abortions – for the first time since 1989 – by 220,000. Also, in 2004 a law guaranteed access to information about abortions, including risks. Nevertheless, despite the scope for family planning after 1989, a reproduction health strategy has been slow to emerge and education on modern forms of contraception is needed. USAID has funded a policy project to support a coalition of NGOs in operating a network of family planning consulting rooms and accessible prices for basic contraceptives. Meanwhile, Romania's position for male deaths from cardiovascular diseases was the second lowest among ECE accession states in 1970 but second highest in 1997; with relatively high rates for tuberculosis, viral hepatitis and syphilis as well.

Men comprised 49.3 per cent of population under communism but now 48.7 per cent (as in 1948); and while one million out of the 1.1m 'missing' men reflect emigration, the rest are the consequence of early death (two to three times the rate for women) from heart and lung disease, cancer and stress. Turning to the children, a decline in infant mortality from 26.9 deaths per 1,000 live births in 1989 to 17.3 in 2002 (though 33.0 in rural areas) has to be compared with the EU average of 4.6. Child deaths often arise through domestic accidents and the failure of illiterate and poorly educated mothers to identify disease. Infant nutrition suffers when low incomes mean cheaper foods with high consumption of bread and low quality cereals. But inappropriate diet makes for high consumption of fats and meat and low consumption of vegetables and fruit: the resulting low intake of vitamins and mineral elements leads to obesity and also anaemic children, tired after minimum effort. Many Romanian children suffer from bronchial asthma and there is also a rising level of youth drug addiction; 8,000 of the 14,000 people affected by AIDS are children (with the largest clusters in Constanța, Bucharest and Galați), although the numbers actually registered are lower in both cases. Nevertheless, even the lower figures place Romania in first place in Europe. However, there is a historic problem of underfunding ($460/pc PPPy in 2001) and a glaring anomaly between good provision for beds (7.6 ptp) in the 1990s and a scarcity of doctors (1.8).

Family Health Care

Attempts have been made to put medical care on a sustainable basis through mandatory health insurance introduced in 1999 involving a seven per cent deduction from wages to the National Healthcare Insurance Fund topped up by budget allocations. There are other funds for the Ministry of Transport and those involved in national security. In 2002, 4.6 per cent of GDP was spent on health (with the state budget accounting for 64 per cent of all spending in 2000) but there is widespread dissatisfaction over the level of taxation that makes up the difference: total welfare contributions amount to 49.5 per cent of wages: 32.5 per cent by employers as a payroll tax with 17 per cent deducted from employees' wages. Any reduction will mean higher injections from the state budget or payments from farmers and pensioners. Meanwhile, doctors and other healthcare providers are contracted by the funds, while it is up to patients to choose their doctor and thereby enrol with the health service locally. However, the response correlates with education with the lowest enrolment ratio for households headed by individuals with no schooling and poor socio-economic background generally. Yet health status is a key determinant of employment and earnings: hence there are 'clear economic benefits to healthiness – probably more so for the poor than the non-poor' (Mete 2003, p.101). Many people have to stop work owing to illness, and so 'chronic illness emerges as a key determinant of employment with startling magnitude', particularly for the uneducated. This is probably because (a) they are less likely to have treatment and (b) their work is more challenging, to the point where illness has 'a more drastic effect on their life' (ibid., p.42), although research is needed to see which of the two factors is the more important for policy formulation. Certainly, access is a problem because 11 per cent of poor households have no health service in their locality (five per cent for non-poor) and they have less capacity for diagnosis through informed informal networks. USAID has made a contribution through its family health initiative (making appropriate use of doctors and nurses and developing an adequate reproductive health system), encouragement of healthy lifestyles and action against HIV–AIDS and tuberculosis. Reference should be made to the EU dimension arising from the 'Access' programme designed for NGOs and non-profit organisations providing health and social assistance for disadvantaged groups with special needs (namely, people who are abused, handicapped, elderly, homeless, illiterate, unemployed or suffering from conditions such as HIV–AIDS). The scheme secures outpatient care and provides local social and community healthcare networks that should improve access to medical care, particularly for rural communities. The Centre for Health Policies and Services campaigned with Phare assistance (through the Development of Civil Society 2000 programme) to reduce smoking in 2003 through better information on its harmful effects, including the danger of passive smoking. And government has co-operated with tourist establishments in providing subsidised vacations at the seaside ('The Black Sea Coast of Romania for Everybody') and some spa resorts ('Health for Everybody'). This boosts occupancy in cheaper accommodation and extends the tourist season.

Hospitals

Hospital underfunding has been a major problem that resulted in massive payouts by patients – mostly 'under the table' – to the tune of 36 per cent during 1989–2001, while the state paid 64 per cent. There was particular dissatisfaction with the state health service in Bucharest because of the need to bribe hospital doctors in order to get attention. However, attempts at reform are showing some positive results. A $207mln reform programme started in 2000 with $44mln of government cash combined with $80m from the World Bank and $82mln from the EIB. Sweeping rationalisation occurred in 2003 when 81 hospitals were closed (11,800 beds): 51 became social care units with greatly reduced budgets, while 19 were re-profiled to cater for chronic diseases. This meant longer journeys for rural people needing specialist care, although a precedent had already been established through the specialist cancer hospital ('Institut Oncologic') established in Bucharest in the 1950s with a nationwide hinterland.

Indeed, Romania has the second highest cancer rate in the world and, with $1.0mln from private sources for a research project, the Institute hopes to provide a cure in ten years. Unfortunately, at the same time as the reform, budget cuts for 2003–4 left many hospitals without funding for medicines, food and heating; resulting in widespread protest over avoidable deaths. The situation is not helped by a 92 per cent level of import dependence (mainly involving the USA and Germany) for medical devices that cost some $240mln each year.

But drugs, for which there is a substantial industry in Romania, constitute a perennial problem that patients often have to solve through their own means. Underfunding in mental hospitals results in increased tension (even cases of patients killing each other), as well as extreme hardship when patients are transferred back to families – perhaps owing to lack of drugs – long after kinship contacts have been broken. The situation is quite unacceptable: not only through shortages, obsolete equipment and low wages but also corruption which seems contaminate even higher education in medicine. President Băsescu has been highly critical, with attacks on corrupt or inefficient hospital directors who cannot be removed from their posts, and claims that health ministry is funding poorly-performing private centres with inadequate equipment. It certainly seems that delayed payments for drugs and equipment increases these prices, while up to 30 per cent of hospital spending has been considered ineffective and wasteful. Nevertheless, a second phase of hospital reform is scheduled to run during 2005–10 to improve access and quality for maternity care (through 180 facility upgrades), and also emergency services through improved communications and 60 upgraded departments. Clinics will be restructured and homes privatised or converted for use by the chronically ill. Psychiatric care remains a concern.

The Private Sector once again has a role through health insurance, available since 1996, and the law of 2003 freezing premiums for young and old, and allowing tax deductibility, with tax surcharges on rich people who do not take out private insurance. Given the huge cost of hospital rehabilitation and re-equipment there is a case for private hospitals since the state cannot find this money. The government has a deal with Euromedic International (the largest ECE investor in the field) in respect of four private diagnosis centres (the first opened in Arad, including a €27mln oncology centre) integrated into the public health system. This $20mln project is supported by World Bank GEF and Dresdner Kleinwort Capital. Other realisations include a Euro-Clinic project for a new wing at Floreasca in Bucharest, with $5.0mln invested by Medisystem (for medical services through specialised clinics) and Interamerican Romania Company (IRC) supported by Dutch financial services group Eureko. This private medical insurance project started with private clinics in Bucharest in 2005 and was extended to major provincial cities in 2006. Bucharest's first entirely private hospital opened in 2005: a €10mln PPPt investment by Eureko for professionals and diplomats. It charges up to €130 a day, with up to €200 for small operations and €1,500 for heart and brain surgery. 70 per cent of Bucharest inhabitants would be interested in private health care if premiums were 100 per cent tax-deductible. Meanwhile, a private hospital opened in Piatra Neamţ in 1999 financed by the wealthy Romanian Viorel Strungariu. And Bucharest's Global Art Clinic was conceived by an Israeli specialist, in order to deliver 'mail order babies' so that men abroad can send frozen sperm to fertilise donor eggs (with good payments to local women!) for female partners.

CONCLUSION

Change since 1989 has been very substantial with the market economy a clear reality and foreign investment reaching dizzy heights: $4.1bln in the first five months if 2008 averaging at double the rate in 2007 and equivalent to the entire (record) year of 2004 boosted by the Petrom privatisation. The years of negative growth, with minimal European funding and constant financial 'blockage' in the SOEs, may seem part of another world when ambitious government plans were repeatedly undermined by lack of resources. Although the trade gap is wide at least exports are now growing faster than imports. The big question now is whether the rapid growth – 8.2 per cent in the first quarter of 2008 – can continue; not only in the context of the global credit crunch but also domestic considerations headed by a labour market that is becoming less competitive since the link between wages and productivity was eroded in 2007 (as unemployment almost disappeared thanks to domestic demand and further labour migration to Europe); although in regional terms the shortage has some benefit in pushing investors away from Bucharest and Transylvanian cities to the relatively 'unknown areas' of Moldavia and Oltenia where it may be possible to tempt more people away from the rural areas. Some migrants will doubtless return as the wage gap declines but the country's poor demographic performance is a matter of concern for the longer term With a labour deficit estimated as high as 500,000 the c.65,000 foreign workers could become 300,000 in the medium term with many more arrivals from Moldova and Ukraine as well as Bangladesh, China and Vietnam (while there is also an expat community of some 10,000 – mostly in middle management – contributing to booming demand in the service sector which registered the fastest growth in the EU in 2007, with rapid gains in IT&C and business support. But investors continue to express confidence in the country's growth potential and its capacity to correct any overheating without a 'hard landing'. But the American Chamber of Commerce in Romania has called for a massive overhaul to make the country more business-friendly as regards fiscal matters and infrastructure, as well as health and education.

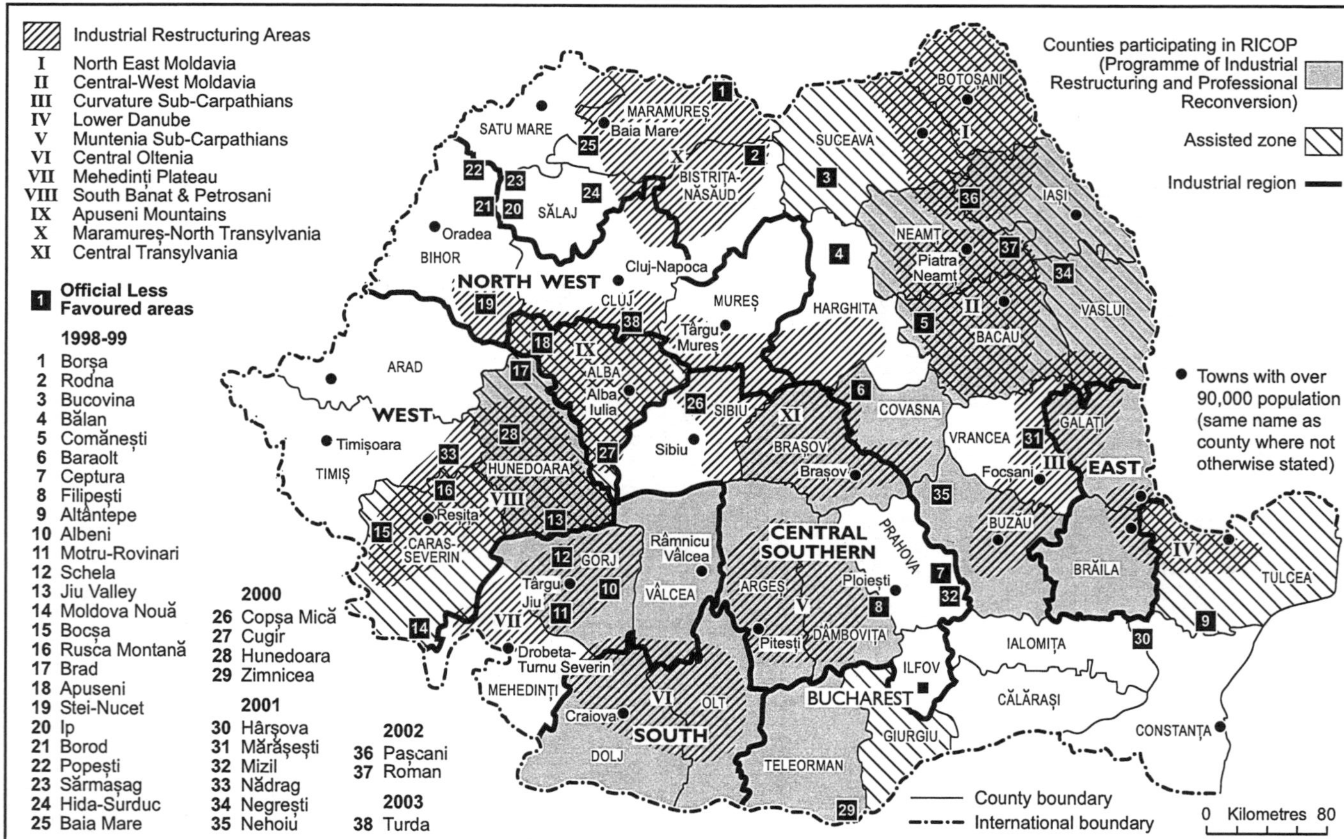

Figure 2.1 Aspects of Regional Development **Source:** Statistical Yearbooks

3. Restructuring Heavy Industry: Mining and Metallurgy

INTRODUCTION: FALLING OUTPUT AND INVESTMENT

This chapter and the three that follow deal with a selection of industries that together form the core of the restructuring agenda, comprising complementary spatial systems evolving over more than a century of modernisation (Figure 3.1), although it should be noted that the first (pre-1914) phase in today's Centre, North West and West regions occurred in the context of the Hungarian economy with the iron produced at Hunedoara (for example) being sent to engineering factories in Budapest. Restructuring has drastically scaled down the state's responsibilities over effective market penetration although there have been considerable misgivings over what is very largely an inevitable trend. Throughout the 1990s there were political objections from neo-communists and the nationalist GRP to selling or liquidating 'national patrimony', while unions opposed any rapid run-down in labour, even if a relatively unproductive workforce was unsustainable in the context of rising wages and production. Restructuring has been unavoidable, given the unforeseen failure to manage SOEs on a financially sustainable basis, coupled with growing external pressure to privatise – fundamentally for its own sake in reducing the role of the state – as a key FME indicator. EU 'Country Reports' highlighted the anomaly (persistent through the 1990s) of heavy subsidies and relaxed financial pressures for heavy industry – with limited restructuring – while the 'engine of growth' was seen as residing among a group of lighter industries concerned with textiles, clothing, footwear, building materials, wood processing and furniture that were privatised relatively early. In the late 1990s, electrical engineering was the only significant representative from the vast heavy industrial complex of metallurgy, engineering and chemicals characterised by declining performance and gradual downsizing. While there were problems over quality and price competitiveness throughout industry, it was in industries like steel where there was a persistent belief in the strategic importance of a significant state sector and hence 'a lack of political will to close down non-viable companies and to reduce the number of companies in line with capacity requirements' (Country Report 1998, p.31).

The following year's report highlighted a significant drop in investment (aggravating a generally low level of capital stock) and shortcomings in human skills. The situation was not helped by Russian melt-down in 1998 and Balkan instability that prevented a stable fiscal regime. Even so there were criticisms over the lack of 'capacity' at the industry ministry and the delay in formulating a strategic industrial policy. The EU noted that there was still no official industrial policy at national or sector level in 1999: although the ministry did have a draft global industrial policy and was progressing towards a more coherent industrial policy through the government's action plan for the implementation of a medium-term economic strategy, the proposals were considered general and beyond the government's capacity for implementation (Country Report 1999, p.63). However the government did move decisively in the mining industry and also introduced a 6.0% import surcharge in September 1998 for two years to protect industry during restructuring (allowable by the EU under exceptional circumstances). It was also seen as desirable to have large enterprises surrounded by clusters of SMEs to revitalise inefficient segments, although it was a matter of careful judgement to establish how far industrial giants should be broken up to eliminate unproductive sectors. Yet in addition to a stimulative investment climate to induce a new generation of technically advanced industries, SOEs needed to show more enterprise in management to attract investors through their 'effervescence': part of a cultural change sought by President Constantinescu to reduce SOE dependence on government and the SOF (although in the end the SOEs proved to be unsustainable). There was also a desire to maintain a substantial R&D effort to prevent the country becoming a 'technological colony' but, again, the finance has not been available; so instead imported technology has enhanced exports and reduced energy intensity.

Problem Solving

The years since 1999 have seen greater purpose, with some continuity through the change of government at the end of 2000. Restructuring strategies were belatedly drawn up for metallurgy, engineering, chemicals, oil refining and synthetic fibres. There was some input through a French social upgrading project to smooth the path for restructuring and upgrading. Nevertheless a further Country Report (2000, p.64) considered that industrial policy was still neither market-based nor predictable and complained of bureaucracy as well as a failure to stimulate an environment of open and competitive markets with any consistency e.g. in terms of product quality and careful identification of foreign markets. Industrial policy has not been able to deal with labour reallocation (Dăianu et al. 2001) apart from ad hoc initiatives of the kind evident in the iron and steel and mining sectors. But under the Năstase government the Agency for the Disposal of State Assets had the task of coordinating sector development strategies on a partnership basis – although there is a lack of information on the state of individual companies apart from monitoring by a post-privatisation directorate. With the state able to grant incentives (within EU rules), provide training and seek to enhance management quality, the reindustrialisation strategy was based on (a) fiscal measures giving 15–20 per cent advantage to encourage high value added in metallurgy, engineering (power sector and environmental protection), glass, pharmaceuticals, textiles and consumer goods; (b) international cooperation in the defence domain and trans-national projects like the Constanța-Omišalj-Trieste crude oil pipeline; (c) regional development measures in high unemployment areas (especially programmes for less-favoured areas and industrial restructuring areas). With EBRD support, government wants the powerful firms to develop (especially those with ambitions to expand into neighbouring countries) e.g. the car industry (after Renault's success) and food processors that should have a good competitive position in the EU.

Table 3.1: *Gross Value Added in Industry (percent distribution) 1990–2004 (note a change in methodology in 1998 with old and new calculations given)*

Year	A	B	C	D	E	F	G	H	I	J	K
1990	0.03	8.0	4.4	33.7	6.3	6.6	4.7	16.6	17.4	1.3	0.9
1991	0.08	8.0	6.2	24.1	11.7	6.9	5.5	12.6	16.2	8.2	0.5
1992	0.23	8.5	4.8	20.4	13.3	6.1	5.9	10.0	17.3	13.1	0.5
1993	0.68	9.7	4.5	18.7	12.7	6.5	5.2	9.7	20.8	11.6	0.6
1994	1.80	9.1	5.5	19.8	11.1	7.1	4.4	10.1	20.4	11.6	0.8
1995	2.37	7.9	5.5	19.6	9.9	7.1	4.3	10.2	22.9	11.6	0.9
1996	3.62	5.9	5.6	20.7	9.2	8.0	4.4	10.7	26.5	7.3	1.6
1997	7.81	7.9	5.5	17.9	8.0	7.1	4.4	9.7	29.4	8.7	1.4
1998	10.31	7.7	4.9	17.7	10.8	7.2	4.7	8.8	27.1	9.6	1.4
1998	9.82	9.9	5.2	18.3	10.5	7.6	5.0	9.1	23.4	9.4	1.4
1999	13.53	8.8	3.4	17.3	8.7	8.0	4.6	9.1	23.2	14.8	1.9
2000	21.95	7.8	4.2	16.6	9.9	8.9	4.1	9.6	25.3	11.9	1.6
2001	32.30	7.1	4.2	17.8	8.8	8.9	4.1	10.0	27.2	9.9	1.7
2002	42.61	7.6	3.6	18.2	10.0	9.3	3.9	10.0	23.6	11.9	1.8
2003	49.49	5.6	2.9	19.4	10.2	9.6	3.7	10.5	25.0	11.4	1.8
2004	60.79	5.5	3.5	20.7	9.4	9.8	4.1	10.3	24.7	11.0	1.9

Notes: A Total absolute value added (bln.new lei); B Extractive industries; C Metallurgy; D Engineering; E Chemicals Oil Refining and Plastics; F Wood, Paper and Furniture; G Building Materials; H Textiles Clothing and Leather; I Food Drink and Tobacco; J Electricity Gas and Water; K Publishing
Source: Statistical Yearbooks: Table 11.9

The state also has some important regulatory functions e.g. to confront the massive counterfeit industry in car parts, cosmetics, clothing and footwear, food drink and tobacco as well as computer games, CDs and DVDs. Government also has a role in improving the legal framework for economic reform and industrial/commercial activity including the harmonising of existing legislation with the EU; securing macro-economic stability as a base for relaunching industrial activity; reducing cross-subsidy in the energy field so that industry no longer supports the domestic consumer; and encouraging export growth through an aggressive foreign trade strategy. There are also tasks for local government: some towns responded well to the challenges e.g. the provincial city of Timişoara but also some of the medium-sized towns like Mangalia in the South East and Paşcani in the North East (Groza 1991–2, 1994). However with the continuance of growth since 2000 and rising levels of FDI much of the pressure on the government for industrial strategies – protective or otherwise – has melted away and individual plants are finding a productive role in multinational enterprise in a way that could hardly be comprehended a decade ago. However the process of adjustment has been severe and it recalls a similar experience of opening-up to a wider economic system in the late nineteenth century when handicrafts were almost totally wiped out by Habsburg and German competition. The impact has varied according to chance as well as available opportunities for the different sectors. Table 3.1 deals with value added and shows that engineering and textiles (with clothing and leather) contracted from a 50.3 per cent share in 1990 to 28.2 per cent in 2002, while chemicals, wood processing, food, utilities (electricity, gas and water) and publishing grew from 32.5 per cent to 56.6 per cent; leaving extractive industries, metallurgy and building materials little changed at 17.1 per cent and 15.1 per cent respectively.

The Problem of Heavy Industry

This chapter deals with one part of a section of industry long considered highly important strategically through its relevance to the military, as well as to the lighter, more consumer-oriented branches that depended on its inputs of machinery. Hence it was ordained under communism that 'Group A' industries should always grow faster than their 'Group B' counterparts. But in a global economy such determinism is inappropriate and in the context of Romania's raw material endowment the inherited capacity was always going to be unsustainable. Mining and heavy industry was in great need of restructuring because of low productivity and the inefficiency of using the large metal production and processing capacities built under communism – heavily dependent on imported raw materials (bauxite and iron ore) and energy (coking coal, oil, gas and electricity) to turn out ships and railway rolling stock for export at competitive prices. Some metallurgical plants were able to expand through imports of cheap iron ore from the FSU, greatly outstripping the scale of the local mines that sustained these industries in their early years. Only a few bulk steel producers will be needed in the future and the smaller and less well-located plants will have to reduce output and concentrate on quality with the use of scrap in electric furnaces. Restructuring seemed unpalatable when there were challenging political issues to confront and when modern technology would accelerate redundancies. Yet subsidised exports were no longer possible, there was reduced home demand and excessive over-manning discouraged FDI. Hence the desperate problem of technological updating, appreciated by the mid-1990s when virtually no FDI was going into heavy industry and the EU provided a period of grace only to 2000 prior to open-market competition. The old technology of the 1980s had somehow to be aligned with European norms.

MINING

Extractive industries enjoyed a privileged role under communism with a philosophy of self-sufficiency and this was very good for the regional development of the Carpathians (despite pollution problems). Management was not trained to minimise costs but rather to realise plan targets covering domestic needs as well as exports of salt, quartz sand, baric oxide, bentonite, refractory clay, limestone and dolomite. But in the context of globalisation and conventional pricing there are very severe problems through low-quality ores, especially bauxite, coal and copper, as well as some obsolete technology and difficult production conditions: remote locations in narrow valleys that make for high transport costs. Markets are relatively sluggish with a collapse of exports – e.g. salt markets have been lost since 1990 in the Czech Republic, Greece, Hungary and Slovakia – and low domestic demand. The quality of the ore was still a problem and the national mining company in Baia Mare (Remin) quoted 0.35 per cent for their copper ore (likewise Cupru/Minvest at Roşia Poieni near Abrud), plus associated antimony, bismuth, cadmium, gold and silver; also 0.70 per cent for lead and 0.90 for zinc. The recovery level from concentrate was 50–75 per cent. The sector declined in terms of its share of value added from 8.2 to 7.5 per cent between 1990–2 and 2000–2, reflecting the protected status of this sector (securing an initial rise to 8.9 per cent in 1993–5) while the decline in the late 1990s was cushioned by the importance of hydrocarbon fuels that have raised their share of value added from 78.9 per cent in 1996 to 84.9 in 2003. Average enterprise employment size came down drastically for non-metalliferous mineraks during this latter period (by 81.2 per cent to 2,006), coal mining (85.7 per cent to 2,016) and other extractive industries (83.5 per cent to 27) but only 46.2 per cent (to 1,148) for hydrocarbons. In this chapter discussion will centre around the general issue of mine restructuring with some specific comment on reserves of metalliferous ores amounting to 2.5mln.t of bauxite, 1.5mln.t of copper, 1.4mln.t of zinc and 0.6mln.t of lead in 2004.

When resolute action was taken in 1997–8 a massive level of subsidy in the mining industry was revealed: 44 per cent overall, albeit an improvement from the level of 75 per cent in 1992 (2.9x revenue) to 65 per cent (1.85x) in 1996, but with great variations between mines reflecting the quality of the minerals, technology and management quality, with only two profitable sectors: Ramin (mineral waters) and Salrom (salt). Production of 43mln.t of coal involved subventions accounting for 14.3–87.3 per cent of costs (0.2–6.9x revenue) compared with 75 per cent on average (3.0x) in the non-ferrous sector – but 90 per cent (9.0x) in the extreme case of the Baia de Aramă mine. Subventions were sometimes sustaining production above the level to demand: for example sulphur was in stock until 1995. Meanwhile productivity in mining was only half the world average because of low automation (two-thirds of the German level for open pit coalmining and one third of the UK level for pitcoal mines). Wages and working conditions were poor. Romanian miners were earning $170/month in 1996 compared with a world average of 5,400–6,000! It was also a hazardous occupation with a poor safety record: 14 miners died in a gas explosion at Vulcan in the Jiu Valley in 2001. Environmental problems arose through tipping and water pollution (with treatment needed to deal with a heavy metal content); also radioactivity at Ciudanoviţa uranium mine in Banat and then at Lisava in the same locality of the Oraviţa Carpathians in Caraş-Severin.

The Restructuring Programme

This was formulated during 1997–8 to reduce the subsidy element to 50 per cent of costs (parity with revenue) and applied to a group of state companies: Minvest (Deva) with copper, gold and iron mining interests; Remin (Baia Mare) exploiting for precious and non-ferrous metals; Lignit (Târgu Jiu), the opencast coal mining company and its pitcoal counterpart 'Huilei' (Petroşani); as well as a rare metals company based in Bucharest and a smaller lignite company based in Ploieşti. The programme would eliminate the hopeless cases and seek improvements elsewhere: increasing productivity to 2004 and reducing subsidies by improved equipment and redundancy (reducing the 183,000 workforce of 1996 by a third) – with massive regional development implications in areas with few other openings; to say nothing of the youth pouring on to the labour market in remote/rough hill country with little alternative employment. The programme marked the start of what was to become a desperate search for ways of maintaining mining communities. Various targets were put forward to address an appalling economic situation. There might well be eventual closure of 279 mines starting in 1997, but in the short term (1998–2000) attention was directed to 110 unprofitable mines and quarries (30 concerned with non-ferrous ores) slated for closure during 1998–2000 at a cost of 120mln.lei. However, it was later expected that the closure process would be completed at only 62 mines and quarries by the end of 2001, while World Bank funding initially related to only 29 closures for which

$44.5mln was loaned: $27.04mln for physical closure and environmental measures, $13.9mln to ease the social impact and $3.16mln for institutional development – plus a Romanian contribution of $12.75mln and a non-reimbursible loan of $4.25mln from the UK government.

There was evidently 'horse trading' in 1997 to the extent that closing highly uneconomic mines might save others: e.g. in the case of the Oraviţa uranium operations, Ciudanoviţa was to close in the hope that Lisava could survive (at least to the extent of a two-year search for new reserves). In the case of iron ore, Ruschiţa would close (with 450 redundancies) in order to retain work at Teliuc. Foreign capital might locate new reserves e.g. to enhance the potential of the Moldova Nouă poly-metallic complex on the Danube and in 1998 Remin envisaged the leasing of 51 mines, supported by the offer of technical assistance. There seemed to be many ways in which improvements could be made by private investment: new technology in coalmining (pits and quarries) and to recover rare ores existing in small amounts like molybdenum; also improved ventilation systems in salt mines and automated sampling systems to improve recovery. In the case of Minvest, better blasting techniques and relocation of first crushing to minimise distance could help with open-pit working at Abrud (Roşia Poieni) and Moldova Nouă. Underground mines in the Apuseni gold 'quadrilateral' (and the ironstone mines of Bocşa and Iara) could secure economies in power consumption; adopt new roofing methods; assimilate 'Alimak' digging equipment to improve productivity along with continuous conveyor belts. With five-year exploration concessions on offer for gold, silver, lead, copper and uranium, Minvest thought that new technology could give good results in processing low grade copper, gold, silver and poly-metallic ores. On this basis a fair number of mines might be retained with production and productivity improved. With losses of $75.5mln during 1993–7 and activity subventioned at 60 per cent overall, Minvest thought that seven non-viable mines would close, while 15,400 jobs might be secure in 2005 (with five profitable units and 16 others operating with reduced subventions until their ore reserves were exhausted): the best prospects were for copper in the Abrud area (Roşia Poieni), gold at Brad and Baia de Arieş, polymetallic ores at Zlatna and iron ore at Bocşa and Iara. Meanwhile it was hoped that pitcoal expenses would fall from 1.8x revenue to 1.5x i.e. with subsidies reduced from 45 per cent of costs to 33 per cent, with monthly production of 0.25mln.t (plus 2.5–3.0mln.t. of lignite) after restructuring and a productivity rise of 10–15 per cent.

Recovery Strategies

Insofar as financial blockages were a problem there were suggestions that large vertically-integrated units might cover the entire range of operations from geological research to ore extraction and preparation of ore and smelting to produce ingots, wire or sheet. Thus Minvest would include the Baia Mare

(Phoenix) and Zlatna (Ampellum) copper smelters, while Remin would include the Baia Mare (Romplumb) and Copşa Mică (Sometra) smelters. Indeed the two enlarged companies might be combined and other manufacturers brought in like Elcond (Zalău) and ICME (Bucharest). There could also be vertical integration in the aluminium industry combining geological research, bauxite mining (Dobreşti), alumina production, by Alor (Oradea) and Alum (Tulcea), aluminium smelting by Alro (Slatina), rolling by Alprom (Slatina) as well as welded parts and cables by Altur and Elcar in the same town. This would certainly have allowed a trade-off within the company between the high costs of the early phases and income from sale of the final product, but losses would still have escalated where costs exceeded world market prices and rich new ore bodies could not be found. Such large companies would also have attracted political support and the lobbying capacity to press for favours such as preferential tariffs for electricity in the case of the aluminium industry. Finally, under pressure from local miners Alba County Council sought a separate company for the Minvest mines in its area (initially agreed in 1998 but subsequently retracted) on the grounds that subventions were relatively modest and, with further financial decentralisation (to deliver local enterprise taxation), the local authority could do a better job in seeking new investment.

A recovery package was also worked out by the ministry, Minvest and Tulcea County Council to save the Altântepe copper mine with financial recovery through funding for pumping and ore preparation. But applications for redundancy (particularly among the flotation workers) began to undermine the operation to the point where activity virtually ceased in 1997. It was easier to shut down the money supply for the new Chituc titanium mine 20kms from Constanța: 80 per cent complete in 1998 and the only such mine in Europe, it was intended to work sand from a sea platform and despatch the material for processing at Giurgiu. This followed the bituminous schist operation at Anina linked with a 900MW power station where there was no further capital to solve the daunting technical problems of ash disposal posed at the end of communism. But other targets were difficult to meet. In 2001 there were still mines with levels of subsidy over 80 per cent (i.e. costs 5.0x revenue) and the ministry was looking for more than 2.5x the money sought for investment to be ploughed into subsidies in the hope that the j.v. formula would eventually attract funding for non-ferrous ore operations from strategic investors by 2002 e.g. at Roşia-Poieni (producing 4,000t of copper concentrate annually for smelting by Ampellum (Zlatna) and Phoenix (Baia Mare) when a foreign partner was required to inject the $85mln needed to relaunch the enterprise. Altogether 210 mines and quarries were closed during 1998–2002: 77 mines and 41 quarries (12 and nil respectively for coal; 23 and 36 for lignite; six and two salt; and 36 and three for minerals); also 23 preparation plants (two for coal, seven for salt and 14 for minerals). While mining employed 350,000 in 1989 (and 700,000 indirectly) the total was down to 183,000 in 1998 and then 68,800 in 2002 after incurring net losses of $5.25bln during 1990–2002. The union naturally deplored the situation – complaining about the lack of a sector strategy and inconsistent social assistance – but strike actions and paramilitary 'mineriada' tactics failed to produce any worthwhile benefits while tarnishing the country's image abroad.

Further Closures involving 63 units were then envisaged for the next period to 2004 (with some operations to be placed on a care and maintenance regime) including investment of 10.0tln.lei to reduce losses by 20 per cent to 2004 (with annual decreases in subsidies of 10 per cent each year). In the case of Minvest costs would be reduced from 3.5x production value to 2.6x (i.e. subsidies would go down from 78 to 72 per cent. Meanwhile Remin would bring down costs to 2.4x (70 per cent). Mining redundancies were part of a wider picture of decline the SOE sector negotiated with global financial institutions e.g. 6,000 mining lay-offs (out of 24,000 in the state sector) were expected in 2003, supported by unemployment benefit and 15–17 monthly salaries. In this context Minvest planned to cut its workforce from 8,000 to 6,800 with the closure of Altântepe, Baia de Arieş and Roşia Montană (though the latter was postponed through the new gold mining project referred to below). Compromises were possible whereby production ceased but mines were retained (across the whole mining sector) on a care and maintenance basis in 2004 against the possibility of future private investment: this involved all the 63 closures scheduled for 2004. Then the 2005 deal involved a further 6,000 miners with lump sum payments of $7,000 each to reduce the total employed to 41,000. 30 new mine closures have been announced in the Baia Mare, Deva and Ploieşti areas and this contributes to a total of another 133 mines closed or effectively stopped on the top of the figure quoted above. Meanwhile the old workings, along with unexploited geological reserves, were placed in the hands of the National Agency for Mineral Resources (NAMR) for possible leasing to private companies.

This was all meant to prepare the industry for operation in a free market economy with European management standards with state subventions eliminated by 2007. There was still some hope of privatising and revitalising viable mines (e.g. through public-private partnerships negotiated through the NAMR) but the more likely scenario would see social problems arising from closures eased by economic regeneration through new uses for old mines and a combination of retraining and environmental improvement for investment in light industry and tourism (the latter by farm, forest and fish resources; not to mention the offering from the former economy through 'flori de mine' which have been protected since 1924). But the future remains bleak and it has to be said that despite desperate efforts to subsidise the building of new enterprises, the programme since 1998 has been a disappointment both socially and economically with the best opportunities for redundant miners having been found abroad. Needless to say, the attitude in the mining areas is one of bitter resignation, most evident in the Jiu Valley coalfield (Kideckel et al. 2000; Sauleanu & Parlea 1997). The results have generally been disappointing in terms of foreign investment with Minvest being eventually forced to close all its mines by 2007 after sustained EU pressure in the run-up to accession leaving only some 250 employees (for conservation work) out of the 40,000 present at the start of the exercise. Unable to reduce its debt to the state (135bln.lei) augmented by 232bln.lei in penalties, the only ray of light appeared to be the takeover of Cuprumin Abrud by the private smelting company Cuprom, although the accounts were again daunting with 67mln.lei of debts (of which 39mln arose from penalties) which are separate from the Minvest figures.

The Case of Remin (Baia Mare)

After 43 closures during 1998–2002 – including 17 mines, one quarry and six preparation plants – Remin is trying to rebuild during 2004–10 with higher productivity through concentration on the better quality material and equipment with greater capacity and performance as at Şuior, Turţ and the gold recovery project ('Aurul'). The Maramureş area, in the immediate vicinity of the company's Baia Mare headquarters, has 19 flotation plants that include the major tailings ponds at Borşa (Colbu and Novăţ), Băiuţ (Bloaja), Cavnic (Răchiţele). the central flotation complex (Tăuţii de Sus near Baia Sprie) and Săsar (Aurul). Some of these are now mothballed with activity now concentrated more heavily on the central flotation complex where $2.0mln was invested by Remin in 2000 (along with the enterprises of Baia Sprie, Cavnic, Herja, Rodna, Şuior and Turţ). The central flotation has given up handling low-grade pyrites – for which there is virtually no market – in order to reduce preparation costs. Costs were reduced overall from $135.3mln in 1990 to 73.4 in 2000; scoring a profit of $0.2mln in 2000 after a $39.5mln loss in 1990. The workforce was reduced by 23,000 or 67.6 per cent (including Aurul) to 11,048 – with variations between Rodna (49.3 per cent to 812); Băile Borşa (61.1 per cent to 3,056); Baia Mare East (62.3 per cent to 5,383); Baia Mare West (73.7 per cent to 1,202); and Gura Humorului/Bucovina (80.2 per cent to 1,703) (Bălănescu et al. 2002). Investment was desperately needed from all possible sources including the state budget, the company's own funds and partnerships with foreign firms. But this has not arisen and Remin found itself in 2007 with employment down to 730 (deployed in the few remaining workings and also in conversion work in mines and processing units) and a debt burden of 27mln.lei (15mln for electricity alone) augmented by government penalties to 67mln.

On the environmental side there have been improvements over accidents, silicosis and sickness. With 215 mine tailings ponds – many disused, with some under conservation like Malaini-Cavnic and others still operational like the pond at the central flotation complex of Tăuţii de Sus (Baia Sprie) and others at the mines of Băiuț, Colbu-Borşa, Herja, Rodna and Turț – it was appropriate that there should be a project involving Romanian and Dutch specialists, along with a special collaboration with Austria over the Novăț pond at Băile Borşa. Modern technology is being used to separate copper and lead concentrate and also for sulphuric acid production and smelting, with a positive effect on the condition of the rivers in Baia Mare (especially the Săsar below the lead smelter). To improve air quality filters have been introduced at the central flotation complex (the Phoenix copper smelter already has a 351m chimney to help minimise fallout over the town). Meanwhile environmental programmes include the IBRD-funded 'Proiectul pilot pentru Reconstrucție şi Dezvoltare' through miniparks at Borşa and Şuior. In the latter area an important innovation is 'Complex Turist Şuior' at 688m with its 1,200m piste (and a chairlift under construction to cope with the 550m difference of level). The new resort also offers tennis and swimming as well as walking to Bodi Lake and the local peaks: Mogoşa, Poiana Boului, Guțâi Pass/Hanul Pintea Viteazul (983m), Creasta Cocoşului with its nature reserve (1,428m) and Vf.Guțâi (1,443m). Mines are being 'ecologised', like the old Dâlga coalmine in Petroşani (not however part of Remin) where 12ha available for industrial use were purchased for €2.0/sq.m for an Italian furniture factory.

Gold Production

As regards new mining ventures the best prospects appear to lie with gold. Indeed the j.v. Aurul (owned 50 per cent by Esmeralda Exploration of Australia and 44.8 per cent by Remin) originated in 1992 and proceeded to an environmental assessment in 1993 with construction starting in 1997 followed by plant opening in 1998 and the start of production in 1999. The enterprise has in effect taken over Remin's western branch of Nistru-Ilba-Săsar, reducing the workforce from 4,563 to 1,202 in the process. The idea was to retrieve gold and silver by cyanide leaching applied to crushed ore from a 450m thick seven-kilometer seam processed at a \$28mln recovery plant based on the processing of old mine tailings to yield 1.6t gold and 9.0t silver annually. However at the same time it was decided to clear material from three decantation lakes that were causing trouble (especially in dry weather) through dust and heavy metal leaching that (especially in the case of Meda Lake at Săsar) affected the 5,000 inhabitants of the Dragoş Vodă neighbourhood on the western edge of Baia Mare. A new pond at Bozânta with a 20m high dam would clear the way for the processing of 4.43mln.t from Meda (yielding 0.60gr/t) as well as 10.05mln.t from the central flotation complex (0.48gr) and 8.50mln.t at the older Bozânta facility (0.30gr). Processing at a rate of 2.5mln.t/yr would take 10–12 years and realise 1.6t of gold and 9.0t silver. Meda was linked by pipeline with a new plastic lined lake at the Săsar-Lăpuş confluence at Bozânta so that slurry from

Meda could be taken to the new Aurul pond and metal extracted, with cyanide returned to Meda as a 'closed circuit' (although Meda pond was not lined and so cyanide routinely leached) (Brewer et al. 2002).

However in January 2000 it was the new pond that breached over a 25m section when efforts to raise the dam failed to keep pace with the growing discharge provoked by heavy rain and rapid snow-melt, whereupon 100,000cu.m of contaminated water were released into tributaries of the Tisa river, with 50–100t of cyanide in the process; resulting in pollution and fish death. The disaster was then compounded by the Novăţ dam failure in the Borşa area two months later when 40,000t of tailings were released during torrential rain and snow melt. Gold production resumed in June 2000 but Hungary filed a $180mln compensation claim and during a subsequent lawsuit in 2005 seeking $146mln damages the company (now Transgold, with a 17.2 per cent stake by the UK company Oxus Gold with interests in Central Asia) claimed that it was not cyanide that killed fish (since there was no problem in Romania) but an overdosing of antidote in Hungary. Ordered by a Budapest court to reduce gold production by 85 per cent, the company argued that it operated under Romanian law and was still permitted to process 2.0mln.t of material annually. It should be added that cyanide has been used for processing for 60 years and pollution at Săsar is long term, with doctors alluding to damage to children's immune systems that increases vulnerability to disease. However huge improvements have been made in Baia Mare since 2000 and it seems unlikely that such an accident could be repeated even though cyanide leaching continues. It has been argued that although the consequences of the disaster were very serious, they merely compounded 'much longer term problems associated with many decades of poorly regulated and largely untreated industrial mining and urban discharges into local rivers' (Macklin et al. 2003, p.256), for pollution was occurring regularly downstream of Băiuţ, Borşa and Cavnic mines as well as Săsar and it was found 'highly likely that floodplain sediment is a major secondary source of contaminant metals' (Brewer et al. 2003, p.78) with 'contamination from present mining activity probably having a more significant impact on water and sediment quality than the tailings dam failures themselves' (ibid, p.82) – though further downstream the rivers comply with the EU water quality directive. However the plant was reported working at only 15 per cent of capacity after a legal battle in Hungary in 2005, before freezing conditions and credit restrictions in 2006 meant lay-offs for two-thirds of the 100 remaining workers.

Gold Production at Roşia Montană.

Cooperation began in 1995 between Minvest and Gabriel Resources over 12sq.kms of waste tips at Roşia Montană and Bucium with a view to redeveloping an active mining area where underground operations had stopped in 1985 in favour of the open pit operation at Cetate: previously started in 1970 with obsolete technology. This operation, now closed, is to be replaced by modern plant belonging to Roşia Montană Gold Corporation (RMGC) owned by Gabriel (80.0 per cent), Minvest (19.3 per cent) and small investors (0.7 per cent) who planned to operate not only at Cetate-Gauri but also elsewhere in the local area at Cirnic, Jig and Orlea during 2006–24 following phases of pre-construction (1996–2003) and construction (2003–5). Although the material is low grade (containing 1.52gr/t of gold), 225.7mln.t of reserves should yield a total of 331t of gold and 1,600t of silver (using cyanide). Indeed, the site is seen as one of the world's top ten undeveloped gold mining projects in the world and it could arguably bring total benefits to Romania worth $1.6bln. The impact would be considerable through 500 jobs during the operational phase plus a multiplier of 3,000 jobs: good news for the high unemployment Apuseni mountain area that could attract several such projects. However much resettlement will be needed (over 2,000 people in some 880 dwellings) and small farms will disappear especially in the Corna valley where conversion of land for the dumping of tailings and overburden is being opposed by many small property owners despite the offer of new homes and land parcels in the immediate vicinity, or monetary compensation adequate to allow some families to move into apartments in the county town of Alba Iulia.

The production process is also controversial (all the more so in view of the Baia Mare incident) although reassurances are compelling since water used in processing will have cyanide removed before going to the tailings pond (using a system commonly employed in mining areas). Moreover, further acid rock damage – which has been going on for many years – will be prevented. The project has divided both the community and the wider public including politicians and experts. There are also mixed signals from Europe with a favourable report by the European Parliament – recognising the economic importance of the project, as well as the $8.0mln spent on an archaeology and ethnography programme (Popoiu et al. 2004) – balanced by EU concern over slow progress in transposing environmental legislation: projects initiated before accession must not prejudge the effectiveness of EU environmental legislation after accession. While much has been done to evaluate and protect the archaeology of the Roman period there is a notion of 'social licence' regarding large mining projects that RMGC may well have difficulty in securing. Total costs are high – estimated at €1.8bln of which €200mln has already been invested – and the failure to win IFC support in 2004, while not crucial, was widely seen as a declaration of 'no confidence' given the sensitive environmental and social issues. On the other hand, the world's leading gold producer – Newmont – acquired 10.2 per cent of Gabriel stock in 2004 and offered their expertise on technology, finance and permitting. The environmental impact assessment (EIA) is clearly crucial and although submission was originally scheduled for 2002 – with the start of ore commissioning in 2004 – the procedure has been repeatedly delayed, partly due to its 'transboundary' nature, since water drains eventually into the Danube via the Arieş, Mureş and Tisa (thereby involving Hungary). It was predicted that EIA would be successfully completed in time to start the construction phase in 2007 and production in 2009. Work continued initially to secure archaeological discharge certificates and to acquire all surface rights within the planned mine perimeter (43 per cent of properties were bought) but the process stopped in 2004 pending progress on environmental matters.

The project remains in the balance with some 300 local farmers still refusing to sell (including Eugen David who has assumed a prominent leadership role) and enjoying international support after the issue became better known as a result of the Dracula Park tourism controversy and the visit of the Swiss-born environmental journalist Stephanie Roth – writing for 'The Ecologist' – who was able to link the local 'Alburnus Maior' opposition group with global ENGOs including Greenpeace and obtain funding for their campaign initially with a grant from the US Global Greengrants Fund. In 2005, while the Soros Foundation was able to help through its interest in open government. The company's promise of an environmental clean-up has been countered by an expert view that despite the promised detoxification the project will inevitably produce other toxic byproducts including heavy metals (not to mention the local landscape changes arising from four large pits). The division within the community in general – and individual families – is expressed by rival signs saying 'RMGC property' and 'property not for sale'. More seriously however there is an effective brake on any development since the status of the village as an industrial zone (since 2002) prevents rural development (e.g. in tourism), which the Soros Foundation wishes to promote, while rejection of the company's long-awaited EIA in 2006 has brought the mine project largely to a standstill (including exploration drilling), pending a further application. Perhaps the remaining owners will eventually sell 'at a price' and certainly neutral opinion anticipates that some organisation (like Gabriel's Toronto mining engineers) will take the gold eventually. But while the company was confident enough to launch its 'Mind Your Own Business' campaign, playing down local opposition and the landscape implications, the project is now badly behind schedule since EIA acceptance was anticipated by 2007 to allow mine building during 2007–9. Two-thirds of the 325-strong workforce is now laid off, although work continues on new housing in Alba Iulia and locally at Piatra Albă.

Other Gold Projects

In order to assess the prospects, European Goldfields Romania (EGR) have been awarded a three-year exploration licence for the 31.3sq.km Căinel perimeter in the 'gold quadrilateral', following public tender. It lies 10kms northwest of the Certej perimeter, where EGR has an 80 per cent interest in a pre-feasibility study completed during 2005. Promising signs have been uncovered in this area – 18–20g/t for gold and 100g/t for silver – through the j.v. Deva Gold established in 1999 between EGR and Minvest (similar to the initial collaboration at Roşia Montană). The same j.v. also examined the Zlatna perimeters but that site has been abandoned after exploration found no basis for viability. Meanwhile International Goldfields have carried out initial drilling for copper-gold ore at Sacu (also in the gold quadrilateral) and are now committing $1.0mln for further study in the hope that it will prove similar to Certej and Roşia Montană. This initiative arose out of the worldwide copper-gold search by BHP World Minerals who retain an option to buy back the Sacu field. Finally, Carpathian Gold (Toronto) are prospecting for gold (and copper) in Oraviţa and also in Maramureş, given underutilised ore processing capacity in the latter's 30km axis of base metal working. Activity is concentrated at Baia Sprie and in the area 25kms to the east at Văratec; also Băiuţ – where promising results suggest an open-pit project – and Jereapan, 6.0kms northwest of Băiuţ.

METALLURGY

Copper-Lead-Zinc

Following growth under communism, there have been environmental problems since 1989 as well as high costs for processing domestic low-grade ore compared with the imports. Indeed the Romplumb lead smelter at Ferneziu (Baia Mare) was found to be using Polish concentrate in 2004 whereas it is traditionally dependent on the local mine of Herja. During 1985–9 copper production averaged 40,000t, lead 29,000t and zinc 39,000t, but experience during transition has varied with copper output falling to 20–30,000t during the 1990s and even further to 15,000 during 2000–3, while lead fell to 10–20,000t in the 1990s with subsequent recovery. Meanwhile zinc collapsed to an average just 13,000t during 1990–4 but subsequently recovered and has exceeded the 1985–9 average since 2000 though not necessarily from Romanian ore (Table 3.2). Smelting and electrolytic refining of copper involves capacities of 35,000th.t/yr at Phoenix (Baia Mare) and 13,000t/yr at Ampellum (Zlatna). In 1998 Allied Deals (subsequently renamed RBG Resources) bought 70% of Phoenix, the only integrated copper smelter/refinery and precious metals plant in the region; paying $37mln for shares and taking over debts of $30mln, with the intention of investing $38mln in upgrading the plant. They also acquired the Elcond (Zalău) copper wire producer in 1999. Problems were encountered in 2001 when regulations preventing the import of scrap caused a three-month stop

Table 3.2: *Production in the Metallurgical Industry (mln.t) 1985–2005*

Year	A	B	C	D	E	F	G	H	I	J	K	L	M	N	O
1985	9.21	13.79	4.15	6.69	2.95	9.90	1.51	2.29	4.74	n.a.	40	30	35	n.a.	247
1990	6.35	9.76	2.12	5.27	2.38	6.79	1.94	2.00	3.70	93.10	25	13	11	247	178
1991	4.52	7.13	1.29	3.87	1.96	5.16	0.63	1.46	2.39	68.92	26	10	9	200	167
1992	3.11	5.38	0.89	2.83	1.66	3.86	0.45	1.23	2.65	67.23	27	9	12	175	120
1993	3.19	5.45	0.96	2.94	1.55	4.10	0.41	0.86	2.40	70.20	25	12	14	186	116
1994	3.50	5.80	1.01	3.28	1.51	4.51	0.47	0.95	2.66	85.23	22	15	19	184	122
1995	4.20	6.56	0.97	4.09	1.50	4.96	0.54	0.86	3.16	84.45	22	18	28	175	144
1996	4.02	6.08	0.94	3.85	1.39	4.48	0.59	0.86	2.95	77.87	29	14	28	175	145
1997	4.56	6.67	0.93	4.55	1.19	4.81	0.63	0.76	3.11	73.82	23	13	30	127	164
1998	4.54	6.34	0.67	4.69	0.97	4.39	0.66	0.46	2,93	59.84	21	15	29	162	175
1999	2.97	4.39	0.32	3.23	0.84	3.38	0.35	0.13	1.59	60.48	21	13	29	.	174
2000	3.07	4.67	.	3.45	1.22	3.69	0.46	0.12	1.53	56.30	15	25	52	.	181
2001	3.24	4.93	.	3.68	1.26	3.64	0.66	0.22	1.34	n.a.	18	22	48	.	185
2002	3.98	5.49	.	4.51	0.98	3.95	0.56	0.25	1.68	n.a.	11	23	38	.	191
2003	4.15	5.69	.	4.54	1.15	4.76	0.45	0.24	1.55	n.a.	17	28	51	.	205
2004	4.24	6.08	.	4.68	1.40	5.19	0.49	0.23	1.57	n.a.	25	25	53	.	229
2005	4.10	6.28	.	4.51	1.77	5.31	0.53	0.22	1.78	n.a.	21	27	57	.	258

Notes: A Pig iron; B Steel (all): C Steel (Siemens-Martin steel only); D Steel (convertor steel only); E Steel (electric steel only); F Rolled steel; G Tubes; H Iron ore; I Metallurgical coke; J Copper-Lead-Zinc concentrate (th.t); K Electrolytic Copper (blister copper only 1985–9) (th.t); L Lead (th.t); M Zinc (th.t); N Bauxite (th.t); O Aluminium/Alloy (th.t)

Source: Statistical Yearbooks: Table 16.3

(and a search in Romania for recyclable materials and blister) but production was eventually restarted after three months using recyclable materials as feedstock. Upgrading then resulted in the commissioning of a new electrolyte purification plant where residual copper in the waste electrolyte could be transformed into high quality commercial or recyclable copper; bringing the plant into line with standard electrolysis plant around the world. The improvement also eliminated the secondary effects of the cementation process through water pollution, following installation of a Scheibler-type filter in 2001. However the main shareholder was arrested in 2002 for involvement in embezzlement of $600mln whereupon the assets were eventually resold to the Romanian company Cuprom in 2003. This company has maintained association agreements with two mining enterprises (Cuprumin Abrud and Moldomin Moldova Nouă) and – led by H.Sima and H.Pitulea (former vicepresidents of Citibank Romania) and supported by Deutsch Bank and Merril Lynch – it was successful in 2007 with its $400mln bid for the Serbian copper company of RTB Bor (with $150mln to be invested in modernisation over 15–20 years). Meanwhile, Ampellum, producer of copper sulphate and electrolytic copper, was treated to a government-supported environmental programme prior to privatisation. The company's preparation plant at Abrud, linked with the Roşia Poieni copper mine has reopened with new equipment and viability is enhanced by profitable foreign sales of wire.

The lead smelter Romplumb (Baia Mare) has also made significant environmental improvements to reduce pollution of the Săsar river but it has not yet been privatised. Because of its appalling pollution record the lead recuperation section (processing old batteries) was closed in 1990 and the manganese peroxide installation followed in 1992, while filters and sewage systems were installed during the later 1990s with new processing technology now anticipated. The substantial accumulation of waste at this historic plant was reduced through reprocessing at Baia Mare's main flotation installation in the 1960s and also by use on local roads. On the other hand the Sometra (Copşa Mica) refinery, with capacities of 42,000t/yr for lead and 66,000t for zinc, now has Mytilneos Holdings (Greece) as the 88% majority shareholder, undertaking a $15mln update to increase metal production, reduce production costs and safeguard the environment – with technical assistance from British and German companies including Lurgi Metallurgie. High performance electric filters will retain toxic emissions while technological gases with high sulphur dioxide content will be used in a new sulphuric acid plant, while the 2,000 jobs available in the year 2000 will fall to 1,600. Metrom (Braşov) invested 10mln.lei in 1996 to convert its non-ferrous metallurgical plant to civilian use; producing goods presently imported for the engineering industries (and so saving $10mln/yr) while also exporting rolled metal.

Aluminium

This successful new branch started in at Slatina (near the Oltenian group of lignite-burning power stations) in 1961 with technical help from Pechiney (France). Preference for a small town rather than the regional city of Craiova made good sense in the context of industrial spread to new county centres formally established in 1968. The first aluminium was produced in 1965 and output in 1989 stood at 263,000t before an initial fall in production to 110,000t in 1990 and 1991 (as 10 electrolysis bays were reduced to four), recovering slowly to 140,000 in 1994 (using five electrolysis bays) and 174,000 in 1996. A further bay was modernised in 1997 – again in cooperation with Pechiney – to reduce power consumption by 1,000kwh/t to one of the lowest world levels, while recovering and reusing all the fluorine gas to secure a 10 per cent reduction in overall costs to $120–150/t. Another bay was upgraded in 1999 with rising profits secured by the upward trend in aluminium prices. Elsewhere in the plant, a new line for the casting and homogenisation of extrusion rods was opened in 1998. In all this work Alro committed $50mln of its own funds. There was further restructuring at the smelter in 2000 to reduce losses by updating the casting lines for slabs and alloy (hence a modest increase in production from 174,000t in 2000 to 178,000 in 2004): also the shedding of some auxiliary activities with consequent staff reductions to reduce losses in 2000. However it was crucial to bring calcined alumina and electricity costs into line with the competition. Hence when electricity prices were liberalised in 1997 a special tariff was negotiated and by 2005 the company invested $30mln from earnings to reduce energy consumption by a tenth to 1.0MWh/t (through use of computer systems) and increase value added by switching from blocks to finished products (with new casting lines for alloys including AlMgSi rods first produced in 1995) and slabs. The environmental was improved by removing of toxic gases with longer shifts (from six to eight hours) then boosting productivity.

Privatising the Slatina Smelter

The financial situation was difficult at the end of the decade when the government was forced to economise and the alumina suppliers located in Oradea and Tulcea also faced difficulty. Output fell to 43,000t in 2000. But privatisation of this 'jewel in the crown' was supported by PSAL with foreign interest from Alcan (Canada), Alcoa (USA), Pechiney (France) and Ruskii Aluminii in 2001 – not to mention possible Romanian bids from the Copos (Ana) or Voiculescu (Grivco) families – but the process was completed in 2003 in favour of Marco Industries (based in The Netherlands) who gained a 41 per cent interest by 'aggressive acquisition' of shares, whereupon the state had little choice but grant them a majority. Marco now own 87 per cent of the company and the state 10 per cent. $70mln were committed to environmental protection (to reach EU environmental standards in 2005), in the context of a total investment of \$170mln during 2000–5 with productivity by the 3,700 workers (retained by the company until 2006 under the privatisation deal) improving annually by around 10 per cent. The company's capital has increased by €52.4mln (to a total of €110.3mln) in a bid to make the aluminium smelter more profitable after EU accession. Indeed, Alro is now eminently viable with profits of €32.6mln declared in 2004. Marco will now invest \$300mln at Slatina by 2008 to raise production from 180,000t in 2002 to an anticipated 250,000t in 2006 (after negotiating loans worth \$105mln from HVB Bank and Bank Austria Creditanstalt in 2004) and eventually 420,000t. But the later announcement indicates that an investment of \$145mln during 2002–5 will be increased to \$700mln over five years to achieve a capacity of 450,000t. Constraints lie in the shortage of engineers and high energy costs which mean that the company will build its own power station (burning high grade coal) for opening in 2013. The bulk of the output of refined aluminium (ISO9002 standard), is exported mostly to Austria, France, Germany, Greece, Italy, Turkey and countries in the region. There is now a much more assured future for Slatina as the largest aluminium producer in the region outside Russia, accounting for some eight per cent of the national electricity consumption with the additional benefit of a long-term power agreement with nuclear and hydro generators (as well as the company's own capacity). It is a vertically-integrated producer working in partnership with overseas bauxite mines given the interest of Russian oligarch Vitaly Machitsky in Belize-based Pioche Consultants as well as Alro (since Marco – now controlling Alprom and Alum too – is owned by Machitsky's Rinko Group). The Russian connection is also evident in O.Deripaska's Ruskii Aluminii (Rusal) while M.Cernoi controls the Rafo oil refinery near Bacău.

The smelter is fully integrated with the Alprom rolling mill after a takeover was agreed in 2005. This latter factory opened in 1970 using American and Japanese equipment and initially produced just 6.8th.t. But capacity rose to 92.5th.t through the rolling mill in the 1970s and production for the aircraft industry – as well as aluminium foil – in the 1980s, although the maximum output achieved was 78,100t in 1980. The factory struggled to compete in the 1990s with exports of just 1,000t monthly to Italy, Japan, Turkey and UK secured in 1999. Output averaged 23,200t during a financially unstable period from 1997 to 2002 (mainly rolled strip) before rising to 31,300t in 2003 serving markets in the automotive and aerospace industries as well as electrical engineering and the food industry. Following privatisation in two stages (1995 and 2002) there was a powerful logic in combining with the smelter and since Marco already owned some 90 per cent of Alprom the formal merger agreed in 2005 was relatively straightforward. With \$36mln invested during 2000–5, a rise in output to 50,000t is expected in 2006 and ultimately 120,000t, with improved technological and environmental standards and a workforce of 1,600.

Looking further downstream, the problem of capitalising incomplete projects is evident at Artrom, making seamless pipes for the engineering industry and oil extraction. This enterprise was established in 1984 and produced its first pipes in 1989. But although most facilities were operating by 1989, further equipping of the factory lapsed until 1992 when a DM29mln loan was obtained, followed by a 0.5mln.lei loan from SOF for auxiliary equipment in 1994. The factory was then complete, but the capacity of only 65,000t (instead of the design capacity of 120,000t) complicated the loan repayment due during 1999–2002. Currently SOF is trying to sell its 58 per cent stake. Petrom is the main customer but exports have increased with the end of anti-dumping duties by EU in 1998. Alumil is a Romanian company with private capital active in the field of aluminium structures and accessories, with a network of stores in Bacău, Brasov, Bucharest, Cluj, Constanţa, Galaţi, Iaşi, Slatina and Timişoara. It also built a production unit in 2000 at Filipeştii de Pădure (near Ploieşti in a less-favoured area with fiscal incentives) costing $15mln and employing 200 people. Can-Pack (at Bucharest and Tecuci) produce aluminium cans – initially 0.66bln/yr but with a capacity for 1.0bln – with recovery of half Romania's used cans. But a €120mln aluminium foundry projected for Cluj by Mountupet (France) in 2004 (creating 2,000 jobs) was lost.

Alumina. This upstream alumina section is more problematic. Tulcea-based Alum opened in 1973 using the Bayer process with 0.25mln.t capacity rising to 0.40mln.t in 1979. It used imported ore and commissioned the first vertical alumina furnace entirely designed and built in Romania: a $2.6mln investment (but allegedly $5.0mln if built by a foreign entrepreneur and 15mln if German technology had been used). With production of 800t daily and savings in alumina production costs of $10/t the investment cost has been recouped quickly, with the project completed on schedule. The plant now yields the new grade of alumina required by international standards (as well as the upgrading process at Alro) though some of the alumina is exported. Capacity then increased to 0.50mln.t in 2000, with a switch from the Floury to the Sanday system. But full integration with Slatina was widely seen as a precondition for the aluminium industry's survival and after a period of closure, a 68 per cent majority interest was acquired in 2004 by Machitsky's interests from Balli Metals (part of a transport group that became the majority shareholder at Alum in 1999). Capacity was set to rise to 0.60mln.t in 2006 and eventually 1.0mln with further cost reductions. There was second alumina works (Alor) at Oradea with a smaller capacity of 0.25mln.t originally processing bauxite from Dobreşti in the adjacent Pădurea Craiului mountains. But production stopped when Alor closed in 1999 and 900 miners went off on leave (with 48,000t of bauxite in stock). It was claimed that Dobreşti bauxite cost only $25/t compared with over $30 paid by Tulcea for Australian, Greek or Yugoslav bauxite. The factory was reopened by Cemtrade using imported bauxite but even this proved unviable and the factory is closed. Oradea attracts foreign investment in new industry and commerce but the end of domestic bauxite production is another element in the picture of catastrophic decline of mining in the Apuseni Mountains.

The Iron and Steel Industry

This is the main section of the metallurgical industry that witnessed an initial rise in the share of value added from 5.1 per cent during 1990–2 to 5.4 per cent during 1994–7 cancelled out by overdue restructuring to 4.0 per cent in 2000–2. Enterprises have increased in number from 322 in 1996 to 481 in 2003 while the average employment size has declined sharply from 509 to 166 given the decline in the total workforce from 163,800 to 79,700. Steel production slumped initially from a record high of 14.4mln.t in 1989 to 5.4mln.t in 1992 before recovering to 6.7 in 1997 and falling to a record low of 4.4 in 1999 (Table 3.2). It has now recovered somewhat to 5.5mln.t in 2002 and 6.3mln.t. in 2005. Exports have been important: 2.33mln.t in 1995 – including 1.24mln.t for hot rolled sheet and strip, 0.39 for concrete iron and rolled wire and 0.19 for steel pipes – rising to 3.0mln in 1997; with scrap a significant item as well. The industry is certainly capable of alignment with EU quality standards and prices, while it retains special local importance through the supply of gas for heating at Călan, Călăraşi, Galaţi and Hunedoara. Much of the industry is now well-equipped e.g. there are new electric ovens of world standard at Călăraşi, Câmpia Turzii, Reşiţa and Târgovişte, while Târgovişte also has a modern stainless steel mill and capacity is available to produce the full range of tubes. The mill at Galaţi for 4.5m wide thick sheet is a facility only found elsewhere in Germany and USA; while technology at IMGB (the Bucharest heavy machine works) for 450t ingot casting exists elsewhere only in Germany, Japan, Russia and USA. However, energy costs are very heavy and although Reşiţa has its own hydropower stations the thermal power station in the Galaţi complex was allocated to the national power company. There is heavy dependence on imports of both iron ore and coking coal. Very little coking coal was produced even under communism but iron ore production has declined rapidly since 1989 because the low-grade domestic resources are no longer acceptable. Initially the Poiana Ruscă continued producing and also Căpuş near Cluj-Napoca, but the Bocşa-Dognecea mines closed during the 1990s along with the iron-manganese operation at Răzoare (south of Baia Mare) which has been worked intermittently during the twentieth century: the Hungarians never completed the planned funicular link with Ileanda during World War Two and although a new mine and quarry operation started in 1988 the underground component closed in 1992 due to high costs and the opencast working (delivering 40,000t/yr to Galaţi) stopped in 2001. However all iron ore production in Romania has now ceased.

Restructuring

The process started with Phare support and involved the industry ministry's metallurgical department, the Siderom (Bucharest) planning company and French consultants Safres. The plan for 1993–2002, adopted early in 1994, ambitiously proposed an investment of $2.6bln in steel – out of $3.2bln for metallurgy as a whole – taking into account the challenge from Europe arising from the protocol signed in 1993: abolishing quotas on Romanian exports in 1995 with gradual elimination of customs duties to reach a free trade situation in 2002. The plan would secure 90–95 per cent of the steel needed for the home market and allow efficient use of productive units at 80 per cent of capacity, with higher quality processing (using technology closer to world level) and reduced energy consumption and pollution. But the plan did not stay on course due to chronic undercapitalisation and lack of financial support, although it was important that upgrading should be completed before liberalisation of scrap iron exports (that would inflict a substantial shock on all works). In 1996 75 per cent of output came from LD converters at Galaţi based on iron ore; and 25 per cent from electric furnaces at Câmpia Turzii, Oţelul Roşu and Târgovişte (later Călăraşi and Reşiţa also) and Siemens-Martin furnaces at Hunedoara and Reşiţa. Four specialised holdings were deemed the optimum framework for competitive marketing by the industry, with auxiliary operations hived off and privatised. First, two integrated works on the Danube had the benefit of low-cost raw material delivery and supplied 72.2 per cent of national steel production. Sidex (Galaţi) produced thick sheet, flat products and semi-manufactures for re-rolling with 6.95mln.t capacity; supplying steel to other works including several tube mills – Bucharest (Helitube), Galaţi (Infor), Iaşi (Tepro) and Zimnicea (Zimtub). Meanwhile Siderca (Călăraşi) operated its own electric furnace for long products (including rails) and semi-manufactures with 1.7mln.t capacity. Second, there was a small (1.55mln.t) integrated works at Hunedoara (Siderurgica) near domestic coal and ore supplies, turning out long products and allied steel profiles. Third, four 'mini mills' dealt with long products and profiles: Industria Sârmei (Câmpia Turzii), Socomet (Oţelul Roşu), Combinatul Metalurgic (Reşiţa) for railway discs and rims; and COS/Oţelinox (Târgovişte) for stainless and other special steels. Fourth, there were six rolling mills and tube factories processing semi-manufactures – e.g. unwelded tubes from Artrom (Slatina), Petrotub (Roman), Republica (Bucharest) and Silcotub (Zalău) – dependent on the other groups for their inputs.

A major investment of $2.6bln was to be generated domestically through the budget, bank credits and the SOF, starting with the continuous casting line at Târgovişte and the plant for coal injection (blowing dust into ovens) for furnace six at Galaţi (on the model of furnaces four and five) but other aspects of the plan fell two to three years behind schedule due to cash shortage, with serious consequences for competitiveness. There was also a diversion of scarce funds to help Moldova over the first production line at its Protos (Faleşti) tubemill opened in 1996 in cooperation with the Iaşi tubemill, with finance from the special Romanian government fund for Moldova. By 1996 the prospects were bleak with no real restructuring achieved and major problems loomed over a future in Europe with regard to quality indicator ISO–9000. Enterprises had no funds of their own, while budgetary and SOF funding was quite inadequate and there were very few external sources (with or without government guarantees); yet investment was crucial for eventual competitiveness. The situation was complicated by low prices and trade barriers intended to block exports, since scrap was selling at $90–100/t on world markets but only $45–50 in Romania: so final produce was attracting anti-dumping measures. Romania also had to face the withdrawal of EU benefits for steel exports in 1998; with liberalisation of scrap costs driving up prices to world levels; and greater competition on the home market with customs charges reduced or abolished. There was little interest from potential investors although ThyssenKrupp (Germany) were looking at steel, engineering and railway infrastructure (especially the possibilities for cooperation with Hunedoara and the Jiu Valley). Hence the prospect, envisaged in 1993 but never implemented, of closing unprofitable units to concentrate investment on plants like Sidex (Galaţi) using most of their capacity and able to export, where efficiency gains and quality certification were most effective. Sidex made 4.55mln.t of steel out of a national total of 6.40mln.t in 1997 (4.05 out of 5.83 in 1996) and exported 70 per cent.

A Revised Programme was based on a Phare study for 'Technical Assistance in Restructuring the Romanian Iron & Steel Industry' starting from an anticipated laminates' consumption of 270kg/pc in 2004 and 360–380 in 2010 (comprising 50–55 per cent for flat products; 35–40 per cent for long products and 7–12 per cent for tubes). The plan also allowed for a greater positive trade balance, taking advantage of Romania's geographical position enabling exports to be directed to traditional markets in neighbouring zones that could be important for the future EU. 'Apparent laminates consumption' in 1998 was calculated at 120.7kg/pc (60.9kg of flat products, 45.3kg of long products and 14.5kg of tubes) compared with 377.2 for Czech Republic and 395.3 for EU-15. This suggested a maximum steel capacity of 12.00mln.t for 9.50mln.t production, including 8.24mln.t of hot rolled metal (5.51mln.t for the internal market and 2.73 for export). Thinking at the Ministry of Industry & Commerce in 1999 envisaged a national metallurgical company to invest $1.0bln in updating and spend $1.6bln in social costs, linked with the downsizing of the seven steel makers (Călăraşi, Câmpia Turzii, Galaţi, Hunedoara, Oţelul Roşu, Reşiţa and Târgovişte) and nine tubemakers in Bucharest (Helitube, Icem, Improlam and Republica), Galaţi (Infor), Roman (Petrotub), Slatina (Artrom), Zalău (Silcotub) and Zimnicea (Zimtub). A halving of the workforce from 140,000 to 70,000 over five years would include disposal of subsidiary activities accounting for 40 per cent of share equity. Privatisation was now making progress at the tube mills but only at two steelworks (Oţelul Roşu and Reşiţa). However it seemed that a single national steel company might best enable the state to modernise the industry in order to raise productivity (three to four times lower than in updated plants) and compete with Kazakhstan, Russia and Ukraine.

Public Sector Adjustment Loan. A slightly different gloss was applied in the light of the PSAL in 2000. The government's view was communicated by the manager of the Ministry of Industry & Commerce Metallurgical Division who noted the disappointing recent history of partial restructuring driven variously by the ministry, factory managements, employers' associations and trade unions. He now introduced a more radical approach to extend privatisation from downstream units like the laminated tube mills: Artrom (Slatina), Petrotub (Roman) and Silcotub (Zalău); welded pipe mills: Helitube (Bucharest), Tepro (Iaşi) and Zimtub (Zimnicea); and rolling mills at Beclean, Brăila and Focşani. Among the steel producers only Oţelul Roşu and Reşiţa were now privatised, but PSAL could now deal with Călăraşi, Câmpia Turzii, Galaţi, Hunedoara and Târgovişte. He also criticised 'static management' unable to respond quickly to market demands as well as inefficient below-capacity working and unreasonably low export prices. And while he was hopeful of privatisation in favour of large European manufacturers, he also foresaw a scenario where the producers of long products would be doomed to loss-making with the threat of bankruptcy eventually forcing mergers and closure of whole units. More positively, by taking account of the needs of downstream steel users, the expectation was that Galaţi would consolidate as the major producer of flat products and thick plate, with an upgraded capacity of 4.5mln.t aided by a $300mln investment over three years to introduce continuous casting and cold rolling. It would continue to supply the car industry – Dacia and probably Daewoo also – as well as the shipyards and agricultural machinery firms. Hunedoara would remain the main producer of carbon and low alloy steel with a complete module (electric furnace, continuous casting and rolling mill) of 0.6mln.t capacity; while Târgovişte and Câmpia Turzii would consolidate as regional producers of wire and wire products from alloyed and highly alloyed steel respectively, with an investment of $180mln. From 80,000 at the end of 1999 employment would fall to 44,000, though 12,300 might find work in enterprises hived-off and those made redundant would benefit through RICOP. Another issue was the Krivoi Rog investment at Dolinskaya: a communidt project to boost Ukrainian production of iron ore with investment from participating countries. After Ukraine withdrew, Romania was left with an investment of $800mln that would require a further $150mln to 2004 to gain any result, with abandonment producing only a modest financial recovery.

The Usinor Study (2000) examined the PSAL programme in more detail and emphasised the need for ongoing state support. With steel production likely to rise from 4.21mln.t in 1999 to 6.50–7.69mln.t (taking pessimistic and optimistic forecasts), capacities totalling 7.93mln.t were allocated to: (a) the large Galaţi producer (5.40mln.t); and (b) the state-owned producers of long products: Călăraşi (0.50mln.t), Câmpia Turzii (0.40), Hunedoara (0.90), Reşiţa (0.45) and Târgovişte (0.48). This left aside privatised companies – like Ductil (Buzău), Gavazzi (Oţelul Roşu), Oţelinox (Târgovişte), Petrotub (Roman) and Tepro (Iaşi) – for which information was lacking. Total restructuring costs were estimated at $1.44bln (of which Galaţi would account for 925mln) and employment would fall from 55,000 to 35,800. Galaţi made a loss of $412mln in 1999 but was expected to show a profit of $39–65mln (according to pessimistic and optimistic forecasts) while the four smaller units – Călăraşi, Câmpia Turzii, Hunedoara and Târgovişte – might see their combined losses of $23.1mln (ranging from Hunedoara's loss of $18.2mln to Târgovişte's small profit of $0.04mln) turned into profits of $40.6–49.8mln of which Hunedoara and Târgovişte would account for $32.1–37.0mln. The global situation was unpromising with low demand and falling prices leading to protection in the US market where customs taxes of 8–30 per cent threatened to eliminate steel imports – with serious implications for Galaţi especially (delivering 80 per cent of its production to the USA) but also Câmpia Turzii and Târgovişte and the tubemills of Iaşi and Roman. Altogether some 15–20mln.t of world steel production might be kept out and therefore potentially redirected to Europe where the EU would be forced to take protective measures; given that mergers were taking place e.g. between Hugovens and British Steel to form Corus; and between Arbed and Asslaria to create Usinor. Romanian steel was now struggling between the US and EU 'poles'. Exports to the USA fell from 352,000t in 2000 to 134,000 in 2001, while the situation in Europe was held.

The Union of Steel Producers (the metallurgy employers) was by contrast more optimistic in arguing in 1999 that economic growth would be slower in the pre-accession period (3.00 per cent rather than 4.75) with Romanian industry therefore modernising more slowly and requiring more steel. They thought that domestic demand was artificially low (with engineering requiring only 2.1mln.t of steel) after three years of falling GDP. They also observed that steel was doing well in EU markets and could do even better if it was allowed more time to adjust after the communist years of extensive growth for a closed economy with little scope to meet the needs of specialised markets. They also thought that privatisation was premature and wanted the suspension of PSAL for the units at Călăraşi, Câmpia Turzii, Galaţi, Hunedoara and Târgovişte in favour of a state steel programme with lower tax liabilities and more favourable accords with EU and CEFTA. But this seemed highly unrealistic given EU insistence on a radical restructuring agenda. The 2000 'Country Report' (p.63) was critical of the fact that a national steel programme was still undecided and that only one minor steel company (Reşiţa) had been privatised: 'due to the delays in restructuring and the unrealised privatisation of Romania's main steel company – Sidex (Galaţi) – the general situation in the steel industry has worsened'. The situation was now handed over to a new government after 2000, taking stock of a decade of subsidy ($1.2bln during 1993–2002) with capacity halved (16.0–8.0mln.t since 1989) and production hovering around 5.0mln (only 4.5mln in 2000) with just 2.0–2.5mln for the home market with activity spread across 33 factories.

The Inter-Ministerial Committee – involving industry, labour and public finance along with the new privatisation agency APMSH – considered a strategic restructuring programme in 2001–2 for the efficient operation and management of the industry, with debts rescheduled or converted into shares. Recovery over five years to 2005 was expected to increase production to 8.5–9.0mln.t with 2.0mln.t destined for export, while employment would be reduced from 77,000 in 2002 to 65,000 (after 150,000 in 1990). An eventual production of 9.10mln.t was allocated as follows: Galaţi 6.00; Hunedoara 0.90; Târgovişte 0.65; Reşiţa 0.45; Câmpia Turzii 0.40 and Oţelul Roşu 0.30. Problems were expected at the five smaller units through heavy debts of 650bln.lei to the state budget and over 2,300bln to gas and electricity suppliers. Private funds were also considered – especially a 'serious investor' for the Câmpia Turzii wire industry – but comprehensive privatisation was still not anticipated, perhaps because of the difficulties at Oţelul Roşu and Reşiţa referred to below. With the prospect of the industry reaching the European technical level an annual profit of $100mln was anticipated, but further investment would be needed over the five years for upgrading in long products and pipes. Various forecasts were made including a further $1.2bln of subsidy to 2010 to reduce raw material and fuel costs, hive-off non-core activities, promote value-added products, close unprofitable lines (e.g. hot rolling at Hunedoara and Reşiţa) and solve environmental problems. At this stage problems were encountered over the EU competition chapter that ruled out subsidies (covert and overt) in support of unprofitable enterprises after 2004. A revised plan emerged at the end of 2004 to save another 0.82mln.t of capacity and reduce total rolling capacity from 11.25mln.t 1993 to 9.20 in 2008.

Privatisation

Quite quickly the situation changed decisively (in a manner quite unforeseen) with a renewed commitment to privatisation in the context of national economic growth and a more favourable global climate for investment. Of the 33 factories that shared national steel production in 2000, 20 were privatised by March 2002 including seven integrated units, four for rolled tubes and three for welded tubes. The transformation occurred quite successfully although the Galaţi case was extremely complex both economically and politically. This key transaction involved Mittal, who also acquired Siderurgica (Hunedoara) and the tubemills at Iaşi (Tepro) and Roman (Petrotub), while COS Târgovişte and Industria Sârmei Câmpia Turzii went to Conares Trading (part of the Conares Trading Group holding a portfolio of metallurgical businesses owned by Russian investors). Călăraşi was privatised as Donasid with Beltrame (Italy) as principal shareholder, although it has now passed to Tenaris (Luxembourg) along with Silcotub (Zalău). Two relatively early privatisations –Reşiţa and Oţelul Roşu – caused problems due to short-term marketing difficulties and the change in government at the end of 2000 with disputes arising over the precise terms of the agreements struck with American and Italian interests respectively. However, Reşiţa was privatised a second time and – following the fiasco over Noble Ventures (USA) which precipited very serious local problems extending over two years – it is now owned by Russian interests through Sinara Holdings-TMK, while Oţelul Roşu also experienced a phase of renationalisation between the first sale to Gavazzi (Italy) in 1999 and the second to Ductile Steel (Italy) in 2005. Privatisation has accelerated the rundown in employment: 52,000 2004 with 43,500 planned for 2008. The recent change has been quite dramatic and almost overnight curtailed further state planning given the mammoth transformation that took government planning and subsidy out of the equation. Perhaps the impending end of subsidies created a will to sell for whatever could be obtained at the time; with the government now ready to respond to EU pressure with only the nationalists to oppose them on the issue. Meanwhile the return of growth helped stimulate potential buyers – after some early expressions of interest e.g. by the merged group KruppThyssen that considered Romanian steel, engineering and railway infrastructure enterprises, with the possibility for cooperation with Hunedoara and Jiu Valley enterprises following two j.v. experiences in Sibiu in the late 1990s. There was also a good result for the small Brăila rolling mill (Laminorul) which was purchased by Donau Commodities (Austria) from ARSA, while Russian interests have taken over at Câmpia Turzii, Reşiţa and Târgovişte as already noted. Unemployment problems have eased e.g. at Hunedoara where the rate was reduced to 5.4 per cent in March 2007 after 10.7 per cent in January 2006. Many were engaged during 2005–6 by the automotive industry (especially cabling), as well as the clothing and footwear sectors, while others went abroad. New problems have arisen through rising coal and ore prices in 2007 although these have been eased by workforce reductions linked with technological upgrading. But future prospects have been brightened by the Voest Alpine's €7.0bln steel project (5.0mln.t) on the Black Sea coast to employ as many as 12,000.

Studies of Individual Plants: Danube Locations – Sidex Galaţi

This great communist project reflected a determination to industrialise in the face of constraints implied by Comecon specialisation proposals. Construction began in 1960 with the first charge five years later. By the early 1980s, six blast furnaces (1,700–3,500cu.m) produced 7.0mln.t: half the national steel output. Sidex scored the lowest material and energy costs in Romania with energy consumption only seven per cent below the most efficient European plants. It became the main flat steel supplier of the vehicle and metal processing industries; also providing long steel (billets and blooms) for further processing in other steel shops The enterprise generated substantial exports (40 per cent to Southeast Asia) and attracted large orders such as material for the Isaccea-Negru Vodă pipeline (carrying Russian gas to Turkey: 16bln.cu.m by 2000 rising to 30bln in 2010) that helped reduce the company's debts of 95.4mln.lei to the power company. From the trough of 3.0mln.t in the early 1990s, production recovered to 4.2mln.t in 1995 and 4.6 in 1997, but financial results were compromised by barter deals (typically) priced lower than cash deals: only 27 per cent of production was sold for cash in 1996 and 15 per cent in 1997! The average price for steel was only $300/t in 1997 when plates (accounting for 45 per cent of Sidex production) did not sell for less than $370 worldwide and 450 in Europe. Huge discounts could not be justified and the profit margin in 1997 was just 0.3 per cent. Liquidity problems – overdue payments to state budget of 100mln.lei at the end of 1997 – kept raw material stocks low and resulted in inefficient plant use, higher operating costs and loss of orders. But $280mln (internal sources $130mln and loans $150mln) went on upgrades during 1993–7, including one of the three basic oxygen steel shops in 1995.

Further Upgrading and Privatisation was envisaged by the new government from 1997. To achieve profitability (at a time when large debts of 80mln.lei were cancelled out by the 100mln owed by end-users) thinking was geared to a $100mln bond issue through Nat-West Bank (UK) in 1997 – tied to shares in the privatised company – to finance upgrading with steel converters and casting machines with help from Mannesmann Demag (Germany), increase efficiency and reach international norms including computer operation. This developed the following year into $1.0bln of finance from Flemings Investment Bank (UK) for a three-year updating programme from 1998 with steel production limited to 5.0mln.t/yr because of falling orders from Asia but with hopes of reaching 6.5mln.t at the end of restructuring in 2000. There was a prospect of some new jobs eventually, but initially employment of 36,000 would be cut to 25,000 over four years, partly by hiving off functions (cumulatively employing some 6,000 workers during 1998–2000) to new companies: Alimserv (canteens); Dunosi (comprising a hotel and the Garboavele-Ţigăneşti accommodation complex); Salvosid (security and fire services) and Seredile (for cleaning, tailoring and greenhouses): all would enjoy one year of privileged relations with Sidex who would remain as the main shareholder in each case in order to control priorities and costs. Reference should also be made to j.v. initiatives in 1997. First, Sidex Trading, involving the Balli Group of London (a transport and distribution firm that was – at the time – also the majority shareholder in the bauxite processing enterprise Alum of Tulcea) that enabled Sidex to negotiate directly with raw material suppliers through Balli's global network of trade offices; and second Sidex Monolitique: converting slag into refractory products with the help of the French cement maker Lafarge. Repairs and spare parts would be hived-off later, leaving only the basic production flow by 2003, plus the Mahmudia limestone company and the local power station that Sidex was able to acquire.

The privatisation process was delayed, but upgrading went ahead to the extent of $700mln for modernisation during 1998–2000 (of which $200mln came from internal sources): this involved three of the six blast furnaces in 1998. But the situation was difficult at the end of the 1990s. In 1999 production fell to 3.2mln.t and the workforce was reduced to 33,000: 3,500 compulsory redundancies were anticipated on top of 1,600 job reductions through request or retirement. Several units were closed: two coking batteries, one blast furnace, three oxygen converters, two casting machines, one thick sheet roller and one continuous casting installation. Much more radical downsizing was envisaged with labour cut to 10,000. It was only in 2001 under the new government that APMSH proceeded with privatisation – through the agency of Fieldstone (USA) – with a 90 per cent holding taken by the INM Holdings, including Ispat International (now rebranded Mittal Steel) – a branch of Indian Holding Lakshmi Niwas Mittal (LNM) – the world's fourth largest steel producer with 70mln.t capacity in the USA (International Steel Group) and Kazakhstan (Karmet) – plus projects in China and India – and annual turnover exceeding $6.0bln through business with China, Indonesia, Mexico and Europe. The deal, which significantly enjoyed UK prime minister Blair's political endorsement, comprised a total package of $500mln: $50mln for the purchase, plus working capital of $100mln and $350mln investment over ten years. A period of grace until 2005 was allowed in respect of welfare contributions, profits tax and VAT (on imported equipment and raw materials; also domestic market acquisitions related to technological and environmental upgrading) but only three years for other transactions. Debt-equity swaps were negotiated at discount rates (shares valued nominally at 2.5lei/share were sold at 0.33lei) and global advantage was secured by avoiding USA's 30 per cent surcharge on imported steel (due to its affiliates in developing countries). Finally RICOP resources were made available to support 7,400 voluntary redundancies through monthly payments of $1.3mln until the end of 2004. The only competition came from a Romanian group that sought favourable terms over debt conversion into shares and the possible delivery of ore pellets from Krivoi Rog (Ukraine). In the latter case Romania retained an interest in a former Comecon project for long-term expansion of steel production in member states lacking domestic ore resources.

Successful Results. Mittal Galaţi (Arcelor-Mittal in 2006) has become Romania's largest company with $3.0bln turnover in 2005 (after 2.1 in 2004 and 0.75 in 2001 when Mittal first took over) due to a buoyant Asian market demanding more steel than it has capacity to produce. Profits have risen since 2003 to reach €47.2mln in 2006 and €97.0mln in 2007 (though there was a small loss in 2005). At the same time the plant is hailed as one of Romania's 'Top Ten' culture-changing investments thanks to the input by multi-millionaire Lakshmi Mittal (worth $25bln in 2001) and his son Aditya Mittal who initially sat on the board. Since privatisation the company has cut costs, improved efficiency and increased output. Domestic sales have doubled through an improved service to customers over technical matters, quality and marketing. Large customers like the carmaker Dacia who cancelled orders due to poor quality have now returned. Barter has been eliminated in favour of direct sale to end-users and identified distributors and furthermore, while meeting 90% of the domestic demand for flat products, more emphasis is now given to higher value-added products such as high quality plate, galvanised sheet and both hot and cold laminated sheet for large diameter welded pipes. Assisted by an EBRD loan of $100mln, plant efficiency has been improved by a $350mln five-year investment to remove high temperature oxide residues by switching from sulphuric to chloric acid in the production of thin sheet, with production to increase 0.8–1.4mln.t/yr mainly for export. Reheating ovens have been automated to reduce fuel consumption and improve casting. Efficiency in the blast furnaces (1x2,700cu.m and 2x1,700cu.m) has been achieved through more stable raw material procurement and output has increased from 2.7mln.t in 2001 to 3.5 in 2002. But $50mln is also being invested to reconstruct blast furnace three with 17,000cu.m capacity (Romania's largest) so that all six blast furnaces will be operational with a total capacity of 5.1mln.t. This latter improvement will boost steel production by 20 per cent to 14,000t/day and help the plant in its ambition for benchmark status as regards steel in the CEE region. Current steel capacity of this basic oxygen operation is 5.5mln.t with downstream options for plates (capacity 2.3mln.t), bloom and billet mills for hot and cold rolled products (4.3mln.t), galvanised sheet (0.22mln.t) and large diameter welded pipes (44,000t). However, actual production fell some way behind: 3.7mln.t 2001 with 5.2 'anticipated' in 2005. Upstream the works operates six coke oven batteries (2.1mln.t/yr) and sinter plants (8.0mln.t). After 1,000 voluntary redundancies in 2006, employment now stands at 14,000 (half the level at the time of privatisation) although production (running at two-thirds capacity) is only 303t per worker compared with 2,200t in Germany and 1,000t in Poland. The employment target is 10,000 in 2012 as a further modernisation (€1.0bln. during 2008–14) starts to impact e.g. coking with technology unchanged since the 1980s. The company has an eye on welfare through a building programme of flats for sale to employees and environmental improvements are ongoing.

Studies of Individual Plants: Danube Locations – Siderca Călăraşi

A decision made to establish Siderca in the 1980s envisaged an eventual massive annual steel output of 10mln.t but the project was evidently downgraded amidst the economic problems of the last communist years. However even the revised steel capacity of 1.7mln.t for long products seems not to have been achieved before 1989 when the first phase evidently involved an electric furnace that could have used scrap or else worked up inputs from Galaţi. In the 1990s the factory was linked with the production of heavy profile Type 49 rails and indeed 1997 saw the production of the first heavy rail of 60kg/m needed for modernising the Romanian railways and also for export to Brazil, Egypt, Pakistan and Turkey (previously such rails had to be imported). DM100mln of new equipment was provided by Mannesman: an electric oven, a continuous casting machine and heavy rail mill; linked with a major programme of professional training in 1998. The oven doubled the production; also over a much shorter period (45–60mins per charge compared with six to eight hours) and with lower consumption of power (200Kwh/t) and refractory materials, while the steel quality improved because slag was no longer discharged into the casting pot. There were also environmental benefits through dust extraction. There was talk of delivery of 100,000t of rails per annum for 25 years if the right type of steel could be delivered, but the economics of the project became horrendous as debts mounted to 100mln.lei and – with no prospect of privatisation – the heavy financial pressure on the government in 1999 meant closure and the prospect of liquidation. But the incoming government of 2001 suspended bankruptcy proceedings and allowed a new management team to restart production on the basis of a restructuring plan, given that there was much modern equipment available and the plant was the only iron and steel works with state majority capital technologically equippd to produce heavy rails for the home market and export at competitive prices. Steel billets were also supplied to tube makers at Brăila (Laminorul), Roman (Petrotub) and Zalău (Silcotub).

There was foreign interest from India and also from the Swiss Duferco Corporation and Corus – the world's biggest railmaker – given the EU decision to replace wood and concrete sleepers with metal. But the necessary cash injection of €20mln eventually came largely from Beltrame Investment Company of Italy (€14mln) as principal shareholder in the Donasid j.v. owned by Siderca and the Romanian Railways (CFR). This brought the transition years of stagnation to an end with 500 workers re-employed and the prospect of growth to 1,000, with further employment of some 700 through a nearby industrial park project in 2002. The plant received orders for bars and rails and produced steel from scrap in 2003. Rationalisation included the hiving-off of Sidertrans and Repsid, concerned with metallurgical equipment repair, metal buildings and spare parts. After improvements in technology, training and outlets, the mill was privatised by Tenaris (Luxembourg) who paid €37mln for a

97 per cent stake in Donasid (plus €6.8mln to pay off long-term debts and €25mln for investment in the 0.47mln.t/yr steel shop). Steel bars are now produced by an electric arc and continuous casting, based on scrap that Romania currently exports. The aim is to secure high value steel supplies for Silcotub and for the owner's Italian operations at Dalmine tubemill (Bergamo). The local canal has reopened since Danube river transport is essential.

Studies of Individual Plants: Inland Locations – Reşiţa

This plant has a very long history dating back to 1771, when the Habsburgs were pushing back the Ottoman Empire and implementing a mercantilist policy in a border province (the Banat of Temesvár, now Timişoara). Extensive raw materials were discovered and a basis created for both non-ferrous metallurgy and iron production, with the latter based on minerals and fuels drawn from an area extending from upper Bârzava valley southwards to Doman, Lupac and Anina; also Secu and Delineşti to the east and Bocşa, Dognecea and Ocna de Fier to the west. A major engineering industry also developed in the nineteenth century which was of great strategic importance. The complex passed to Romanian control after 1918, but the modest local resources were greatly outstripped when Second World War steel production of 200,000t required substantial quantities of scrap – and even more so under communism when iron ore and coke were brought in from the Soviet Union to sustain 1.0mln.t of steel production by the late 1970s (although this level was reduced to 0.74mln in 1989). Imports were unavoidable and although an extended coke-chemical plant (allowing for self-sufficiency) had reached an advanced stage when the revolution occurred, large imports of coking coal would still have been needed. The works therefore faced a bleak future under market conditions, but it did control a hydropower system in the area that held out the promise of viability on a mini-mill basis. Steel production fell back to 323,000t in 1990 and 185,400 in 1992 before reaching a relatively steady state in the middle years of the decade whereby production averaged 152.2th.t, with scrap the main input (not without its hazards considering that sufficient artillery missiles to destroy the complex were uncovered on one occasion!). In 1990 the blast furnaces were closed along with the coke ovens (apart from some small-scale production that ended in 1994). Work on the new coke batteries also ceased and the possibility of coking for the Smederevo furnaces in Serbia (although not finally abandoned until 1996) was effectively scuppered by UN sanctions against Serbia (Hillinger et al. 2001). Decommissioning of Siemens-Martin furnaces began in 1992 at a time when a credit from a consortium of Spanish banks for an electric oven and casting installation was first mooted, although it was only in 1995 that the substantial credit (including $34.9mln from foreign sources) was received, after formal approval the previous year. Also work started in the 1980s to increase hydropower on the Bârzava (suspended after 1989) was resumed (Figure 3.2).

The Spectre of Liquidation. Despite progress with modernisation, escalating debts (increased by money owed by the state electricity and railway companies and the Brăila shipyard) brought a threat of liquidation in 1997 from the new government if activity was not satisfactorily relaunched. It seems that in 1997–8 production costs were roughly in line with selling prices, but further downward movement in market prices then produced a situation where the loss rose from $74/t of steel in 1999 to $114 in 2000 (when accumulated debts reached 130mln.lei). Production plunged to just 117.5th.t in 1999 and 0.46 in the first half of 2000. The likelihood of bankruptcy was all the greater because the enterprise found itself obliged to work through predatory middlemen who paid the minimum price for the production they sold while demanding the highest prices for goods delivered. At the time there was talk of a j.v. involving French banks based mainly on the hydropower system with $15mln participation, but the projected doubling of capacity at the Crăinicel power plant (scheduled for 2001) was never completed. Fortunately the danger was averted and the new electric steel furnace with continuous casting was inaugurated in 1998. This offered a basis for profitability by delivering round billets across a wide dimensional range (230–300mm) needed for tubes when the dimensions required by at least one tubemaker – Petrotub (Roman) – were being imported. The plant was now exporting 12–14 per cent of its steel to EU countries, plus Bulgaria, Serbia and Turkey, and the prospects for further international trade seemed good. Upgrading had now cost $45mln (as a state-guaranteed credit) plus $5.0mln of the enterprise's own capital, with a further $6.0mln still needed.

The Noble Ventures Debacle. Max Aicher Bau (Germany) now showed interest in the plant, but at this juncture it was privatised in favour of Noble Ventures (USA) – run by former managers of Bethlehem Steel – for $4.5mln (for a 94 per cent stake) and an $85mln investment over three years, while government agreed to reschedule $35mln of taxation and utility debts that were now equivalent to four times the nominal share capital. With the new investment the company hoped to turn the complex into a world leader in ingots and blooms, rails and railway accessories, tyres, wheels and other hot-treated products. However the new regime began at a highly unpromising moment with the domestic market sluggish and world markets over-supplied. It was expected that the company would be divided into five sections for steel production, wire rolling, energy, transport and maintenance. But production stopped early in 2001 through non-payment of wages and there were recriminations between company and government over mutual non-compliance with the privatisation agreement (complicated by the change of government at the end of 2000). Noble Ventures were later to argue before the World Bank Arbitration Panel that the new government halted the debt rescheduling exercise on the grounds that privatisation officials had agreed only to 'seek' rescheduling from government creditors with no explicit guarantee. However the company contended that no real effort was ever made and that without the rescheduling it was almost impossible to run the business: it was clearly under-capitalised, with insufficient resources to settle debts with electricity and gas suppliers, pay full salaries and break the grip of middlemen.

A decision to earmark a third of production for sale to Petrotub without first settling all outstanding obligations towards its 1,500 workers caused further problems and brought charges of 'highway robbery' from a government representative in 2001. The company was also accused of creating more redundancies than had been agreed and the business was then paralysed by the 'Vatra' union's strikes accompanied by demonstrations and blocked roads around the city; while the government provided some social aid to relieve a desperate situation but otherwise showed reluctance to get involved. There was no progress in expanding exports, paying off debts and making investments. Legal action to cancel the sale was restrained by a 'cheque of good intentions' from the American ambassador, but the privatisation was eventually cancelled in 2003 after the contractual investments were not made and the scheduled payments due at the end of both 2001 and 2002 were missed. In 2003 the enterprise was taken back into state ownership and production restarted. Then in 2004 it was sold through Sinara Holdings to the Russian tubemaker TMK (selling pipes to Gazprom and other markets in Kazakhstan) for a nominal €1.0 plus €25mln to pay off debts and secure a €10mln investment. The aim is to reach 450,000t annual steel production after modernisation and the plant is now profitable although gas emissions from the electric arc constitute an environmental problem (as at Oţelul Roşu) and the whole site could be cleared up to make way for an industrial estate. Meanwhile Noble Ventures failed in its $350mln claim to the World Bank's International Centre for the Settlement of Industrial Disputes in 2003 on the grounds of abusive renationalisation.

Studies of Individual Plants: Inland Locations – Hunedoara

This second integrated works (chronologically-speaking) is located at the eastern end of the Poiana Ruscă with substantial ironstone resources at Ghelar and Teliuc and relatively poor quality coal in the Petroşani basin to the south. To support the development of heavy industry in Hungary, five blast furnaces were built during 1882–1903 (the first three for charcoal), rather closer to the iron ore supply (thanks to a new branch railway) than an earlier unit at Călan (1863) on the main line from Simeria to Petroşani. The intention was to deliver pig iron to the engineering industry in Budapest and it was only with steelmaking in 1941 that this state ironworks became an integrated unit. It was greatly extended under communism as Romania's leading metallurgical works (prior to Galaţi) with new coking and blast furnace facilities starting in 1950 and building up to a total of eight blast furnaces (ranging between three of 213cu.m and two of 1,000cu.m) while steel making was enlarged by eight 50t Siemens-Martin furnaces. Output reached 3.0mln.t by 1970, supported by new rolling mills of increasing scale in 1958, 1962 and 1968. Local iron ore was delivered through a tunnel connecting the two main mining units with the Teliuc-Hunedoara funicular while a further supply came from Căpuş (Cluj) and from imports. Coking coal was imported but maximum use was made of low grade coal from Petroşani in the Jiu Valley: indeed, the closer linkage of the complementary centres of Hunedoara and Petroşani was the first great inspiration of the communist period. But after the building of Sidex at Galaţi, Hunedoara began to specialise in long steel products: 44 per cent of all such exports by Romania and a 28 per cent share of the domestic market for such products in 2000. Also Siderurgica is now a major Romanian producer of carbon steel products, construction steel and steel for the car industry. Rationalisation began by blowing up the 1,000cu.m blast furnace built 1962 and used until 1992 to produce 0.5mln.t.p.a. But the whole blast furnace platform closed in 1999 when two other furnaces were demolished – providing more scrap for the steel furnaces that now use about 45,000t of iron annually.

The Mittal Strategy. In the context of market pricing for energy, fuel and scrap metal the only future lay in the 1998 decision to close the Siemens-Martin furnaces in favour of an electric furnace. The following year Danielli (Italy) were contracted to update the second wire rolling mill for $46.5mln (obtained through a foreign credit without government guarantee), a project that allowed the processing of special steel and boosted labour productivity. By 2003 the wire rolling mill was updated with 300,000t/yr capacity. Hunedoara also obtained a government guarantee for a $5mln credit for the commissioning of a new electric furnace in 2001; also sales of scrap deriving from closed units have been used for capitalisation of the plant rather than the payment of debts to the state. With a DM21mln credit falling due in 2000, privatisation was attempted with the help of the US Recovery Group (Boston, Mass.), specialising in stabilising and rationalising commercial companies. However there were no solid offers from foreign investors although Nippon Steel of Japan expressed interest in 2002. But in 2004 an 80.9 per cent holding was sold to Mittal Steel for $22.4mln plus debts of $21mln. Although attracted by the packaging of Siderurgica with Petrotub, the plant was an obvious candidate for the Mittal strategy of turning-round ailing state plants through the mini-mill principle with costs reduced below the rising cost of scrap by use of 'direct reduced iron'. The company will now concentrate on steel casting and rolling (750,000t capacity for billets, bars and wire) while the old company is liquidated and left to deal with the scrap and a third module covers auxiliary activities hived-off as separate businesses. The strategy involves the operation of two electric furnaces: one for steel for forging and 800mm rolling and the other for continuous casting of billets for long rolled products and seamless pipes. There is a ten-year programme to invest $12mln in modernising the furnaces, upgrading the finishing and implementing environmental projects. The workforce will be reduced by 2,000 but there is a prospect of some new jobs arising from the industrial park linked with the restructuring programme.

Studies of Individual Plants: Inland Locations – Oţelul Roşu

Formerly Ferdinandsberg, this plant has no recent history of iron production, although it is the sole legacy of a former, scattered metallurgical industry in the central and western parts of the Poiana Ruscă with late eighteenth century origins (linked with more prolific iron ore workings on the eastern side of the range after a remarkable rack railway was built thorugh the pass from Hateg in 1908). But the ironworking plant was transferred by Hungarian owners to Őzd in 1916 and the works was restarted after the First World War with steel furnaces that could have used scrap (or pig from Hunedoara using the Subcetate-Caransebeş rack railway already mentioned) in an electric furnace drawing power from local hydropower plants especially Marul. This small unit was retained and enlarged during communism and then, under the name Socomet, contacts with Italy blossomed after 1989 through the Romanian-Italian j.v. Easteel Siderurgica Romană. Gavazzi Steel (owned by the brothers Marco and Stefano Gavazzi) obtained a majority interest in Socomet after an offer of 1999 to invest $20–30mln in an electric furnace to produce steel for metallic constructions for export. There has been an improvement in infrastructure with a surfaced road to give vehicle access from the town (for which the old name of 'Ferdinandsberg' is now remembered) to the Colonia Veche (otherwise known as Baia and Valea Ohaba), linked with the old factory between the Bistra river and 'Canalul Turbinelor' that still delivers part of the power required. A total of $60mln was invested with EBRD assistance during 2000–5 through a new rolling mill and installation of a new 300,000t/yr electric furnace from Tehint (Italy) to replace three older units. Privatisation did not succeed however and the plant was renationalised by the Năstase government after a dispute (over the initial deal in 1999) about revision of the payments schedule to allow for inflation. Italian-owned Ductile Steel of Buzău then acquired the plant in 2005 for $6.5mln.

Studies of Individual Plants: Inland Locations – Industria Sârmei

This venture started in 1920 at Câmpia Turzii – a railway junction near Turda – producing wire and needles. Rapid expansion in the 1970s made it the fourth steel works in the country with electric and Siemens-Martin furnaces and a new rolling mill. It was then known simply as the metallurgical works, but reverted to its traditional name in 1991. The company markets electric steel in the form of ingots, billets, and finished rolled metal goods; also welding electrodes, cables, barbed wire and nails; though it has many rivals for wire products scattered across the regions including Cablu Românesc (Ploieşti), Cord and Ductil (Buzău), Griviţa (Bucharest), Promet (Beclean) and Sârme şi Cabluri (Hârşova). An opportunity for upgrading arose through a j.v. for automatic welding wire attracting foreign capital with the worldwide prestige of Trefilerie di Cittadella (Italy) in 1998. This also led to the upgrading of the steel furnace, with continuous casting and a new wire rolling mill in 2000. Like COS Târgovişte the factory is now part of the Moscow-based Mechel Group of coal and metallurgical companies that has accumulated a portfolio in ECE comprising Swiss-based Conares Trading Group. The new owners paid €2.5mln in 2003 and promised to invest a further €24mln to produce wire and cable while also rolling carbon and low-alloy steels for the engineering industry.

Studies of Individual Plants: Inland Locations – Târgovişte

Special steel complex 'Combinatul de Oţeluri Speciale Târgovişte' (COST) began in 1970 to produce steel (including alloy and special steels) from scrap in electric furnaces at a location with adequate labour and energy/transport infrastructure convenient for important centres of engineering in Braşov, Bucharest, Craiova, Piteşti and Ploieşti. A major problem after 1989 was the cost of power at $50–60/MWh compared with $30 in neighbouring countries, but alloy steel bars and sheets found a steady market in the automotive industry and component factories; also agricultural machine and electric motor makers like Ana IMEP (Piteşti), Electromotor (Timişoara), Electroprecizia (Săcele, Braşov) and Subansamble Auto (Sfântu Gheorghe) – and the chemical and food processing industries. Privatisation was energetically pursued in 2002 when it seemed that a Romanian consortium might emerge ahead of a foreign investor given the attractive location in the domestic market. But there was a strong bid by Erdemir (a branch of Turkey's Erdemir Eregli iron and steel company), planning a $15mln investment over three years to upgrade the strip mill to 100,000t/yr from the present 40,000t, with export to neighbouring countries as well as Italy and the Middle East. The competition was won in 2002 by Mechel (through Conares Trading) – a Russian mining and steel company producing rolled products in carbon and alloy steel for the engineering, automotive and construction industries – hoping to increase production at Târgovişte to 600,000t in 2002: much closer to the 750,000t capacity than the 340,000t achieved in 2000. Employment fell from 12,000 in 1989 to 6,700 in 1999 and 5,700 in 2001 but a further decline to 5,000 is expected; linked with a $35mln investment programme extending to 2011. Meanwhile a majority stake in the associated stainless plate and special steels producer Oţelinox was acquired in 1997 by Samsung Deutschland, an affiliate of Samsung (South Korea), with a view to trebling production and improving quality. The enterprise was planned in 1974 and opened in 1979–80 with a Japanese-built cold rolling mill for stainless steel strip and sheet (60,000t/yr now) and a unit for hot rolled single profiles and wire rod (now 100,000t/yr). Up to 2002 $18mln went on upgrading and training 1,040 workers for competition over an extended product range.

Studies of Individual Plants: Tube Mills

The tube industry that covers both unwelded pipes – e.g. Artrom (Slatina), Petrotub (Roman), Republica (Bucharest) and Silcotub (Zalău) – and welded pipes by Helitube (Zimnicea), a section of Sidex (Galaţi) and Tepro (Iaşi). Demand has been strong with rising gas and oil prices in 2000–1 stimulating interest in new pipelines (encouraging technological restructuring of long products and pipes at Sidex). Republica (Bucharest) is the oldest unit: opening in 1938 within the Malaxa engineering complex before separating in 1948. High performance control installations were imported to meet the American Petroleum Institute standard (although their monogram quality mark was first held in 1940, though briefly suspended after the war). Output under communism was 200,000t/yr but fell after 1989 desspite some retooling (modernisation of the thread-cutting machines and import of high performance control equipment) leading to acquisition of the Germanischer Lloyd ISO9000 standard as well as the Russian standard. Exports to Russia were maintained until 1994 but contacts were lost during 1994–7 and output slumped to 16,000t.

Republica and the Moody International Trading (USA) Contribution. MIT support was very significant during 2000–1 when they were present in Romania (in connection with the first Pepsi-Cola factory) and were able to arrange orders accounting for 80 per cent of production, including some from Russia where Moody's contacts were crucial (later Belarus, Singapore, Slovakia and Ukraine): 62,000t in 2001 and 50,000 in 2002. The Russian orders also required MIT assistance over raw material since Republica's financial condition did not allow bank guarantees and letters of credit. This partnership between a state enterprise and foreign investor also included the supply of steel, finance for investment for the first and second rolling mills and help over human resources in 2001. Products for the oil industry were assimilated: indeed Republica became the only factory in Romania producing solely for the oil industry. As production returned to 100,000t, with the workforce cut from 3,000 to 1,200 in 2000, the factory was able to operate not only one mill ('the Moody') but the second as well. Moody then showed some interest in buying Republica – a welcome move since they were operating over a broad segment of the market, while maintaining particularly close links with Russia. But slow negotiations dismayed the Republica management and a Russian company eventually prevailed. Meanwhile a separate company Sidcom Metal (set up in 1997) producing hot extruded stainless and refractory steel pipes from billets supplied by COST – replacing Republica in this domain because the latter's Tubinox section was hived off in 1997 due to financial blockage and a separate workshop acquired to use cheap, obsolete equipment from abroad. The billets were broken down and the pieces heated to 1,100degC and pressed by the force of 2500t. Production reached 100t of stainless pipes monthly for export to Germany, India and Turkey, with the home market still lacking liquidity in 2000. This separate company was privatised by Tenaris in 2003 and additional capital acquired for expansion, before being sold on to Viraj Alloys (India) in 2006.

The Rise and Fall of Tubman International (Gibraltar) Empire. Tubman planned a $7.0mln investment at Laminorul (Brăila) in 2000 for advanced thermal treatment for higher value added and also with a view to gaining a majority shareholding. In addition to tubes the factory was producing wire and equipment for the wire industry: under licence from Hi-Draw Group (UK) using top technologies in thermal treatment, phosphating, chemical cleaning and scaling. However Tubman were sued by APMSH for failing to make all promised technological and environmental investments; apparently making do with second-hand equipment from their Silcotub mill in Zalău in which Tubman also acquired a majority holding. With interest also in Petrotub (Roman) Tubman became associated with a 'club of pipemakers' during 2000–1, linked in turn with Siderca as a potential steel supplier for the group. Investments were made at Zalău in 2002: $16.9mln for a manufacturing line for 50,000t oil pipes/yr, a line for precision pipes (8,000t/yr) and an extended range of hot, rolled pipes to take operational capacity to 200,000t/yr with ISO9002 and 14001 certification. At this time the US International Trade Commission started an anti-dumping investigation into the Roman and Zalău factories, although it was subsequently closed (at the request of the foreign affairs ministry through the Romanian embassy in Washington) and exports continued. However, Tubman were hoping to sell Silcotub to Tenaris in 2004, reflecting the latter's special interest in seamless steel pipes (for the energy, automotive and mechanical industries) at a time when their purchase at Călăraş*i* would make for vertical integration. Tenaris then invested further in new technology at Zalău to reach international standards (and also acquired Tubinox for a few years as noted above) while Tubman abandoned their Romanian project completely by leaving the Roman mill to be privatised by Mittal Steel (it is now known as Arcelor-Mittal Tubular Products) and allowing their 16.3 per cent minority interest in Laminorul to be overtaken by complete privatisation of the mill (at the sixth attempt) in favour of Donau Commodities of Austria in 2006 after Tenaris had failed to assimilate the unit and had returned it – free – to the state. Evidently, having failed to acquire a steel producer of their own Tubman sold-out to companies better able to secure the benefits of integration.

Tepro (Iaşi) meanwhile had a particularly stormy privatisation history in view of the initial takeover by the Czech company Železarny Vesely; whereupon a company profitable in 1997–8 was bankrupted by the Czechs interested only in removing a rival from the market. When obligations were not met the deal was cancelled and interest then came from Russia's Metalexportimport Magnitogorsk until the competition was won by Mittal in 2003, providing a close technological link with Sidex and an investment programme of almost $10mln in technology and environment. A big increase in output raised internal market share from 17 to 60 per cent in 2004. The Iaşi mill has a capacity of 380,000t of welded carbon steel tubes and employs 1,400. It will expand output of high value products following American Petroleum Institute recognition opening up new markets in the oil and gas industry. As already noted, Mittal are also investing in Petrotub (Roman) where a 70 per cent holding was acquired in 2003 from APMSH for $43mln plus $40mln of debts. It can produce up to 500,000t/yr of seamless carbon and low-alloyed steel pipes with 3,100 employees and the intention is to invest $31mln over 10 years (including $13mln for environment) and cut the workforce by half.

Studies of Individual Plants: Other Units

Sidermet (Călan) proved highly problematic with 120mln.lei debts that no investor is keen to acquire. With World Bank agreement (since Sidermet is a PSAL company), the solution lay with a $17mln investment envisaged in 2000 in a new centrifugal casting installation and production of ductile pig iron pipes. Sidermet was partially privatised in 2001 through separating the cast iron pipe shop (where production will be resumed) with an injection of share capital increase by a foreign investor (after two firms have expressed an interest) to create 800–900 jobs. The Saudi-Arabian Amiantit Group are to establish a pipe production centre (for water supply and oil industry) involving a $20mln j.v. ($12mln by Amiantit for a 58 per cent stake) with Sidermet for production of malleable iron pipes requiring the import of American machinery (with American finance of $17mln in 1999 to produce ductile pig iron pipes at Călan for water supply networks and avoid import). Sidermet also plans to takeover pipe production by the Orăştie-based Romarm company that uses German equipment to produce malleable iron pipes. Orăştie Mechanical Plant (UMO) has a 'state of the art' casting shop (capacity 40,000t/yr) thanks to a €30mln investment (that should be recouped in seven years) with a government-guaranteed loan from Germany's BHF Bank in 2002. Pipes are zinc- and tar-coated and cement-filled to carry industrial and drinking water, rain water and sewage. A quarter of the output for five years will be taken by Fritz Werner (Germany). In 2002 there was a possibility of a rail-road link for liquid malleable iron between Călan and Orăştie, linked with the offer of $9mln investment for Sidermet to update two furnaces needed for the production of iron tubes presently too costly to import. Now known as 'Cilindrul', employment has recovered from a low of 230 to reach 300 due to growth in the 'bobinaj' shop but suffered an audacious act of sabotage in 2007 when 230m of gas pipeline was removed as scrap and the power supply cut. Among downstream activities, Max Aicher Bau (Germany) – interested in steel production from scrap for the engineering industry – acquired the Lamdro bar mill in Drobeta-Turnu Severin in 2000 with an eye on Balkan reconstruction and also became involved in the privatisation of Combinat de Utilaj Greu in Cluj 2006 (now disputed with the Turkish company World Metals). Foreign capital is also present at Lindab Construcţii (the Romanian arm of Sweden's Lindab) manufacturing and distributing thin metal sheets, air vents and ducts: set up in Cluj in 1994, it transferred to Buchares in 1996 and opened a new factory there in 2002. Among the service industries, Electrocarbon is the sole regional producer of mini-mill graphite electrodes following the demise of Polgraph (Poland), but with competition from China, India and Russia.

CONCLUSION

Employment has been reduced substantially in this problem sector during 1996–2005: from 266,500 to 134,200 jobs in the extractive industries and from 163,800 to 66,800 jobs in metallurgy. Meanwhile enterprise numbers have grown from 168 to 676 in extractive industries and 322 to 438 in metallurgy; so that employment per enterprise has been reduced dramatically from 1,586 to 198 and from 509 to 152 respectively. Metallurgy has virtually completed its restructuring in the hands of successful private companies and there is even the prospect of development at new locations given the Voest Alpine (Austria) plan to invest €5.5bln in a new steelmill on a 50ha site at Agigea near Constanţa: highlighting the logic of a Black Sea location for Central Europe as well as Romania (though it is interesting to see the focus on Constanţa – the leading port after communist-era decentralisation of investments to Călăraşi, Galaţi and Tulcea; admittedly before completion of the Danube-Black Sea Canal). Meanwhile mining remains in a desperate situation with Minvest and Remin owing huge debts which neither enterprise can handle since foreign investors show little interest, even with employment drastically reduced and mines in conservation. Non-ferrous ore mining remains in desperate state with few assets attractive for privatisation (excepting of Cuprumin (Abrud) with a basis for takeover by the smelting company Cuprom) and even gold production ventures (Baia Mare and Roşia Montană) have experienced difficulty with the former's pollution disaster in 2000 and the latter's inability to silence local opposition to a venture scheduled for a 2007 start.

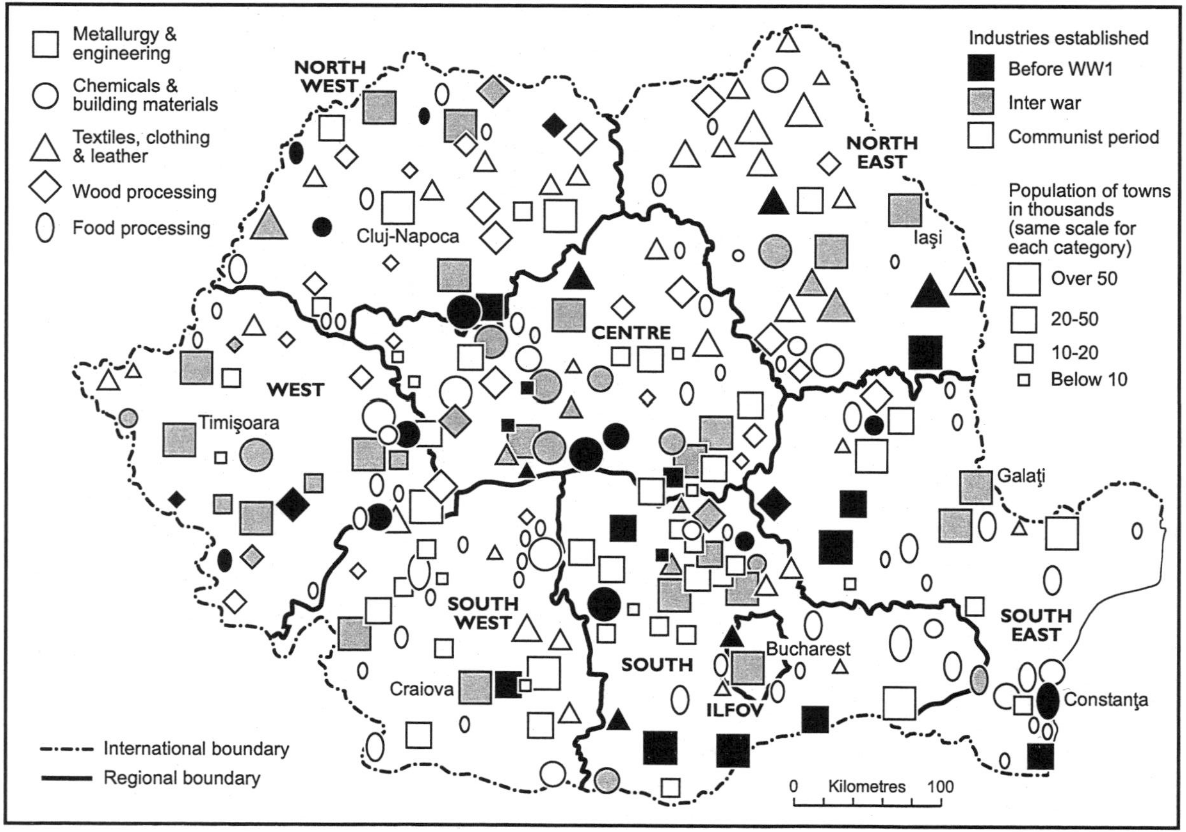

Figure 3.1 Industrial Centres in Historical Perspective Source: Popescu 2000

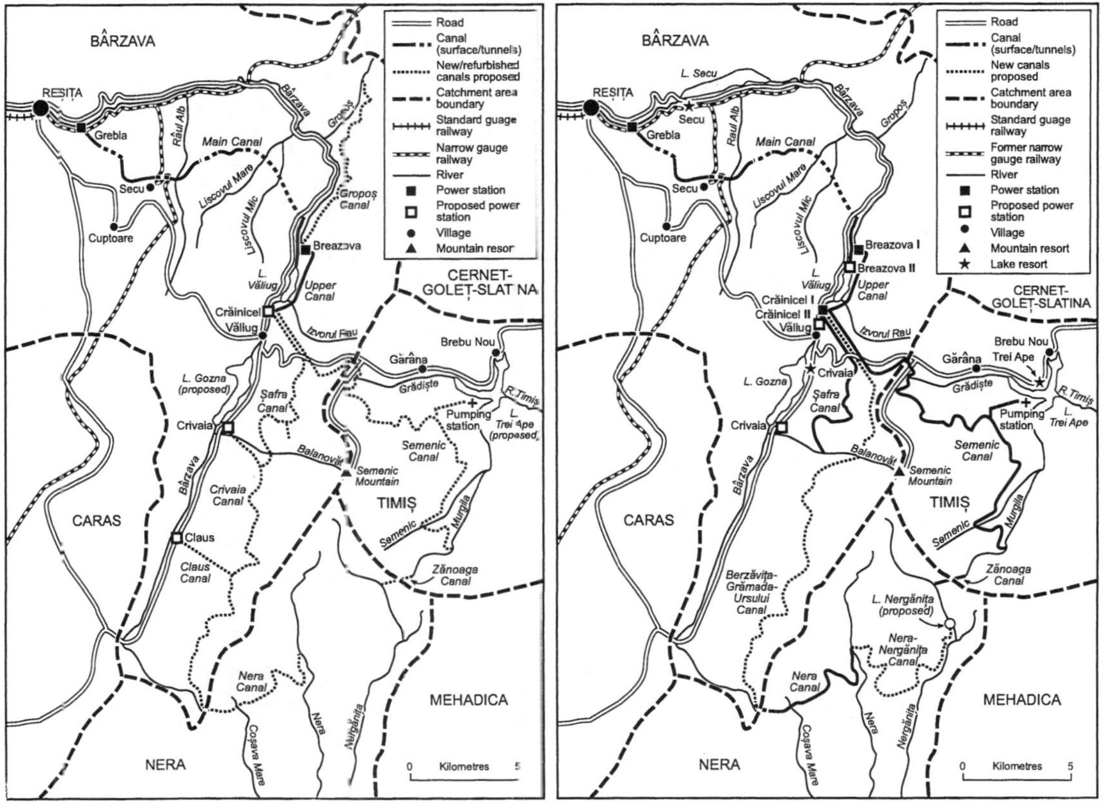

Figure 3.2 Hydropower on the Bârzava River to supply Reşiţa: showing (left) the first (pre-1914) phase and Pavel's proposals of 1942-3; (right) post-1945 developments and the 1983 plan
Source: Hillinger & Turnock 2001; Hillinger et al. 2001

4. Engineering and Transport Equipment

This sector is of massive importance after the expansion during the communist period to maximise self-sufficiency while securing exports of relatively basic goods, especially to Third World countries. However, there are nineteenth-century origins linked with the foundry industries of Transylvanian towns such as Oradea, while railways provided a stimulus through workshops in Griviţa (Bucharest), Reşiţa and elsewhere. Transformation was relatively rapid after 1996, with virtually no FDI going into the industry to update technology and the prospect of only a short period of grace (to 2000) before starting the process of opening the home market to EU competition. The number of enterprises increased 2.4 times (well above the industrial average of 83 per cent) during 1996–2005, while employment decreased by 36.8 per cent (more than the industry average of 30.5); hence the average employment per enterprise has decreased very sharply by 67.5 per cent (from 153.8 to 40.0) against the average of 61.8 per cent (83.7 to 32.0) for industry as a whole. Engineering contracted sharply during the early 1990s, from 26.1 per cent of valued added in 1990–2 to 19.7 in 1993–6 (when extractive industries and metallurgy were protected), followed by slower decline to 17.8 per cent in 1997–9 and 17.5 in 2000–2, when trade advantage was exploited especially in electrical engineering. Thus, trends also vary greatly between different sections: electrical goods have gained ground strongly (6.4–14.2 per cent of total value added between 1990–2 and 2001–3), along with road transport equipment (11.0–18.7), with smaller relative increases for IT and office equipment (0.9–1.1), radio, TV and communications equipment (5.0–5.7) and metal (17.9–19.4); the big loser has been machinery and equipment (41.0–26.7 per cent), along with medical equipment and precision goods (6.9–4.1) and other transport equipment (10.7–10.0). The average number of employees per enterprise is highest for road transport equipment at 164 in 2003, down from 706 in 1996, followed by 149 for other transport equipment (490), 104 for machinery and equipment (422), 84 for electrical engineering (179), 48 for radio, TV and communications equipment (108); 20 for metal construction (43), 15 for medical and precision equipment (90) and six for computing (15). In this chapter a short summary, with examples covering heavy machinery, defence industries and electrical engineering, is followed by more detailed attention to transport equipment (locomotives, railway rolling stock and shipping). The following chapter then covers the automotive and aerospace industries. Table 4.1 covers both chapters.

Table 4.1: *Production in the Engineering Industry (th) 1985–2005*

Year	A	B	C	D	E	F	G	H	I	J	K	L	M	N
1985	5.1	70.2	6.8	4.1	17.9	400	124	8065	134	1664	20.8	91	191	12782
1987	5.0	37.9	6.4	1.1	19.6	420	164	9107	129	1965	12.7	159	317	14061
1990	3.7	26.0	4.1	1.5	9.0	393	132	5115	85	1327	8.5	121	129	7500
1991	2.9	22.0	1.3	1.0	6.0	389	147	4030	74	1005	7.6	34	141	3780
1992	1.6	21.0	0.6	0.6	5.0	402	154	2185	64	633	4.5	.	150	1916
1993	0.5	26.0	0.4	3.1	10.0	435	171	1201	82	420	4.4	1	199	566
1994	0.3	14.0	0.6	2.2	11.0	383	115	1302	80	462	3.0	.	4	444
1995	0.5	15.5	0.7	1.7	7.3	435	145	1787	82	532	3.1	1	14	51
1996	0.6	13.1	0.3	1.3	4.6	446	231	1987	93	492	3.1	.	27	38
1997	0.7	10.5	0.2	0.4	4.5	429	202	1716	106	260	2.0	.	17	10
1998	0.6	3.6	#	1.0	3.4	366	206	1767	103	321	1.3	.	10	383
1999	0.3	4.5	.	0.8	2.2	323	165	1484	88	82	0.9	.	.	543
2000	0.3	5.4	#	0.7	2.9	341	160	1704	63	45	0.8	2	.	1128
2001	0.4	5.3	0.1	1.1	n.a.	313	157	2110	71	102	0.4	1	4	1458
2002	0.3	5.5	0.1	0.8	n.a.	390	127	1865	65	74	0.5	5	23	1429
2003	#	3.7	0.1	0.8	n.a.	522	108	1998	76	7	0.3	8	4	2019
2004	#	5.4	#	1.2	n.a.	700	112	2012	99	3	0.3	.	6	2177
2005	#	5.5	0.1	0.9	n.a.	826	318	1512	175	.	0.2	.	13	1924

Notes: A Lathes; B Tractors; C Combines; D Cultivators; E Sewing Machines; F Refrigerators and Freezers; G Vacuum Cleaners; H Electric Motors (0.25Kw and over); I Cars; J Buses and Trolley Buses (units); K Lorries; L Diesel and Electric Locomotives (units); M Railway Coaches (units); N Railway Wagons (units). # - less than 0.1

Source: Statistical Yearbooks: Table 16.3

HEAVY ENGINEERING AND EQUIPMENT

The Case of Intreprinderea de Maşini Grele Bucureşti (IMGB)

Romania inherited a large engineering works in Reşiţa when former Habsburg territory was annexed in 1918 and this plant was a source of expertise for the growth of the industry in the old kingdom. A major feature of this spread was the opening of a heavy machinery plant in Bucharest (IMGB) in 1963 and subsequently in Cluj, Craiova and Iaşi. IMGB was created to produce for the traditional energy sector with an associated factory (FECNE) for the nuclear sector. The enterprise acquired licences in 1967 from Rateau-Schneider, Alstom and Delas for 330MW steam turbines first produced in 1973 for Rovinari power station (followed by 15 more over 20 years, along with smaller capacities ranging from 3.5MW to 150MW). In 1977 IMGB produced turbine shafts and generator shafts for the six Kaplan 175MW units installed at the Iron Gates, on the Danube, and from this time IMGB became a major supplier for Romania's hydroelectric schemes. In 1979 a General Electric licence was obtained for 700MW steam turbines for Cernavodă nuclear station (the first completed in 1987), along with others from AECL and Ansaldo for other Cernavodă components. Other interests were ship propellors and rudders, cement mills and heavy excavator components, and also metallurgical industry equipment for rolling and pressing. Although divided into five companies after 1989, the massive core business combining metallurgy and heavy machinery was kept together; but, whereas IMGB produced 150,000t of steel and employed 15,000 workers before the revolution, the 1998 figures were down to 15,000t (from two electric 50–70t arc furnaces) and 3,100 employees – utilising only 15–20 per cent of productive capacity while accumulating debts of 21mln.lei as 'the cost of survival'. In that year both IMGB and FECNE were sold to Kvaerner (a company registered in Norway, with a London-based international operation) after three years of consideration. This was an ideal arrangement since Kvaerner was clearly a global leader in technology-based engineering and construction services (maritime industries, mechanical engineering and environment-friendly solutions for processing natural resources including woodlands – paper-pulp technologies – hydrocarbons, hydropower and minerals).

The Kvaerner Privatisation

The deal involved a $10mln payment ($9.5mln to cover debts and $0.5mln to buy 90 per cent of IMGB shares) and a $60mln four-year strategic investment launched in 1999 for technology transfer and staff training (with employment further reduced to 1,600 by the end of 1999) intended to turn the factories into profitable world producers working to western quality, environmental and labour security standards. Steel melting (at 70,000t) and forging and machining sections matched market share and product profile (while power generation, compressed air production, galvanising and scrap processing were restructured) and non-core activities were sold: the oxygen factory, electricity distribution, food production and the social club; along with vacant land, scrap iron and redundant machine tools. Cooperation programmes were launched: with Kvaerner Energy and Voest Alpine for hydro turbine blades and turbine assemblies; with Kvaerner Oilfield Products for forging technology for well-head equipment; and with Kvaerner Metals for assemblies for steel mills and cement mills. The company hoped to open a design centre and get involved with Romanian and foreign companies in extending the Bucharest metro system and other infrastructure projects. Indeed, contracts were obtained from Romania (RATB, and Sidex) and from abroad (for example, Hitachi, Sulzer and Voest Alpine) although the steelworks and casting shop could not be used at full capacity. Nevertheless, the deal was a major achievement, marking a new stage in privatisation with largely symbolic payments for assets against promises of substantial investment. It was hailed as a breakthrough 'to change the black image of a country with high investment risk' with the power of a global company – previously involved (with Timken) in the privatisation of 'Rulmenţi Grei' (Ploieşti) – to boost the competitiveness of the two ailing factories and perhaps open the way to disposal of other major assets such as oil refineries.

Faltering Steps. This positive start was almost immediately overtaken by the announcement of poor financial results for Kvaerner as a whole in 1998, and the need for restructuring including the sale of IMGB and FECNE – through the German consulting company Roland Berger – to buyers with a good reputation in machine building. Twenty interested companies were reported in September 1999, but the difficult international business climate discouraged new contracts, reflected in a falling steel market as prices fell by half. Meanwhile, fiscal reform in Romania eliminated customs-free equipment import facilities and raised property taxes and social insurance; moreover, the company's own restructuring prevented significant growth of international contacts (and some of Romania's own energy-related projects were soon to be frozen in 2001). Yet it was fortunate that no deal could be struck because the company then decided to retain its Romanian assets and embarked on a two-year programme in 2000–1 to make IMGB profitable by concentrating on sectors with significant added value (while still hoping to sell FECNE). Money injected by the company was largely absorbed by debts, taxes and working capital (also assisted by the sale of non-core assets) to the detriment of direct investments, although the company remained committed to the remainder of the investment programme ($54mln over four years), while employment sank to only 900 in 2001 and 580 in 2003. However, Kvaerner's confidence rested on the very large machinery for which it had a competitive advantage, and orders were eventually obtained for hydro projects in Canada, China and USA by 2003: e.g. runner blades for turbines for hydro plant at Three Gorges in China to be made in Bucharest in one piece rather than by welding two halves (previously necessary in France and Canada).

Consolidating Progress. IMGB was also able to accomplish a 206t stainless steel charge for the crown of a Francis turbine for the world's largest hydroplant: Itaipu on the Parana in Brazil. There was also involvement in the Brazilian Tucurei hydroproject: a $4.1mln contract for parts of eleven 330MW turbines; also parts for turbines at Sirikit hydro project in Thailand. Shipbuilding work – picked up through shafts for Denmark's Odense yard and parts for Mitsubishi Heavy Industries' yard in Japan – also helped to sustain the investment programme. Additional work was obtained on components of Francis turbines for the Grand Coulee hydropower plant (6,809MW) on the Columbia river in Washington (USA) and also for the Castaic station in the San Joaquin Valley near Los Angeles. Further Francis turbines are now to be supplied for the Long Tan and Tai An plants in China, as well as replacements for the Beauharnois (Canada) rehabilitation. Voith Siemens have ordered ten Kaplan turbines for Wannapum hydro project on the Columbia River (worth $6.0mln over ten years), while further turbine and generator shafts are needed for Romania's own Iron Gates rehabilitation project being undertaken by Vatech (Austria). Some the company's fortunes have revived and employment has crept up to 600 despite redundancy through new technological equipment in 2002. Romanians have been restored to three of the top five positions in management after all were taken by foreigners immediately after privatisation. Meanwhile Nordex and Gildemeister (Germany) are interested in Fortus (Iaşi) in order to manufacture wind-farm stations and crane counterweights (the latter requiring the foundry section), although the huge debts of 150mln.new lei (130mln to the state budget) are a major disincentive. Max Aicher (Germany), interested in steel production from scrap for the engineering industry, are in competition with World Metals (Turkey) to secure CUG (Cluj–Napoca).

Reşiţa and Bocşa

The Reşiţa machine building complex (UCMR) developed in the nineteenth century on a site adjacent to the metallurgical works (discussed in the previous chapter) when it was owned by Staatseisenbahngesellschaft: an the Austrian railway company. It diversified after 1918 from steam locomotives and railway bridges to electric engines and generators (1922–94), steam and hydro turbines (1951), engines for diesel and electric locomotives (1962) and finally marine engines (1977). At the same time it lost certain lines of production to other works: railway wheels, points and bridges along with oil drilling equipment and small electric motors in the 1950s, cranes, steam turbines and power generators in the 1970s and railway bogies in the 1980s. But as state orders dried up after 1989, the export share rose quickly from only seven per cent in 1996 to 35 per cent in 1997 and 50 per cent in 1998, on the basis especially of collaboration over diesel and electric engines with GM (USA) and ABB (Sweden); also with Sulzer Hydro (Ravensburg, Germany) which had already ordered hydromechanical and hydraulic equipment from UCMR; and with Arab countries seeking industrial equipment for the chemical and metallurgical industries. On the domestic front marine engine capacity increased with the testing of a prototype 3,510hp marine engine (4L35MC) built under MAN–Burmeister und Wein licence using a new computer programme and destined for a 3,000dwt cargo boat under construction at the Severnav shipyard in Turnu Severin in 1997. Meanwhile the j.v. Reductoare Reşiţa Renk made a loss (working at 40 per cent capacity due to reduced home market of ship reductors), while demand from the chemical and building materials industries was slack.

UCMR was privatised in 2003 in favour of Inet (Switzerland) who intended to make the works a world leader in heavy machines within five years, with particular emphasis on hydropower units, electric machines, welded structures and R&D services. Meanwhile, similar problems arose at the nearby heavy fabrication enterprise in Bocşa (CMB), which originated under communism through the hiving-off of functions once discharged by UCMR. While working on travelling cranes and contributing to the construction for the new Mara Hotel in Sinaia and Petrom's Ploieşti headquarters, as well as industrial and domestic buildings in several other towns and the bridge over the Danube–Black Sea Canal at Cernavodă (1,300t), the company became more focused on exports after 1990, with goods to Bangladesh (metallic structures), Egypt (hydromechanical equipment), Qatar (cement factory equipment) and USA (coffer dams). It has also been focusing on bridges and port equipment and work for road and rail modernisation linked with projects undertaken with the Bucharest railway construction company (CCCB) and UCMR. It wants to modernise by acquiring modern cutting machines, sanding and welding installations; also by updating internal transport with tractors and electric stackers. Its main suppliers are of course the domestic steel and tube mills. Privatisation was actively sought over several years along with an industrial estate, to mop up the space no longer required by this dinosaur of the communist era. But this strategy has not succeeded and a belated attempt to run a private business quickly collapsed and the old state business is now liquidated.

Other Equipment Producers

This section of short profiles shows a range of experiences. First, Unio (Satu Mare) – a leading producer of mining equipment for underground and surface operations – fell on bad times through lack of orders after 1989 and employment fell from 10,000 in 1989 to 2,460 in 2000, although exports picked from 1998 (paradoxically when Romanian mines were being restructured) through cooperation with American corporations such as General Electric and Morgan. Second, Rotec (Buzău) – a maker of industrial equipment, privatised in 2000 – has also done well in export markets, with up to 85 per cent of production going to the EU: it has supplied the Danieli iron and steel works (Italy) and was involved in supplying a new cement factory at Calucso (Italy) in 2003. Third, Upetrom 1 Mai (Ploieşti) is a producer of oil drilling equipment with modern technology working to ISO9001 quality and co-operating with Asian countries with hydrocarbon resources (Indonesia, the Philippines, Thailand and Vietnam): CEE (including FSU) and Africa as well in 1995. Fourth, the Mechanical Complex Plant (Timişoara) has survived by diversification through links with Caterpillar (France), while its salvage and rescue equipment remained appreciated on the domestic market in 1996. Finally, Beta (formerly the Buzău Technological Equipment Works, established in 1925) designs and manufactures equipment for the chemical, food, paper, power and environmental protection industries including pressure vessels, heat exchangers and filters. Well placed for shipment by rail, river or road, it has British and Italian shareholders, plus a Quality Assurance Programme since 1993.

Defence Industries

These developed in Bucharest in the late nineteenth century and were extended in the 1930s to more sheltered locations in the Carpathians e.g. Cugir and Plopeni, while further diversification in the communist period included several small towns in Prahova county. In 1989 some 30 companies employed around 200,000, thanks to large state orders plus $500–800mln of exports annually during 1985–89, when Romania was the world's fifth arms exporter. The aviation companies will be considered below, which leaves Romtehnica and the former Ratmil (defence and aeronautics) organisation, restructured as the national Romarm company comprising 22 separate enterprises brought into the 'civilian circuit' and slated for 30 per cent privatisation in 2000 through a $120mln four-year reorganisation to reduce the workforce drastically from 60,000 in the late 1990s (when 45,000 were described a burden). Romarm includes the Arsenal ('Arsenalul Armatei'), an independent corporation with subsidiaries, such as Carfil, Cugir, Mizil, Moreni, Plopeni and Tohan, forming a special department within the industry ministry that retains a majority stake. Some enterprises were taken over by Romanian management, such as the Mizil tank factory – the first to go private (2003) – which went to an employee association. But Rheinmetall De Tec (Germany) were interested in the privatisation of the weapons and ammunition producer Arsenal (Reşiţa) and the Clinceni Centre for Integration and Production of Electronic Systems. The challenge is all the greater because Romanian armed forces need equipment that meets NATO standards – hence the importance of funding to upgrade. At the same time, new conventions require externalisation: Romania's tanks are being upgraded with the involvement of several foreign companies through a feasibility study by Krauss Maffei (Germany), although there are chances of export contracts for Romanian manufacturers as well as Romanian army orders.

Arms exports average $30–40mln/yr but could reach $70–100mln with a more aggressive sales policy. Apart from the maintenance of Croatia's MiG planes, business is mainly tied to the US market (light infantry weapons and ammunition). The technology deficit is a problem that could be eased by a niche in specialised production and maintenance capacities absent in neighbouring states: for example, IAR might undertake Eurocopter maintenance for the entire region. In 1999, Cugir weapons works received a $20mln credit from Eximbank (plus $3.5mln from its own sources) for new technology to produce ammunition and military equipment to NATO standards. And in the same year Expomil saw displays from Romarm, and from Electromagnetica and Romtehnica, featuring new products including the TR85M1 tank, the MLI84M infantry fighting machine, the 'Hamster' motor vehicle and the 'Zimbru' amphibian armoured transporter. However, there is a strategy to compensate for redundancies through industrial parks at Mija, Moreni, Ploieşti and Vălenii de Munte created in 2002, while promising links were made in the same year through contracts negotiated by Ghimbav–Eurocopter and Daimler-Chrysler (Cugir), the latter producing parts for the M271 Mercedes engine. Tohan (Zărneşti) also has potential as Romania's only bicycle and motorcycle maker. Motorcycle production, at 15,000/yr, stopped during 1987–90 when the supply of engines could not be maintained but recovered to 3,000 machines in 1995. In 2003, the company went on to launch 'Hero Winner' and 'Hero Puch' scooters – the first to be made in Romania – following a contract with the Indian company Hero Honda in 1999. With 49cc engines and an $500–750, they should be popular in western cities. But redundancies exceeded 2,500 in 2006, mainly at Romarm which is now limited to 2,700 workers (2,296 fewer than in 2005), while Avioane (Craiova) is limited to 300 (150 below the 2005 level), and Uzina Mecanică Orăştie to 40 (60), with similar situation at Uzina Mecanică Filiaşi.

MACHINE TOOLS AND HOUSEHOLD GOODS

This is a highly varied group that starts with machine tools and bearings where reorganisation has been quite radical with substantial downsizing leading to the sale of unwanted equipment and production space, for example at Bacău's machine tool factory in 1997. Some firms retain a market niche without such radical change. Robinete Industriale (Bacău) began in 1919 as Alter Davidovici's cast iron workshop and foundry and developed into Bacău Metallurgical Plant in 1949. It specialised in cast iron industrial taps for the water distribution programme; a trademark was registered in 1966 and much German equipment was acquired later in the decade. Under its present name, adopted in 1992, export outlets were found in Europe, North Africa and the USA. Industrial taps for use in connection with drinking water, sea water and oil are made of grey cast iron and nodular graphite cast iron, but during 1995–96 the company developed electro-static field painting equipment to cover the inside of taps (necessary in the case of drinking water) and reached ISO9001 standards in 1999. Meanwhile Aversa (Bucharest) supplies pumps to leading Romanian companies (e.g. the oil drilling enterprise) and foreign customers. However, financial injections have often been crucial. Izoterom (Baia Mare) purchased a majority holding in the town's Ramira tool factory, which faced liquidation in 1997: it had the resources to relaunch production by taking on several hundred new workers despite the serious risks this strategy entailed. On the other hand, links with western business have often opened up new horizons. Some companies have arrived to set up new units: for instance, Durkop Adler produce fine mechanical parts for sewing machines in Târgu Mureş, while Wisconsin Machine Tools (USA) have set up in Târgovişte. But many existing firms have been taken over: for example, Bosch (Germany) extended from their headquarters in Băneasa (Bucharest) – distributing tools, heating equipment and auto parts – to buy the machine tool maker IAMU Blaj (a successful export enterprise established in 1972) from the Banat-Crişana investment portfolio. Bosch subsequently announced a €10mln investment in Blaj involving a 40,000 sq.m. factory for machine tool parts, expected to employ 300 workers in 2007.

Some Bearing and Component Producers

These have been greatly assisted by foreign investment after finding themselves far behind world leaders such as FAG, Koyo Seiko and SKF, although ahead of Chinese and Russian producers. Rulmenţi (Bârlad) managed to get its export share up to three-quarters but was compromised by recession in Asia, whereupon the company was able to compete – with good quality at low prices – in American and European markets to secure an operating profit (albeit wiped out by outstanding debts) in 1999. The company is now successful enough to embark on €11.5mln in acquisitions in Germany, Hungary and Turkey. And after FAG Kügelfischer Georg Schaefer (Germany) showed interest in the 60 per cent SOF shareholding in 1998, it was Kombassan (Turkey) that became the majority shareholder and introduced the latest technologies (including ecological facilities to be introduced into the manufacturing process) in 2000. Meanwhile Koyo Seiko (Japan) acquired an interest in Rulmentul (Alexandria) – and took over the firm's debts – after they had built the factory in 1971 (and also enlarged the Braşov factory: a major privatisation headache resolved by liquidation). Finally, Timken (Ohio, USA), world leader in the production of bearings, gained a majority holding in Fabrica de Rulmenţi Grei (Ploieşti) and invested $17mln in equipment, computerisation and new products (mainly for heavy industry and shipping) in 2001, with another $24mln to follow.

Sterom (Câmpina)

As the Romanian subsidiary of Precision Castparts Corporation (PCC) of Portland, Oregon (USA) – market leader in castings and components for jet engines – this factory is becoming a manufacturing powerhouse for Europe with the relocation of production from 15 units in Canada, Italy, The Netherlands, Switzerland, UK and USA, after considering new acquisitions in India or Mexico. Sterom is seen as the main Romanian manufacturer of oil rigs and other oil equipment, with a century of experience in the industry. With potential as a launching pad for PCC sales to the former Soviet Union – and possibly the Middle East, Latin America and Europe – Sterom has worked with factories in Canada and Italy since privatisation in 1999 and has done well in operating the new Reiss valve production line. Câmpina will now go into new lines such as high precision components and machinery for the aerospace and the pulp and paper industries. In 2000 the company received ISO quality certification for management systems in regard to design and manufacturing, and a new foundry was commissioned in 2002, with the expectation that employment would rise from 750 by more than 2,000 over three years in sympathy with a large growth in exports (after updating of the pumping rods factory with computerised accounting to cope with American orders). A modern training centre has been opened and $10.5mln invested to solve environmental protection problems.

Mefin (Sinaia)

This factory – in which DCI Walbridge & Partners have a majority holding –. specialises in the manufacturing and trading of diesel engine fuel injector systems and components, exporting to Bulgaria, Egypt, Iraq, Pakistan and Turkey in 2001, while foreign influence is also evident in Celsius 2000, a successful manufacturer of 7,000–86,000kcal/h boilers successful in export markets especially the UK – given incentives to replace outdated heating systems with modern condensing boilers – as well as Italy and The Netherlands (with only five per cent going to the home market). The business started in 1990 as a Romanian–American j.v. producing boiler components. This led to a new condensing boiler in 1993, and was followed by ISO quality certification and diversification of the boiler range. Turnover increased by on average 30 per cent annually to 2002. An Italian corporation was interested in a j.v. with Termorom (Cluj), which was due for liquidation in 1997. Most production (of boilers and heaters) went to the Russian market during 1980–95, but there are now big opportunities in Romania through modernisation of heating systems and a switch from central to district thermal stations evident by 1999. At the lighter end, Romtoys – the Romanian Association of Toy Manufacturers – was set up in 1997 and was exporting widely to Europe by 2000.

Household Goods: Arctic (Gaeşti)

This firm claims a leading role in the field of household equipment through the manufacture of refrigerators; the firm was established in 1968 under a Thomson-Houston (France) licence, producing 200,000 units annually and doubling to 400,000 in 1981 when vertical freezers were assimilated. It represents a development in the communist period when belated attention was being given to consumer goods and it came at a time when location policy was changing from a focus on large regional centres with the restoration of the county system (although the small town in Dâmboviţa county chosen as the location of this new factory was only 70kms from Bucharest – the main market – with a direct railway connection). Forty per cent of its output is now exported to France, Germany and the UK, with expansion in 1999 expected into Cyprus, Greece, Italy, Moldova, the Netherlands, Portugal and Spain, and the Middle East. The company adheres to the Montreal Protocol (1994) through an ecological emphasis in using non-polluting cooling substances instead of Freon, thanks to SOF help with a 110,000 lei injection in 1994 and 135,000 in 1995 to build a new microprocessor and dyeing lines. Negotiations were then conducted to secure $15mln of EBRD investment in 1997–8 for updating and restructuring. At the end of 1999 Arctic concluded a $20mln investment to modernise equipment. Production and quality control are now certified by ISO, while negotiations also provided for privatisation in 1997 in favour of EBRD and Group Société Générale (France) with a 51 per cent stake, but Arcelik (Turkey) has emerged as a major shareholder since 2002, and alignment immediately brought a new range of products to consolidate the company's position in the Romanian market for both refrigerators and freezers. This was a major boost for a company that had struggled through the 1990s with low demand through competition from cheap Chinese imports. Improved marketing ensures that Arctic's professional team maintains a 70 per cent domestic market share. Further investment of $25mln has been made to increase production from 0.4mln units in 2003 to 0.9 in 2005 using the new 'diffusion' technology, and this should make Arctic the region's largest producer of refrigerators. With 4,000 units daily, the product range has extended to include washing machines, stoves and vacuum cleaners in 2003 and TV sets in 2004 (but not yet dishwashers owing to low home demand). There are exports to Europe and North Africa (perhaps North America in future). Meanwhile, Electrolux of Sweden (owners of Zanussi of Italy and AEG in Germany) acquired Samus (Satu Mare), producer of cooking stoves, with a €19mln investment since 1998 to boost annual production to 1.2mln stoves for the home and export sales under the 'Samus Zanussi' label, with assembly work followed by the production of parts (with the 2,400 workforce reduced to 1,900 during 1998–2001). With further capacity in Hungary (refrigerators) and Poland (washing machines), Electrolux is also building a new domestic appliance plant on a 40-hectare site near the future Transylvania motorway at Turda, which will create 2,000 jobs.

ELECTRICAL ENGINEERING AND ELECTRONICS

This branch experienced rapid growth under communism with a focus on the larger towns throughout the country but especially in towns within or close to the Bucharest-Braşov-Piteşti triangle. Privatisation was well on the way to completion by the millennium, with much concern for ISO9000 and adjustment to EU guidelines to meet competition from western firms, such as ABB, that started to make a marketing presence in Romania. The challenge has been formidable through falling home demand for Romanian radio and TV sets, communication equipment and computers – given the invasion of imported products – and limited export potential. The CEFTA Accord of 1997 was not a great help because the Czech Republic, Hungary and Poland were considered to be 20 years ahead of Romania, with huge capacities (a Polish TV factory can produce 1.5mln sets annually) and cheap labour. In this sense CEFTA was seen as 'a much more aggressive commercial relationship for Romania than Western Europe'. But some firms have done well: Emailul (Mediaş), IMEP (Piteşti – included in the Ana Group) and Romlux (Târgovişte). But others disappeared, including Contactoare (Buzău), Electroconstruct (Botoşani) and Electroturis (Turnu Măgurele). IPRS (Bucharest–Băneasa), Electromotor (Timişoara) and Tehnoton (Iaşi) encountered great difficulty – although the latter was successfully privatised in favour of Omega and became Omega–Tehnoton in 2003. Electro-Argeş (Curtea de Argeş) and Electroaparatej (Bucharest) maintained their activity, though small export volume reduces vitality. Bucharest Electrical Engines (UMEB) faced liquidation in 1997 but attracted an Israeli company the following year, while TMC (Filiaşi) is noteable as a successful producer of 11–250Kw electric engines exported to Germany and Italy in 1998. Some stabilisation occurred among SMEs e.g. for accumulators since simple assembly technologies favour small local producers; and electric lamps and lighting equipment (as well as household appliances referred to above). The Elba (Timişoara) electrical lighting company invested over $1.0mln in 2001 to launch a new range of products the following year, including car lights, ornamental lighting and fluorescent industrial lighting; it also offers free design of lighting systems, and installation and upkeep. Thus some welcome momentum was achieved – thanks to research and professional training – in a non-polluting sector where rapid global growth and diversity are conducive to the creation of niches. Luxten Lighting has also been very successful, with many large urban contracts generated through PSD political channels.

Electronics and Computing

Romanian products were initially below world standards owing to old technology, lack of product renewal and inadequate quality control discouraging to skilled workers. But improvements were being made by 1998 in the face of penetration by western companies with imported equipment and technology financed by enterprises' own funds, the SOF restructuring fund and state budgetary support for R&D. Romanian companies successfully switched their emphasis to telecommunications and electronic consumer goods at the expense of automation and control. The change was brought about by Romanian private companies and others through links with foreign capital such as Alcatel, EMCS and NEI. The Romanian–French company Alcatel Network Systems, producing electronic equipment for medium and small capacity ISDN telephone exchanges and Alcatel telecommunication centres, expanded in Timişoara, with a 6,000sq.m. facility for research activities in 2000 staffed ultimately by some 200 young experts. With its high quality management and assimilation of new technology, Electromagnetica (Bucharest) can supply telecommunication equipment to Romtelecom, with considerable potential growth for the home market since 2000 – likewise for TV sets if the popularity of second-hand products can be halted – and also exports to Austria, Germany, Italy and The Netherlands plus Lebanon and North Africa. The company was founded in 1930 as Standard Electric Romania and the employees' association gained a majority holding in 2001. Electromagnetica has established the Emcom j.v. with Siemens and Romtelecom for digital telephone units. NEI is the Romanian–British j.v. Network Electronica International: after the deal was signed in 1992 Electronica exported Romanian-made black and white portable TV sets to the UK and their goods were also well received within Romania. Electronica also assembled refrigerators, freezers, washing machines and radio-cassette recorders, before going on to colour and monochrome monitors, video security systems, alarm systems and closed circuit televisions by 1995.

Strategic Partnerships
Some American and West European producers of hardware equipment and applications for electronic processing are looking for partners in the region, but this means that Romanian and other ECE companies have to operate as subcontractors to the global players: only small companies can survive independently by occupying territorial or sectoral niches. A strategic partnership has been established between Rank Xerox Romania (successful in multifunctional equipment for offices and colour laser equipment) and Compaq Computer Romania with respect to staff training, marketing and distribution in Romania. This brings together the largest world distributor of digital systems and solutions for document management and the top world distributor of calculation systems to provide the most efficient IT integrated solutions. The arrangement extends the strategic partnership concluded internationally in 1999 and should allow economic agents in Romania to become more competitive internationally in terms of enterprise management. Posada (Curtea de Argeş) has a j.v. with Gantner Electronics of Austria producing security cards with imbedded electronic chips (rather than a magnetic strip). Electroprecizia (Săcele, Braşov) is active in international markets thanks to improved product quality (ISO 9001 standard) and competitive pricing for the production of optical fibres – for Romtelecom and SNCFR in 1998, for example – in collaboration with an Italian company (after previous emphasis on motorcar electrical equipment and spare parts as well as small washing machines). Finally, Marconi Selenia Communications (Finmeccanica Group) and Electromecanica Ploieşti (a branch of Romarm) set up the Elettra Communications j.v. in 2004 to provide a permanent transmission network for the Romanian Army; the Italian partner will supply telecommunications equipment from the Ploieşti production line. The Group has been in Romania since 1981, initially through Ansaldo Energy working on the Cernavodă nuclear power station. By 2004 it had also set up a €200mln strategic military network and helped to modernise the Super Puma helicopters produced by IAR Braşov (fulfilling an important North Atlantic alliance integration criterion). Flamingo Computers was set up in 1994 and by 2001 was supported by Flamingo International, a Romanian-capital company engaged in import and export activities. In 2006 a FlexLink (Sweden) assembly line was opened in Chiajna (Bucharest) to enable Complet Electro Serv to supply 10,000 computers monthly to the Altex store chain in a €1.4mln project assisted by a Raiffeisen €1.1mln loan. And in 2007 Siemens took over the automation company Frosys of Cluj – their partner since 1996 – with a full upgrade in mind.

Solectron and the 'Timişoara Phenomenon'. As American and West European companies such as General Electric opened sales and distribution facilities, the government hoped that investment would follow and that the boom in high technology would change the country's image and slow down the brain drain that sucked out 400,000 Romanians during the 1990s. Several projects have followed. Solectron Corporation, an American company from Silicon Valley, started operations in Timişoara in 1998, with 3,500 employees (expected to double in two years) producing mobile phones and computers for export to Europe at its 18,000sq.m. facility on a 16-hectare campus with 1,000 trained associates. The company is the world's premier supply-chain facilitator for customised electronics technology, manufacturing and service solutions. The facility also provides a comprehensive range of product development, manufacturing and distribution services (design, supply-base and logistics management, printed circuit board and systems assembly, custom packaging and distribution management). Attractive for labour and infrastructure, Timişoara provides a low-cost manufacturing hub – with rapid start-up and government assistance in 1999 – for the company's rapidly growing European customer base, already supported by facilities in France, Germany, Ireland, Sweden and the UK. The Timişoara plant has been granted the TS16949 quality standard issued by ISO and the International Automotive Task Force (IATF), which includes such leading companies as BMW, Daimler-Chrysler, Ford, GM and VW. However the plant has not been financially successful and was sold to Singapore-based Flextronics in 2007 after €5.3mln losses in 2005–6.

Internet business Auctionwatch is also based in Timişoara as well as in Kathrein (Germany), producing large antennae for picking up radio and TV broadcasts. Siemens–Matsushita negotiated for a modern 3.0ha electric components and semiconductor factory in Timişoara to employ 400 in 1996. They now employ 1,200 and have moved on to Iaşi to employ 500 in 2006 in a €20mln R&D centre on 2,000sq.m. at 'Technopolis' industrial park in 2006. Siemens have expanded further in Romania by acquiring Elcaro (Slatina) which produces electric cables with enhanced scope for home market and export business after technological updating. At the same time the Swiss company Eastern Technology – a producer of industrial electronics – created 300 jobs on a two-hectare site acquired in Arad in 1999 for an electronic components factory to follow Lucas in producing exclusively for export; and Super Mod (Oradea) makes the electronic products of Hyundai (South Korea): TV sets initially in 1998, with microwave ovens and car tape recorders and CD players to follow. Meanwhile, Samsung's Hanil Electronics (South Korea) are investing up to €40mln in Oradea (overcoming competition from several towns in eastern Hungary) to make flat LCD screens for the company's plasma TV modules.

Contor Zenner invested $5.0mln in 2000 in a 2.5ha factory site – the most modern complex in its field in CEE – to produce water and thermal energy gauges, while Wenglor (Germany) has set up in Sibiu to produce high fidelity sensors for home security systems. Celestia (Canada), maker of electronic subassemblies, is building a factory at Borş through a $100mln investment programme to create 500 jobs by 2007. Elcoteq mobile phones, using the Nokia mark, have invested €50mln in Cluj industrial park to provide 1,000 jobs, and Weidemüller electric connectors are investing €5.0mln in Maramureş in a factory to offer 200 jobs by 2007. But probably the greatest development to date has been the relocation of mobile phone manufacture by Nokia (Finland) from Bochum (Germany) to a €200mln development at the Tetrarom industrial estate at Jucu northeast of Cluj-Napoca, encouraged by the local airport runway extension and a link with the Oradea-Braşov motorway under construction. Employing 11,500 eventually but 3,500 by 2009 after an initial investment of €60mln, four types of phone will be made at this stage, using some parts from Komárom (Hungary). However, component producers are also expected in the Nokia 'village' including BYD (China) with a 15ha site generating 500 jobs; and a j.v. by Hansaprint and Elander (Finland/Sweden) employing 150 on a 7.0ha site.

The Software Industry

This involves 2,000 companies and 100,000 IT specialists (8,000 high school graduates are trained each year), making Romania one of the best-placed transition countries for growth in this sector; with a National Association of Software Industry and Services. German companies were prominent by 2001, attracted by a favourable business milieu with low costs and young, skilled labour. There has also been a rapid growth in US investments in the software industry, with activity by Compaq, Hewlett-Packard, IBM, Oracle, Microsoft and Cisco. Projects have been located in Bucharest and also Braşov, Cluj, Iaşi, Oradea, and especially Timişoara. Romania offers highly skilled workers, extraordinary competence in foreign languages, relatively low costs and proximity to western markets. There are also large software exports to USA by American and Romanian companies, worth $18.4m in 2000. Scala Business Solutions, a world leader in the development of software solutions to achieve high performance local and global business management, has a Romanian subsidiary in Timişoara in 2000 that presented Scala solutions to business management, seen as an area of great potential. At the same time Motorola opened a software development centre in Bucharest for digital signal processors (DSPs) used in the most advanced communication teams – the first such development in R&D – demonstrating the intensive USA–Romania contact for IT. The centre will collaborate with the polytechnic universities of Bucharest and Timişoara, with the number of engineers eventually growing to 50 from the initial 15. SAS Institute, the world's largest private software company, opened an office in Romania in 2002, while in 2004 Microsoft (USA) acquired the intellectual property and technological assets of GeCAD software (Bucharest) concerned with anti-virus technology.

SHIPBUILDING, LOCOMOTIVES AND STOCK

Shipbuilding

This industry is heavily dependent on exports given the very low domestic demand in this field, compounded by the problems encountered in restructuring the large but ageing Romanian fleet. And while Romania works to Lloyds, Bureau Veritas and Det Norske Veritas registers, the value of Romanian ships is (as elsewhere in the region) lower than world market prices by 20–30 per cent thanks to a cheaper workforce and reduced reliability: labour costs are 10 per cent lower than in Asia and Western Europe, with labour costs only 24–28 per cent of total cost in Romania compared with 43 per cent in Western Europe. It is usual for the state to support shipbuilding so that costs can be paid from revenues earned by the ships in service, while other concessions may apply like VAT exemption on spare parts. Privatisation has brought new investment and competitiveness while earlier partnerships with foreign shipowners gave export opportunities (especially to Belgium, Germany and Norway), albeit for ship-bodies fitted-out overseas for lack of good quality equipment. In 2000 Romanian yards supplied 22 fully-equipped ships. Of the 11 yards, Brăila, Galați, Oltenița, Orşova and Tulcea were privatised with Constanța (part of PSAL), Hârşova and Drobeta-Turnu Severin following in 2001–2, while Mangalia was managed by a Romanian-South Korean j.v. (Daewoo Mangalia Heavy Industries) with privatisation in hand and Giurgiu was undergoing liquidation having accumulated large debts to the state with no buyers in sight.

Santierul Naval Constanța

This yard occupies a 70ha site and was developed during 1975–80 to build ships of up to 250,000dwt in a dry dock of 360x58m and to repair ships of up to 150,000t in another of 364x48m. For the last 20 years it has built bulk carriers of 55,000dwt and 170,000dwt; oil tankers of 85,000dwt and 150,000dwt; and ferryboats of 12,000dwt. Traditional customers are Deiuleman (Italy), Exmar/Bocimar (Belgium), Ferrostaal (Germany), Lampton Investment (Hong Kong), Nikimen (Japan), Petroklav (Norway) and Safmarine/Safore (South Africa). Technology from the early 1970s is complemented by some recent innovations e.g. cutting machines with digital control that contributed to the award of ISO9001 quality from Germanischer Lloyd in 1998. The yard worked at around 35 per cent of design capacity through the early 1990s, rising to over 60 per cent in 1999 and subsequently came close to the record of 73 per cent achieved in 1989. Labour was reduced from some 4,100 in 1997 to 3,150 in 1999 and some debt-reduction was achieved in the run-up to privatisation in 2002 for $17.4mln in favour of the holding company Resources International, comprising two Romanian and six foreign companies (five based in Valletta and one in Limassol). $2.0mln was invested in the first year. The yard has been building a diverse range of ships recently: LPG transporters of 3,800–5,600cu.m, special trawlers, a minibulk ship of 7,850dwt, a 5,000dwt Ro-Ro vessel, a 1,100dwt coaster and a port container for food liquids, as well as barges and tugs (the latter for Rynwald of The Netherlands) – much smaller than vessels launched pre-1989 until a Taiwanese owner ordered three 75,000dwt ships. German owners use Constanţa (and Tulcea as well) with the first 'Attika' ship of 5,400t (108m long and 9.0m wide with 6.7m draught and a speed of 12knots – for grain, timber and containers) arising from cooperation with Ferrostaal who has also taken container and LPG ships: indeed the first launch after privatisation was the container ship 'Tharos' – the last in a series of six for this customer.

Daewoo Mangalia Heavy Industries (DMHI)
This yard lies further down the coast as a j.v. involving Mangalia's '2 Mai' yard, with its three large dry docks (360x60x13m) in 1996 with $51mln contributed by the South Koreans for a 51 per cent share (but actually $20mln in cash plus Korean components of ships to be assembled locally using Romanian labour). The 3,300 workers – including 26 South Korean specialists – were initially paid $650/month (plus facilities and social protection) in return for improved productivity: reducing the building cycle for a 20,000dwt ship from three years to six months and raising capacity from one to eight ships each year, albeit for relatively small vessels. 1,300 workers have been sent for one to six months training at the Okpo yard in South Korea. Thus Daewoo contributed know-how that would otherwise have been prohibitively costly. An expansion in ship repairing was also anticipated. $32mln investments were made by the company during 1997–2000 in modern production equipment and improved manufacturing processes while non-core business like cleaning and transport was outsourced. During 1997–2001 55 new ships were delivered – including 13 barges, 25 multipurpose transport ships, ten containers and four tankers for chemical products – with a total value of $91mln to customers in Cyprus, Greece, The Netherlands, Norway, UK and USA. And in 2001 when a 42,500dwt orange juice carrier (the biggest in the world) was built for Norway's Kleven Floro company, the yard had orders for 31 new ships to take it through to 2003. DMHI entered the US market as a result of the contract signed with Metro Machine Corporation regarding a $20mln floating dock delivered in 2002, thanks to a quality certificate relating to the company's competence over repairs/conversion work on US navy ships. Contracts worth $850m have also been signed with Hamburg and Gebab for 10 container carriers for 2008–9. With good opportunities in a developing global market orders are expected to reach $0.5bln by 2009 – four times the cumulative level reached in 2004.

Meanwhile the state tried to sell its remaining holding in Mangalia and succeeded in 2006 after failing to attract offers early in 2005. Losses of €28.7mln in 2005-6 were disappointing but there was a return to profitability in 2007 thanks to strong world demand despite rising raw material prices.

The Danube River: Galați-Brăila

Dredged to a depth of only 7.3m, the limitations are such that Galați has been building 35,000t oil tankers and 55,000t ore carriers (with an upper limit of 65,000) whereas Constanța and Mangalia can produce vessels of 150,000t and 85,000t respectively. Santierul Naval Galați was established in 1891 which makes it the oldest shipyard in Romania. It has two dry docks of 235x35m and builds and overhauls both river and sea vessels. There are separate assembly lines, warehouses and body shops for ships of up to 7,500t and those of 7,500–40,000t. There are launching slips for ships of up to 7,500 and 15,000t while larger vessels are launched from a dry dock. All sales were initially for the domestic market, but foreign orders (from Belgium, China, France, The Netherlands, Norway and Taiwan) have been secured through good quality, competitive pricing and 'in time' delivery. Equipment was updated by 1999 but maximum efficiency was then constrained by the failure of Romanian suppliers to deliver on time. Privatisation occurred when a 51 per cent stake was taken by the Dutch Damen Shipyards Group (which holds 22 yards in Europe and Asia) after a $7mln investment during 1990–9. The yard was still delivering complete ships in 2000 (including on-board installation) with the adoption of new technology and working methods to shorten completion time. Electrical work was contracted to a subsidiary (Ekels) while painting was outsourced to an independent company. However in 2000 the yard launched a 9,000t freighter and a 5,000t mini-bulker supplied as shells to Aker in The Netherlands for equipment and sale to third parties, with 14 mini-bulkers of 4,250t for the parent company to follow. The yard, which has links with both Constanța and Mangalia, has suffered badly through the loss of some 300 skilled employees to the USA in 2007 and would like to compensate with Vietnamese workers who will accept €200/month or less. Meanwhile, specialising in the building and repair of sea and riverboats of up to 8,700t, Brăila yard was fully privatised in 2000 by Scandinor of Norway (taken over in turn by Aker-Kvaerner in 2002). Arctic trawlers have been built for Norway, with German 'Westfalia' engines, and the owners Soviknnes have evidently been pleased with the technical level as well as good stability and manoeuverability (following a j.v. with the Dutch Gefonzo company and the French national company for navigation on the Rhine). Other ships have gone to The Netherlands and Turkey. Aker are also building a €31.3mln platform service vessel for delivery to Volstad (Norway) in 2007.

The Danube River: Tulcea, Olteniţa and Turnu Severin

Further downstream Tulcea shipyard (Santierul Naval Tulcea) moved away from the domestic market in 1991 (except for repairs) since no orders were being placed and built ships for Greece and Turkey (1991–4) and later for Belgium, Germany, The Netherlands and Norway in competition with yards at Turnu Severin, Giurgiu and Olteniţa (taking advantage of the world demand for ships of 15–30,000t). But it has progressed from 15,000t ship-bodies to fitting-out larger vessels of 20–30,000t. When a $3.0mln investment improved technology and productivity (with a modern installation raising ships on to the shore) there were some initial recruitment problems because local high schools turned away from engineering after 1990 and ceased to cooperate with the yard. In 2000, ten ships were built for export through contracts with Germany and Norway and after Aker purchased a majority shareholding in 2001 (prior to taking over at Brăila the following year) there was a $15mln investment for technological flow and management restructuring – and partly for employee housing – so that ships now leave the Aker Tulcea yard on a monthly basis. In 2000 the yard was building five ships for Aker and also 20 'Zeus' port-containers for Reederei Lauterjung (Germany). The latter use some Dutch, Danish and German equipment but also Romanian products from Laminorul (Brăila), Petrotub (Roman) and Sidex (Galaţi). Moving up-river, there are floating docks (800t) and workshops at Turnu Severin, Giurgiu, Hârşova, Olteniţa and Orşova. Olteniţa has built 3,000t ships for The Netherlands suitable for river and sea transport and the yard was purchased by Dutchman Karel Jan Boersma in 1998 after a period of cooperation that began in 1992. He invested $1.6mln and employed 130 workers on 8.5–18.0m luxury yachts for rich Europeans costing up to DM2.0mln. He has secured a good order book and hopes to enter the American market. Meanwhile Severnav (Turnu Severin) was privatised by EMBO and also turned almost exclusively to export orders e.g. 8,600cu.m ethylene tankers, LPG vessels and oil tankers of 3,500–7,800t, small cargo ships (3–6,000t) as well as tug boats and speedboats. Until 1992 Santierul Naval Orşova, with a smaller capacity of 3,000t, concentrated on repairing river ships but subsequently more attention was given to shipbuilding and export with updated equipment. A weak point in 1999 was that building still did not take place under cover, but after the yard was privatised through 'Navol' raised $1.0mln in bonds for investment.

Locomotive and Railway Rolling Stock Builders

Faur (Bucharest)

Faur is one of the leading locomotive builders, founded as Malaxa in 1921 (Holban 1991) and then known as 23 August under communism. Until 1914

Romania had generally imported locomotives but after 1918 Resita was able to extend its activity from narrow-guage to standard-guage locomotives; while subsequently – beginning as a mobile workshop – Malaxa was able to expand rapidly expanded to become an industrial giant producing both locomotives and railcars for the state railways. It now builds diesel-electric and diesel-hydraulic locomotives, railcars, trams, diesel engines (with Alco, Maybach, MAN, MTU and Sulzer licences), braking systems (Knorr–Bremse licence), industrial plant for metallurgical, chemical and cement industries (an emphasis acquired after 1950) and a wide of range of components and semi-finished products. A hunt for strategic investors in the USA and Austria stimulated investment by GEC Alstom to create the GEC Alstom-Faur Transport partnership in connection with bidding for the upgrading of SNCFR diesel locomotives for the non-electrified Cluj-Oradea main line in 1997; also for other modern equipment to meet Romanian and third country requirements. But since the demand for new locomotives has declined the company has refurbished and upgraded trams in the late 1990s for the Bucharest transport undertaking (RATB) to avoid the expense of new trams from abroad, although many of the old trams are beyond repair. The firm also joined in the bidding for the updating of the Bucharest-Braşov railway modernisation in 2000. Meanwhile massive repair programmes have been undertaken in other countries. Privatisation was attempted in 2001 under PSAL but did not succeed until 2003. Under the Crişteseu Brothers (Bega Group) the halls will be modernised and space consolidated to make some 20,000sq,m space available for residential development (though currently surplus space is rented for manufacturing by other companies).

Electroputere (Craiova)

This enterprise was set up in 1941 to overhaul steam locomotives following the loss of installations in southern Transylvania in 1940. In 1949, with the lost facilities regained, it went on to build trams and mine locomotives (until 1960) but took up diesel-electric and electric locomotive building in 1954 (as well as electric engines, generators and transformers). As the centre of the large but rekatively backward Oltenia region, the communist authorities were committed to accelerate economic development in an area relatively poor in raw materials. In addition to food processing based on the local agriculture, the expansion of engineering was a rational choice given the linkage with Reşiţa in the adjacent region while coal from the Jiu valley (Petroşani) provided an energy base before the local lignite resources were exploited on a large scale. Electroputere assembled the SNCFR fleets of 2,100hp diesel electric locomotives (under Sulzer and Brown-Boveri licences) and 5,100kw electric locomotives (Asea licence). Both projects were highly successful and generated exports: 925 diesel-electrics for Bulgaria, China and Poland and 148 5,100kv electrics for Bulgaria and Yugoslavia. It is the only Romanian producer for some appliances whereas in other cases (medium/high voltage appliances, transformers, engines and generators) there is competition on the domestic market. Its main foreign collaborators include Adtranz and Siemens (Germany), Holec (The Netherlands) and Pawels (Belgium). But it has been undermined by the lack of new locomotive orders since 1989 (Table 4.1) and was forced (like Faur) to concentrate on overhaul and upgrading work, notably through cooperation with SNCFR and General Motors' Canadian Subsidiary in London (Ontario) for upgrading 20 2,100hp diesel-electric locomotives after an initial seven with EBRD funding. Japanese financial help was mooted on a scale that might have allowed refurbishment of electric and diesel-electric locomotives to run into several hundred (even 500) over the years from 1998. However this has not happened, primarily because of the purchase of new Siemens railcars for a new generation of mainline passenger services. However upgrading work has also affected electric locomotives with the first two EGM621s tested in 2000 to show excellent reliability and attract interest from Bulgaria and Poland. The company intends to develop new equipment and advanced technologies for higher quality and productivity.

It already has reached the ISO quality standard for some products and benefits from the national R&D agency's cooperation agreement with General Motors in 2000 over a $50mln five-year investment for export/import, technology transfer and training in the traction rolling stock field. The company has also a j.v. with its traditional partner Adtranz (the latter holding 51 per cent) for asynchronous electric generators: 30 3,000Kw generators were produced in 2000 with 700 at 5,000Kw planned in 2002. There was also cooperation with China in 2001 over new technologies for electrical/electronic equipment. But Electroputere remained a major outstanding privatisation case needing an investor of 'significant financial power' to provide capital and technology. Offering railway locomotives, power transformers and electric motor sections, the Craiova enterprise stood out as a potential premier CEE service centre for railway equipment trading with ECECs (Bulgaria, Croatia, Poland and Serbia) as well as China. In 2001 there was interest from Alstom, GE, GM, Karsdorfer Eisenbahngesellschaft and Siemens, along with Mitsui of Japan (on behalf of a number of companies it represents). There was a further push to privatise in 2005 after the business slumped financially from a 10,000 lei profit in 2001 to a 13.1mln loss in 2004 following a sharp fall in turnover. Interest came from DAB Electromec (Greece) as well as Horvath Holding Investment (Hungary), Siemens (Germany) and Telemania (Israel). But the accumulated debts posed a formidable problem as well as the government's commitment to sell the business as a single unit to avoid investors 'cherry-picking' the profitable sections. After four failures it seemed that this option might have to be adopted, but in 2007 Al-Arrab (Saudia Arabia), part of the consortium involved on the Saudi infrastructure programme, bought a 62.8 per stake for €2.3mln and paid

€60mln to cover debts and provide €57mln for working capital. At present, in addition to work for Saudi Arabia, the company is assembling trains for the Bucharest metro and, like Astra (see below), could work with Bombardier (Canada) on trains for the Romanian railways.

Astra (Arad)

This famous rolling stock company, founded in 1891, was initially highly diversified with interests in locomotives, aircraft, tanks and cars up to nationalisation in 1948 (when it was named for a time after the Bulgarian socialist Dimitrov). The post-1989 slump led to a prototype Astra IK trolleybus on the strength of a 1995 contract with the Bucharest public transport company RATB. Privatisation in 1999 resulted in a split between passenger and freight business following the desires of interested parties. Trinity Industries (USA) bought a 70 per cent stake in the freight company Astra Vagoane Marfă, including the local Wagon Research & Design Institute. They transferred wagon production from Studenka (Czech Republic) in 2001 along with equipment for the railcar production (since production costs were cut by two-thirds) with the intention of turning Astra into a European strategic centre. New wagon types were assimilated and important business secured through bogies for container wagons and other stock for inter-modal transport including parts for Ro–La wagons manufactured at Debrecen (Hungary). There is tough competition in western markets where Astra has sought to compete following the collapse of the former Soviet market. Trinity also acquired Meva (Turnu Severin) and invested $6.8m in 2001 to improve the design, production and repair of freight cars. Wagons are also repaired for the railway freight company Marfă.

Competition for Trinity comes from Romvag (Caracal) established in 1973 with an annual capacity of 5,000 wagons in 1990, mostly for export. With employment reduced from 3,500 to 650 it is now engaged heavily in wagon modernisation (especially bogies and couplings) and won an international competition for the updating of 750 Marfă freight wagons – helped by collaboration with a Belgian partner (Technorail) who have two experts – permanently present in Caracal where prototypes of three updated wagon types (Hbikklls, Shimms and Rills) were produced. Romvag has also obtained high performance cutting and welding installations from Germany (1999) and the company was included in PSAL (2001) and privatised in favour of Karsdorfer Eisenbahngesellschaft who acquired a 60 per cent stake in 2002 with the hope of making Caracal a large CEE rolling stock maker. The firm is repairing 2,200 wagons for SNCFR (France) in addition to work on a contract for 3,000 wagons for Kazakhstan. The company hopes to penetrate the American market with models of freight cars currently being checked out in USA; bringing the prospect of increased employment. Other repair companies are Remar (Paşcani), who also maintain and modernise coaches and were privatised in

2004 by the railfreight company GFR; Rova (Roşiorii de Vede) who also do some coachwork; and Umerva (Ploieşti). Another competitor for Astra is the rolling stock plant of Balş that survived a traumatic period of massive dismissals to reduce the workforce (from 8,000 to 2,700), achieve efficiency gains, and renegotiate contracts with suppliers. As a result exports of wheels and bogies (to EU standard ISO 9000) were under way by 1997. New technology is coming in gradually including digitally-controlled lathes and automated welding. The company also retains some welfare functions: meals, a single men's boarding house and a holiday house.

The Astra passenger company – Astra Vagoane Călători (AVC) – was constrained by the absence of hi-tech carriage components and the high price of imports. However technology for 'Corail' coaches (with Y32 bogies for 160km/h running) was assimilated under licence from De Dietrich Ferroviaire (France) when financial problems curtailed the programme initiated by the 'Călători' railway passenger company: an initial order was for 30 coaches (IRU standard passenger cars, restaurant cars and sleeping cars) for international services at a unit cost of $1.3mln, financed by part of a $350mln state-guaranteed EBRD credit in 1998. Astra had to fall back on the repair and upgrading of coaches for short/intermediate domestic journeys: 100 passenger coaches (30 first class, 60 second and 10 bar–restaurant coaches) were updated during 2000–2 by an Alstom Transport Romania-AVC partnership. The work was done at Santierele CFR Griviţa (Bucharest) but AVC produced the Y32 axles for high speed running (160km/h) where the rail infrastructure will allow this, with other component suppliers from Europe and Romania including the aircraft companies Aerofina (Bucharest) and Avioane (Craiova). The main partners acted as subcontractors of Alstom–De Dietrich Ferroviaire, using components from Europe and Romania, as part of a railway rehabilitation programme financed by a $250mln IBRD credit in 2002. AVC exhibited an upgraded passenger train at Bucharest's Gara de Nord and the coaches now operate on inter-city and international routes. There was also a reference to the updating of 180/200 coaches in 1999 by AVC as well as Griviţa and Remar (Paşcani) linked with the subcontracting by Aerofina already noted. New work is now being done through 'Desiro' railcars for Romania and coaches for Iran.

Other Railway Businesses

This includes the Buzău railway equipment manufacturer Apcarom that has attracted interest from Austria (First Alpine), France (Cogifer) and Germany (BVG). In the mid-1990s Cogifer were interested in expediting the production of switches made from manganese (essential for high-speed traffic). The Bucharest-based railway construction company (CCCF) is building a reinforced concrete sleeper factory for Romanian railways with production starting 2001 at Blejoi (Prahova) costing 0.5mln.lei; with an annual output of 100,000 sleepers –

enough for 60kms of railway – suitable for speeds up to 250km/hr. Previously such sleepers were produced only in Braşov. Meanwhile, due to lack of orders, the former workshops of Construcţii Feroviare Moldova at Iaşi-Nicolina (privatised in 1995 but then acquired in 2002 by the French company Colas – a member of Bouygues Group and one of the world leaders in railway building) have reduced employment from 6,000 to 2,300 and changed their activity to production of road equipment in cooperation with French, German and Italian companies. Modern information systems allow for computer-based management. They retain a small amount of railway work through cooperation with Siemens for high-speed passenger coaches in 1996. Reloc (Craiova) repairs diesel and electric locomotives and participated during 1996–7 in an unusual barter deal involving repair of 15 5,100kw electric locomotives for Serbia in return for bauxite for the Romanian aluminium industry.

CONCLUSION

Engineering has struggled to cope with a transition away from the steady orders placed by former communist states and relatively undemanding markets. It is also a relatively unknown sector that attracts little comment from the economic press. It is of course extremely diverse and fortunes have varied from branch to branch as the chapter has indicated (while the next chapter extends this perspective by combining a – generally – highly successful automotive sector with the much more problematic aerospace industry). Foreign investment has been geared very heavily to privatisation deals so that relatively cheap labour can be used to secure higher quality production following technological upgrading; although this strategy may not always be viable since the Damen shipyard in Galaţi has recently transferred its port container business to China (bringing a 33 per cent cost reduction) while falling back on small naval vessels and pleasure boats. However, a major feature of the industry's changing profile has been new growth in electronics, exemplified by Solectron in Timişoara, and major investments in the Cluj area where Nokia's mobile phone project (controversially transferring jobs from Germany) started production in 2008 – initially with relatively simple assembly products – is being followed by Emerson Group's five electrical engineering plants (to be built during 2008–12) serving European and Middle Eastern clients. Thus, in some respects the 'classic' engineering industry inherited from communism is being overshadowed the revolution in electronics and computing which is boosting the large cities (and particularly Bucharest and Cluj) in the context of business services linked with expanding BPO (Business-Process-Outsourcing) activity.

5. The Automotive and Aerospace Industries

THE AUTOMOTIVE INDUSTRY

This is an expanding and successful industry in many respects, especially for car production and parts worth €2.0bln in 2005 and some €6.0bln in 2006. Domestic car sales have been buoyant (with 42 per cent growth in 2004 alone) while exports are increasing and the production of parts is growing fast (Table 4.1). The industry began in Romania with the assembly of Ford cars in Bucharest between the world wars. Large-scale production started with tractors in 1946 and lorries in 1953 (both at Braşov) followed by 'jeeps' in 1957 at Câmpulung (by Aro) and buses in Bucharest (Autobuzul, now Rocar) before car production started at Piteşti-Colibaşi (now Mioveni) by Dacia in 1968 (in a j.v. with Renault). It was then extended to Craiova in 1982, this time through collaboration with Citröen – hence the Oltcit brand – and shortly afterwards to Timişoara through an experiment with a small car, known as the Lastun, which was unable to make an impact by the time the revolution occurred. The number of motor vehicles has surged since 1989: in 2005 there was approximately one car per six inhabitants (and one vehicle per 4.3) in the Bucharest area – nationally, one car per 11 people and one vehicle per 7.3 – although the average age of vehicle is 11.3 years: bad for pollution in terms of carbon oxide concentrations, unburnt hydrocarbons and suspended particles. But Romanian factories have had to cope with competition from the global players and it has been a struggle to get the industry privatised on a sustainable basis. When the DCR government came to power in 1997 Aro, Dacia and Rocar had no links with foreign companies, although during the previous year Škoda had been considering a j.v. production of the Beta car and Liaz truck. The situation is better for cars because, although no greenfield assembly project has materialised (despite Daihatsu's expressed interest in building cars in Romania and the further possibility of a factory in Romania built by a Chinese automobile company in 2007), solutions were found for the survival of the Craiova and Mioveni factories with a ratio of total output to home market shares of roughly two to one. This could hardly have been taken for granted, considering that the car market was transformed after 1989 by the import of second-hand cars that met 40 per cent of the demand in 1995 and, along with increased market penetration by new cars from abroad, limited output by domestic producers.

The Motor Industry in the 1990s

In the mid-1990s the motor industry was providing 135,000 jobs in the car industry: 40,000 in assembly plants, 34,000 in the production of spare parts and the rest in various supply, service and retail functions. But there were challenges ahead with the pressure to increase quality, reduce the amount of energy-consuming technologies and reach international comfort and security standards. Closer links with Europe had implications for protection regimes against imported vehicles, while new environmental standards would make the fitting of catalytic converters mandatory for Romania during 2000–2. There was talk of tax incentives for cars with catalytic converters and for the less-polluting imported second-hand cars (rather than a blanket ban on all cars older than eight years) as a political move to stimulate domestic car production. The industry then ran into crisis towards the end of the decade, with negative growth reducing incomes at a time of more open trade, with a dramatic reduction in domestic sales and a big increase in the number of foreign imported cars (especially Renault, Volkswagen and Škoda) favoured by new legislation and some advantageous leasing offers in 2000 while Daimler–Chrysler announced its interest in building commerce logistic centres for storing and distributing goods at the ports and leading cities in 2003. The 48,156 cars sold in 2000 (including 2,270 exported) was 44 per cent fewer than in 1999 and production dropped 36 per cent. The decline was most evident with Dacia, given price increases and outdated design, but Daewoo sales also dropped. Dacia retained 62 per cent of the market, but a massive loss at the Dacia plant in 2001 was only just cancelled out by Renault's investment. At the beginning of 2002 government provided some relief by ruling that that only imported cars of Euro Three pollution standard (not mandatory for domestic car makers – and the EU in general - until 2006) would be accepted for registration. Coming hard on the heels of rising imports of new cars in 2001 – when Renault was followed by Škoda (through the success of the Fabia), Volkswagen, Fiat, Peugeot and Ford – it meant that more people would buy Romanian cars for a similar price, thus reversing the decline in home-produced car sales. There was a growth in monthly sales during 2003–4 (4,100 for Dacia and 2,800 for Daewoo), while leading imported makes were Renault (1,100), Škoda (800), Peugeot (600) and Volkswagen (500).

Vehicle Design Capacity

It is unfortunate that Romanian vehicle design capacity has been largely wasted. The Institute for Road Motor Vehicles (IRMV) in Braşov suffered from a decline in research contracts after 1989 and there is regret that firms like Roman (within whose complex the Institute is accommodated) turned to foreign designs to make their products more competitive in the shortest possible time, whereas the Institute could have helped them update their products. The Institute needs the industry ministry's help for building prototypes through collaboration with an association of components suppliers including Rocab (Întorsura Buzăului) for cabs, Imasa (Sfântu Gheorghe) for gears and transmissions, and Automecanica (Mediaş) for the chassis element. The Institute did in fact set out to design a vehicle that could be used for a wide range of functions: hence the INA900 which was shown off in Timişoara in 1996: a small, 960cc vehicle of 40hp, 140km/h maximum speed and 4.8 liters/100km fuel consumption. It may have a future because Romania was not producing small-capacity cars (below 1000cc) that could be marketed in the West as well as in Romania and the Mecatim (Timişoara) premises were also available for components (used to only a limited extent on work for Dacia). Hence the hope that IRMV and Mecatim might launch the INA900 cars in 1997 using the latter's experience with the Lastun (a small car that did not prove popular and was abandoned before the revolution, with just 3,800 built in 1989), and possibly incorporating a Volkswagen engine. However, this did not happen and instead Daewoo acquired 50 per cent of Mecatim in order to produce components (steering-boxes, air conditioning installations, drum braking systems and alternators) for Craiova and other Daewoo plants in CEE, with an investment of $100m during 1998–2000 to increase employment from 95 to 550. It had earlier been thought that, following the Daewoo project at Craiova, Oltcit production might be transferred to Timişoara (and renamed Oltim) to realize the Lastun's potential to compete with the Daewoo 'Tico' with annual production conceivably as high as 20,000 by 2000. But presumably Daewoo decided that it would not be desirable to allow their predecessor's products to create competition with their own output, and so they absorbed Timişoara's capacity for their own purposes. Very large funding was needed, with a new model required every year to 'look like other new vehicles'. But the fiscal climate discouraged investment with such rare exceptions as the IRMV-related prototype car 'Gerula' with a diesel engine, rust-free light body and simplified construction costing below $10,000.

Car Production: Dacia

The government was very concerned to get the best deal for this company. Renault had expressed interest over several years but on terms that were initially unacceptable. Instead the government tried to sustain a special development fund of 150bln.lei to upgrade the production line. Annual production fell from 67,500 units in 1989 (144,000 nationally) to 51,300 in 1992 (64,000), but then rose to 100,400 (106,000). Following the initial 1100 model, of which 37,500 were built during 1968–72 and the 1300–1410 range involving 1.96mln during 1975–2006 (plus 319,000 for the Dacia Pickup during 1975–2006) a 'Dacia Nova' was designed and produced in Romania with 1300, 1400 and 1600cc variants; also with air conditioning, centralised locking and improved aerodynamics. A third of the production incorporated non-polluting engines, catalytic exhaust and modern ignition for export to Germany and ECE, but mainly to northern and southern Africa, Asia (especially China) and South America (Argentina and Uruguay). There was interest in the Peugeot diesel engine for Dacia cars: 400 in 1997 rising to 1,500–1,600 in 1998. Meanwhile, the traditional Dacia remained popular through the mid-1990s, and the company was considered profitable. However, quality suffered and, with increasing obsolescence, exports contracted to a tenth of production in the mid-1990s and fell below five per cent at the end of the decade. For a time there was a problem of black market sales at premium prices for the Dacia Nova through insufficient capital to meet the home demand, but by the beginning of 1999 short working of one to three days per week was necessary as stocks increased. The government sought the help of a partner interested in cars for the Romanian market with modest purchasing power and variable road surfaces. Some progress was made through a contract negotiated in 1997 with Hyundai, to produce a new D33 car to enter mass production in 2000 for foreign and domestic markets (presumably the government could find the means of supporting this in the context of negative growth). There was also some opportunity for components, since Dacia manufactured electronic circuitry for BMW (through the j.v. RomAutoParc Piteşti that generated special freight trains to Regensburg). But there was particular interest in Renault after the rewarding experience of 1968, when the Dacia became highly efficient for Romanian conditions, generating a powerful demand (under conditions of a market with little choice that was chronically under-supplied – 280 cars per day to 1989) and ensuring that each car was sold four to five years in advance.

Successful Privatisation by Renault

When Constantin Stroe persuaded Louis Schweitzer (Renault president) to take over the company, the Dacia privatisation was an important success for the Vasile government after the premier had given his personal support to the French connection. It was appropriate since Renault had given birth to Dacia 30 years previously and the company still appreciated the adaptive capacity of Romanians towards modern technology. Renault was also well received on domestic and foreign markets. So, at a time when some western car makers were interested in Dacia only as a spare parts producer, the Renault team headed by Christian Estève was prepared to take 80 per cent of the company for $50mln in September 1999 – and to invest while sustaining further losses to 2004 – thereby helping Dacia join 'the large family of world automobile producers'. The two negotiating teams agreed a French investment of $270mln to update production and assimilate a new model. Dacia General Manager Constantin Stroe was personally involved and supplied the 'quicksilver' with constant interventions and 'total sincerity' to both the French and the workforce, including close collaboration with the unions. François Fourmont's success as Dacia Renault general manager then ensured that Renault's intervention would stand as one of Romania's ten top culture-changing investments. Rather than suppressing the Dacia name, the brand was relaunched in a western quality context, while the 'Super Nova' emerged within ten months, with expectations of selling 6,000 during 2000 and 35,000 in 2001 (including exports to China, Turkey and Venezuela) in three variants: Clima, Confort and Rapsodia. With a Renault Clio diesel engine produced at the beginning of 2001 (using Renault parts from all over Europe including Spain and Portugal – with more from Romania expected to reduce production costs by 12 per cent in the future) and a Renault Laguna gearbox, the car offered low fuel consumption (15km/l) and the price was considered accessible in the context of a reviving Romanian economy; with trade-in deals for owners of Dacia cars over 12 years old. Various fiscal concessions were made: Renault would not pay customs taxes on imported goods or VAT on goods acquired from the domestic market; they also received exemption from profits tax for five years (with the period beginning only with the first profitable year, provided the latter came within three years of privatisation); also no VAT on cars sold on the domestic market for three years – all provided that investment in the first year reached $127m. The deal also maintained of sale volume at home and abroad, with a rise in quality and replacement of the 'Dacia 1310' over three to five years (with the 'Dacia' marque subsequently retained as Renault's second trademark) with a new model for the ECE market. After 38,100 Dacia Novas were turned out during 1995–2000, 60,200 Super Novas were built during 2000 2003.

Production Plans. With imports from France, Renault hoped to sell 35,000 cars in 2001 including 7,500 exports to ECE, Latin America and China (half of total Dacia production). Much use was already being made of Romanian suppliers, many of whom were now collaborating with western car makers. Progress continued under Estève's management for almost five years (1999–2004), with €300m invested in upgrading, retraining and development that saw the launch of not only the Super Nova but also the Solenza variant that also sold well in the region and in North Africa. At the time losses were sustained each year, albeit by declining amounts but with no profit expected before 2004. There was also the prospect of a new 'X90' model in 2003–4 costing €5,000 and geared to Central Europe and Latin America, with new standards of sturdiness and performance incorporating elements of the Renault Clio and Nissan Micra II. This materialised as the Logan, which appeared on the streets of Bucharest early in the autumn of 2004 when 40,000 orders had already been secured. Moreover, in 2003 Renault were planning Dacia plants in Russia (Moscow) – also in Morocco and Colombia – with the Logan to drive Dacia's international ambitions as a centre for car development in the region. By 2005 (when production in these three countries was due to start) output was also being planned in Iran for 2006 – with some sourcing of parts from India – to achieve a total sale of a million Logans by 2010. Indeed, from 2007 Dacia could be producing one-eighth of all the cars made by the Renault Group – essentially 750,000 Logans (150,000 in Romania and the rest in Russia and Morocco, and later in Colombia and Iran) – and a range of parts that will facilitate new models to secure a total of four million units by 2010. The Logans for manufacture outside Romania would be assembled from CKD (completely knocked-down) sets of parts and components despatched by the company's export centre in Romania (30,000 units in 2005 rising to 150,000 in 2006); however, this programme has been delayed. Meanwhile, the Solenza finished in April 2005 when the production line was adjusted for the Logan. Altogether 79,200 Solenzas were built during 2003–5; followed by the Logan of which 505,600 were turned out from 2004 until completion of 3.0mln cars overall in 2007.

Rising Sales and Productivity

Dacia is now moving into quite a strong position, with 2005 sales up 39 per cent on 2004 when 95,296 units were sold (2.5mln since 1968) including 15,000 abroad; the company enjoys Renault's full confidence, according to Estève, who is now Renault's director for Eastern Europe. Dacia's 46.5 per cent share of domestic market was boosted by the diesel version of the Solenza offered from 2003. Inevitably the workforce has been reduced from the level of 30,000 before privatisation, when behind each employee there were 9–10 other salary earners in other companies (underlining the massive social role of the plant that government had to support). From some 22,000 just after privatisation, the new management had to reduce the level massively to 16,300 at the beginning of 2004 and 9,000–10,000 a year later. Marian Ghita (Director of Progress) saw a change in worker outlook after lists of absentees were posted on notice boards! However, labour was cheap enough to make robots too expensive (hence only one was actually used – to put putty on windshields), although a German-style tidy and clean production hall was considered essential – also a fully-trained sales team. Redundancy was supported by a Technical Re-employment Unit and an Assistance Mission for Business Creation, in collaboration with Bernard Brunhes International. Daily capacity increased from 460 to 750 units (against only 280 before 1989) but productivity remained low despite pressure from workers for higher salaries: whereas Renault produced four million units with 140,000 workers, Dacia needed almost 22,000 workers for 52,000 cars in 2001 (still an improvement over 30,000 workers producing 40,000 cars in 1999).

The Current Picture. The trend is moving in the right direction with the expectation of 12,000 workers producing 180,000 cars in 2005 given further upgrading to include a €350m investment by 2004 in preparation for the Logan, with production of components by specialised companies. This is a remarkable after the initial growth under communism (16,200 in 1970 to 79,700 in 1980) and the downward drift under transition from 62,500 in 1990 to 52,200 in 2002 before expanding again to 94,700 in 2004 and 188,500 in 2006 (virtually on target); with 350,000 planned for 2008. After taking 17 years to produce the first million cars (1968–85) and 13 for the next (1985–98), the third million marker was reached in 2007 (after nine years) with the fourth due in 2010 (three). And 11,000 job losses the employment trend is again positive with 600 new jobs to be filled by the end of 2008. Dacia won a fresh ISO certificate in 2002, with Renault keen that all plants should develop quality management systems; likewise its suppliers, who include Michelin and Continental along with Johnson Controls (for automotive interiors). 2004 was still not profitable, but the company hoped to break even or make a small profit in 2005 based on the original target of 180,000 cars (including at least 60,000 exports) with a Dacia market share of 40–50 per cent). After 61,400 Logans were sold in Romania in the first half of 2005, 110,000 sales were expected for the year from a 240,000 total including exports to 35 countries. Moreover, Logan sales – achieved at the expense of the Solenza as well as Daewoo's Matiz – were to be integrated into the company's Indian operations in 2007 and subsequently in Brazil, Colombia, Iran, Morocco and Russia, using some Romanian components and sub-assemblies. Meanwhile Volkswagen is seeking to challenge the Logan with a saloon car at a target manufacturing price of €3,000 that could sell in China in 2008 and also in Southeast Asian and Latin American states. This undercuts the Logan's projected sale price of €5,000 that has not yet been achieved (even the new €5,500 'basic version' planned for mid-2005 was postponed because customers seemed to prefer more expensive cars).

However, Renault is now committing €215mln during 2005–8 for a Renault–Nissan gearbox factory that should bring total investment at Mioveni to €2.0bln (double the level of mid-2005 and roughly trebling the €700mln reached at the end of 2004). By 2008 Mioveni should be the largest centre of the Renault–Nissan alliance, with an annual output of 0.3mln cars, 0.4mln engines and 1.0mln gearboxes. The first profit under Fourmont's management (€57mln on a turnover of €1.2bln) was secured in 2005 after greatly increased sales (up from 98,300 in 2004 to 157,400 in the third quarter alone) and a good export performance, with the 50,000 mark for exported Logans (worth €420mln) passed in November after a big success by this model at the Bucharest International Auto Show earlier in the year. Profit should rise to €60mln in 2006 with 200,000 sales expected (exceeding the 2005 national production of 193,400) and 88,000 exports, including the first Logan exports to Italy (5,000 through selected Renault dealers) and with total Logan production passing 200,000 by the year's end. Logans were also sent to Bulgaria in 2006, with the expectation of 2,500 sales during the year: at €6,500 the Logan is the cheapest car available apart from Fiat Seicento and some Ladas. The plan seems to be on course, with 33,900 vehicles sold in the period January–April 2006, including 29,500 Logans, 40 per cent of which were diesels costing €1,000 more than the 1.4l petrol type and so surpassing the company's greatest expectations. With a light van option appearing on the market in 2007, the model could well be an appropriate icon for Romania as a new EU state and certainly the management (including Constantin Stroe, who is now Dacia vice-president) is delighted at the prospect of the country's fame resting on the Logan – and its extension as the Sandero announced in 2008 – which is bringing renewed growth in employment after a fine export performance (two-thirds of all production in 2007) and the boost to domestic sales through the heavy tax imposed on the first registration of second-hand cars (raising their cost by some €600). After a €1.2bln investment in the Pitesti area in eight years since the Renault acquisition (which delivers two-thirds of the budget for the town of Mioveni), the company's confidence is also being expressed through a multi-million Euro development centre (complementing two others in Brazil and South Korea) to occupy 500ha and provide 2,000 jobs announced in Târgovişte. It was operating in the Pipera area of Bucharest early in 2007 with the intention of moving to the western part of the city (convenient for Piteşti) later in the year; remaining there until the move to Târgovişte in 2009. 'Hundreds' of jobs have already been reported including transfers from Mioveni.

Car Production: Daewoo

Until the Dacia privatisation, pride of place in car industry investment was occupied by Daewoo (South Korea) with an initial cash injection of $156m in the former Oltcit factory in Craiova, in addition to $33mln for a 51 per cent stake in the factory. As Romania tried to create a favourable environment for investment and entrepreneurship, with low wages as a powerful incentive, the liberal foreign investment law of 1991 was followed by the 'Daewoo Law' of mid-1994, designed expressly to attract a company known for hard bargaining over tax incentives. 100 per cent foreign ownership of business was allowed, with repatriation of profits, tax holidays and exemptions from customs duties. Automobile Craiova was abandoned by its French partner Citroën in 1991 (when the 'Oltcit' became 'Oltena'). The technology inflow stopped, with difficulties over raw materials and spare parts compounded by falling orders and capital shortage (unrelieved by the SOF and the banks), depressing output to 14 per cent of capacity in 1994 when the search for a foreign partner interested in an almost bankrupt company was becoming desperate! From 30,300 units in 1989, production fell to 6,500 in 1994: export value from 35.0 to 6.0mln lei and profitability from 35mln.lei to a loss of 188mln (Nica-Guran 1998).

Daewoo's 'Frontier Spirit'
Rodae Automobile was created in that year as a j.v. (Rodae Automobile Craiova, renamed Daewoo Automobile Craiova in 1996) between Automobile Craiova (with assets of $150mln) and the Daewoo Motor Company. Daewoo's decision reflected the frontier spirit of the group's founding chairman, Woo Choong Kim, who saw Romania as a promising company with big growth potential thanks to its population and its strategic position (a) between Central and Western Europe and the Caspian Sea region and Central Asia (on the Rhine–Danube–Black Sea route) and (b) between the Baltic and Balkans; it was also boosted by CEFTA and EU and NATO enlargement. Daewoo also recognised the well-educated and technically competent workforce and the solid support base provided by auxiliary firms. The privatisation challenge was taken up with high motivation on the basis that 'no cure' (for an ailing industry) would mean 'no pay' (in other words, no profit for Daewoo). But the manager also remarked that the company arrived not only to make a profit but also to get integrated into social life and play a partnership role. Hence a family approach: flats for employees and nurseries for children, alongside refurbishment of the park, local sponsorship and donations to children's foster homes. Total investment reached $870mln during 1994–2002, with 50,000 jobs retained and 4,000 new jobs created. Meanwhile Mangalia shipyard (see below) offered the prospect of improved productivity and quality, now being achieved with the building of Panamax bulk carriers. But Daewoo had no wish to persevere with the Oltena that was taken over by a new company Axa with the intention of transferring production to the Mecatim premises in Timişoara, although this did not happen.

New Investments. Some $83mln was spent on the first assembly plant, with over $500mln to follow to double capacity (from 20 to 40 units per hour) and provide an engine and gearbox factory employing the highest technology within the company with serial production in 1998. Production started at the end of 1995, although the idea of producing Cielo, Damas, Espero and Tico cars as well as 1.0–3.0t lorries was disappointing as only 22,000 Cielo cars were made in 1996 (rather than the 50,000 initially expected). The Espero and Tico models followed in 1997, when some 92,000 cars were produced, although there was production capacity for 200,000 cars. There was also capacity for 300,000 engines and 240,000 gearboxes (allowing for an export surplus for factories in Europe, the Middle East and North Africa), although 1998 production was only 150,000 engines and 100,000 gearboxes, along with 200,000 transaxles. The total production surface is 228,000sq.m. on a 1.09sq.m site, with high quality standards imposed on over 60 Romanian suppliers, located mainly in Wallachia between Bucharest and Craiova, but with some in Transylvania, including Compa (Sibiu) and Sinterom (Cluj). There was actually Daewoo investment in some suppliers: Plastor and UAMT (Oradea), Roman and Tractorul (Braşov) and Roţi Auto (Drăgăşani). The Cielo was to use 35 per cent Romanian components (80 per cent over five years) while the 6,000 employees in 1990 fell to 3,783 in 1994, but rose to 4,906 in 1996 and 7,700 in 1998. Quality was maintained by above-average wages for Craiova factories, though major investment in the painting shop included ten robots assisted by human operators.

Exports Commence. There was no difference between Korean and Romanian-made cars (although problems reported with Romanian-made batteries reflect the widespread need for massive re-equipment for quality exports at a competitive price). Wider problems of quality arose in connection with Romanian raw materials, plus the risk of client dissatisfaction through accelerated change and price rises linked with inflation. Cars such as the mini Tico sold well through 106 authorised distributors for sales and service with a three-year guarantee (maximum 100,000km), with distribution concentrated first on the zonal centres of Braşov, Bucharest, Cluj, Constanţa, Iaşi and Timişoara. But production was always geared to foreign trade, with the intention of exporting half from the outset. The first lot of 500 Cielo cars was shipped to Rostov early in 1997 as SKD (Semi Knock-Down) to be mounted at destination. The aim was to export 20,000 units to Russia – and the same number to Poland – during 1997 (with a total export target of 75,000). However, 1997 exports were later assessed at 15,000 cars to Poland and Russia, with 35,000 planned for 1998 (partly for developing markets in Moldova and Latin America), with Romanian engines and axles (exported from 1997) destined for Poland, Uzbekistan and other countries. But falling domestic sales due to three years of reduced buying power meant an even greater emphasis on exports. In the first half of 2000 Daewoo exported widely to the CEE countries (Bulgaria, Croatia, Hungary, Macedonia, Moldova, Poland, Russia, Slovakia and Slovenia), especially the Matiz. Also, exports were planned to China, where the Nubira was to compete with Audi, Citroën, General Motors, Renault and Volkswagen, plus engines and gearboxes to Egypt and Poland – also with Matiz car frames to the latter (reflecting the efficiency of new investments in pressings at Craiova).

The Daewoo Parent Company Crisis

The years of negative growth prevented any expansion of output in the late 1990s, and the optimistic expectation of 200,000 units proved hopelessly unrealistic. Home market sales rose with a return to growth, and consumer confidence was strong in 2002 when the Matiz was the most popular model, followed by the Cielo, with the new Tacuma launched in the middle of that year: a large family car produced for Europe (while Daewoo did not interfere with the 1,100–1,400cc range covered by Dacia). The new millennium saw Daewoo reasonably well placed, with a successful team strategy providing flexible and dynamic organisation and a technical centre (incorporating computerised laboratories and a metallurgy laboratory) creating prototypes and models: a Cielo ambulance and light lorry, a Matiz van, a Musso truck and a Nubira ambulance. But with $430mln of debts at the start of 2003, the parent company became over-extended in its bid to launch new motor car technology and there was a possibility of a South Korean withdrawal at this time. With the collapse of Daewoo and the takeover of the main company by General Motors (GM), the Romanian government was left with responsibility for Craiova. Most of the suppliers were kept on, but employment at Craiova was reduced to 4,000 in 2002 and subsequently to 3,600. The factory supplied the Cielo, Matiz and Nubira to the home market – and gained about one sale for every two by Dacia – but plainly needed new models to boost exports. Although the Tacuma was hailed as an innovation 'saving the company from drowning' in 2002, at a time of sluggish home sales, little further mention has been made of it and (like the Lanos) it was evidently not assembled in 2003 as once projected. Meanwhile, production of the Tico ceased in 2002, and the Matiz was then offered at the same price as the Tico: indeed, the Matiz proved extremely popular – the best in its class (exports began in 2004) – along with the Cielo and the Nubira. Although Romania did not have to comply for another two years, Euro Three engines were introduced 2004 for the Cielo (with an LPG version that was a substantial boost for this model) followed in 2005 by the Matiz and the Nubira (the latter with an LPG version also) – still ahead of time. The Cielo was to continue for at least two more years towards the Euro Three deadline, with the Nubira and the luxury Laganza. Sales inched upwards from some 20,500 in 2002 to 22,000 2003 and 24,000 in 2004. Competitiveness comes from reliability, low maintenance costs and a good spares service through the current network of 83 sales and service centres, plus discount schemes and buy-back for new cars (with dealers selling the old vehicles secondhand with guarantees).

The Ford Takeover

The Romanian state acquired the Korean share of the j.v. in 2006 and set about privatising the company in 2007 with the prospect of competition between Ford and Renault–Nissan spiced by possible intervention of China's Chery Automobile and India's Tata. Ford emerged victorious as the sole bidder with a deal involving €57mln for the purchase of the plant plus an immediate investment of €675mln rising to €1.2bln by 2012; while the number of units should double over the 300,000 target for the first year with the workforce (which has already increased from 3,500 in 2005 to 4,000 in 2006) should reach 9,000. Craiova will certainly experience a property boom in housing and commerce in the Bănie area (where local businessman Constantin Dâlgoiu was farsighted enough to invest €9.0mln in the site of the old Tufon foundry business) and this should extend across the city boundary into Cârcea commune 10kms from the factory. Also more component manufacturers are likely to move in, such as Johnson Controls in respect of seating and carpeting as well as Kirkhoff sub-assemblies. It will also be interesting to see how land values increase from the present (2008) levels of €240/sq.m in Craiova and €25 in Cârcea. Finally it should not be assumed that greenfield car plants will not be set up in Romania in future. Currently Daimler (who separated from Daimler-Chrysler in 2007) own Mercedes-Benz and plan to supplement their Rastatt plant with a factory in Poland or Romania with the latter preferred on the grounds of logistics. Various locations have been mentioned including Cugir and Suceava, with Jucu near Cluj the most likely choice. And Romania is a possible engine factory location for Peugeot.

Other Vehicles

SUV Production by Aro Câmpulung

This 'Landrover' enterprise started at Câmpulung in 1957 and two-thirds of production was exported to about a hundred countries. But maintaining unsubsidised sales around the world after 1990 proved impossible and from 20,000 at its height employment slumped to 3,500 after a further 1,250 dismissals in 1997. New models emerged in 1999 with ISO9002 certification using imported or licensed engines from BMW, Chrysler, Daewoo, Peugeot, Renault or Toyota. Aro also organised collaboration with the French company Matériel et Appareillage Mécanique for trade with the French market including supply of Peugeot and Renault engines. And experts from Toyota and Mitsui studied collaboration possibilities for an Aro prototype with engine, gearbox and transmission from Japan. But numerous attempts at privatisation failed because the process was highly contested politically and substantial prices were expected; going well beyond what East European Imports (USA) was prepared to offer in 1997 on the basis of assembly of 1,000 Aro24s monthly at Brunswick (Georgia) combining a Romanian chassis with an American engine and transmission. Aro gained considerable experience as a small, flexible production facility using foreign engines including Ford, Toyota and Volkswagen in 1998, in addition to the Romanian-made Daewoo and the French engines already mentioned. But 1999 was a poor one for exports because of the severe financial restraints limiting the acquisition of engines. However, export orders were secured in 2000 from Bulgaria, the Czech Republic, France, Hungary, Norway and Slovakia, and also Argentina, Costa Rica, the Dominican Republic, Mozambique and Venezuela. This phase of resumed exports in 2001 was based on new engines to meet Euro Three pollution norms: a Renault turbo-diesel engine for the 10 type (with a new body design) and a new Toyota Andoria engine for the 24 type, with further new models in the pipeline: a 29 type pick-up truck with a 1.5t payload, to be followed by the 264 and 266 types. It was hoped that half the production would be exported by the end of that year through cooperation with interested companies in Switzerland, Turkey and the USA. It was also hoped that there would be continuing sales to Serbia reflecting quality and price; further penetration of ECE markets using a Toyota engine (also for the home market); and continuing sales in France using Renault engines: 16,000 over ten years or five per cent of the French 'all roads' market. There was also cooperation over auto moulds for Volkswagen vehicles and at this time of relative optimism Aro was included in the 2001 PSAL programme.

The Cross Lander Debacle. In 2002 there was a prospect of assembling the 24 type in Brazil, in the Manaus (Amazonia) assisted area, involving up to 10,000 vehicles within three years. This would arise through a j.v. named Cross Lander involving the Brazilian Group Samambaia and Lacaro Auto Distributors (USA). Seventy per cent of components were to be manufactured in Brazil, including some under licence from third countries (including a 2.8l engine licenced from an American company) while the body and chassis would be sent from Romania. Half the production would be exported to the USA, which is where Lacaro come into the picture, with possible marketing potential in other Latin American countries. There were plans for a new model based on the 24 type. In 2003, agreement was reached with Cross Lander to transfer technology related to the assembly of sub-aggregates for the 264 prototype, in the context of Aro's falling turnover (with losses of $30mln incurred in 2002). Production slumped, and during the first four months of 2003 turnover of $7.1mln involved losses of $3.0mln! Assisted by PSAL, the fifth privatisation attempt required Cross Lander to pay $150,000 for a 56.7 per cent of Aro plus non-returned credits and commercial debts of $11.4mln and a small investment (total $15.8mln), while over $10.0bln was to be invested in Brazil on the Cross Lander assembly unit. However, the privatisation proved problematic, with shortage of funds linked with poor sales and reduced deliveries generating further losses. Nothing was paid from 2003, with allegations of cheating by the company President John Perez for allegedly selling-off parts of the business. Cross Lander said that they had fulfilled all their obligations, but the sequence of events became highly confused and a $5.0mln investment for new technology, environmental protection and working capital in 2005 was missed. The privatisation was cancelled and the company was liquidated the following year: a sad end for an enterprise that could not attract a really serious foreign buyer linked with a realistic political consensus. The site is now an industrial park and there is interest from several companies who might continue the automotive tradition in some form: indeed one UK company has acquired the Aro name.

Truck Building: Roman Braşov

The Braşov lorry factory started up under communism in 1953 with the name Red Flag ('Steagul Roşu'), later changed to Roman: the name of the truck that followed the early Carpaţi and Bucegi models of 3.0t and 5.0t respectively. The enterprise has had great difficulty in holding its market without new models. No fewer than eight new models were considered for assimilation after 1989, culminating in a 'total multipurpose vehicle' in 1996: boasting 30 functions, this model incorporated a choice of foreign engine (Caterpillar, Renault or Steyr) and an Eaton (US) gearbox as well as new manufacturing technology (requiring $6.0mln of investment during 1995–96 alone) in a bold quest for export growth. The company also participated in international rallies including Dakar (1997), and arrangements were made with Navistar International Corporation (a major US truck producer) to equip lorries with the non-polluting 65hp Navistar engine, initially to be imported from the US against the prospect of Romanian components exported in exchange. Subsequently a j.v. was set up with Navistar for the manufacture of 160–370hp engines in Braşov to meet European norms and make Roman trucks competitive on the world market. Ten thousand engines were to be produced over two years, with 60 per cent of the necessary parts manufactured in Romania. Roman also won a contract with Pesaka Astana (Malaysia) in 2000 to supply 1,000 trucks over five years (including some exports to the Malaysian Ministry of Defence) while a Roman–Ikarus Autovehicle company (involving the Ikarus factories in Budapest and Székesfehérvár in 1999) produced buses for Romania and for export. Another opportunity lay in car components, quantities of which were produced for Belgium, Denmark, Hungary, Italy, Spain, the United Arab Emirates and the USA by 2000.

The Mirage of Privatisation

In 1999 the state holding of share capital was increased by 20mln.lei to finance truck production in the hope that European production standards would make Roman more attractive in the context of PSAL in 2000. In 2001 it was one of the largest companies in the hands of APMSH (8,600 employees, down from 21,000 in 1990) but struggling against stiff competition and falling production (430 trucks in 2001 represented only five per cent of the 1989 level) and a heavy burden of debt ($140mln) in the form of bank loans and interest. Restructuring and privatisation, actively sought from 2000 onwards, was allegedly delayed by 'managerial hesitations' and powerful union opposition, leading to special administration in March 2002 with the imminent risk of bankruptcy eased by BCR credits. The strategy in 2002 was one of hiving off sections as separate companies to repay debts, with privatisation of the core to follow; and under PSAL, Pesaka Astana was prepared to pay a single euro for the plant plus

€45mln of debts and non-returned commercial credits and a commitment to spend €4.0m on environmental investments. Privatisation in 2003 would also be linked with an industrial park that would rent the surplus space and help to provide new jobs for those laid-off by the truck company. At the time MAN (Germany) were interested in assembling trucks in ECE with a view to selling 15,000 vehicles to the region each year from 2007. Romania was not chosen and the Roman option may well have been declined (against the greenfield alternative) due to the high upgrading costs as well as the radicalised work force. Liquidation proved the only option, with local magnate Ioan Neculae acquiring the bulk of the old platform in 2004 to create a new 'Autocamioane şi Autobuze' business, with some 3,000 qualified workers reportedly re-engaged to make lorries and buses for military use in Afghanistan and Iraq on the basis of tendering organised by the USA in 2005. The Romanian military could be another source of business along with Asian markets in general. Evidently $100mln of business in 2006 made the venture profitable after a loss in 2005.

Buses: Rocar (Bucharest) and Robus (Reşiţa)

Rocar was set up in south Bucharest under communism and went into transition as the maker of urban and inter-city buses as well as tourist coaches, trolley-buses, minibuses, ambulances, vans and station wagons at prices 20–30 per cent below those of West European competitors. Links with Mercedes-Daimler emerged in 1994 (after the company had previously failed to make progress with Roman Braşov in 1991) but the joint building of a modern town bus – designed for use in Eastern Europe and manufactured in Turkey by Mercedes Benz–Turk – contemplated in 1996 as a means of gaining some assembly work failed reportedly for lack of space. And the company developed a new bus in stainless steel with a MAN engine and Voith gearbox in 1997, when the Bucharest transport company RATB was looking for 300 new buses and Rocar competed with Ikarus, Mercedes, and Volvo. Rocar also hoped to sell 200–300 buses to Africa in 2001, following contracts with Saudi Arabia and Venezuela: high quality vehicles at half the cost of MAN, Renault or Škoda products while fitting engines of these companies' provenance. But evidently no links have come to fruition and the company became insolvent in 1992. Meanwhile the Reşiţa engineering enterprise UCMR has allocated a hall at Mociur to the Robus company which was set up in 2006 (with partners from Hungary, Russia, Serbia and Slovenia) with the aim of producing price-competitive urban/inter-urban buses under a Russian licence, but incorporating Euro Four UK or US engines. 200 buses are planned for the first half of 2007, facilitated by the Russian partner's commercial and technical experts placed at the factory on an on-going basis. This is an entirely new line for the Reşiţa engineering complex which has not previously been involved with motor vehicle building. Finally, Automecanica (Mediaş) builds special vehicles for maintenance and technical assistance using standard truck chassis from Roman and materials from Alprom, Petrotub and Sidex. Fuel distribution companies are supplied, as are the military and road maintenance teams.

Tractors and Farm Machinery

The Braşov Tractor Factory (UTB)

Manufacture of tractors started in Braşov in 1946 at what became the Ernst Thälmann plant (in memory of the German socialist) before reverting to 'Tractorul'. It became a major loss-maker after 1989, and despite attempts at restructuring from 1994 debts rose to 15mln.lei in 1998, whereupon nine auxiliary activities were hived-off from the core business the following year. Exports included annual sales to the USA of 2,500 and Turkey of 5,000, although allegedly the figures might have been 3,500 and 11,000 respectively given more money to finance greater production: hence the 1.5mln.lei credit from RDB and a $2.0mln loan from a Viennese bank to produce for export in 1998. And arrangements were made to deliver 1,125 tractors to USA in 2002–3 under a contract with the US Company Long Agribusiness. Meanwhile the home market was depressed, with only 1,300 tractors sold in 1997, against a potential demand for 10,000 annually (based on agricultural needs). From 1997, government envisaged subsidies of up to 40 per cent to assist farmers to buy tractors, with further work related government orders, but the scheme could not be financed and instead facilities were advertised in 2000 for purchase by instalments or in exchange for agricultural products. In this connection a company was set up to store and market cereals received through barter, with five shareholders drawn from tractor and farm machinery producers: UTB along with Aro (Câmpulung), Hart (Miercurea Ciuc), Mat (Craiova) and the National Land Improvement Company, although it does not appear to have operated on any significant scale. However, a useful innovation was the production of equipment for small farms: a 17hp Titan 2,000 tractor was launched with a Lombardini engine and gearbox, plus a range of compatible equipment, including a trailer of 750kg capacity, a plough, a cultivator and a bulldozer blade. The equipment was suitable for smallholdings and could be secured with monthly instalments of 130lei through county agriculture departments in 2001. Meanwhile, UTB developed contacts with Fiat (Turin) in 2001 to reactivate cooperation dating back to the 1960s, possibly through a j.v. with a Fiat majority shareholding or Fiat purchase of the factory.

Interest from Landini and Mahindra. Under the second PSAL a deal was actually struck with Landini (Italy) to sink €45.25mln into Tractorul (€28mln for investment plus €17mln for debts and unpaid credits in addition to the purchase price of €250,000) but with no immediate reduction of the 3,300 work-force. But the deal was declined (amidst claims that the accord was not adequately respected on the Romanian side) despite a partial debt write-off and arrangements for subsidised sales to Romanian farmers. Other offers came from Italy and Turkey, with Mahindra & Mahindra (India) the most likely foreign buyer against the domestic challenge from Myo-O, the agricultural machine maker referred to below. While the company has debts of 614mln.lei ($208mln) plus 550mln.lei for delayed payments to suppliers – and continuing losses amounting to 66mln.lei in 2004 – Mahindra are keen to penetrate West Asian markets while securing a low-cost manufacturing base for Western Europe and the CIS. However all these hopes were disappointed. With only 750 tractors sold in 2006 (370 of them under special subsidy arrangements) it seems clear that relatively high fuel consumption – still 20l/ha: down from 35 but still high compared with the attractively-priced Czech 'Zetor' offering 'western technology for eastern prices' – requires new prototypes and diversification (to offer both high and low capacity) for which the required €10–15mln is simply not available. The enterprise then went into voluntary liquidation with the remaining workforce of some 2,000 laid off. The factory site has been acquired for development by Flavius Investiţii owned in Cheyne Capital (a UK investment fund). Meanwhile, other Romanian producers operate on a much smaller scale. Craiova Agricultural Machinery and Tractor Company exported a high-power tractor in 1996, with a 195hp engine produced in Braşov (while looking abroad for the same engine at a lower price), while 15–25hp tractors were made by Praser (Călăraşi) in co-operation with China in 1997. Also, after poor sales forced a drastic reduction in employment from 5,000 to 800 in 1999, Mecanica Ceahlău (Piatra Neamţ) was successful with ecological tractors of 46hp with a Euro-Three engine from a company owned by Detroit Diesel. Thirty per cent of Ceahlău's production was exported, mainly to Argentina, Hungary, Sweden, Russia and the USA in 2001. It also formed a strategic alliance with Strojna Industrija (Slovenia) in 2002 to manufacture new products and serve joint interests in international markets.

Agricultural Machinery

Particular reference should be made to Semănătoarea (Bucharest), established in 1949 through the rationalisation of workshops previously owned by Fichet, Nibo and other private companies. Initially simple equipment was produced for animal traction but in 1968 the self-propelled 'Gloria C12' harvester went into serial production under a Laverda (Italy) licence. By the 1980s, 10,000 harvesters were being produced annually by a work-force of 7,400 in the 40ha factory complex with railway access in central Bucharest. But restructuring has been a painful process. By 1996 production was down to just 350 harvesters with only 2,680 employed, although there were plans for irrigation installations and a range of small- and medium-capacity harvesters for a diverse range of crops in plain and hill environments. At this point, New Holland (Fiat Group) offered to invest $50mln in combine harvester production, but workers objected to redundancies and management also adopted a confrontational attitude. Rather than negotiate directly with New Holland, the government sensed hostility by machinery importers whose 'supremacy' was threatened by the company's intention to produce their combines 50 per cent cheaper in Romania; while in 1997 the union demanded privatisation by tender with a quota of shares and voting rights on the management board. The deal was abandoned but this eventually led to a threat of liquidation after the EMBO option was declined. In 2001, with the firm now in the grip of bankruptcy, a local buyer – the Romanian Myo-O company, created in 1993 as a distributor of farm machinery and one of Semănătoarea's old dealers – offered to invest $1.2mln, with the prospect of much more a further in the future. New SEMA 10 and 140 combines were launched in 2001, costing $41,000–50,000 – a third of the price of imported machines – with the eventual prospect of matching the price of second-hand machines from abroad. The owner consolidated production to free space for foreign company partnerships but the under-use precipitated a relocation decision with sale of the site for redevelopment. Among other companies, Metalurgica (Reghin) serves private farmers: e.g. animal-driven equipment such as a two-row maize-sowing machine and a maize-weeding machine in 1996.

PRODUCTION OF COMPONENTS

Romanian Companies

This section highlights several cases of where Romanian companies have been able to develop to keep pace with the requirements of the vehicle builders through capital investment and collaboration, especially with foreign companies. In the field of plastic and rubber parts, several domestic companies developed in close proximity to the Craiova and Mioveni assembly plants (Nica-Guran 1998): Flexiplast and Rolast in the Piteşti area close to Dacia, and Spumoplast in Craiova, with products including carpet and polyurethane that formed the basis of a j.v. with Daewoo in 1996. There are also links with Aro and Roman. From 1989 fortunes improved with new management and collaborative links with Romanian factories of similar profile, such as Spumoplast's link with Subansamble (Piteşti) that in turn started a j.v. with the Belgian Solvay Group (world leader in polyethylene fuel tanks) to produce and market plastic fuel systems for the car, truck and tractor industry in 1999. Resources for qualitative improvements are obviously crucial. An electric wiring company in Târgu Mureş established in 1950 was absorbed by Electromureş in 1969 but then separated in 1995 as Romcab, and when Paneuro became the majority shareholder in 1999 there were technological improvements in 2000, a quality management system in 2002 and a new car wiring extrusion line in 2003; while Paneuro itself developed a national network for import and distribution of car parts through agencies and associates from a 5,000sq.m. warehouse in Târgu Mureş in 1995. Electroprecizia (Săcele, Braşov) began manufacturing electrical sub-units for the Daewoo Cielo because, thanks to an SOF credit, prototype starter and alternator units were tested in 1997 prior to mass production (with updating in 1999). The company has cooperated with China in 2001 over new technology for electrical equipment and asynchronous engines. In 1991, Iorom began making truck parts in Timişoara but developed primarily by distributing parts for all vehicle types, with stores near Bucharest (Săbăreni in Joiţa commune) and in Iaşi and Timişoara.

Gerom (Buzău) is Romania's largest glass-making company, producing windows for all models of cars made in the country (as well as bottle production, including producing eco-friendly glassware to replace plastic bottles in 2002). And a new factory for car industry sintering products – sustained by a $20mln investment based on a credit from Fortys Bank (Belgium) – has been opened in the Giurgiu free zone by Contransimex of Bucharest (a state company created in 1971 and privatised by EMBO in 1994, with diverse interests in building, international road transport, container fabrication, plus the treatment, bottling and marketing of Biborţeni mineral water). Having participated in the rehabilitation programme for railway carriages, the company has negotiated with SNCFR (developing a programme with Siemens) over the future use of sintering products. Meanwhile Sinterom (Cluj – part of the Serviciile Comerciale Române Group controlled by Cluj businessman S. Vuza – was producing parts for the Logan and also for Bosch and Caterpillar in 2004. Cugir Mechanical Works has collaborated with Mercedes since 1995; after installing new technology, the factory produces gear wheels and other components. Co-operation with Japanese companies also became a possibility in 1998. Conductoare (Buzău), a cable maker founded in 1975 and privatised in 1991, sought work for Volkswagen in 2003. It is also worth mentioning design companies such as Delta Invest, established in Mioveni in 1994 for design and moulds for plastic components: it now gets work from abroad e.g. ABB France outsourcing design and production of elements for their robotics business.

Compa (Sibiu)

This company has achieved a much larger scale of activity, originating in the private Datky company in 1886 that became a state-owned metallurgical plant in 1948, concerned with armaments, tractors and farm machines. As 'Uzina Automecanică', in 1964 the company shifted its focus to car parts and household appliances: using Romanian spring steel from Târgovişte, rods and wire from Câmpia Turzii, along with bearings and forgings from the Braşov-based companies Roman and Rulmentul to supply the vehicle industries – Aro, Rocar and Roman as well as the car plants – with springs, engine valves, injection pumps and windscreen wipers. Restructured as Compa Sibiu in 1991 and fully privatised by 1999 (with the employees' association the majority owner), it was then the largest component factory in Romania, producing dampers for Dacia and Mercedes (with German ISO 9001 and 9002 certification) and a range of other products – including springs, brake gears and cylinders, shock absorbers and steering columns – for all branches of the automotive industry and for the railways. The search for assistance over state-of-the-art technology to continue development programmes, including assimilation of spare parts for Dacia, Daewoo and Tractorul, led to links with Krupp in 1996 and culminated in the j.v. ThyssenKrupp Compa Arcuri in 1998, between Compa Arcuri Sibiu (27 per cent) and ThyssenKrupp (73 per cent), making shock absorbers for Aro, Dacia and Daewoo, but with 60 per cent of production exported to Jaguar and Mercedes Benz, also reflecting Compa's policy of reducing costs with a reorientation for foreign markets through partnerships with prestigious German companies (although cooperation with Japanese companies was also seen as a possibility at that time). The German partner then turned Compa into the main European producer of lamellate springs (with production exceeding 30,000 tonnes per year in 2000) not only for existing customers – Mercedes Benz and Daimler–Chrysler – but potentially Ford, MAN, Scania and Volvo as well. In 2001 ThyssenKrupp Romania planned further investments in car springs and shock absorbers to turn the factory into the largest of its kind in Europe (although the ThyssenKrupp truck springs factory in Sibiu has been taken over by Styria Federn of Austria). But Compa's exports are also linked with agreements with Piroux Industrie and Bergerat Monnoyeur (France), while the partnership over steering gears concluded with Koyo SMI (the French bearings maker and a traditional provider for Renault) enabled Compa to resume supplying Dacia, with involvement in the launch of the Logan. Fiat gets spare parts from Romania through CLR Denis Montaj (Bocşa), assembling bolts with the latest equipment and technology, Fiat's own raw materials and rigorous quality control. Employment was set to rise from 26 to 150 (in 2000) with rising production.

Foreign Takeovers

There are cases where foreign firms have taken over Romanian firms in preference to greenfield developments. Italy's Magnetto group acquired a majority stake in the 'Roţi Auto' car wheel company of Drăgăşani in 2000 and invested €24mln to upgrade production during 2002–4 to 1.5m wheels, with attention to information, quality control, management and accountancy; this should start to generate profits in respect of its business with Dacia, as well as exports to Hungary, Poland and Ukraine which have now justified a third production line raising capacity to 5.0mln (half for Dacia). Michelin started a programme in 2001 to double production over three to four years in plants acquired in that year from the Tofan group, a Romanian company set up in 1992 to buy, restructure and re-equip tyre factories in a pollution-free environment (securing ISO14001 environmental certificates from the British Standards Institution for all its units). Tyres for cars and vans are made by Victoria (Floreşti) and for trucks at Silvania (Zalău) where Michelin have now opened a new steel cord factory. The company also controls the Automaxima distribution network and the Recap company for retread tyres in Bucharest. Pirelli is also making metallic cord (one of the key elements in tyre production) on the premises of Cord (Buzău), established in 1976 on the basis of a GCR Italy licence and privatised in 2001 as a j.v. with the Russian–Bulgarian consortium EP Commerce. Pirelli does not intend to make tyres in Romania but is improving its distribution network and has also launched a major new cord project at Slatina in cooperation with Continental.

Greenfield Projects with FDI

There is also scope for relocating production in engineering from Western Europe to reduce costs. Initially Hungary offered better quality, but rising labour costs have given Romania greater opportunity in recent years, and foreign capital is now enhancing efficiency. Thus Solectron (Timişoara) has been granted appropriate quality recognition by ISO and the International Automotive Task Force (including BMW, Daimler–Chrysler, Ford, General Motors and Volkswagen), though the factory was taken over by Singapore-based Flextronics in 2007 after losses of €5.3mln during 2005–6 when employment was reduced by a quarter to 2,100. Parts for the automotive industry are prominent in Romanian international trade, with exports of €318mln in 2003 against imports of €213mln (a surplus of €105mln) and most trade is with Germany in both directions. Exports have grown from €90mln in 1998 and reached €600mln in 2004, although the import ratio (imports as a percentage of total trade) doubled from 1997–98 to 40 per cent in 2003. Moreover, for trade in vehicles there was a large import surplus of €652mln at this time, making it particularly important that Logan exports should do well and that more component manufacturing should be attracted to Romania. So far, it is the labour-intensive production that is being outsourced: cabling, steering wheels, upholstery, tyre cord (although there is also automotive software by Siemens), and western locations in Banat and Transylvania are particularly prominent, with some growth in Oltenia through the Pirelli–Continental project at Slatina and the takeover at Drăgăşani noted above. However, Romania is in competition with Bulgaria in such fields as customised software and electronic components for the automotive industry; and, with the component sector working at only 30 per cent of its potential, there is a danger that competitiveness over labour costs will be eroded in four to five years.

German Projects

These typically involve investments of about €100mln or more. Continental Automotive Products acquired a site of 170,000sq.m. that once belonged to the Timişoara Mechanical Works (UMT), a producer of heavy machines and mining equipment. Investment of $100mln in a 6,000sq.m. factory during 1999–2001 resulted in the employment of a thousand workers (500 in 2001) producing some 8.0mln tyres annually using the latest technology. This was after the investment had been threatened by the new fiscal régime at the end of 1999 preventing customs-free import of the ultra-modern tooling and thermo-power plant. Arrangements were also made with the city's Polytechnic University for a master's degree in tyre technology. The company will now increase tyre production in Timişoara to 10mln units a year and open a new factory in the city for pressure hoses and transmission belts, and another in Sibiu for braking systems. Along with other factories in Arad and Carei the total employment generated in Romania has now reached 7,500. Siemens Automotive invested DM120mln in a factory in Timişoara employing 500 workers to manufacture electronic parts for Daewoo Cielo cars in 1996; it also started producing software for the German vehicle industry in 2003 and plans a future headquarters in the city. Three medium-sized German companies should also be mentioned. After considering Sibiu, Suceava and Timişoara, INA Walzlager Schaeffler invested $150mln during 2002–6 in Braşov, with 3,500 jobs in bearings (anticipating cooperation with the local Rulmentul company).

Leoni Wiring Systems have transferred cable production from Eger (Hungary) to a new factory in Arad in 2000 (originally a German project but now part of the British Lucas company): the 6,000sq.m. factory employs 470 producing for car makers (including Rover in the past) and other customers. It is situated on the western side of the town for easy export by road. The company went on to invest €25mln in a second new factory in Bistriţa to produce circuit boards for BMW and Mercedes. Given the German tradition in the town, the location seemed acceptable for JIT delivery, with 2,500 jobs expected by 2005. And Lisa Draxlmaier began on a modest scale at Piteşti before expanding at Satu Mare in 1999, securing 2,000 jobs, a figure that could increase by a further 500 in the second stage. The investment was helped by the highly skilled labour in the town and the presence of German speakers. Further capacity was opened in Braşov and Timişoara, employing 1,000 at the latter, with a DM4.0mln investment to employ a further 300 in 2000. The company's East European headquarters will also move to Timişoara. Most recently, in 2004, 600–1000 jobs were created in Hunedoara. The company produces electric cables and systems for Audi, BMW, Mercedes and Volkswagen cars and the total of 19,000 jobs is largest attained in Romania so far by a foreign investor. Smaller German projects include a €17mln investment within the Arad airport zone by Bos Automotive (Stuttgart), producing car interior parts; Daimler-Chrysler created 3,000 jobs in 2004 at a gearbox factory on the Cugir industrial park; and in 2005 Bosch invested €15mln on a 25ha site in Cluj to employ 3,000 people making auto components (where Ruwel also intend to make an investment), while Marquardt Schaltsysteme started producing gearbox components in Sibiu in 2005 with a €20mln investment to employ 500 by 2008. Schlemmer is investing €10mln at Satu Mare in a greenfield cabling project to employ 80, and Stabilius have made a similar investment in a factory in Braşov producing springs and shock absorbers for car seats. In 2007 Optibelt announced a €20mln investment at Tăuţii-Măgherăuş near Baia Mare.

Other Firms

Montupet decided not to locate their €100mln factory for aluminium (including cylinder heads) in Romania, but another French project by Auto Chassis International (Renault Group) worth €68mln did go ahead at Mioveni. Autoliv (Sweden), a world leader in the production of car safety systems, started producing webbing and safety belts in Romania in 1997 for Dacia and Daewoo and went on to invest $1.5mln in 1999 in a factory in Braşov to produce safety belts and air bags, transferring production from Germany in 2005. The company now has an 18,200sq.m. complex in Braşov, enlarged from 500 to 1,200 workers with a $22mln investment. Siber Group (Amsterdam), producing engines and electric components for Bosch, Electrolux, Philips, Rowenta and Volkswagen, invested in Lipova in 1998 in order to export to Italy. EJBL (Austria) rented capacity in Timişoara in 1999 to produce cloth and leather materials for cars before moving to their own production hall on a 2.0ha site in a DM5.0mln development. Cabling factories by Zoppas Industries (Italy) – and Delphi Packard (USA) mentioned below have absorbed all the available labour in Sânnicolau Mare and attract other workers from Romania and also from Hungary (given cross-frontier cohesion arising from the local Danube-Criş-Mureş-Tisa Euroregion. Cefin (Italy), a distributor of Iveco trucks and Dunlop and Sava tyres, is active in Romania with a €4.0mln project for tyre distribution (both new and retread) and a service network for cars and lorries, starting at Otopeni, with Cluj, Constanţa, Deva and Braşov to follow in a total network of twenty by the end of 2006 (when further units will develop by franchise). They aim to take the lead in tyre distribution with production of 100,000 a year. Cefin – also active in Bulgaria and Hungary has a partnership with Marangoni Ringtread Systems Romania, turning out 400–800 retread tyres each month at Otopeni (with a Timişoara operation to follow).

A €40m steel cord factory opened in 2006 at Slatina (chosen for its low costs and rapid authorisation – as well as easy access to the assembly lines at Mioveni and Craiova) on a shared basis between Pirelli (80 per cent) and Continental (20 per cent): the 100,000sq.m. development (on a site five times this size) could employ up to 1,000 by 2010 (using advanced non-robotic technology) and increase metal cord production from 6,500 to 30,000 tonnes per annum through four growth phases to 2010. Initially only the finishing processes are operating, using imported material from Germany and Italy but 2.0m tyres should be produced in 2007 against a total capacity of 4.5 (90 per cent for export). Cord will be supplied to the region (with Continental interested especially in the Timişoara factory) by the two companies, which have co-operated since 1972. The Slatina project is now being extended through a second factory to take total tyre production from the initial 2.0mln (2007) to 8.0mln. Pirelli will recruit another 1,500 staff in 2008 although a proportion of the 500 skilled workers will be sought among Romanians in Italy. Spanish investments involve Automobile Componente Electrice (ACE) with a $20mln cabling factory in Cluj, with employment increasing from 1,600 to 2,000 in 2005 in four stages, and the company will build three new factories by 2011, transferring all production from Spain (while retaining a factory in Mexico); meanwhile Mapsa and MMF (Manufactura Moderna de Metales) are investing €10mln nearby at Turda to provide 250 jobs producing pipes and tubes; while Bamesa-Arcelor (Spain) are investing €30mln on a steel service centre at Topoloveni serving the auto/appliance industry. Other interests are located in Sibiu (Caucho Metal) and Timişoara (CIE-Matricom). A Swedish company from Trolleborg is to produce automotive anti-vibration parts at an undisclosed location, while the American company Delphi Packard, already present in Ineu and Sânnicolau Mare, plan to relocate all their French and Spanish production to Iaşi by 2010, starting with €100mln to employ 1,000 workers on diesel injectors and engine components. Japanese companies include Sumitomo Electric Wiring Systems, with car wiring factories opened since 2000 in Deva and Orăştie (producing for Renault and Honda) followed by a €7.0mln investment at Alba Iulia in 2004; and Takata Petri transferred the business of putting leather covers on Mercedes steering wheels from the Czech Republic to Arad in 2002 and then brought over the manufacture of the steering wheels themselves in 2004 in a €35mln investment. The production is geared to Audi, BMW, Iveco and Nissan as well as Mercedes. Yazaki (Japan) have a $16m project at Ploieşti park, while Hyundai (South Korea) opened a factory in Oradea in 1998 for electronic products, starting with TV sets and expanding into microwave ovens and car tape recorders, including radio tape recorders and CD players. Finally Colicab (Tunisia) have a €25mln project for cabling at Timişoara.

THE AEROSPACE INDUSTRY

In 1990 the aeronautics industry amounted to 17 companies and 33,000 workers with capacities roughly equal between Bucharest and the provinces. For Bucharest attention will be concentrated on Turbomecanica, set up 1975 to make aircraft engines and components with licences from Rolls Royce and Turbomeca (for Viper and Turmo engines respectively) and from Aerospatiale for Puma helicopter gearboxes and rotorblades; while struggling to produce all its components in-house which was hardly efficient. There are other Bucharest enterprises including Aerofina, Aeroteh, ICMAV and Metav. The provincial companies are: Industria Aeronautică Română (IAR) or Romaero based at Ghimbav, Braşov dating back to 1925 with an interest in helicopters and gliders and also the production of engines following the acquisition of a French Lorraine-Dietrich licence in 1927; Aerostar (Bacău) founded in 1953 as a repair factory only (at a time of Soviet political interference that temporarily stifled the Romanian aviation industry) before taking up manufacturing; and the Craiova aircraft factory (Avioane), created 1976 to build the IAR-93 in collaboration with the former Yugoslavia – a collaboration eventually hit by the UN embargo. These companies have worked mainly for the Ministry of National Defence but they are also involved in the supply of components as well as R&D and project coordination. In 1970s investment was grounded in the western technology of British Aerospace/Rolls-Royce: the ministry took 80–85 per cent of the output but there was some export to Iran and Iraq as well as Puma helicopter sales. But Russian know-how was sought in the 1980s when priority was given to paying-off foreign debts. In 1985 Turbomecanica began to cooperate with OMKB Omsk over a helicopter turbo-shaft and a separate facility was opened to avoid contact with western technologies. However this was not a good strategy because the revolution left Romania in 1990 with no ministry orders and no exports.

Upgrading

In the mid-1990s a number of upgrading programmes were under way: MiG21s occupied Aerofina, Aerostar (cooperating with Elbit of Israel) and Comoti R&D Institute of Bucharest; the IAR-99 trainer and attack jet fighter was handled by Aerofina, Avioane and Orcas; the IAR-93 fighter-bomber concerned the same three companies plus Aerostar; while Aerofina, IARB and a Piteşti company were involved with the IAR-330 helicopter in cooperation with Elbit. There were still hopes of selling Romanian aircraft and Expomil 1999 displayed several products including Aerostar's MiG-21 'Lancer', Avioane's IAR-99

'Soim' and IAR's IAR-330 Puma-Socat helicopter being further developed through a second prototype with a capacity to launch anti-tank missiles. There was also talk of a proposed aeronautic association to increase the sector's potential and maximise opportunities presented by Euro-Atlantic structures. But huge losses were sustained with no clear perspective for the future of this strategic industry and under the prevailing mentality it was assumed that the state would provide any necessary finance (e.g. for 75 per cent of the salaries of 2,500 Aerostar workers in 2001) and secure orders even though better quality aircraft could be secured from abroad. The big question by 2002 was whether the industry should develop a set product and look for a market or settle for strategic partnerships in respect of structures and sub-assemblies (like the niche found by Romaero) producing what the market required. Evidence suggested that Romania could hardly sell planes on her own given the sophisticated political lobby required: hence the strategy of linkage with large western companies through repair work and the supply of components and sub-assemblies. On this basis the major companies, including Aeroteh, Glar and the Company for Aircraft Economic & Technical Development came together in 1999 for efficient promotion, marketing and licensing to implement a national programme for aeronautics. This might enabled a relaunch 'towards 2005' but without large unitary programmes or stabilisation of the workforce at the prevailing level of 13,500. Some scope arose from trade-offs e.g. cooperation with UK over defence to offset Romania's purchase of two British frigates. BAE systems – managing the regeneration and upgrading of the frigates – will cooperate with Aerostar, IAR and Turbomecanica. Also, the European Aeronautic Defence & Space (EADS) company is supplying €650m of border security and surveillance equipment and will coordinate helicopter, sea vessel and equipment upgrading.

Industria Aeronautică Romană (IAR), Ghimbav, Braşov

IAR is the only civilian and military helicopter maker in the region (and the only factory in Romania) to have manufactured and exported Romanian-developed and Romanian-made planes. By 2001 the factory had manufactured over 370 helicopters under Eurocopter licences starting with Alouette Three and Puma licences in 1968 and 1976 respectively; also 850 gliders and motor gliders as well as 150 aircraft completely developed by Ghimbav specialists. In connection with Romania's acquisition of nine ATR 42-500 planes there was an agreement in 1996 with Sogema (a branch of Aerospatiale) to make 200 'shipsets' for 'Galaxy' business plane bodies and for the Israeli aircraft industry. And as a result of a link with Carpatair services in 1996 and their overseas orders IAR made subassemblies for Bombardier CL-415 planes built in Canada (and Craiova produced spare parts). However major decisions had to made in the late 1990s over the helicopter business with impending withdrawal of Alouette and Puma licences in 1997 threatening further export markets. At this time there was talk of cooperation with the Franco-German Eurocopter company, involving Aerospatiale and Daimler-Benz Aerospace (DBA) of Munich, over assembly of 80 Ecureuil helicopters on the lines already established for the Alouette and Puma; while in 1997 DBA were also interested in cooperation with IAR (and other companies including Aerofina, Avioane and Turbomecanica) over the 'Dornier' plane and helicopters built on 'purchase and offset' terms. Another idea was diversification into Volvo buses at a price of $140–150,000 per unit (much lower than in Western Europe). However President Constantinescu and some members of the government in power in 1997–8 were keen on relaunching economic relations with the USA through a takeover of IAR by a 51 per cent stake from Bell Helicopters. The Bell Cobra light assault helicopter (informally named 'Dracula') seemed appropriate for Romania's future role in NATO and could be manufactured at Braşov for the Romanian army by 2000. The fuselage would be made at Braşov while the engine, transmissions and other flight systems would come from Turbomecanica, with Bell supplying the high-tech equipment. Helicopters made in Romania could also be sold abroad, including ECE, Latin America and the USA. The deal was finalised in 1998 in respect of 96 advanced AH-1 Super Cobra-Dracula attack helicopters using airframe and engines by Bell-Textron and assembled in Romania. But the enormous cost of $1.45bln (against an annual defence budget of around 1.00bln) called for a bond issue launched on international capital markets. Some thought this price was far too high – including the finance minister D.Dăianu, who was forced to resign.

Eurocopter

Unfortunately the whole deal eventually fell through and left IAR in a situation where it could not be sustained by the Romanian army work, while lacking money to launch a new Romanian programme (and with only a small market in any case for combat helicopters in the event of purchase of a new licence). There was no prospect of a buyer which left the sole possibility of a j.v. for series production, spare parts and upgrades for Puma and Alouette Three helicopters compatible with NATO. On the strength of the good results achieved by IAR in upgrading the Puma attack helicopter for the Romanian National Defence Ministry, a Eurocopter Romania joint venture was set up in 2001 between IAR and Eurocopter (a subsidiary of the EADS company): the latter (holding 51 per cent) would supply advanced technology and a licence for the EC135 helicopter while Ghimbav (with 46 per cent – leaving three per cent for three private investors) would supply the production hall and licences for Puma and Alouette helicopters. This provided scope for revitalising sales of new Puma helicopters for domestic and foreign markets with the aid of the Eurocopter network and trading expertise – though IAR could not compete directly with Eurocopter. Moreover in 2000 there were hopes of supplying light civilian helicopters for the Ministry of the Interior and the Ministry of National Defence. With technology transfer for the manufacture of latest-generation equipment crucial for the company's future, IAR will produce EC-235-type light choppers for police and rescue work in Romania; and Eurocopter will gradually transfer to Ghimbav technical assistance activities for Puma and Alouette helicopters (but there were only two helicopters on the order book in 2002). It will also maintain and repair Puma and Alouette helicopters in respect of Romania's helicopter fleet. This work is currently going ahead in respect of the IAR-built air force/navy fleet of 330 Puma helicopters that involves cooperation with Elbit through a $25m contract for advanced avionic systems needed for the EADS system. This follows Elbit's input for MiG upgrades in 2001 and IAR-99 trainers in 2004 (while the Romanian airforce is now buying second-hand Lockheed Martin (USA) F16i and F16b fighters from Israel to replace its MiGs). As for foreign markets a $125mln deal was struck in 2002 to upgrade Emirates' fleet of 25 Pumas to the highest international standards over four years: 75 per cent of value for Romania after allowing for some work by Cubic Defence Systems/Rockwell Collins (USA) and Turbomeca (France). Two years will be required for R&D and certification and two years to deliver one helicopter per month. The contract is seen as the first step towards the relaunch of the Ghimbav plant within the Eurocopter consortium. Ghimbav began production of the IAR330 Puma naval helicopter in 2005 and the first three were tested in 2007 prior to entering service with Romanian frigates (for anti-submarine and rescue purposes) in 2008. It is claimed that the cost is half the €30mln needed to buy each machine abroad.

Privatisation Remains Elusive

The company is now more soundly based with some 73 per cent of its stock acquired by Britten-Norman (UK) in 1999 in a $80.5mln deal linked with new investment. This follows three decades of cooperation involving IAR production of Islander aircraft (enabling Britten-Norman to reduce their manufacturing costs for passenger and cargo planes made at Brasov), not to mention other UK links over the One-Eleven (Rombac) passenger jets built under British Aerospace licence. The company now operates with a profit centre for helicopters involving revitalised sales of Puma helicopters and licences for light civilian helicopters, with a new assembly hall opened in 2004 that could be used for EC-135 helicopters in addition to modernising Eurocopter helicopters and producing components. The factory is also fully competitive to work in the Puma market with upgrading through the Socat system to provide a modern combat support helicopter. In 2000 a fixed wing profit centre saw the launch of the two-seater IAR-46 designed and built by Ghimbav for pilot training, for sporting and entertainment use and also for monitoring and coastal patrols (with some export potential given US certification). Four were built for Romania's air-club and it is hoped that production may eventually run into hundreds. A third interest, that follows prototype testing in the UK, is IAR's dirigible airship linked with the Sky Cat Project conceived by UK's Advanced Technologies Group jointly with ten American and British companies. The contract, signed at the Farnborough Airshow, is worth $0.75mln and should facilitate the transport and landing of 200t payloads on desert or swampy terrain. It was also considered in 2000–1 that Sky Cat might also be built in giant form to carry 1,000t loads. This new generation of dirigible airships should fly in Romania in 2004 with IAR designing the cargo module. The company also supplies Sabca (Belgium) with 31 components for the Airbus A-380 under a $2.0mln contract; while also supplying components to BAE Systems (UK), Bombardier Aerospace (Canada) and Israel Aircraft Industries (for the Galaxy business plane in the latter case – under a $30m five year contract signed in 2001), along with wings for some Boeing aircraft. Romaero was also maintaining Boeing, BAC-111, MD-80 and BN-2 Islander planes in 2003 and diversified as a major producer of LPG cylinders. Even downsizing went on relentlessly from 4,300 workers in 1990 to 1,700 at the end of 2001 and 1,200 in 2005. A strategic investor interested in privatisation remains elusive but a major effort will be made in 2006 despite heavy debts to local utilities.

Aerostar (Bacău)

This company first produced school and training planes but it was certified as a MiG-21 repairer in 1972, while the first Romanian fighter (IAR-93) was launched in 1974 and four years later production of the Soviet Iakovlev IAK-52 training/acrobatic planes began under licence: 1,800 were built up to 1989 and 20 per year continue to emerge from a modernised production line, with modern versions for US and UK customers or variations such as the IAK-52W or IAK-51TW. But after 1990 Aerostar was selected to upgrade 100 MiG-21 fighters – and also made the variant MiG21 Lancer – capable of using both standard and latest-generation armament – in cooperation with Elbit Systems (Israel). Starting in 1995 with a World Bank project for 100 MiG-21 Lancer upgrades for the Romanian army using Russian R-73 air to air missiles, this now features the MiG-29 Sniper (meeting NATO's requirements for compatibility and interoperability) in cooperation with Daimler-Chrysler Aerospace (Germany) with standards raised through the 'A-E Electronics' j.v. launched with Elbit in 2000 for high-tech mechanical and electronic systems, following earlier collaboration. There is also a joint venture Aerothom Electronics with the French company Thomson CSF Communications for electronic products for communications and navigation. And the Bucharest R&D Institute (Comoti) is working on an upgraded engine design. Although the record was tarnished by the crash of some Aerostar-upgraded MiGs, the Bacău company gained international recognition in 1999 for its repair/updating activity as well as light plane manufacturing, electronic equipment and avionics. Aerostar have also repaired and upgraded 12 Croatian MiG-21s and built radar components under a Lockheed Martin licence in 2003. The company also makes landing gears and hydraulic, pneumatic, electrical and electronic equipment; also parts for Daewoo and work for agriculture as well as the metallurgical and oil industries.

Prototype Work

Since the early 1990s this activity has gone beyond four variants of the MiG-21 Lancer and one for the MiG-29 Sniper to include the IAK-52W, IAK-52TW and the Aerostar-01. The first flight of the IAK-52W aircraft took place in 2001 – a western variant of a well-known plane for training and aerobatics of which 1,800 have been built by Aerostar since the start of the 1980s. The first sale was made on the Australian market to Red Star Aviation (of Camden, New South Wales) and Aerostar hopes to exploit other western markets given the plane's safety record and its reputation in Western Europe and North America. The company would also like to collaborate with an eastern partner over a plane to be certified and sold on the western market and there is thought to be potential for the ultra-light (480kg) WT-01 plane: a low-priced two-seater family pleasure plane, designed and built entirely by Aerostar. It has made its maiden flight from Bacău (with the prototype displayed at the 2001 Paris Air Show) and – with a maximum speed of 170km/h and a price of $30–40,000 in 2003 – it could attract interest in North America, Europe, Australia and East Asia (a US order for 15 was secured in 2003). It is currently being built for a German partner. Aerostar is also the sole manufacturer of aviation hydraulic equipment for the IAR-93 (also the 99, 316B and 330) and IAK-52 (cooperating with India over dual use hydraulic equipment). It also produces defence systems and has set up a joint company with Stork Fokker Aerospace (The Netherlands) to make aircraft parts. The company was privatised in 1998 with Iarom (Bucharest) the main shareholder, although the state holds a golden share.

Avioane (Craiova)

In this case there has been a struggle to recover from the setback over cooperation with Serbia (arising from the UN arms embargo) through its training aircraft of 100 per cent Romanian design and manufacture: 15 planes were produced annually and supplied to the Romanian army or Warsaw Pact, but there was no market after 1989. However an IAR-99 prototype to meet western standards was shown at Băneasa and Farnborough 1990; and France in

1991. Collaboration with Israel produced the IAR-109 'Swift' in 1993 (exhibited in Singapore in 1994) but, after collaboration collapsed, the IAR-99 'Soim' (i.e. Falcon) was produced in 1996, with advanced avionics incorporating components from Turbomecania (engines), Aerostar (hydraulic systems) and Aerofina – with a maiden flight in 1997 followed by appearances at the Farnborough and Paris airshows in 1998. It is easy to fly and compatible with both eastern and western weapons systems. In 1998 the government approved a 17mln.lei factory update to assimilate new manufacturing technology and obtain ISO9001 certification. Much interest was shown by ambassadors of Latin American countries who visited Craiova in 1999 (also African & Middle Eastern countries) but no foreign or domestic orders transpired. Meanwhile the factory gained a railway order in 1998 to update coaches and hopes to retain such business. 2002 saw Avioane still hoping for an order of eight IAR-99 Soim aircraft linked with a foreign credit contracted by the Ministry of National Defence ($40m for Avioane but also benefit for Ghimbav and Aerostar) but the ministry started thinking about second-hand UK Hawk planes instead. Meanwhile the workforce has been radicalised by lay-offs reducing employment from 1,800 to 1,400. A McDonnell-Douglas delegation visited Avioane in 1996 in the context of possible Tarom purchase of their aircraft balanced by Romanian components and subassemblies but this contact did not develop.

Privatisation

This goal has not yet been achieved since the first failure in 2003 and renewed attempts in 2005 were compromised by the company's substantial debts of 5.5mln.lei. Progress remains elusive although interest is reported from Saab (Sweden) – already involved through subassembly deals with IAR in connection with Airbus A380 and the supply of aircraft for Carpatair – as well as AGI Group (UK) and Ramses Romania. ARSA stipulate that any buyer must submit an investment plan for modernisation and development for at least €5m extending over at least five years. Several foreign companies are interested including Aero Vodochody (Czech Republic), Alenia (Italy), Saab (Sweden) and Sabca (Belgium), as well as Metav (Bucharest) and others from Romania.

Turbomecanica (Bucharest)

This company is still concerned with the design, testing and production of aircraft engines (in competition with Pratt & Whitney, Short Brothers and Westland) with gas turbine aircraft engines a speciality (note the TurboIVC engine which involves the company in overhauls and component supplies). As already noted the company took out a number of licences for the manufacture and repair of engines, including one for the Rolls-Royce Spey engine in 1980 (in connection with the Rombac project). But the company is now best regarded as a component manufacturer e.g. helicopter mechanical components – gearboxes, rotor blades: parts for Rolls-Royce and mechanical assemblies for the IAR-33 helicopter. By the end of the 1990s, sales had been secured in the USA, Europe, with some success in the Middle/Far East (UAE and Israel) and Latin America and an intention to penetrate Africa and CEE – given the decline of the FSU market and lack of orders from the Romanian Ministry of Defence. Regarding NATO opportunities, General Electric Group aircraft engine division agreed to the manufacturing j.v. Turbomecanica Combuster Products in 2002 with Turbomecanica manufacturing combustors and other aircraft parts transferred from USA. A programme of re-equipment for higher productivity should help in penetrating new markets: a 0.2mln.lei investment envisages an experimental workshop and laboratory: now a production hall will be renovated and equipped to produce engine parts concerned with burning energy (for engines for medium-sized carrier planes). Turbomecanica also produces aerospace components and since 1998 has been a GE Aircraft Engines and Power Systems supplier; also a supplier for Boeing engines. In 2004 a long-term contract was signed for the supply of components to Rolls-Royce beginning in 2005. Privatisation was attempted after the failure to finance the Bell Helicopter deal (under which Turbomecanica would have built engines for Dracula helicopters) when GE announced it would buy a fifth of the stock, while Pratt & Whitney showed an interest in privatisation in 1999. Currently there is interest from Avion Systems (Israel). Meanwhile Aerofina, also based in Bucharest where it set up in 1980 for the design and fabrication of control systems, has had to go into railway work (for Arad, Griviţa and Paşcani) with reference to doors and windows. And the Metav company has now diversified as a business park near Băneasa, although the name appears as a possible Avioane buyer.

CONCLUSION

The chapter is clearly a story of two halves with a highly successful automotive industry that could yet include a new greenfield car plant (by Fiat) as well as expansion at Craiova and Mioveni (not to mention Renault's regional engineering centre and testing facility) and an ongoing second wave of investment by component suppliers. There is even a prospect of farm vehicle production at the old Aro platform in Câmpulung. Meanwhile the aircraft factories still await acceptable privatisation offers, with most current interest coming from the Czech Republic's Aero Vodochony company (with respect to Romaero and Avioane) but with no substantial employment increase likely.

6. A Traditional Growth Industry: Food, Drink and Tobacco

INTRODUCTION

This is a traditional sector that remains of key importance today, accounting for 57 per cent of all household spending (44 per cent in Bulgaria and below 30 in more northerly accession states). Also, in 2005 the UK's Economist Intelligence Unit estimated that Romanians spent $24bln on this sector (presumably including fresh produce) out of $57.4bln for all spending (though Romania's own National Institute for Statistics quoted $20.2bln and $44.0bln respectively with the latter including health and education. Furthermore while it takes some 4.0mln people to generate the 12–15 per cent of gross value added contributed by agriculture only 170,000 (admittedly full-time salary earners) contribute a further 8.0 per cent through processing. However the industry is not in the best of health. There was contraction after 1989 reinforced by the poor harvest of 1992 but growth returned in 1994. In any case the decline was not as steep as in some other branches so that the share of industry's value added rose from 17.0 per cent in 1990–2 to 25.4 per cent in 2000–2 with a peak of 27.7 per cent during 1996–8. Some local brands have gained a solid foothold while recovery has been further aided by FDI; partly linked with privatisation that took off from 1997, albeit at a slower pace than expected with 184 commercial companies sold by March 1998 while 240 still remained in state hands. Investment following privatisation has flowed successively into soft drinks, beer, bakeries, sweets and more recently dairy and meat products, although – encouraged by developing supermarket networks – there has been a preference for low risk/high value added ventures in alcohol, beer, coffee, soft drinks and sweets. Early in transition, the industry as a whole languished way below EU quality standards. EU 'Country Reports' highlighted a lack of transparency, with transfers to private owners without adequate capital and management skills, while the privatisation of grain storage enterprises did not encourage the emergence of fully competitive marketing channels accessible to private producers. On the whole the industry was slow to adapt to the restructured farm sector and exploit its export potential (mainly because of poor linkages both downstream and upstream). There has been a persistent trade deficit for food and beverages, especially for high value added processed products as opposed to raw materials where there is an export surplus. The overall gap amounted to some €1.0bln in 2005 – two per cent of GDP – with processed products comprising 43 per cent of imports but only 23 per cent of exports.

Stimulated by increasing purchasing power since 2000, growth has been crucially important in the run-up to EU accession and the removal of all protective barriers, with the added value of rising meat and milk sales to maintain the recovery of livestock farming (although agriculture in general needs stronger market-orientation and more value-added through business contracts with the food processing industry). Consolidation is awaited with many more mergers and acquisitions previously discouraged by uncertainties over raw material supplies and agricultural policy. Change may be anticipated especially in the meat industry where the top 10 firms hold only 31 per cent of the market at the turn of the millennium, compared with 55 per cent in milling/baking and dairying where there is better scope for development. This is partly related to privatisation that – at end of the 1990s – was relatively slow in such branches as fish (20 per cent), preserves (23) and meat (38) characterised by old technology and surplus capacity. Even in 2005 only some three percent of Romania's 2,170 meat and milk processing plants were complying with EU standards. More foreign investment is taking place and although the SME stake is contracting, more small firms have been taken over during the final pre-accession years: indeed there is an important role for SMEs in niche activities and a considerable number have been assisted by SAPARD. Moreover in 2003 a joint project between the Romanian government and the UN Industrial Development Organisation was launched to support SMEs in the food industry with €663,000 of funds for quality improvements, diversification and exporting for beef, dairy products, and processed fruit and vegetables. Overall the number enterprises has increased by 25.5 per cent during 1996–2005 to 10,841 while employment fell by 27.4 per cent to 204,600 with the employment per enterprise falling from 32.6 persons to 18.9 (significantly less than 32.0 applying to industry as a whole). However there are some very large firms like European Drinks, with three factories in Bihor county, and InterAgro – links cereal storage, milling and baking with a meat cannery at Poroschia (near Alexandria) and a group of factories in Zimnicea concerned with alcohol, milk, sugar and tobacco (also stakes in fertiliser production and the insurance market). Many Romanian companies have been acquired by foreign investors and Nestlé for one have expressed interest in going further.

DAIRY PRODUCTS

A review in 1997 referred to 51 companies handling 13mln.hl of milk for direct consumption or processing into fresh dairy products, including 120,000t of cheese, 80,000t of butter and 60,000t powder milk. At the time it was difficult to compete with subsidised imported milk powder from EU. Compared with Western Europe Romania had higher costs due to the large number of collection points and the use of small tankers (while Friesland have improved cooperation with farmers over this matter). There is also a problem of seasonality with tough competition for milk in winter while a summer surplus has to be used for powder manufacture and cheese which generate stocks that are problematic in terms of working capital. Only some 35 per cent of milk was being processed industrially in the 1990s because many small producers were selling milk in nearby towns unchecked in plastic bottles (likewise some cheese and cream): stopping direct sales would mean more milk for processors. It was suggested that milk for consumption would increase with privatisation along with dairy products but the growth has been somewhat delayed. Cheese production has increased from a low of 29,000t in 2000 but the 49,000t figure for 2003 is way below the 94,000t produced in 1990. Fresh milk products declined sharply from 4.26mln.hl in 1990 to 0.82 in 1998 before recovering (particularly in 2000–1) to 1.74 in 2003. But milk delivered by the processing industry fell catastrophically from 5.69mln.hl in 1989 to 1.17 in 2001 before starting a modest recovery to 1.44mln.hl in 2003 (Table 6.1). Dairy products are currently growing fast and increased their share of all food sales from 14.4 to 16.0 per cent in 2006.

Foreign Companies

€10–15mln was being invested annually in modern factories in the late 1990s when international companies arrived. Danone (France) entered the Romanian market in 1997 with imports and launched 'Delicios', 'Natural' and 'Natural de Băut' yoghurt in Bucharest in 1999 (processing milk from 25 farms) to claim half the yoghurt market in 2001, with 80 per cent recognition from Romanian consumers. Their $15mln investment (employing 300) was considered 'a genuine growth propeller' by the group that was also marketing fresh dairy products in Bulgaria, the Czech Republic, Hungary and Poland. Danone eventually lost their leading position to the Dutch company Friesland Coberco Dairy Foods acquiring Nutricia Dairy & Drinks in 2001: comprising Belcar (Deta), Industrializarea Laptelui (Târgu Mures) and Someşana (Satu Mare). They were already undercutting imported yoghurt in the mid-1990s but now diversified successfully into fruit yoghurts distributed nationally, with four factories employing 1,400 in all. There was also an interest in baby/invalid food, while further diversification arose from a 40 per cent interest in Napolact (Cluj-Napoca): a major ice cream company with a new factory in 2003. Friesland have now expanded their distribution to eastern Romania and are carrying out further updating. In 1998 the German Hochland company, based at Heimenkirch (Allgäu) specialising in cheese spread, purchased (from SOF) and

Table 6.1: *Production in the Food, Drink and Tobacco Industry (th.t) 1985–2005*

Year	A	B	C	D	E	F	G	H	I	J	K	L	M	N
1985	986	17.0	328	33.1	n.a.	n.a.	582	n.a.	87	5765	n.a.	5349	9847	32
1987	1006	20.0	393	42.3	n.a.	n.a.	646	n.a.	79	5530	n.a.	8055	10364	33
1989	686	8.0	248	48.0	n.a.	n.a.	693	n.a.	82	5687	n.a.	4632	10573	33
1990	947	35.0	270	28.7	2623	306	538	366	94	5222	4264	8221	10527	27
1991	855	22.0	236	26.5	3006	175	348	338	71	4084	2707	6944	9803	26
1992	623	11.0	216	19.8	2784	107	290	250	49	3843	1510	5739	10014	26
1993	626	9.7	213	20.7	2625	85	185	130	50	3188	1443	6549	9929	23
1994	601	4.8	194	16.4	2725	80	231	191	47	3855	1505	8425	9046	22
1995	604	6.0	224	17.4	3030	91	266	207	51	3964	2250	7351	8768	23
1996	607	4.4	236	21.9	3772	105	396	244	48	3491	2051	6709	8118	25
1997	496	3.1	246	25.8	3668	96	243	205	42	3070	1457	7314	7651	26
1998	374	1.5	173	36.1	2945	81	321	185	37	1864	825	5071	9989	29
1999	361	1.3	245	36.1	2763	83	246	114	31	1750	922	5661	11133	31
2000	259	1.5	253	38.0	2275	87	476	55	29	1608	905	5453	12664	33
2001	202	4.5	296	45.6	1382	101	493	74	36	1168	1306	5463	12663	39
2002	167	3.1	228	60.0	1297	109	514	66	43	1281	1665	5488	11627	35
2003	204	4.7	243	68.2	1603	115	460	59	49	1442	1740	5457	13292	36
2004	210	9.0	258	60.9	1828	145	506	50	53	1577	2708	7071	14406	35
2005	265	8.8	264	65.8	1742	166	539	64	61	1600	3171	2602	15295	33

Notes: A Meat; B Tinned and Semi-Tinned Fish (tinned only 1985–9); C Edible Oil; D Margarine; E Wheat/Rye Flour; F Confectionery and Pastries; G Sugar (all); H Sugar (from sugar beet only); I Cheese (th.t); J Milk (th.hl); K Fresh Milk Products (th.hl); L Wine (th.hl); M Beer (th.hl); N Tobacco
Source: Statistical Yearbooks: Table 16.3

updated the Sighişoara dairy in a DM20mln investment for high quality cheese production using German recipes (with local ones to follow). The factory is processing 50mln.l/yr of milk from local farmers, though (as in the case of other foreign investors) problems were encountered over the primitive methods of milk storage, collection and transport. Parmalat (Italy) negotiated with the local authorities in Timişoara for a j.v.with the local Untim company in which Parmalat Romania now has a majority shareholding and a $250,000 investment has given rise to UHT and pasteurised milk under a Parmalat licence. The venture includes cattle farms (20,000 animals) and production of fruit juice in Periam and Sânnicolau Mare; also a $50mln EBRD investment to help extend the range of products. A Danish company has opened a new milk powder factory at Rimetea (Harghita), close to an older factory dating back to 1954, while Tnuva (Israel) employ 300 at their €55mln milk and cheese factory at Popeşti-Leordeni near Bucharest (annual capacity 60mln.l) with a 35 per cent stake held by EBRD. It has also invested a further €5.0mln in its dairy farm nearby at Adunaţi-Copăceni, supplying a third of the milk required. It supplies the Bucharest area (including deliveries to supermarkets) and also distributes in Cluj and Timişoara. They also intend to double their product portfolio in 2008 through dairy desserts and niche products. Market leader for ice cream is Delta (Greece), who arrived in 1998 and spread through the Balkans (through Nestlé's company – based in Greece – which has offered €111mln for the Romanian business) while Unilever sell their Cornetto, Magnum and Vienneto brands.

Romanian Companies

These include Maralact (Baia Mare): a diversified business selling ice cream and yoghurt as well as milk, butter, cheese and cream. Supplied by local farmers and the former state farm of Ardud, it was able to provide some competition for Friesland at the end of the 1990s. Plarom (Arad) has expanded by acquiring the powder milk factory of Chişineu Criş (opened in 1975 but placed in conservation in 1994 due to a sharp fall in milk production) for conversion into an ice cream factory. An EBRD credit for the Mureş dairy in Târgu Mureş helped to upgrade production (with modern packaging for butter, powder milk and fluid products) and open an ice cream factory in Reghin, complete with sales vehicles and stands. Prodlacta (Braşov) is another example of a recently-privatised company that originated in the communist era or earlier. It was originally the Jensen dairy of 1900, nationalised as Industria Laptelui. It was privatised by EMBO in 1994 but is still managed by Mariana Eftimie and Eugenia Panait as in 1990. It produces milk, butter and cheese as well as ice cream (modernised with EBRD help) for a sales network in Braşov and surrounding counties served by refrigerated vehicles. Other prominent players in the ice cream market are located in Brăila (Mercur), Bucharest (Cam) and Piatra

Neamţ (Kubo) in addition to the foreign companies already referred to. Meanwhile SAPARD funding has also made a big impact e.g. InterAgro modernised the Zimnicea dairy in 2004 in a €2.5mln project with SAPARD assistance. Another example is the 10.4mln.lei investment at the Ilvas (Vaslui) milk products factory, opened in 1971 and acquired in 2002 by the Racova Group (a diverse business with hotels and trade interests, as well as dairy farms at Bădeana and Pogoneşti with 1,000 Holstein-Friesian cows). The Vaslui dairy was modernised to European standards with German and Italian equipment in 2003–4 with annual capacity increased from 50,000 to 120,000hl; followed by an integrated management system for quality and food safety in 2005. With improved collection and transport systems to boost export potential, milk and dairy products are sent to a warehouse in Bucharest and also to Bacău, Galaţi, Iaşi and Suceava.

As regards current trends, Albalact (Alba Iulia) is a particularly go-ahead company that started in 1999 when the state dairy (opened in 1971) was purchased by Petre Ciurtin (though it is now run by his son Raul). Faced with rising demand (with turnover rising from €2.3mln to €29mln during 2000–2006, arising in part from the success of 'Fulga' UHT milk) but unable to acquire another company with a similar profile, the family sold the old town-centre factory (in a rewarding land deal realising €6.0mln for 16,000sq.m) and started a €11mln project on the edge of the town, now being enlarged to 0.3mln.hl/yr. And because the milk collection system has fragmented, as the leading players look after their own requirements, it is necessary for dairies to depend more on their own farms: hence the company (which has been importing 15 per cent of its milk from Hungary) is spending €7.0mln to acquire new farms, in addition to the three which it already owns, but with a doubling of capacity at its Vaidei (Hunedoara) farm to 20,000l/yr, while maintaining existing contacts with local farmers. The aim is also to develop sales in southern Romania through a logistic centre near the capital at Afumaţi. Finally, there is a trend whereby Romanian dairies are producing for West European partners e.g. Lactag Câmpulung supply cream and yoghurt to Meggle (Germany) and also work for Nordex Foods (Denmark); while Covalact Sf.Gheorghe are linked with Campina (The Netherlands). There is also diversification (already evident in the case of Racova): dairy producer Dorna is growing 7,000ha of cereals on the Brăila Great Island under a three-year lease from the State Assets Agency which includes investment of up to €3.0mln in 2008 for irrigation and other infrastructure. It is unclear how far there is still a role for small producers; although in 2002 the agriculture minister (I.Sârbu) encouraged local communities to come up with programmes to promote local specialities (such as cheeses in the Sibiu area) and secure the domestic market.

SUGAR

This is a classic case of an industry that developed under the cover of total protection afforded under communist central planning. 6.77mln.t of beet was harvested in 1989 but the impact of globalisation was devastating, despite calls for a ceiling on duty free imports and reduced VAT on sugar, because the harvest fell to 3.28mln.t in 1990 and then averaged 3.03mln during 1990–8 with the exception of a particularly poor year in 1993 when an extremely small area of 97.2th.ha yielded 1.78mln.t of beets (18.3th.kg/ha) processed for just 129th.t of sugar: the combined production of 33 companies (of which only four were privatised at the time) with a total beet processing capacity of 8.5mln.t/yr. Rationalisation reduced this to 50th.t/day in 19 factories (or from 8.5 to 6.0mln.t/yr) which meant that many state processors were forced out of business. Even so there have been losses for the regional holding companies. When 2.84mln.t of beet were processed in 1996 (still only 60 per cent of 1991) due to reduced cultivated area, the domestic sugar production of 450,000t met only 52 per cent of home market requirement. The rest was imported at costs below that of Romanian production: $342/t on the London and Paris exchanges compared with $395 at the Oradea factory gate and national exchange prices $434–468 (reflecting intermediary chains between producer and customer). Higher costs arose partly because Romanian factories had lower extraction rates than those in other CEFTA states and needed modern equipment. Further problems arose through floods in 1998 when only 108.5th.ha out of the total of 121.7 cultivated could be harvested; with further losses for the Carei, Luduş, Târgu Mureş and Teiuş factories that had invested in seed, fertilisers and pesticides. With only 225,000t sugar expected against consumption of 420,000t five factories were geared to processing imported crude sugar that was coming in duty-free from Moldova (including some re-exports of Ukrainian sugar).

Foreign Companies

These have been prominent in privatisation. Sucrière Cooperative de Bazancourt (France) bought half of Zahar (Arad) for $8.1mln, of which $6.1mln was the value of a two-year investment programme (with 30 per cent dedicated to imports of materials and seeds for a relaunch of sugar beet production). The move was linked with the objective of self-sufficiency in sugar compared with a 50 per cent level in 1997. The French see a problem in the lack of a legal framework to protect domestic sugar production (for the world market price of $250/t prevents competition by a European producer; especially with high energy costs). The factory made agreements to process Hungarian beet from Békés. Man (UK) bought Zaharul Mureş (Târgu Mureş) in 1998 with a supply area of 8,000ha in Alba, Cluj and Mureş). Tate & Lyle's Cukrownia Grabow Lublin acquired Zaharul (Buzău), which was opened in 1971 and diversified in 1991 with acquisition of the soft and alcoholic drinks section from Sucros (Râmnicu Sărat). The aim in 1998 was to introduce modern technology on farms (including mechanised harvesting) as well as the factory. But Agrana Zucker (Austria) played a major role in privatisation by first taking majority holdings from SOF in the Beta (Ţăndărei) and Urziceni factories for $11.25mln plus debts. The Austrians were keen to settle debts, update the factories and support local beet producers through consultation and financial support. They also campaigned for fiscal measures against imports and productivity growth in the sugar beet industry. Agrana later bought the Zaharul (Buzău) and Danubiana (Roman) factories, paying $9.0mln for a half stake in the former case, but sold Urziceni to local interests (after it had originally been abandoned by the state due to financial inconsistencies). In 2004 Agrana Zucker combined their three Romanian companies to form Zaharul Românesc, thereby reducing costs and increasing competitiveness. Currently Agrana's factories (including a sweets factory at Roman and a starch/glucose factory at Ţăndărei) hold a third of the market, with an investment programme of €30mln from Raiffeisen/Creditanstalt (on top of a previous €50mln) to invest in raw materials, higher quality production and diversified products/services. Foreign capital has also been invested at Zahar Oradea in favour of French-German Cristal Diamant Group.

Recent Trends

But privatisation has now taken place throughout the industry as a means of overcoming financial blockages and generating capital for modernisation. With around a dozen further factories to be accounted for it is impossible to be comprehensive but Marr Sugar took over at Urziceni in 2002 and reopened the factory the following year after a major modernisation programme while InterAgro now run the Zimnicea factory. Other prominent players are the companies at Bod, Călăraşi, Corabia, Luduş and Paşcani; while it is probable that some other units like Bucecea, Carei, Lechinţa, Sascut and Teiuş have closed. Programmes have been launched to stimulate farmers with help over seeds, fertilisers, herbicides and irrigation equipment. A good example was set by Nectar (Paşcani) that gave growers free seed plus 50kg of sugar for each tonne of beet delivered: this helped to increase the area sown in Iaşi county and the surrounding counties of Bacău, Botoşani and Neamţ. More efficient use of energy is important because power represented 20–25% of the cost of sugar at the factory gate in the late 1990s when the government was under pressure to impose further increases. Higher yields were obtained in 2004 with 5.0t/ha after only 2.6 in 2003. But whereas sugar from beet was expected to double in the late 1990s, the situation deteriorated to 1.41mln.t in 1999 and an average of only 0.81mln during 2000–3. Competitiveness is a problem with Romania the only country unable to meet its EU quota: 329,000t with 109,000t from beet. Sugar consumption in 2004 was 570,000t: 50,000t from Romanian beet; 80,000t from imported beet and 440,000t imported raw sugar. Capacity might decline to four or five factories, but no recent closures are reported.

Sugar-Based Products

Products like chocolate and sweets involve a handful of companies producing 100,000t of sweets in 1997. The complex history features the Bucharest companies of Peleş (1914) and Nicolae Anghelescu (1920) brought together as the nationalised IISB by 1954. But Braşov can claim to be slightly ahead through the 1889 Frank chicory processing factory – a subsidiary of Heinrich Frank (Linz) – and enlarged as Frank Kaffe in 1940 (amalgamated with the Inka factory opened in 1920) and subsequently nationalised as part of Avantul and later as Cicoarea (that also included the Zamfirescu business established in the town in 1912). Privatisation then featured Kraft Jacobs Suchard (KJS) who purchased Braşov's Poiana Produse Zaharoase in 1994 and invested $22mln in modernisation and marketing (they now own 82 per cent of the shares). In the mid-1990s Mars (UK) and Nestlé (Switzerland) were also active on the Romanian market but did not have production facilities. A further $7.0mln was then spent on launching the new Milka chocolate (as well as Poiana Suchard) while Jacobs 'Kronung' coffee was relaunched in 2001 with new packaging and design, along with soft drinks. KJS became the first confectionery manufacturer in Romania to receive ISO9002 certification (gaining recognition for both domestic and international markets) joining over 60 other Kraft Foods International companies; while employment was reduced slightly from 1,220 to 1,020 mainly by retirement. The company provides facilities for staff and is involved in the community e.g. through child nutrition educational pilot programmes during 1998–2000 with support from N.N.Paulescu Institute of Nutrition & Metabolic Diseases. It has also organised a Sweets Festival in Braşov – dedicated to Children's Day and five years of activity for the company in Romania (also 100 years of chocolate production in Braşov) – and opened 'Silvana Castle' in 1999 as an entertainment space for children in Titulescu Park. Competition for chocolate now comes from Stollwerck who opened a sales office in 1997 and planned to open a chocolate factory in Romania in 1998 with a DM20mln investment over five years in collaboration with a Romanian partner; while Nestlé's interest was extended through the Czech chocolate maker Cokoladovni Prague (80 per cent owned by Nestlé and Danone) operating through its trading company Mega Tech in respect of sweets with high vitamin content and other special products. Alka (Alka GM Amir Krenzia) produce Kandia Excelent chocolate (after a merger of Kandia and

Excelent in 2004, with a subsequent takeover by the UK company Cadbury Schweppes) as well as Gold Mocca coffee and Alka wafers. Kraft import their chocolate from Germany but will start doing some production in Braşov – and after acquiring Danone's 'cookie' business globally they now intend to develop this product extensively in Romania.

MILLING AND BAKING

In 1997 the key milling and baking sector (accounting for 22 per cent of all spending on food) was headed by 17 large companies producing 11,300t of bread daily and 650t of biscuits and pasta (with a 50 per cent increase expected in the latter case during 1996–2000). Privatisation occurred through EMBO after 1989, subsequently boosted by mass privatisation. It led to increased productivity and lower energy consumption thanks to new equipment from Italy (Pavan) and Switzerland (Buchler) installed at Bacău, Cluj and Craiova – presumably to replace Pavan paste machines of late 1960s vintage (subsequently built in Romania under licence in the 1980s). Meanwhile the grain market formerly dominated by Romcereal was split into county Comcereals privatised after 1996. Emerging companies include Cargill (USA) which has 0.60mln.t of cereal storage capacity in Brăila, Călărasi and Corabia (Olt) plus networks in the counties of Dolj, Galaţi, Giurgiu, Ialomiţa and Teleorman counties (25 units in all) complemented by oil and fodder interests; while the very large, vertically-integrated Romanian company InterAgro has 0.72mln.t of cereal storage at 28 locations in Bacău, Ialomiţa, Prahova and Teleorman counties; also bakeries in Bucharest (two) and Ploieşti as well as Giurgiu and four towns in Teleorman: Alexandria, Roşiorii de Vede, Videle and Zimnicea. They are supplied by mills at Buturugeni and Zimnicea (the latter a new €6.0mln investment opened in 2003) which send their residual material to the group's pig rearing company Suinprod.

Foreign capital made its first major appearance through the Loulis Group (Cyprus) in 1999 when they acquired the Titan company of Bucharest (two years after it had first been bought by the Greek company Saint George Mills Commercial) as well as Mopan (Târgu Mureş) to complement their assets in Albania, Bulgaria and Greece. They also launched an investment in wheat and corn mills (including the first hard wheat mill in Romania) at the 100,000sq.m. Cernica complex opened in Bucharest in 2003. The company now produces bread (200t/day – enough for half the city's needs) and pasta as well as cornflakes and frozen dough (the latter sold with various fillings through the Loulis 'Belforno Fresh' chain for home cooking). Loulis have 22 per cent of the Bucharest bread market (43 per cent for sliced bread and 45 per cent for flour) after launching their 'Beforno' sliced bread and pasta, 'Fortza' breakfast cereal and 'Titan' flour through a retail network of 30 family stores in Bucharest. In this way 'Moara Loulis' was able to mount a challenge to the leading Romanian milling companies like Boromir, Craiova and Dobrogea. However, 60 per cent of Loulis was acquired in 2007 by Raiffeisen-controlled Leipnik Lundenburger Invest (LLI) Euromills who have restored the Titan name and have extended the Belforno shops in Bucharest from 30 to 50: serving up to 30 per cent of the city's packaged bread market they now account for 14 per cent of the firm's total turnover (up from eight per cent before).

Broadhurst Interests: Vel Pitar and Pangram

Vel Pitar is a dynamic business owned by New Century Holdings through the Broadhurst Fund. With a tenth of the bakery market, the business includes majority holdings in 10 associated companies such as Libertatea (Bucharest), Panem (Giurgiu) and Postăvarul (Braşov) operating a total of seven mills, 11 bakeries and 174 retail outlets with 4,500 employees. The company was launched 1999 and has expanded through buyouts and upgrading; poised to take advantage of increasing EU funding with €4.5mln earmarked for new bakery production lines (after the $10mln invested over the past three years). The company is based in Râmnicu Vâlcea with partners Panem (Giurgiu) (eight outlets) and Postăvarul (Braşov) as well as branches in Bucharest (33 outlets including Libertatea Centre), Cluj (16), Iaşi (10), Piteşti (16), Târgu Jiu (26) and Tecuci (13). Business increased substantially in 2004, notably with a new €1.5mln line at Berceni (presumably the former Libertatea factory) for sliced bread that sells very successfully as 'French Toast'. Each month the company mills 12,000t of wheat while producing 10,000t of bakery products and 500t of biscuits and pasta. During 2004–5 the company invested €9.2mln in modernising its retail chain. With 16 shops in Râmnicu Vâlcea and an unknown number in Braşov the total is now well over 150, mostly in the relevant large towns but including smaller towns like Mioveni and Topoloveni near Piteşti; Băbeni, Balş, Călimăneşti and Drăgăşani near Râmnicu Vâlcea; as well as the village of Ghidigeni near Tecuci. Investment in 2007 concentrated on new works in Iaşi and Râmnici Vâlcea. There is also a keen interest to expand into Bulgaria, Moldova, Serbia and Ukraine. Meanwhile another Broadhurst interest lies in the large Iaşi baker and confectioner Pangran at the end of 2001; a business that emerged from the break-up of the former state bakery enterprise privatised by EMBO in 1994 before succumbing to 4.2mln.lei debts owed to RDB and the government. A massive increase in capital from 6.9 to over 21.0bln.lei gave Broadhurst two-thirds of the business with funding for new technology including an integrated IT system and modernised van fleet; also the resumption of operations in Paşcani in 2002.

Other Companies

Boromir is primarily a major milling company that has acquired an extensive portfolio beginning with a new mill in Râmnicu Vâlcea in 1994 which expanded capacity from 24 to 180t/day over a decade, with further mills acquired in Sibiu (1998), Buzău (2000) and Deva (2002) raising total daily capacity to 1,300t and supporting countrywide distribution of flour with representatives in all counties. There are also other units producing glucose and paste in Sibiu and paste in Buzău, Iaşi, Mediaş and Sibiu and the company is now rationalising to reduce the number of units (currently five) and sell off city centre sites such as the former Amylon glucose factory site in Sibiu acquired by Immoeast. Racova, with extensive farming interests in cereals (Comcereal Vaslui), oil and vineyards – as well as dairying (already referred to) – took over the Suceava milling chain Mopan in 2002, refurbished the Suceava mill with German equipment and reopened the old Dorneşti mill in order to distribute bread and confectionery to 145 shops throughout the county from bakeries not only in Suceava but also in Câmpulung Moldovenesc, Fălticeni, Gura Humorului, Radăuţi, Solca and Vatra Dornei. Racova also have a new milling complex in Bârlad for 6,000t/yr and the local Andreea bakery (1,500t/yr); also a new bakery opened in Vaslui (2,000t/yr) in 2003 – with local distribution to its own shops in both cases. Other bakeries have been privatised as Romanian companies but low margins in many cases suggest further rationalisation although there are some strong players at the bottom end with good retail locations. Pan Group Craiova is a specialised bakery company producing at two locations in Craiova, as well as Calafat, Filiasi and Segarcea, with sales assisted by 43 of its own shops, though it also runs a fodder plant. Further interest lies in some new developments occurring in LFAs through investments by the biscuit maker Hay (part of the Alka Group already mentioned): a DM10mln biscuit factory in the Stei LFA in 2001 was followed by DM15mln at the Filipeştii de Pădure LFA the following year. Dr Oetker made a €7.5mln investment in Curtea de Argeş during 2000–2 for pastry additives (e.g. baking powder) and desserts after acquiring Regal (Domneşti) in 1998. Arnos quality pasta is distributed from Oradea throughout Transylvania – and also to Bucharest, Gorj and Mehedinţi. The large Dobrogea Group has moved from bread and biscuits into cereals and frozen products (with some export successes). And finally, Star Foods at Popesti-Leordeni near Bucharest were acquired by Pepsi-Cola in 2004 with an automated chip production line installed to boost crisp production while the acquisition of the Bulgarian company in 2007 has prepared the ground for exports.

MEAT PROCESSING

There were 65 commercial companies in 1997 with a capacity of 1.0mln.t for meat, 250,000t for meat products and 70,000t for canned meat. Consumption was low at 52kg/pc (compared with 79kg in the Czech Republic and 90 in Hungary) and it was expected that production of beef, pork and chicken would rise by about a quarter from 0.58 to 0.73mln.t during 1996–2000 in order to reduce dependence on imported goods by the emerging middle class. Growth in demand would provide a stimulus for modernisation given the low level of compliance with EU standards at the start of the millennium, although there was a constant threat posed by low cost imports from EU (below normal production prices) for which customs taxes did not adequately compensate. The failure of the old state processors can also be seen in Prahova county where competition from private processors along with financial blockage (preventing purchase of live animals) forced Incaf (Ploieşti) to sell its abattoirs in Buşteni, Câmpina, Mizil and Vălenii de Munte in 1999, retaining only the central installation in Ploieşti eventually acquired by the Lebanese company Cold Chain in the same year. The new private firms have encountered varied fortunes. Some old abattoirs have been modernised e.g. by Decebal, a local privatised company that updated the Deva factory and others in the area at Brad and Haţeg (increasing employment by 600) before moving on to Petroşani in 2000 to reopen the local abattoir forced to close in 1998 (with the benefit of LFA incentives that also applied at Brad). Tempus Vit Cominpex (Cluj) was forced to stockpile chicken because of import competition and changing consumer taste. It sought to reduce its costs through purchase of the Nutrex fodder factory in 1999. Two years earlier Avicola (Buzău) completed work on a fodder factory and modern slaughterhouse and was able to reduce costs sufficiently to export poultry meat in addition to supplying Bucharest and such provincial towns as Buzău, Craiova, Galaţi and Ploieşti. The process started with technological redevelopment of the hen farm in 1997 with Belgian equipment to allow automated feeding, watering and heating. Some new SMEs have emerged to provide local markets for finished animals like the Sergiana Prodimpex salami factory opened in 1996 at Poiana Mărului near Zărneşti and the Alber meat factory at Zalău in 1997 (part of a complex that includes a bakery and dairy.

Smithfield

At the other extreme the outstanding case of foreign investment concerns the American company Smithfield Foods that wishes to expand in Europe (at a time when there was little scope for further growth in the USA). Appreciating Romania as the potential 'Iowa of Europe' and recognising ECE as the logical area for the development of meat production, they see West European producers located in the wrong half of the continent! Smithfield arrived in 2004 to acquire the old Comtim pig-rearing unit along with its processing section Agrotorvis (now 'Smithfield Procesare') for €27mln. $850mln of investment will extend to 2011 on the 'Noul Comtim' farm complex: ten units each turning out 260,000 pigs/yr – subject to some delay in getting the necessary permits – complemented by contracts with private farmers and grain producers. One of the production centres is Masloc near Timişoara where local opposition has arisen over nitrate pollution worries. Processing is located at the 75,000sq.m Freidorf factory with 1,800 workers handling 4.0mln pigs/yr, while initially importing frozen meat to establish brand awareness. In 2005 Smithfield also acquired half of the Bucharest transport/distribution firm Agroalim: ten logistics bases were rebuilt and retooled in line with EU norms with storage and distribution capacity enhanced while Transfrigotren acquired in 2006 has been rebranded as Agroalim Logistic. Along with a half share in the Frigorifer cold store at Tulcea, the company can service the home market as well as its Danube port for export to the EU.

The Charcuterie Business

Funding is now available from SAPARD and this is boosting the leading players whereas the top ten meat producers could claim barely a third of the market at the start of the millennium when a process of mergers and acquisitions was awaited. A good example is Cris-Tim Group's 'Recunoştinţa' salami/sausage factories at Filipeştii de Pădure LFA in 2003 involving a total investment €2.0mln to provide 500 jobs; a venture that complements their ecological dairy farm. The business is a remarkable one having started through the decision of Cristina and Radu Timis to expand from their food shop opened in Bucharest in 1993 to process their own meat two years' later; working up from 500kg/day to 25.0t in a 5,000sq.m Bucharest factory (with German equipment) by 1997; followed by relocation to the LFA where their two factories now process 90t daily. They have 450 employees in the factories, 13 shops (nine in Bucharest plus Constanţa, Ploieşti and the villages of Cornu and Filipeşti) and their nationwide distribution from warehouses in Bucharest, Cluj, Constanţa, Craiova, Iaşi and Timişoara with their own fleet of trucks and vans. In 2003 Cris-Tim was market leader for meat products with sales worth €44mln and they are holding this position with a further €7.0mln investment to boost output from Filipeşti at a time when all the leading players are gaining some benefit from the closure of enterprises that lack the resources to upgrade to EU standards. Cris-Tim are now interested in strategic partners for faster growth and spoke to several foreign interests including Campofrio (the largest multinational) and Reinert before entering into a partnership with former supplier – Tulip Food of the Danish Crown Group – to have their 'Gusturi Europene' products made for the Danish and German markets. It is hoped that traditional Romanian varieties will do well in Europe when all restrictions on the export of charcuterie products are removed.

Another company with metropolitan origins is Caroli which started in Bucharest in a small way in 1994 before acquiring Indcarf abattoir in Pitesti in 1999 (including refrigerated storage for 5,000t of meat). The businesses relocated to Piteşti in 2002 and a major investment programme resulted in the greatly-enlarged Caroli Foods Group (2005) with distribution nationwide from Bacău, Brăila, Braşov, Cluj, Constanţ and Timişoara as well as Bucharest and Piteşti. Medeus is a smaller Bucharest company which has recently moved production from the city centre to a new suburban factory in Chitila: it is too expensive to remain near the Crowne Plaza Hotel when their 16,800 site could bring in €1000/sq.m for real estate! Turning to the provinces, Aldis Călăraşi is a major producer (after Cris-Tim and Caroli) with a national distribution system, although they have decided to sell their national network of 50 shops in the face of supermarket pressure and the expectation of higher quality fresh meat sales in future rather than charcuterie. In Moldavia the Apostol family's Kosarom business grew out of the pilot privatisation process in 1992 which brought together the Paşcani abattoir (subsequently modernised with SAPARD funding) with the pig-rearing unit at Ştefan cel Mare (Neamţ) as well as poultry farming and arable land at Târgu Frumos. Meanwhile 'Principal' have sausage factories at Filipeştii de Pădure and Salonta (forming part of Signus Romania business which includes Murfatlar wine) while two other companies also combine charcuterie with other interests: Elit (Cugir) is a leading firm owned by Dorin Mateiu (a partner in La Stejaru property company, building a hotel by the golf course at Pianu de Jos near Alba Iulia); while Carvil (Mizil) features Iustin Paraschiv's processing and distribution companies combined with the Oltchim chemical company's former pig and poultry farms and fertiliser production.

Foreign Companies

These have now become very prominent in the sector and Cris-Tim experienced stiff competition after Spain's Campofrio took over the Tabco fish processor in Tulcea in 1997 and, following a factory upgrade (thanks to a €2.0mln SAPARD project), expanded from selling in seven counties (Tulcea and adjacent areas) to the whole country in 2001 with regional warehouses in Bacău, Braşov, Bucharest, Cluj (Floreşti), Constanţa, Craiova and Timişoara as well as the central warehouse in Tulcea. Competition gave rise to a court case over the ownership of the brand 'salam săsesc' which both companies were using. Another early entrant was the Swiss 'Angst' company which arrived in 1991 and now has factories in Buftea and Sinaia supplying a regional network that includes around 15 of the company's own shops in Bucharest and expanded through the acquisition in 2006 of the 'Discovery' chain of 14 shops in Cluj, where a further factory will be built. Orkla (Norway), selling meat products and margarine, established a Romanian subsidiary in 2002 with the acquisition of Topway Foods followed by the takeover of the country's second largest meat processor – Ardealul – with annual sales of €10mln for the 'Bunică' and 'Laminuț' brands of paté as well as canned meat. Preferring to buy market share rather than launch a greenfield venture, Orkla were attracted by Ardealul's brand new factory (fully compliant with EU regulations) built by entrepreneurs O.Costea and S.Olteanu with previous experience in the industry. German and Italian equipment was also installed in the new Avistar poultry plant at Baia Mare in 1996 owned by a Romanian-Israeli company. Most of the 110 employees are shareholders and enjoy western working conditions. Other assets have emerged through the disposal of former state poultry and pig farms linked with processing facilities. Thus Comtom (Tomeşti near Iaşi) – the biggest meat producer in central Moldavia – was sold by the SOF to the Danish Agro Group Global who paid off the firm's debts and invested in technological updating. After previously importing 80 per cent of the meat needed for its 'Gourmet' and 'Familia' products, a Romanian-Austrian j.v. meat processor Gourmet Prod made a \$2.0mln investment in 2001 in a European-standard slaughterhouse (at Tunari, where it currently operates) and ten pig farms. H.&E.Reinert of Versmold near Osnabrück (Germany) built a greenfield meat/sausage factory at Feldioara in 2006. On the other hand Vivatis (an Austrian charcuterie firm) consider a greenfield project is too risky and so they plan to make an acquisition in 2008. There may well be a growing threat to Romanian firms, especially in the light of new EU regulations over mechanically-recovered meat, although there is some potential in the cities (as home cooking declines) through the niche market for semi-cooked food and salad contracts.

VEGETABLE OIL

This is a branch with a relatively high level of concentration. By 1997 18 companies were responsible for an edible oil capacity of 525,000t (plus 44,000t of margarine) with consumption expected to increase by some 50 per cent from 270–400,000t during 1996–2000. A leading role was acquired by Craiova-based Topway Industries (market leader in vegetable oil, margarine and ketchup). The company improved its 'Olpo' Podari factory on the edge of the city with a state-of-the-art sunflower oil refinery (marketing 'Olpo' cooking oil in one litre plastic bottles from the new Italian bottling line) and then attracted $9.5mln from the Baring Central European Fund – dedicated to Central European enterprises – to finance expansion of its vegetable oil and margarine output in 1999 and come up with new products. Meanwhile Topway acquired the large sunflower and soybean oil producer Ultex (Ţăndărei) in 1997 but then sold a $30mln majority stake in Olpo to Cargill (USA) in 2004. Bunge, another American firm, acquired a third of the market through acquisition of the Unirea (Iaşi) oil factory in 2002, followed by Muntenia (Bucharest) in 2003, which also delivered Interoil (Oradea), and finally Agricover (Buzău) in 2007. This compares with 19 per cent for sunflower oil producer Argus (Constanţa) and a smaller share for Racova who operate the Ulerom oil press in Vaslui. However, oil producers are having a difficult time through foreign currency fluctuations and some factories have been sold (like Ultex now owned by Ilie Nitescu) or switched to biodiesel. Bunge closed their Bucharest and Oradea factories in 2007 – and Iaşi will follow in 2008 – while production will concentrate on the Buzău plant currently undergoing a €25mln modernisation that will easily be paid for out of property development since the sale of the 6.0ha Bucharest site to GEA Prasa (Spain) raised €29mln. 700 jobs will be lost in the process but after the efficiency gains the company is looking to sell a fifth of its output in Bulgaria. In the case of margarine a key player is Unilever South Central Europe which acquired and modernised the Precomb (Târgu Mures) margarine factory in 1998 to produce the Delma, Flora and Rama brands initially imported from Hungary (though the company also assimilated the Knorr products factory at Otopeni near Bucharest acquired from the US multinational Bestfoods in 2001). A new margarine factory with Romanian and German capital started at Craiova in 1995 while European Drinks (see below) are diversifying into margarine at their complex in the Beiuş-Stei area of Bihor.

TOBACCO

This is a sector blighted by illegal activities mostly involving organised crime in smuggling cigarettes to European black markets and also the Romanian home market as demonstrated by some notable detections by the customs. There is also a long tradition of consolidation in this branch through the state monopoly Tutunul Românesc (TR) that was being prepared for privatisation in 1998. Competition had been allowed by this time but TR still accounted for more than half the national production and made a massive contribution to the state budget. The company has six factories – Bucharest, Iaşi, Râmnicu Sărat, Sf.Gheorghe (modernised in 1997 through TR's own funds and j.v. capital using German machinery from Hauni-Korber Maschinenbau of Hamburg), Târgu Jiu and Timişoara – as well as the Arad, Bârlad, Carei, Craiova, Ocna Mureş, Titu, Urziceni and Vlăduleni fermentation units and the Bucharest Central Station for Tobacco Culture Research & Processing. However the TR empire was unable to modernise (for complete re-equipment of Romanian cigarette factories with 1960s machinery would have cost $80–100mln) yet cigarette prices remained low to compete with imported cigarettes evading customs duties. Competition also came from legally-imported brands and a subsidiary of Philip Morris who set up an office in Romania in 1993 and then started work in 1997 on a new $100mln factory on a 15ha site on the Bucharest belt road near Otopeni using state-of-the-art technology for tobacco primary and secondary processing; creating up to 600 jobs by 2000. Four international brands – Bond Street, L&M, Marlboro and Red & White – and the Romanian Callatis brand were launched at this time after studies revealed the receptivity of Romanian consumers to a genuine national trade mark offering high quality at an accessible price. Meanwhile British Tobacco considered manufacturing high-quality cigarettes in Ploieşti in the mid-1990s, whereas Papastratos Romania now produce Assos cigarettes in Bucharest to replace Greek imports and encourage local tobacco growers. Avoiding high import duties contributes further to lower prices.

Privatisation of TR became controversial in 2000 when the competition for a 90 per cent stake was won by InterAgro, a Romanian conglomerate active in agriculture and insurance, making a bid of $40mln (plus $35mln investment) on condition that there would be no closures until after the conclusion of a five-year investment programme. The problem arose because Ioan Neculae's InterAgro company was preferred to the Greek consortium Michailides Leaf Tobacco (MLT) offering $32mln for the purchase with $113mln of investments to follow. Although recommended by the government's private advisor (the Dutch bank ABN Amro), MLT would have split up brands and factories and hence the agriculture ministry (who scrutinised the tendering) preferred to keep a well-known company intact and in Romanian hands. However the sale was annulled although InterAgro people were installed before privatisation and were already stopping unnecessary imports and planning increased productivity among domestic tobacco pickers. Other actions included the introduction of new Italian machinery, while retaining the workforce of 3,500 workers thanks to profits from the insurance subsidiary Asirom. A new upmarket brand was launched to meet foreign competition (dented when Bucharest's general mayor T.Băsescu removed illegal street kiosks selling black-market material). With the cancellation of Neculae's bid in 2001 the company was then sold to the 'Tobacco 2003' consortium involving firms in the British Virgin Islands and Italy, albeit with suspicion that Neculae was behind them. The matter was investigated since any fraud could have relieved the government of its obligation to pay €5.6mln of TR debts. But TR does not control all activity because InterAgro opened a new tobacco factory in 2002 producing 'strips' for cigarette production; thereby overcoming Romania's lack of tobacco processing technology in collaboration with Tecnoimpianti of Italy.

THE DRINKS INDUSTRY

The transition started with a boom in Coke as Coca-Cola launched Romanian operations in 1991 with factories in Bucharest, Ploieşti and Braşov (though the latter closed in 2002) and subsequently in Iaşi and Oradea (1992) and Timişoara (1995): all merged in 2000 into the one Coca-Cola Hellenic Bottling Company (CCHBC). Fanta was launched in 1994 (now in several flavours) and further diversification included 'Cappy' fruit still-drinks and the energy drink 'Burn' in 2002, while the mineral water company Dorna Apemin was purchased in 2002 for €39mln (including the Izvorul Alb and Poiana Negri mineral water brands). Coca-Cola have invested $300mln (including CCHBC) and employed 2,200 in 2003. However a study by an American business college estimated that 23,900 jobs were supported by the sale of Coca-Cola since each job created directly by the industry created 11 elsewhere, mainly through 20–25,000 kiosks and small retail shops started or maintained because of Coke sales: cumulatively a major base for the free market activity. New trucks and bottles (PET bottles were manufactured in Romania in 1992) suggested high quality and made people feel better about themselves; while fears of 'Coca colonisation' were balanced by the advantages of MNEs as a vehicle for transferring organisational and management skills. To save space, the Bucharest factory is now used for storage while the daily production capacity of 0.66mln.l has moved to Ploieşti.

Other soft drinks operations were started by Schweppes distributing orange, lemon, bitter lemon, grapefruit and tonic water nationwide by 1996 from units at Chiajna in Bucharest (using 1.5l PET bottles) and Topoloveni (250ml bottles). Quadrant Amroq Beverages (USA) bottle and distribute Pepsi, Prigat and Mountain Dew soft drinks. Fruit juices make greater use of Romanian raw materials with Sucmerom (Reghin) investing its own funds in a Swiss superfiltering installation to process local produce into natural apple juice concentrate for sale competitively in Austria and Germany (17,000t seasonal capacity). But a key player is the private Romanian-Swedish company created by Ioan and Viorel Micula investing well over DM1.0bln (with an EBRD stake of €250mln) to develop three factories in the Beius area of Bihor including 'European Drinks' at Rieni, 'Scandic Distillers' at Sudrigiu and 'European Foods' at Stei (the latter producing tomato paste, ice cream powder and biscuits under the 'Regal' brand) with a total employment of some 5,000, including its own logistics – Transport General Import-Export – with over 2,000 trucks and over 200 warehouses nationwide. A range of soft drinks led by 'Frutti Fresh' are sold in PET bottles of 0.2– 2.5l. Another leading player is Parmalat (Italy) who sell Santal soft drinks (some 17mln.l in 2007) with a base at Tunari near Bucharest and regional distribution from Cluj, Iaşi and Timişoara as well; while Maspex (Poland), who arrived in Romania in 1996, produce their 'Tymbark' juices in a former canning factory in Vălenii de Munte acquired in 2001 (as part of a portfolio including cappuccino, pasta and instant products). Given the growth of the sector, breweries are starting to diversify with URBB expecting a big sale of its 'Orangia' product given the demand for natural fruit juices. The same trend is event among mineral water companies with Harghita (Sâncrăieni) launching non-carbonated juices in 2007. The hot summer 2007 also boosted sales of energy drinks: the latter led by Red Bull (who set up a domestic unit in 2004); also Coca-Cola with 'Burn' (already noted) and Dacardi Impex with 'Power Horse' and 'Red Force' as well as low-price producers led by European Drinks with 'Reinergy'. The quite new ice tea business involves European Drinks, Romacqua and Tymbark Maspax.

Mineral Water

This segment suffered a depression because despite an abundance of quality natural resources, the industry was initially left to deteriorate in a grossly undercapitalised state. Endemic financial blockage in the state sector prevented new drilling and technological updating, but production decline was reversed after 1993 by the new company Regina Apelor Minerale (Ramin) with a rising output using 1970s technology at full capacity, although energy and packing costs were high and there was only a small export (to Ukraine). In 1997 Ramin was transformed into the National Mineral Waters Company (NMWC) responsible for both research and exploitation: leasing water sources to more than 20 privatised bottling companies and 10 spa companies. However the payments made for water were traditionally very low and it was revealed in 1999 that poor supervision enabled Dorna Apemin to work the Izvorul Alb spring near Vatra Dornei with inaccurate documentation and claim the water as 'technological' rather than 'mineral' water; thereby evading all payment for the water – and raising both fiscal and consumer protection issues. However, the most important area is in eastern Transylvania based on Miercurea Ciuc (covering Braşov, Covasna, Harghita and Mureş counties) with other prominent branches at Deva and Vatra Dornei.

Recovery was underlined by a seven-fold increase over ten years: 0.12bln.l in 1993 to 0.46mln in 1998 and 0.84bln in 2002 (5.5 to 36.5l per head of population, compared with 55 in ECE and 255–200 in Western Europe which gives an indication of the potential). Since then the upward trend has continued to 1.10bln in 2007 with 1.25bln expected in 2008. Exports to Canada, Greece, Israel, Saudi Arabia and USA are worth $1.5mln. Covasna and Harghita bottling companies are looking to exports in the CEE region and also in Asian and Middle Eastern markets with emphasis on high-profit table mineral waters: Romaqua (Borsec) issued foreign currency bonds in 2000 to attract funds to replace old technologies and build a new 'flat' water factory. European Drinks are also active in the business with a DM200mln investment to bring water through a 25km stainless steel pipeline from Izvorul Minunilor-Stâna de Vale for processing and bottling at the factory at Rieni where products include natural, carbonated and non-carbonated waters. In 2002, European Drinks led the market with 22.6 per cent followed by Borsec (17.2 per cent), Perla (6.4), Harghita (9.8), Biborţeni (5.4) and Dorna (5.2). There is a hazard arising from fake products (marketed by ghost companies) that are certainly not natural mineral waters; while Vitarom Impex – producing Perla mineral water – had to withdraw one lot that was not microbiologically pure. But prospects are good with investment in new NMWC-licensed springs, pipelines and bottling plants. Petrom is a relatively new player through its Carpatina company bottling at a spring at Toşorog near Rădăuţi (trebling daily capacity to 10,000 bottles in 2001) and selling through its filling stations and supermarkets (Billa, Carrefour, Gima and Metro) as well as exports to the Emirates and Israel. Meanwhile the established companies are increasing capacity: Harghita now have five production lines at Sâncrăieni and sold 75mln.l of mineral water in 2006.

Brewing

Here is a story of outstanding success with substantial investment and expanding sales. From 10.5mln.hl in 1989 production fell to a low of 7.7 in 1997 but there was a dramatic recovery to 11.1mln in 1999 (over a period of negative growth in the economy as a whole) and production has continued above the level of the communist period to 13.3mln.hl in 2003 (26.5 per cent up on 1989) (Table 6.1) while capacity is estimated at some 20mln.hl. Beer has gained significantly in popularity since 1989: over 70 per cent of Romanians were drinking beer once a fortnight in 2001 compared with just over half in 1997, thanks to promotion campaigns and advertising at a time of rising purchasing power among lower and middle income groups. Consumption has now reached 100 litres/pc – close to Austria (111) and Germany (118) though modest by comparison with the Czech Republic (160). The industry continues to expand, encouraged by the hot summer of 2007: total sales reached 19.4mln.hl 2007 (worth €1.0bln). Meanwhile the number of breweries has declined. In the early 1990s Romania boasted some 75 breweries with total capacity of 1.59bln.l but there has been much reorganisation of communism's protected regional production and marketing system meaning, for example, that Bere Miercurea Ciuc distributed only in Harghita and three adjacent counties. Some weaker units (like Piatra Neamt, Solca and Zimca) have now disappeared because of obsolete equipment and high energy costs plus the failure to privatise in favour of a strong investor with resources for modernisation. Rahova brewery in Bucharest was also threatened with closure in 1997 as a source of pollution; at that time it had failed to get adequate funding to modernise its 1960s technology and compete with other breweries and was working at only a third of capacity: the premises were eventually sold to the World Trade Centre although they are now the subject of a large property restitution claim by the Bragadiru Estate. But many other units are now modernised and enlarged since brewers often favour acquisitions and/or extensions rather than costly, time-consuming greenfield projects involving buildings/equipment, workforce recruitment and a distribution system. Acquisitions also bring established brands with market share.

After a producers' association was set up in 1992, renamed as the beer industry union in 2001, it was replaced in 2004 by two separate organisations: a new association for the four large international companies and a separate association for independent brewers. The 'big four' comprise Heineken, Ursus Breweries, InBev Romania and United Romanian Breweries Bereprod, owned by Tuborg (Denmark). They account for some 85 per cent of the production and achieved a 20.2 per cent growth in 2007 compared with the 17.7 per cent for the industry as a whole. The internationals have been popularising western brands like Bergenbier, Kaiser, Stella Artois and Tuborg while promoting the best Romanian beers under their control like Ciuc and Ursus. Some brand-new breweries have been built like Efes (now InBev) in Ploieşti and Tuborg in Bucharest, while others have been closed through rationalisation like Piteşti (by Bere România, now Ursus) and Reghin (by Brau Union, now Heineken). They have to keep a close eye on other sections of the drink industry, with a domestic sector boosted by the Romacqua project for a €31mln investment in a 1.0mln.hl brewery in Sebeş. All the leading companies have an alcohol-free beer on market. Meanwhile, the independents, who accounted for 100 per cent in 1994, but are now down to 7.5 per cent following the recent acquisition of Bere Mures by Heineken. There are some 15 producers in the group with the most prominent being Azuga (Bere Azuga), Galaţi (Martens), Rosiorii de Vede (Robema) and Suceava (Bermas). Some considerable initiative has been shown. Roşiorii de Vede brewery (opened in 1978) responded to competition from imported beer by improving quality through new pasteurised ales (Probeer and Southbeer) and a change in brand from Arcina to Robema to regain market share by 1997. Suceava brewery, which opened in 1974 and became Bermas in 1991, now uses better malt and invested 2.0mln.lei by 1999 – from its own funds and a bank credit – to provide a new bottling and pasteurisation line while also introducing stainless steel kegs for longer life. In 2000 it still had a majority SOF holding and no contact with foreign partners, but was selling beer throughout Moldavia and also in Bistriţa-Năsăud, Buzău and Constanţa counties in competition with Zimbrul (Iaşi) and Bere Malt (Bistriţa). A modern brewery also survives at Maneciu (Prahova), integrated with an adjacent bakery business, and produces Jager beer using its own spring water and German processing equipment. And in order to increase domestic sales Beverly Hills was produced in Galaţi under licence from the USA in 1997. The difference in the shares between the two groups is accounted for by a small foreign interest: Bere Satu Mare, with the German company Privatbrauerei Franz-Joseph Sailer as the majority shareholder marketing the Sailer brand abroad in 1999; also by European Drinks though their new initiative for a €100mln investment in a 3.5mln.hl/yr brewery at Drăgăneşti that could become the largest in Romania linked with their 'Bürger' beer sold in 2008 in 2.2l plastic bottles. Further competition is due from Bulgarian 'Boliarka' beer from Vel.Tarnovo which is now selling in Romania, with a big expansion planned using plastic bottles.

Heineken

This is the name adopted in 2007 for Brau Union which was built out of majority shareholdings in several breweries privatised by EMBO during 1994–6: Arbema (Arad) in 1997 followed by Bere (Craiova), Malbera (Constanţa) and Silva (Reghin) in 1998–9 with a combined capacity of 2.0mln.hl and 1,865 employees. $80mln was invested up to 2000 to make better use of capacity e.g. a new $11mln industrial hall and bottling line at Arad in 1999 for 400,000hl/yr capacity (also with improvements to brewing, yeast and refrigeration) with more prominence for Arbemer Lucifer, Kaiser and Steffl beers. There was also a canned beer bottling line in Craiova. Attention was also given to reducing costs through use of steam and hot water while improving quality through better raw materials (some imported) and packaging. Then BBAG (a subsidiary of Austrian Breweries International: originating in Linz in 1921 and the second largest brewer in the region) took over Brau Union in 1998 and Heineken's interest arose in this context. The initial 18.6 per cent market share was boosted through the acquisition of Haber International (Haţeg), followed by Bere Miercurea Ciuc (established in 1975 but brewing only 145,000hl in 1999 compared with a 1.2mln.hl capacity) and Griviţa: a Bucharest brewery founded in 1869 by the German Luther family and enlarged under nationalisation in the 1970s, with a j.v. in 1992 through association with Sems Palma de Mallorca. Griviţa produced a beer called Gambrinus (associated with inter-war prosperity). These further mergers, completed in 2000, took the total employment to 2,400 workers and production to 4.5mln.hl, placing the company in the first position. Regional brands were maintained – Arbema Lucifer and Zarand (Arad), Ciuc and Harghita (Miercurea Ciuc), Haţegana (Haţeg), Malbera Mamaia (Constanţa) and Silva (Reghin) as well as Gambrinus (Griviţa) – with all still produced in 2002 (when BBAG was leading the market with 38 per cent) plus standard products: initially Kaiser, followed by Golden Brau, Schlossgold and the new high-quality Gösser.

In view of raw material problems BBAG decided in 2001 to secure the two-row barley needed for the following year's brewing from the Romanian market; thereby helping contracting farmers (mainly in the plains of Brăila, Moldavia and Transylvania) to set up barley and two row barley cultures with seeds, fertiliser and consultancy. But restructuring in 2003 involved withdrawal of poor-selling regional brands (Arbema and Kaiser) in favour of better sellers like Bucegi, Ciuc, Gambrinus, Golden Brau, Haţegana and Silva. Also the Silva (Reghin) brewery – the original producer of Bucegi and Silva beers – was closed, although the group still had enough capacity at Constanţa, Craiova, Haţeg and Miercurea Ciuc for 4.5mln.hl production. In 2003 the Heineken-BBAG strategic partnership under Brau Union (headquartered in Austria) was extended across the region which made the group market leader in five countries in addition to Romania where there is now steady growth after an explosive phase starting in 1997. All the brands are maintained, with Zipfer imported. Meanwhile the workforce has been reduced to 1,300 after a total of €165mln of investment since 1998; with distribution organised regionally at Arad, Bucharest, Cluj, Constanţa, Miercurea Ciuc (for Moldavia) and Ploieşti. But as a result of expansion elsewhere market share fell to 26.5 per cent in 2006–7. However, a substantial lead (31 per cent) was regained at the beginning of 2008 by winning the race to acquire Bere Mureş based at Ungheni near Târgu Mureş (distributing Dracula, Neumarkt and Sovata beer countrywide): a private company arose in 1992 (through management buyout by some people who had built the Reghin brewery in 1974) and introduced PET bottles in 1998, Their capacity of 1.6mln.hl took the group's total to 6.0mln.

Ursus Breweries

This is the name adopted in 2005 for the SAB Miller business that started with the SAB investment of $18mln to purchase 70 per cent of Vulturul (Buzău) from the SOF in 1995 to upgrade the factory over five years to 2000, with quality assured through use of best quality barley, malt and hops. The company also acquired Braun und Brune International (BBI) in 1996 to gain control of Ursus (Cluj), first privatised early in 1992 with distribution extended to Bucharest and Constanţa by 1994 with the launch of Ursus Premium Pils. BBI also included Pitber (Piteşti) and contributed to the company's total production of 1.8mln.hl with 44 distributors giving nationwide coverage in 2000. A further acquisition was made through Bere Timişoareană (Timişoara) in 2003, at which point the company employed 1,115 people at its four brewery locations producing Keller, Timişoareană and Ursus, while also acting as sole importer of Pilsner Urquell. Then Aurora (Braşov) was acquired in 2004 – thought to be the new brewery opened by Ernst Lipps (Germany) 1997 – in search of a 25 per cent market share with rationalisation requiring the closure at Piteşti. SAB's 'Compania de Bere România' almost achieved its target with 3.0mln.hl capacity and 1,300 employees – in Braşov, Buzău, Cluj-Napoca, Timişoara and Tunari near Bucharest – with 24 per cent market share for its Romanian brands (Ciucas, Timişoareană – first brewed in 1718 – and Ursus) and the imported Pilsner Urquell. It has also launched the premier segment product Peroni Nastro Azzurro with Romania only the second European country to be targeted by this promotion after the UK. The company is now launching its own alcohol-free beer (now an essential part of a typical brewery profile) rather than import from Hungary. With 20 per cent of the market Ursus are investing €50mln in their Timişoara brewery to bring total capacity to 6.3mln.hl in 2008.

InBev

Known as Interbrew until 2007, this Belgian company's interest arises out of the acquisition in 1994 of two breweries at Baia Mare (Proberco, replaced by a new brewery in 1997) and Blaj (Bianca) for the production of Bergenbier, plus the establishment of a national distribution company in the same year; with the three elements subsequently brought together as a single Interbrew entity in 2002. In the meantime Efes opened a new brewery in Ploieşti at the end of 1998, following the launch in the previous year of a $65mln greenfield development on land received under concession from the city council adjacent to Coca-Cola. The brewery uses the latest technology from Belgium, Germany, The Netherlands and Turkey) for up to 7.5mln.hl production using Romanian raw materials and providing 300 jobs (that seemed likely to be doubled in line with the firm's aim of providing high quality beer at an accessible price). Initially they produced Efes Pilsener, but other lines were taken up in 1999: Efes Dark, Efes Extra, Efes Light and the local Caraiman. However, consolidation then arose through a j.v. with Interbrew so that 2.4mln.hl/yr would be produced under its own (Efes) trademarks while 4.0mln.hl would be sold as Interbrew brands: Konig and Stella Artois as well as Bergenbier. This would allow accelerated investment recovery for Efes, through use of their spare capacity, and allow Interbrew to produce locally for their market in southern Romania rather than distribute from Transylvania. Without the Ploieşti option Interbrew would have needed an acquisition or a greenfield investment (with less attractive fiscal facilities). In effect Efes granted production licences to Interbrew for Efes and Caraiman in exchange for benefits generated by Interbrew's distribution network. Bergenbier is the best-selling brand, but in 2003 Interbrew obtained a licence for the German brand Beck's (sold in 120 countries and now brewed in Ploieşti). In 2004 five types of beer were making up a capacity of 1.3mln.hl at Ploieşti with 140 employed. The arrangement seems to be working well because Interbrew registered a 9.8 per cent growth (year on year) in the first half of 2005, thanks to enhanced sales of Bergenbier and Stella Artois while the industry as a whole grew only 0.6 per cent. 2006 was also a good year with a big growth in the sale of Beck's after a successful advertising campaign: indeed a feature of recent growth in beer sales beyond 16mln.hl has been the popularity of 'European' beers – both sweet/fruity ales and sweet/black stout or porter. 2006 brought a full merger at Ploieşti when Interbrew acquired the shares in Efes. Other brands are Leffe, Löwenbräu and Noroc, while a recent innovation is Bergenbier Ice with a special cooling effect. Employing 740, InBev lies in third place for production (3.4mln.hl) and market share (23 per cent). The company makes considerable use of PET bottles and has assisted a recycling project in Blaj.

Tuborg

This company operates as URBB (International Romanian Breweries Bereprod) set up in 1994 by Romanian, Danish and Israeli partners to produce Tuborg beer (and premium local brands) in Bucharest and help satisfy the increasing demand for high-quality beer. The production system – as well as the distribution arrangements for beer retailers and consumers – is similar to that used by the company in Denmark. In 1996 EBRD's agribusiness team provided a $43mln loan to URBB to develop a $75mln complex on a 65ha greenfield site development at Pantelimon (similar to a DM33mln loan for a greenfield project in Croatia). Opening in 1999 with ISO9000 quality certification, the brewery is one of the most modern in the Tuborg-Carlsberg International Group and uses Romanian raw materials to operate at a capacity of 500,000hl/yr. In 2003 Tuborg Romania opened a new automatic state-of-the-art bottling line to bring investments to $85mln during 1997–2003 (doubling capacity to 1.0mln.hl for Carlsberg, Tuborg and Skol, with Guinness and Kilkenny imported from Ireland). Total employment reached 520 and an export business started with Moldova and Serbia. The company is also promoting its own Holsten brand and plans to invest €12mln in bottling and distributing Granini natural juices (without preservatives or artificial colouring) owned by Eckes Granini of Germany. Furthermore, having expanded in Pantelimon to 2.0mln.hl, a major new development has been the decision to invest €60–90mln to double production to 4.0mln.hl with the choice (reflecting the differences in cost) between expansion in Bucharest (with a relocated distribution depot) and a new brewery in the west. Altogether the 'big four' produced 15.5mln.hl of the 19.4mln.hl total in 2007, with first place for turnover taken by Ursus (€278mln) followed by Heineken (€208mln), InBev (€188mln) and Tuborg (€90mln), but Heineken was the clear profit leader with the turnover gap narrowed by the acquisition of the independent Bere Mureş (Targu Mureş).

Wine and Spirits

A viticultural basin comparable to that of France makes Romania a major wine producer with high export potential, but it has been difficult reorienting trade away from relatively undiscriminating eastern markets and business declined from 7.35 to 5.45mln.hl during 1995–2000 while beer increased from 8.77 to 12.66mln.hl. with exports reduced to some four per cent in 1998, extremely poor compared with Bulgaria and Hungary. The western market was also constrained by increased competition among the top 15 wine producing countries in 2000 and while exports to Germany (the second largest market) continued, some other markets were abandoned to larger producers. Another weakness was the emphasis on bulk selling because – although understandable through avoidance of investment in bottling lines – it projected a poor image (with Moldova the leading buyer because of resale to Russia). It was therefore considered important to bottle more wine in Romania for sale to Germany and other western markets seeking quality wines. However this needed leadership and coordination at a time when decisive state participation was not forthcoming. The situation was complicated by vineyard restitution, for the new private owners lacked capital for investment while foreigners were still barred from owning land. The emphasis on lower quality vines in the communist period and the sudden need for new noble stock was also a major challenge, while financial blockage in the state sector affected Vinalcool's capacity to acquire large quantities of grapes from private sources. Moreover domestic consumption was reduced by low buying power (given the maxim that 'a good wine has to accompany a good meal' which few people could afford) along with priority for children's soft drinks and the growing popularity of beer and strong liquors among adults.

Patrovitas, National Wine Owners' Association and Vinrom combined into a single organisation in 2000 for more effective penetration, but a trademark to cover all Romanian wines is also needed. Meanwhile the Vinexport Trading Company (Bucharest) is a j.v. including foreign partners from Germany, The Netherlands and UK and ten Romanian wine exporters. After modern technology was introduced in 1999, bulk/bottled sales in USA and Canada, Europe, Japan, Australia and Israel increased in 2000 but there is also scope for bulk supply to Russia with bottling by a Russian partner, bypassing traditional contacts with Moldova. Wine from the Aiud, Apold and Sebeş areas of Transylvania and Dealul Mare northeast of Ploieşti is made at Ciumbrud (Alba) and Săhăteni (Buzău) respectively with a total 50,000hl of storage (2002). The Angelli company of Italy (matching the requirements of grapes with soil and climate) decided in 2000 to prepare and bottle six traditional varieties in the light of trends on the European wine market: white wines based on the Riesling and Dry Muscat of Murfatlar (Constanţa) and Sauvignon of Drăgăşani (Vâlcea); and reds from the Merlot and Cabernet Sauvignon of Tohani (Prahova) and the Busuioaca of Pietroasele (Buzău). UK Halewood-owned 'Cramele Prahova' (currently the largest bottled wine exporter) entered the Romanian market (after a previous export focus) given the success of Murfatlar – and Jidvei – in 2001.

State-Owned Companies

Vinalcool Prahova (Ploieşti) expanded output by investments using their own resources. Champagne output increased and new processes were introduced to reduce costs and improve quality; with increased export for both red wine and champagne in 1999. Cooperation with vineyard owners was extended through partnerships in the Dealul Mare area, while Vinia (Iaşi), the privatised Vinalcool for Moldavia, tried to promote wines from Bohotin, Cotnari and Uricani from 1998 and Vincom Vrancea developed an effective 'Vampire' range using Cabernet, Merlot, Pinot Noir and Sauvignon grapes in 2001. Individual vineyards are also taking action. Following privatisation in 2000, Cotnari in Moldavia (one of five leading companies on the Romanian wine market, with 1,200ha of vineyards, 5.0mln.l/yr of production, 15mln.l of storage and 350 employees) has invested in new equipment and is selling 5–6mln.l of wine annually: 90 per cent at home (representing five per cent of the total domestic market) and the rest to Europe, America and Israel. It has some excellent quality wines in 2004 but needed publicity for more profitability. Meanwhile the Murfatlar company in Dobrogea was established in 2002 with 2,100ha of vineyards and markets in France, Germany, Japan, Scandinavia, UK and USA. Its €1.8mln investment programme in 2004 (half of it under SAPARD) will rejuvenate the vineyards, modernise equipment and improve the product through better quality control. However, as in the case of Halewood's business, greater efficiency means fewer jobs.

Spirits

There is a substantial spirits industry based in the towns and formerly controlled by the state Vinalcool monopoly from which various private companies have emerged e.g. Prodvinalco (Cluj) which is reorganising its buildings and production. Brandy is a leading product e.g. the 'Milcov' brand produced in Bucharest; while wine companies may also be involved e.g. the 'Zareza' by Vinars de Murfatlar. Foreign spirits are also prominent and a flood of South American alcohol was reported in the mid-1990s with trafficking via Italy and Hungary to Elma (Târgu Mureş) for conversion into vodka and rum. Romania does of course have its own alcohol production including InterAgro's new plant at Zimnicea using the latest Italian technology. Quality spirits are distributed through Romanian companies e.g. Prodal promotes Stalinskaya and Wembley as market leaders respectively for vodka and gin, while partnering Russia's state-owned FKP Soyuzprodimport in the distribution of various drinks in 2003. But most people familiar with Romania are aware of the prominence of plum brandy ('ţuică' or 'rachiu') distilled widely across the Subcarpathians wherever plums are available – but with a range of other fruits as substitutes. Traditionally Romanians have distilled privately under licence (with the permitted quantities invariably exceeded!) and while the communist authorities made some efforts to restrict activity to central stills run by cooperative farms they still depended on individual peasant households to deliver the fermented fruit ('borhot'). This measure of consolidation formalised the transfer of brandy from the rural areas to the towns where it could be used as the basis for manufactured spirits, whereas previously it was usual for individual peasants to take their brandy to town by cart to urban markets or direct to hotels and restaurants. Since 1989 licensing of household stills has again become widespread (indeed it continued during communism where central stills were not established e.g. in areas where private farming persisted; not to mention a substantial amount of small-scale illegal distillation in farmhouse kitchens and sheds where the authorities were tolerant). In areas with a copious supply of fruit almost all households make brandy and if they do not have their own equipment they will hire a neighbour's still for a day or two. Indeed some peasants have constructed modest still houses that are regularly rented out on a daily basis to families who arrive with a cartload of 'borhot' (in a specially-constructed cylindrical wooden cask) and the necessary fuel for the fire. But the question arises how far this business can be commercialised beyond the present informal arrangements involving barter and casual sales to locals and travellers, especially as plum orchards (often neglected under communism in preference for apples and pears) are restored. There is also confusion over the name that varies regionally e.g. palinca, horinca or turţ. There is competition with Hungary claiming the double-distilled 'palinka' as a national drink but it is also referred to in a recent Romanian law on fruit trees.

Plum brandy is marketed professionally in some cases. Silviu Zetea of Medieşu Aurit (Satu Mare) distributes 'a few thousand litters' of fine quality brandy annually through élite outlets (Bucharest restaurants and government protocol) and won a silver medal for his exhibit at the Brussels International Fair, facilitated through the support of a foreign company. Zetea would like to establish an owners' association to support production of natural distilled products and similar developments might follow from plum brandy festivals that have been organised by some local authorities (e.g. Vălenii de Munte in Prahova) and rural tourism organisations. Another option is the supply of spirit (particularly strong twice-distilled spirit of the kind produced in many parts of Transylvania) to factories in the towns for working up into standardised products for nationwide distribution and export. A Chinese j.v. has been reported from Buzău, arising out of an official visit. At the moment the variable quantity and quality of production inhibits commercialisation. There are also environmental hazards arising from the careless disposal of the dregs ('boască'). This can have some amusing consequences as at Cuza Vodă (Brăila) in 1996 when ducks ate dregs dumped by a steam and fell into a deep sleep before eventually returning home, while cattle have been known to 'collapse' temporarily for the same reason. Again at Brad (Hunedoara) piped water tasting of brandy prompted a local newspaper headline 'ţuică through the tap' in 2000:

when local environmental and sanitary inspectors investigated they found that peasants had dumped a large quantity of 'boască' by the river immediately above the public water supply abstraction point! The business is adjusting to EU regulation which allows the licences for stills producing for the owner's own consumption: 300l of brandy at 40deg (though usually 50) with a supplement for larger amounts. 300 licenced stills in Maramureş use 10,000t of plums from 1,142ha of orchards plus a million trees scattered through the countryside. Harvests fluctuate between 800–1,000kg/ha in 2005 and 12,000 in 2006, but there is considerable potential for a well-organised rural industry.

CONCLUSION

The food industry can claim major successes with a balance of foreign and Romanian companies and also a mix of updated inherited plants of the communist era and new greenfield developments, with the latter using a range of urban locations albeit with some use of rural settings in less-favoured areas like Filipeştii de Pădure which is still quite close to Bucharest. The two components seem to coexist in what is a very competitive business although the foreign sector has done particularly well in brewing whereas its penetration of the charcuterie business in relatively modest and ice cream has proved difficult through undercutting by Romanian companies which has forced Nestlé to close its factory. Investment has been driven by European standards (required by the end of 2009) and there have difficult decisions to made e.g. in the case of Campofrio whether to modernise their old Tulcea premises or build a new factory close to Bucharest or acquire a Romanian company with an appropriate manufacturing base. But there is also the issue of growth: not only though export potential but domestic consumption which has been increasing with rising incomes. In the case of drinks, the boom was orchestrated in part by the hot summer of 2007 with a surge in sales that is unlikely to be repeated. It is also significant that rapid expansion by the successful companies coincides with the concentration of food retailing on mainly foreign-owned supermarket chains which have now appeared in all but the smallest towns, though it also true that some foreign companies have invested heavily in aggressive nationwide marketing so that Tnuva (Israel) – based near Bucharest – have very quickly gained third place in yoghurt sales after Danone and Friesland. Expanding capacity usually means retaining the initial location as with Tymbark Maspex who are building a second factory at Vălenii de Munte. But big is not always beautiful and there are good examples where small independent companies (like Azuga brewery) have found a niche that has justified substantial investment and diversification.

7. The Energy Complex: Maximising Efficiency and Self-Sufficiency

INTRODUCTION

The electricity, gas and water sector improved productivity as employment fell from 240,200 to 161,300 during 1996–2005 (with expansion only in waste recovery and recycling – up from 6.1 to 12.4) while the average enterprise size declined sharply from 1,213 to 403 for gas and electricity (22 to 10 for waste and recycling) during the same period. After the heavy losses sustained by national companies in the energy sector in the early transition years their financial performance became crucial for financial discipline in the public sector as a whole and became a factor working in favour of privatisation. Not only is this process now well-advanced, but 2007 saw the energy market fully liberalised allowing energy producers to sell as they wish and even small customers now have choice of supplier. Another measure of success arises from the growth of companies able to install efficient energy systems. This involves relevant sections of the building industry but also companies that have revolutionised street lighting and the flood lighting of historic buildings e.g. Luxten Lighting and Flash Lighting using western products including Philips and Thorne. Luxten Lighting (France) bought Electrofar in 1993 (when it was on the verge of bankruptcy) and invested $38mln in upgrading production and improving productivity to achieve a massive growth in output, exporting half its lamps and accessories. In 1997 the company won the international bidding for a 15 year contract to upgrade public lighting in Bucharest, resulting in lower energy consumption and an overall reduction in costs of one fifth. The company went on to Alba Iulia and gained further contracts in Constanţa, Craiova and Ploieşti. They acquired AWM of Timişoara, who produce measuring equipment to help reduce energy losses, and the company hopes to be the most important European producer of measuring equipment. Competition comes from the Dutch-Romanian j.v. between Elba of Timişoara and Philips Lighting who set up the flood-lighting for the historic Black Church in Braşov in 1997, sharing the costs with the local authorities and the electricity company. Another relevant aspect concerns companies in Romania that can handle work in the energy sector at home and abroad e.g. Electromontaj (Bucharest) that is well placed as a privatised company to install electricity transmission lines abroad. Of course much attention must also be given to energy resources and the harnessing of Romania's potentials in all energy domains covering not only the traditional fuels but increasingly the scope for renewable energy.

Environmental Policy

Apart from a number of pollution black-spots which are still attracting remedial action – e.g. the pressure to meet European standards for water quality and waste disposal – the rural landscapes of the coastal and mountain regions is frequently outstanding and the extension of the conservation programme to cover more reserves and national parks is entirely beneficial. Indeed, with a carbon quota of 250mln.t gas (carbon dioxide equivalent) and effective pollution today of 147mln.t Romania could – with appropriate allowance for future growth – sell the surplus for as much as €1.0bln – needed to restructure the power system. However, the oil industry is responsible for a number of problems relating to sludge in Prahova. A Phare programme for 'Cleaner Soil in Ploieşti' provides €750,000 (including €250,000 from the Romanian state) to assess and correct the pollution of soil and water by oil residues in southern Ploieşti as far as the Petrobrazi refinery. The feasibility study was carried out by Iwaco (The Netherlands) with Petrostar Institute (Ploieşti) and Eco-Ind (Bucharest) in 2001. Meanwhile the German Bank for Investment & Development has helped with a pilot plant at Câmpina to treat land containing oil, with the aim of removing 1,700t of oil products from the Fish Lake area.

Land Reclamation

This has also taken place in Gorj, another area damaged by both oil and lignite extraction, not to mention two large power stations (Rovinari and Turceni) and the cement industry at Bârseşti near Târgu Jiu. But some 260ha of degraded land have now been reclaimed in the strip mining area out of a total of 1,700ha of farmland affected in the Rovinari-Poiana area alone after the great quarries were opened up in the 1960s and canalisation of the diverted rivers freed the floodplain lands for mining (Cioacă & Dinu 1998). Substantial areas have been taken up by tipping but some have been partially reclaimed for fruit growing at Beterega and Gârla, while willows have been planted to stop torrential erosion; on the other hand at Berbeşti (Vâlcea) the large Panga Nouă tip (holding 50mln.cu.m accumulated over 96ha during 1979–2002, requiring the removal of 200 families from Vlăduţeşti village) became unstable early in 2008 and suddenly slumped over a further 20ha of farmland, requiring some further evacuation. The Ţicleni oil industry has damaged the Cioiana valley and in 1999 Petrom returned to agriculture some 250,000t of soil polluted by oil residues in this area (with oil recovered in the process!). There are about 800,000cu.m of oil residues ('trash') in Romania and further reclamation is taking place at Suplacu de Barcău (Bihor) and Videle (Teleorman). FAO have approved a scheme for 'Rehabilitation of Polluted Soils' worth $264,000: a two year project to use the most efficient means of improvement for farmland polluted by oil waste, mining operations, pesticides and chemical fertilisers. Action will be implemented by the Institute for Research in Pedology & Agrochemistry and the Academy of Agricultural Sciences & Forestry.

Hydropower

Environmental issues have arisen such as the disappearance of an ancient fish species from the Lotru basin following the construction of the accumulation lakes. But management standards have improved through the Romanian-Canadian programme 'Environment Management for the Romanian Hydropower Sector' launched in 2000 to deal with the prevention of flood, pollution and land degradation through waste management, habitat restoration (to conserve flora and fauna) and pilot projects in land planning at Dăieşti, Râureni, Râmnicu Vâlcea and Vânâtori stations. As a result the various regional branches of Hidroelectrica should now be better able to develop their interest in the management of river basins. And in 2003 the company was seeking ISO14001 environmental management certification after substantial spending on preventing flood and soil erosion, as well waste collection and recycling, environmental studies and assessments. Of course practical problems remain such as damage to hydropower plants at Râmnicu Vâlcea arising through waste and wood mass in the river, including the high cost of unclogging; though here again Canadian experience was harnessed in 1999 given the recommendation by Hydro (the Canadian equivalent of Hidroelectrica) over the value of river councils to bring stakeholders together. Electricity distributors are helping to conserve stalks in Transylvania by collaborating with ornithologists over placing nesting boxes at a safe height above the high tension wires: when birds build their heavy nests directly on the top of the concrete posts they are frequently electrocuted while consumers may suffer from local blackouts.

The Wider Energy Problem

This is many-sided but the backlog in overhauling the energy infrastructure is massive and constitutes an embarrassing legacy of a central planning system that failed to place a realistic value on energy resources while encouraging higher consumption in the economy (though not by private households) as an end in itself. The challenge is all the greater in view of the substantial trade dependence for energy at a time of rising costs without any built-in concessions of the kind that previously favoured communist states importing from the Soviet Union. Electricity and heating prices have been traditionally set below the cost-recovery level, while gas prices in particular have been below the import parity level and further losses have arisen through inefficient collection procedures.

Romania has significant primary energy resources but barely enough for even two-thirds self-sufficiency, with a particular weakness in oil of which more than half is now imported (Table 7.1). In 2002 the requirement was 37.9mln.toe of which only 24.7mln.toe was produced domestically. Moreover the situation is getting worse with primary energy imports surging by 11.8 per cent during 2004 (10 months) while domestic energy grew by only 2.1 per cent. Coal reserves at the end of 2002 were 1.46bln.t – enough to last 48 years at the present rate of exploitation – but much of the coal is low grade and production costs exceed import prices. And despite a policy of support for domestic coal mining imports of coking coal are unavoidable. Meanwhile Romania has traditionally been the region's leader in hydrocarbon fuel output but oil production peaked in 1974. Petrom's reserves are 1.4bln barrels (though not all are in Romania) and substantial import dependence has badly affected the economics of petrochemistry since 1989. Oil consumption reached 224,000 barrels in 2002 with domestic production 124,500: while Petrom spent $330mln on oil imports for their Arpechim (Piteşti) and Petrobrazi (Ploieşti) refineries. Gas production has also peaked with 37.9 per cent of consumption imported in 2002.

Winter Fuel Imports

These are a major trade item and require special financial arrangements. The ABN-AMRO bank has raised a $75mln six-year loan for 20 of the 28 members of the Cogeneration Power Plants' Association to finance such operations. In the case of Distrigaz-Sud (one of the regional gas suppliers) almost a quarter of the company's needs during winter 2002–3 came from imports financed by a $10mln credit from Raiffeisen Bank. At the same time winter fuel bills are a major item of household expenditure which frequently exceeded average salaries in the past. 72 per cent of the population (but only 1.7 per cent in rural areas) depend on power/heating stations compared with 27.9 per cent for stoves using solid or liquid fuel (98.0 per cent in rural areas) and 0.1 per cent (0.3 per cent) have other arrangements e.g. solar panels. Many households are cut off and some people have even lost their apartments because of unpaid bills. And the problem was exacerbated by external pressure on government to raise energy prices to European levels by 2007 – with subsidies to debt-ridden companies eliminated and infrastructure upgraded (at the cost of some €2.5bln) – while imported energy costs were also rising e.g. Russian gas cost $270/cu.m in 2006 when the internal production cost is $110. Sudden rises embarrass domestic consumers and also industry e.g. less-efficient glass producers and the nitrogen fertiliser industry producers like Azomureş in Târgu Mureş.

Consumption Trends

Reduction since 1989 reflects both lower demand and greater efficiency. Electricity generating capacity is 22.2GW although only 16GW is operational

Table 7.1 *Energy Consumption (mln.toe) (A) and Percentage from Domestic Sources (B) 1992–2005*

Year	Total		Coal		Gas		Oil		Wood		Primary Elec.	
	A	B	A	B	A	B	A	B	A	B	A	B
1992	50.94	65.2	12.17	60.4	20.92	82.9	13.86	48.4	0.80	98.4	1.43	73.3
1993	50.68	65.4	10.79	69.9	20.14	82.0	15.25	44.4	1.17	98.8	1.38	81.3
1994	50.16	63.2	11.52	67.5	18.56	79.9	15.89	42.9	1.17	98.7	1.30	88.1
1995	55.94	61.5	12.17	64.8	19.24	75.1	16.27	41.8	3.84	99.7	1.53	95.7
1996	55.94	62.8	12.11	66.6	19.42	70.9	14.56	46.0	4.90	99.6	1.92	89.9
1997	51.27	61.2	11.40	57.9	15.94	74.7	13.41	49.2	3.37	99.7	3.02	97.0
1998	46.20	62.3	9.38	54.9	14.97	74.8	12.93	49.6	3.03	99.6	3.12	96.7
1999	39.79	69.8	9.51	61.8	13.73	81.5	11.09	56.3	2.83	99.7	2.96	96.8
2000	40.36	69.6	8.06	69.5	13.68	80.2	11.48	53.6	2.77	99.7	2.68	97.5
2001	42.66	65.6	8.98	69.5	13.76	79.1	12.16	50.2	2.15	98.8	2.69	97.5
2002	43.99	62.9	9.77	62.6	13.87	74.8	12.94	46.0	2.39	98.4	2.73	98.6
2003	45.38	62.1	9.91	65.9	15.78	66.7	11.66	49.5	2.93	99.0	2.34	96.6
2004	47.20	59.5	9.61	63.4	14.84	68.7	13.68	40.9	3.26	97.0	3.00	92.8
2005	47.35	57.3	9.41	61.6	14.81	64.4	14.88	35.8	3.33	96.9	3.30	93.8

Source: Statistical Yearbooks: Table 16.6

i.e. more than a quarter is not needed, partly because of falling industrial production but increasingly because of more energy-efficient machinery. Nevertheless, energy intensity is still poor. For an equivalent GDP Romania needed 3.25 times the energy used in the UK in 1990, falling to 2.81 in 1993 (2.74 and 2.63 for Germany). These are higher figures than Bulgaria (3.06–2.62 for UK and 2.58–2.47 for Germany) and substantially higher than Hungary (2.06–1.87 and 1.74–1.76) and Poland (2.06–2.06 and 1.74–1.94). Calculations by Kramer (1999) in relating the ECECs to the EU performance over GDP value per unit of energy consumption would assess Romania with 44.5 per cent: better than Bulgaria (42.6) and Slovakia (38.9) but poorer than Poland (49.3), Czech Republic (53.1) and Hungary (55.6). However production prices were driven down significantly from $48–39/MWh over just two years during 2001–3. Inherited systems of energy production are still inefficient: coal and lignite mining, thermal and hydropower generation as well as centralised heating systems inherited from communism that lose more heat than they deliver and do not allow individual consumers to control temperature. At the end of the 1990s Bucharest's heating system had not been overhauled since the 1970s, with many cracks and heavy water losses among the local distribution systems operating from the control points (one per 1,500 apartments) served by the primary higher temperature network. Moreover bills have been traditionally based on floor measurements, the number of residents in the household and local government distribution/processing costs. And in 2003 households without meters were billed for the average consumption of those with meters! The situation in the past has been bad for the government as well as consumers: electricity and heating prices have been below the cost-recovery level, while gas prices in particular have been below the import parity level and further losses have arisen through inefficient collection procedures. Individually-metered heating units constitute one of the many goals to be achieved before Romania becomes an efficient and environmentally clean energy user. But distribution systems are frequently hazardous with a recent explosion at a Craiova heating unit revealing 'chaotically intersecting' underground gas, water, heating and telephone lines.

RESTRUCTURING AND PRIVATISATION

Privatisation of the energy sector was initially unthinkable but has moved quite quickly into the realm of reality since 1997 through various exercises in reorganisation to adjust monopolies and phase out state intervention. Although hydrocarbon exploration was opened up to foreign companies in 1990 through production-sharing agreements, privatisation was long-delayed due to the strategic nature of the business and high levels of subsidy. In 1998 a new energy strategy (until 2020) was approved, adapting to the European single market and taking the first step in restructuring the major utilities and opening up to competition. But prices remained too low and required a further round of increases in 2005 that proved to be a major contributor to inflation. Now there is almost universal acceptance of the need for privatisation 'accompanied by good corporate governance and an effectively-implemented regulatory framework that can deal with monopoly behaviour, secure fair prices for consumers and avoid external over-indebtedness' (Dăianu 2004, p.401). According to the 2001–4 strategy, privatisation was led by the regional companies for electricity and gas distribution in the context of mounting concern over the condition of the infrastructure, with the production sector following on. European money is coming in for technological studies that will form a basis for power station rehabilitation (especially for large stations like Turceni) while American and European companies (e.g. Germany's Ruhrgas) are taking over the Romanian utilities. Meanwhile the Constanţa-Trieste energy corridor, seen as a potential stimulus to the disposal of companies like Rafo, Vega, Oltchim and Solventul Timişoara in 1999 has not yet materialised but realisation has been slow. There is no prospect for privatisation in the coal industry (except for specific fields tied to power stations) and the effort is one of downsizing the relevant national companies to find a basis for viable operation (as already noted in discussion of the mining industry as a whole). Nor is there an intention to privatise Nuclearelectrica, Transelectrica and Transgaz, though the shares of the last two are quoted to stimulate 'market-viable management' (along with two state electricity distributors, Constanţa Seaport Administration and Henri Coanda Airport). The section will now deal with electricity, gas and oil companies.

Electricity

This was first placed in the hands of the vast Renel organisation in 1990, divided into 53 joint stock companies dealing with repair of installations and R&D, in addition to the nuclear fuel and heavy water factories, integrated into Renel which also held 49 per cent of capital in ABB-Energoreparaţii. Major rehabilitation programmes were launched in 1996 for thermal and hydro stations as well as transport and distribution. Renel offered a 20 per cent discount to Alro and Sidex, the leading aluminium and steel companies, to pay for imported fuel. Basic electricity prices were high enough to discourage excessive consumption and cover production costs. In 1997 prices were pushed up to \$50/MWh compared with 35–40 in Ukraine/Russia. Then Renel was restructured in 1998 as two national companies (a) the Conel national electricity company for production, transmission and distribution – but with separate identities (albeit under its umbrella) for Termoelectrica, Hidroelectrica and Electrica (split into 42 separate distribution companies) and (b) a national trading society Nuclearelectrica for the Cernavodă power station, with 'autonomous authority' status for the heavy water producer Romag employing 2,400 workers on its four production lines at Halinga near Drobeta-Turnu Severin; and the Institute of Energy Studies & Consultancy. Unions naturally saw a danger of 'artificial' price rises by separate sectors as the cost of striving for a competitive power market, but crossed subsidies in electricity supply were eliminated in 1999 when industry ceased to support domestic consumers who inevitably incur high costs through the small amounts and low tensions involved. Electrica formed a j.v. with Germany's RWE in 2002 to improve distribution in Bucharest with metering for each household and block stairs.

Restructuring in 2000

Three companies under Conel's umbrella (Termoelectrica, Hidroelectrica and Electrica) became independent and a new Transelectrica national company emerged to deal specifically with the grid. Thus Conel as an over-arching organisation was eliminated in favour of discrete smaller units that could be considered for privatisation; with the proviso that as part of the 'white charter' of 2001 (creating convenient units for privatisation in the electricity, gas and defence industries) the 42 separate Electrica distribution companies were reduced to eight: Moldavia for the northeast (based at Suceava) with 1.29mln customers; Banat for the west (based on Timişoara) with 0.84mln customers, Bucharest and Ilfov with 1.06mln; Dobrogea at Constanţa (covering Călăraşi and Ialomiţa counties as well as Constanţa and Tulcea) with 0.59; Muntenia (Buzău, Dâmboviţa, Giurgiu and Prahova) at Ploieşti with 1.20; Oltenia at Craiova with 1.35 (Argeş and Teleorman as well as the South West region), Transilvania-Nord at Oradea with 1.08; and Transilvania-Sud at Braşov with 1.02. There was a subsequent alteration to reorganise Bucharest and Muntenia by transferring Giurgiu from the latter to the former which became Muntenia-Sud while the rest of the old Muntenia became Muntenia-Nord. Meanwhile, to liberalise the electricity market, the National Regulating Authority for Energy allowed nominated large companies to choose their electricity supplier in 2000 and negotiate the price. The first ten were Alro (Slatina), Arpechim (Piteşti), Automobile Dacia (Piteşti), Azomureş (Târgu Mureş), Cimus (Câmpulung Muscel), Lafarge Romcim (Medgidia), Petrobrazi (Ploieşti), RATB (Bucharest), SMR (Balş) and the ONLC (Oltenia National Lignite Company) Jilţ mine. The initial 10 per cent of the market was increased to 25 per cent at the beginning of 2002 by accrediting more 'eligible consumers': further Oltenia coalmines (Berbeşti, Motru – surface and underground – Peşteana, Pinoasa, Roşia and Rovinari) along with Alprom (Slatina), Ambro (Suceava), Casial (Deva), Ductil (Buzău), Elsid (Titu), European Drinks (Oradea), Gruppo Frati (Sebeş), Ispat Sidex (Galaţi) – temporarily, pending the completion of outstanding payments; Moldocim (Bicaz), Petrotub (Roman), UCM (Reşiţa) and the subsidiaries of Holcim (Aleşd and Turda) and the Lafarge installations at Hoghiz and Târgu Jiu.

Privatisation of the Regional 'Electrica' Distribution Companies

This attracted wide interest from several German companies – Energie Baden Württemberg (EnBW), E.On Energie (Ruhrgas) and RWE – as well as Electricité de France, the Greek Public Power Corporation, ČEZ (Czech Republic), Enel (Italy), Ferosa International (Spain), United Utilities (UK) and AES (USA). The process began with Banat and Dobrogea in 2003–4, following advice under the consultancy programme by the French company BNP Paribas (2002). Enel won the bidding for both these companies with €35.1mln for the 24.6 per cent of the shares and €76.7mln in investment for a capital increase to 51 per cent. There was also a €300mln investment plan to improve infrastructure, starting with €65mln in 2006. In 2004 Moldova went to E.On Energie who acquired a 24.6 per cent stake and share issue equivalent to another 35 per cent in a company selling 4.1bln.MWh annually while ČEZ gained control of Oltenia (6.80mln.MWh) on a similar basis. The intention was to press on through 2005–6 with Muntenia-Sud scheduled for January 2006 (with particular interest from AES, ČEZ, Enel, ENW (Austria), Gaz de France plus two from Spain – Iberdrola and Union Fenosa – and the German trio of EnBW, E.On and RWE). Enel has been successful in this case and the focus is now moving to the three remaining companies: Muntenia Nord and Transilvania Nord/Sud scheduled for 2007–8. Privatisation is also extending to power stations, notably the three major generating complexes of Craiova, Rovinari and Turceni, along with their lignite quarries separated from the ONLC in the teeth of strong union opposition. The need for €8–10bln to complete the upgrade process makes this inevitable with action awaited by ARSA in 2008.

Transelectrica

Urgent rehabilitation of the national grid system is required – 3.74th.kms at 220Kv; 4.54 at 400Kv; and 0.16 at 750Kv – to avoid the risk of collapse which became more serious in the first years of the millennium. There are transformer stations to install and rehabilitate as well power lines to modernise (for a better quality current and higher safety/reliability), not to mention the replacement of obsolete technology at power stations. Modernisation of lines (costed at $105mln in 2002) includes fibre optics, following a US Trade & Development Agency grant of $0.43mln to Transelectrica for feasibility studies on the electricity transport system as a basis for an ITC infrastructure, arising out of a j.v. between the electricity and gas industries in 2003. This initiative – marking the end of the RT monopoly in 2003 – involves a Teletrans company to manage 3,900kms fibre optics by the end of 2004, with the eventual prospect of a 9,000km system. The first bidding organised by Transelectrica – for rehabilitation of 900kms of high tension lines (with Arad/Oradea-Békéscsaba as a priority) plus connection with optical fibres – was won by Electromontaj (Bucharest) and Nokia for €11mln, supported by funding from EBRD, EIB and Phare (2002). The latest estimate of funding needed to modernise the system (2007) called for €2.0bln over five years.

Transformer Stations. In the same year there were credits of $150mln from Swedish companies to rehabilitate transformer stations and reduce maintenance. In 2004 ABB Romania rehabilitated the 400–100–10Kv Constanţa station to international (UCTE) standards using advanced technology; they have also commissioned a substation in Braşov county and have upgraded Bacău substation with the help of a loan from Sweden's Nordic Investment Bank. The Comăneşti 110–10Kv station has also been rehabilitated and a brand new urban type 110–10Kv substation (the first of its kind) installed in a purpose-built structure for the Stadion area of Cluj-Napoca. In 2005 ABB designed and built a 400–200–110Kv station at Gutină to provide a reliable supply to Moldavia ($40mln) and modernised the 400–220–110Kv Sibiu Sud station; improving the power supply to the north and also with western Romania via the 400Kv Sibiu-Mintia line leading to Western Europe. The company is also involved with replacement of the high-medium-low voltage equipment at Piteşti Sud (220–110–20Kv) and Oradea Centru (110–20–10Kv). Altogether Transelectrica needs €900mln (from EBRD, EIB and its own funds) for modernising infrastructure during 2001–13: 320mln in 2001–4; 500mln for 2005–7, with a slowing down after accession. There is also the question of further extensions in distribution to connect outlying settlements. Electrica also launched a programme for remote areas with €300mln of government support during 2003–6: $150mln was needed to connect 94,000 households during 2003–5, covering new housing as well as some 4,000 existing households in 121 localities lacking distribution. But this has not solved the problem entirely and when premier Tăriceanu promised electrification for all villages by the end of 2005 he subsequently had to face reminders e.g. from 12 localities in Hunedoara county including one (Ribicioara in Ribiţa commune) where the old surviving inhabitants (lacking a transformer) can only gaze upwards at the high tension wires above. The privatised Enel-owned Banat electricity company certainly realises the high cost of supplying a few extra customers.

Gas

Although an extensive gas distribution system was built under communism it was not comprehensive and inequality in gas supply became a political issue in view of the convenience of this fuel and the pressure placed on local woodlands where people remain dependent on wood-burning stoves.

Investment was therefore necessary (e.g. $1.0bln for Covasna and Harghita) and again to extend supply in 1997 to the most distant counties like Tulcea to boost the efficiency of key industries like the alumina factory (BBG Alum). This has implications for the quality of service because any reduction in gas pressure in winter can have very serious consequences for large chemical plants that may have to shut down temporarily. Romgaz therefore needed to invest $1.0bln in updating gas transport and distribution, along with underground storage and international gas transit. Storage for winter was increased from 1.3bln.cu.m in 1998 to 2.7 in 2000 with 4.5 anticipated in 2010. The main underground storages are located at Bălăceanca (Ilfov), Bilciureşti (Dâmboviţa) – the largest with its initial capacity of 0.7bln.cu.m rising to 1.2bln, Sărmăşel and Târgu Mureş (Mureş) and Urziceni (Ialomiţa) but further capacity is needed in deficit areas using salt cavities near to intersecting pipelines. Romgaz undertook a $28.8mln investment in an underground gas storage at Ghergheasa (Buzău) to help meet peak domestic demand and to facilitate export to Bulgaria and Turkey; with 100mln.cu.m injected to raise gas pressure from 30 to 50 atmospheres. Meanwhile distribution in the north of the country improved with the arrival of Russian gas supplied through Ukraine, with a possible underground store at Roman-Mărgineni mentioned in 2000.

Romgaz

Restructuring for an era of competition and privatisation started in 1998 and should complete in 2006 apart from storage. By 2000 there were five entities: Transgaz (Mediaş) for transport; Distrigaz-Nord (Târgu Mureş) and Distrigaz-Sud (Bucharest) for distribution. However the National Regulating Authority in the natural gas domain designated eligible consumers – essentially Sidex (Galaţi) and gas-burning power stations – with the right to conclude direct contracts at advantageous prices and thereby open up a quarter of the gas market in 2002 (for technological reasons a minimum consumption of 5.0mln.cu.m was required). Meanwhile production and storage functions were initially separated through Exprogaz (Mediaş) – a commercial company for natural gas exploration and production (covering 65 per cent of domestic consumption – with the balance by Petrom and imports – with access to the storages at Sărmăşel and Târgu Mureş; and Depogaz (Ploieşti) primarily a storage operation but with a tenth of the gas exploitation as well. However the two were subsequently combined to re-create Romgaz, since the disappearance of a name respected on the international scene was considered unfortunate by the new government in 2001. To give an impression of the complexity of the distribution companies, Distrigaz-Sud was responsible for 12,500kms of pipelines 650kms of polyethylene, including 250kms of replacements (financed by World Bank and IBRD in 1997–9 under a scheme that unfortunately did not continue in 2000).

Faced with many more old pipes needing renewal since the 1980s, 500kms of pipes were replaced 2001–2 with planned continuation at 250kms/yr. Further extensions – 150kms of steel and polyethylene – serve some 130,000 new customers. Distrigaz-Sud invested €100mln in 2006 replacing 500kms pipes and providing 450–500kms of new pipes, while gas sources were diversified. Gaz de France was also interested in electricity company Muntenia-Sud.

Distrigaz-Nord/Sud Privatisations. These were scheduled for completion in 2005 with interest from Germany (EnBW, Ruhrgas, RWE and Wintershall) as well as AES, ČEZ, Enel, Gaz de France (with IFC support over Distrigaz-Sud) and the Spanish companies Iberdrola and Union Fenosa. For Distrigaz-Nord Ruhrgas paid €125mln for a 30 per cent stake plus €179mln for new shares to increase its holding to 51 per cent; while Distrigaz-Sud was acquired on similar terms (for payments of €128 and €183 respectively) by Gaz de France with existing interests in Berlin, Hungary and Slovakia already. Both companies need a concession, natural gas licence and distribution licence for the longest time possible by law: 49 years, 30 years and 15 years respectively. Interest was also reported from Gazprom (possibly with Marco) and Wintershall (Germany). Meanwhile E.On will buy Mol's non-core businesses in natural gas supply and storage and will invest €200mln over seven years to modernise Distrigaz-Nord and attract industrial consumers. In addition to upgrading, Distrigaz-Nord/Sud customers will benefit from some reduced gas delivery prices during the 2005–7 regulatory period. After unsuccessful bids for Romanian electricity and gas companies, Russia's Gazprom is interested in partnership with E.On (who bid successfully for Moldova and whose gas unit – Ruhrgas – acquired Distrigaz-Nord) in respect of energy distribution projects in Romania; not to mention possible collaboration including E.On's partner BASF in developing the Yuzhna Russkoye gasfield. But it will some time before E.On can sell its shares.

Other Companies. Small distribution companies are now able to compete successfully among retail and industrial customers and had captured 30 per cent of the market in 2007. A special arrangement concerns Gaz Bucovina – owned by Suceava CC and other local authorities – who received a credit from a Norwegian Bank in 2000 to build Romania's first private methane gas distribution system among the villages of northern Suceava. Finance will cover a methane gas system for 59 localities and the revamping of thermal energy in all urban areas to be undertaken by Hans Gunther Reimer (Germany). Finally it should be noted that bottled gas has been a private operation for some time with companies like Linde Gaz (Germany) and Rubis (France) involved. Linde are based in Timişoara with regional air separators in Cluj, Ploieşti, Râmnicu Vâlcea and Timişoara, plus acetylene lines in Galaţi, Ploieşti and Timişoara and a hydrogen facility in Râmnicu Vâlcea. Meanwhile, Rubis (who acquired Shell's regional LPG interest in 2007 for €90mln), run the Negoieşti gas filling plant at Ploieşti-Brazi. Both companies distribute nationwide through local county organisations. ButanGas, owned by I.C.Drăgan, is a leader in the local LPG market – distributing to isolated houses, hotels and factories without a piped gas supply – with a growing presence at the Midia marine gas terminal. The company had a j.v. with Petrom so that gas could be sold through the latter's network but this arrangement ceased after Petrom acquired Shell Gas. The Borcea family's Crimbo Gas business also lies in the LPG domain and was sold in 2008 to the Dutch Group SHV for €50mln. And with regard to industrial gases, Air Liquide (France) completed a €10mln project at Călăraşi followed by Siad (Italy) with a €5.0mln investment at the same place.

Oil

Petrom

Any notion of privatisation in the oil industry was anathema to Romanian governments prior to 1997. In 1990 separate national companies were created for pipelines (Petrotrans), distribution (Peco) and refineries (Rafirom), coordinating the refineries of Rafo (Oneşti) for the north, Petrobrazi (Ploieşti) for the south and Arpechim (Piteşti) for petrochemical feedstocks plus limited exports. In 1991 crude oil exploitation and production activities were grouped under Petrom (while gas production, transport and distribution was combined under Romgaz), although 12 drilling units were separated and turned into commercial companies in 1992, followed by building and assembling units in 1993. As late as 1996 a decree provided for full state control of the oil and petrochemical industry including the subsoil and subsea resources (with the state to take responsibility for all domestically-produced oil). And in that year the centre-left government brought all production together under Compania Română de Petrol (CRP) chaired by M.Georgescu (former chairman of the Arpechim petrochemical complex at Piteşti) combining the old Petrom with Petrotrans, Rafirom and Peco. This was deplored by the opposition but had some merit through internalising many inter-enterprise debts and overcoming financial blockages. CRP was then reconstituted as Petrom in 1997 and enlarged by acquisition of the Doljchim chemical and fertiliser factory in 1999 after a Burgas (Bulgaria) bidder was disqualified for ignoring conditions imposed by a creditors' meeting. Petrom proposed to invest $20mln over two years and will process gas obtained from the Târgu Jiu region. Altogether there were state holdings of at least 51 per cent in 62 different Petrom enterprises: 43 commercial companies (mainly county offices of Peco), 12 refineries and petrochemical plants, three pipeline and transport companies, three research institutes and the foreign trade company Petrolexportimport. Under new rules (1997) sales of petrol from the refineries required immediate cash payment (previously two months grace was allowed and so – especially in an inflationary situation – customers always preferred to buy from state refineries rather than import). The intention was to process 16-18mln.t of crude and reach 22mln.t in 2000; ensuring products for all branches of the chemical industry (currently 14–15mln.t but with idle capacity to be returned to production). Foreign companies could buy into Petrom but only up to 49 per cent and invest in refineries, but without management control and hence an unattractive proposition!

Delayed Privatisation. The new government in 1997 was keen to restructure the 'monster' created by their political rivals. Radu Vasile, one the centre-right prime ministers of the 1997–2000 period, had stated in opposition that the first measure of a DCR government would be Petrom's elimination, such was the dislike of the company's monopoly status (although it was claimed with some justification to be similar to that of Elf in France or Mol in Hungary, while some facilities like the Black Sea Petrotrans terminal were open to other users). However privatisation was delayed. A 35 per cent stake was offered in 1999 (with the world oil price very low at $9.0/barrel) but management control was again not on offer. There was an international auction at the beginning of 2000 but all five offers were unsatisfactory. It was after the return of the centre-left, with a radically-changed political agenda, that privatisation was achieved in 2004 in the context of a much-improved economic situation: the company's debt was written-off and restructuring was underway with uneconomic sites/wells shut down, crude production from existing fields intensified and offshore/onshore exploration stepped-up. Petrom privatisation was included in the PSAL II project in agreement with the World Bank and IMF: it was a good test of Romania's readiness to sell enterprises of great national importance. Companies selected for participation in the sale of 51 per cent of Petrom in 2003 were: Alon (USA), Conoco Phillips (UK), ENI (Italy), Gazprom (Russia), Glencore International (Switzerland), Hellenic Petroleum (Greece), Mol (Hungary), Occidental Oil & Gas Holding Corporation (USA), ÖMV (Austria), PKN Orlen (Poland) and TNK-BP (UK) with interest also reported from Amoco, Lukoil, Shell and Total. Bidders were required to take a 33.4 per cent stake and invest to raise their shares to 51 per cent, while environmental and cleaning-up costs were taken on by the state. ÖMV (already running 73 of its own petrol stations in Romania) won the competition with a $1.6bln bid after the Mol and Occidental bids were rejected in the final round. The raising of the shareholding to 51 per cent involved a capital increase of €983.3mln. It was agreed that the company would remain integrated for at least five years in return for which there were no restrictions of lay-offs. Interestingly this was one privatisation where domestic clients of the government were not allowed to succeed, although it seems that there was an attempt made by the Tender company through a partnership with Halliburton and a Dutch NATO intelligence officer W.Matser (known to Tender and considered an influential figure – through his NATO connections – who might attract foreign capital). When Matser was forced to withdraw through charges of fraudulent dealings he was replaced by Regal Petroleum (UK): chaired by Frank Timis: a business friend of Tender and an oil/mining entrepreneur. But while Tender was able to project a credible bid, with Halliburton providing 'technical, management and operational expertise', it was weeded out in the first round. However charges of 'croney capitalism' have surfaced in other sections of the oil industry.

Modernisation, at a brisk pace, boosted Petrom's attractiveness – reflected in the high value of $2.7bln in 2003. Upgrading of 146 depots for oil and gas storage started in 1999: 32 were dealt with by the end of 2001 with a further 43 projected in 2002. The process meant that all gas could be recovered instead of being lost into the atmosphere, with savings at Colibaşi store alone equivalent to a well costing 2.0mln.lei to construct. There was also lower electricity consumption because of hot water heating rather than steam heating. Petrom was also investing in its refineries and filling stations (with the company's 600 outlets amounting to about half the national total at the time), while 'externalisation' helped to reduce employment down from a level of 80–90,000 quoted when the company was first anticipated in 1996 to 57,000 at privatisation: this involved 14,200 at Petroserv Bucharest; auxiliary refinery activities at Arpechim (1,980), Petrobrazi (1,155) and Doljchim (375); also the Petrotrans transport branch (1,110) and some energy and mechanical activities at Petromar Constanţa (785). Petrom was also highly active overseas, participating in tenders for oil exploration in North Africa, Middle East and Asia in order to increase its reserves portfolio to 25mln.t/950mln barrels – and foreign production to 2.0mln.t annually by 2005. Particular interest was shown in Kazakhstan through a 25 year exploration and exploitation licence for Jusaly (1998) where production will expand to an industrial level; likewise for Aktas, Tasbulat and Turkmenoy (1999) through acquisition of Tasbulat Oil Company; while acquisition of Oztyurk Munai in 2000 concluded an exploration and production contract for hydrocarbons at Sinelnikovskoe. Offshore drilling in Iran made use of the Fortuna and Orizont platforms (modernised at Sharjah).

Foreign Interests Extended. In India agreements with Essar Oii secured participation in exploration at the Ratna field and offshore (Saurashtra) and a contribution to the building of Vadinar refinery; there was also a j.v. in India with Hi-Tech Carbon (Additya Birla Group) producing black carbon; and technical assistance was provided in Kuwait. The Petrom drilling rig 'Diamonds 1' started operations in Ecuador under Petrom's exploration and production sharing agreement with the Petroecuador Group (after Rompetrol acquired Lumbaqui Oil in 2001) and a drilling area was leased for 20 years with a possibility of a further five: production reached 15,000 barrels/day in 2002 for sale in regional markets. Finally the Fortuna installation undertook drilling in the Sea of Marmara under a contract between Petrom and Turkey's National Petroleum Company in 1996; and the company also worked with Enterprise Oil on an oil derrick for the Bulgarian platform (Bulgarevo Vest) with drilling by Petromar. Under President Wolfgang Rüttenstorfer, this great vertically-integrated company is making profits – €391mln with turnover up a quarter to €2.97bln in 2005; €647mln in 2006 (a 60 per cent improvement on 2005) and €500mln in the first half of 2006 alone. Meanwhile the company invested €1.0bln during 2005–7 (including €100mln/yr on new hydrocarbon sources) to retain 35 per cent of the Romanian market at least (€2.0bln sales in 2003) and an 8.0mln.t refinery capacity. The company has also been supported by the lease of oilfields by the government at a rate below the market price of €0.5/sq.m; not to mention the sale of some oilfields to Petrom under a secret clause of the privatisation agreement, conferring a big advantage on ÖMV.

Reserves are to be increased, production and pipeline transport automated and exports maintained (2.0mln.t/yr including 1.0mln to Turkey). Expansion in the region started with Petrom Hungaria in 1998, leading initially to Nagylak and Szeged filling stations and then the Békéscsaba complex in 2000 including oil storage. Petrom Yugoslavia was founded in 1999 for wholesaling and retailing, with commercial activity postponed until 2001; while Petrom Moldova dates to 2000 with the Chişinău Ceucari distribution complex following in 2001. Relations with competitors eased after ÖMV allowed prices to fluctuate with international trends. But the outlook over employment cannot be too bright considering that Petrom's 50,000-strong workforce dwarfed the ÖMV total of 6,000 across the rest of the region. Petrom's productivity of €43,000 per worker compared very unfavourably with €1.23mln for the company in Austria, although the inevitable lay-offs among the 50,000 employees will occur 'naturally'. The company has sold its Carpatina mineral water interest to Lipomin but it is expanding in the transport field where Rompetrol Logistics runs a road tanker fleet as well as railway operations (with 400 tank wagons and 10 locomotives) in which domain it hopes to become the leading private operator. Abroad Petrom have taken over ÖMV's operations in Bulgaria and Serbia (105 filling stations in all) and seek expansion (for both exploitation and distribution) in Turkey, plus a big growth in Kazakhstan. The aim is to boost oil output by acquiring an oil exploration and production company.

Rompetrol

With gross revenue of $1.6bln in 2004, this company is controlled largely by Liberal politician Dinu Patriciu, an entrepreneur in building and publishing who became majority owner in 1999 and was reputed to be worth some $350mln in 2006. The company was set up 1974 to undertake constructional work in foreign countries but acquired Palplast (producing polyethylene pipes in Sibiu for gas, oil, water and sewage transport) in 1996 and entered into contracts with Turkmenistan in 1997 to develop the Sovetbad gas field. A management buyout in 1992 was followed by asset stripping; until Patriciu took over in 1998 with a $2.1mln purchase (assisted by two Americans: Colin Hart and Phil Stephenson). A radical reorganisation ensued, with the new owner personally tidying up some of his assets, followed by diversification both downstream into filling stations and upstream into oil refining (as noted in the case of Petromidia and Vega below) while Petros Romanian Well Services were taken over in 2000. A stock exchange flotation in 2002 generated high profits amid claims of an artificially low valuation which involved both Patriciu and his associates in charges (unproven) relating to fraud, money laundering, tax evasion and insider dealing. But the company has continued to prosper; operating through the whole chain from extraction to processing and distribution, while recruiting a strategic ally through sale of a 25 per cent interest to ÖMV (returned after ÖMV won the Petrom privatisation battle). Rompetrol is an ambitious company with growing sales in other countries in the region where US and West European firms are relatively inactive. Believing in the potential for profit in a Balkan-Black Sea market of 125mln people, exports to Moldova and Ukraine were followed by business with Albania, Bulgaria and Macedonia, with future plans for Greece and Turkey. Albania in particular is seen as a pristine market in which few large companies have intervened, with scope for expansion towards Kosovo, Macedonia and Montenegro. Rompetrol operates a 14,000t depot and floating terminal in Durrës and spent $3.0mln on filling stations in Durrës and Tirana – with initially 10 (later 20) rented stations brought up to the Romanian level. They hoped to sell 150,000t of products in 2005 (10 per cent of the market) through their own stations as well as 40 others plus 10 small wholesalers). The company also launched a project for petrol stations in Ukraine – initially 200 through company ownership and franchise – and purchased the Dyneff chain in France in 2006 where the Rompetrol label is now used. Meanwhile, exploration work in Ecuador and Kazakhstan was extended to Azerbaijan (Zaisan) and Russia in 2002 and now the Middle East and North Africa as well; seeking to raise foreign production from 11 per cent in 2001 to over 40 in 2003; thereby compensating for falling output at home (carried out by Rompetrol Well Services, formerly Petros). It was access to a range of foreign markets that made Rompetrol attractive to Kazakhstan's KazMunaiGaz company that paid $2.7bln for 75 per cent of the company in 2007: seeking wider outlets for its growing oil production (after Rompetrol had been seeking a capital increase from another company involving up to a 25 per cent shareholding).

INTERNATIONAL TRANSPORT LINKS

Oil

The greatest interest has attached to a Constanța-Trieste oil pipeline linked with increasing exports from the Caspian zone with its 60–75bln barrels of reserves. With shipping through the Straits nearing its maximum (requiring additional Caspian output to be transported through pipelines only), Romania was in a good position through capacities at Constanța with an oil terminal and capacity for ships of 200,000dwt. There were also refining capacities because thanks to Ceauşescu's hobby of developing petrochemistry 33/34mln.t/yr could be processed for markets in the region. 13.16mln.t of oil flowed through the Constanța terminal in 2004 including crude oil, black fuel (for Renel) petroleum and petrochemicals: this takes account of domestic processes, foreign companies (like Lukoil who send Siberian crude to their Romanian refinery) and exporters like Oltchim (also Lukoil who declared an intention to export half their production at Petrotel refinery). A pipeline – already in place as far as Piteşti – could be extended first to Pančevo in Serbia (reputedly for less than $1.0mln) and then continue to Trieste, supplying some 15mln.t/yr for Austria, the Czech Republic and southern Germany. ENI (Italy) calculated that with transport costs of $12/t for a route via Romania, Serbia, Croatia and Slovenia, Romania could make $30mln/yr in transit dues. International cooperation began in 1995 with the EU study of 'Opportunities for the Promotion of the Project on the Oil Pipeline for the Transport of Crude Oil on the Constanța-Adriatic Route' – targeted on countries receiving Phare assistance (Celac 1998). Outline agreement was negotiated 1995–8 and signed in Kyiv (where a technical secretariat was set up) in 1999 by 13 states. Meanwhile 'Silk Road' ferry traffic was expanding through services to Poti from Constanța and Ilichevsk.

The Constanța-Trieste Pipeline

It was argued that 1998 was a critical year. Crude would arrive at the Black Sea in 2002–3 (via the Tengiz-Novorossiysk pipeline); the flow from Central Asia to the West could be 80mln.t/yr by 2003 with 40mln.t maximum through the Bosporus. So a Balkan pipeline would need to be started in 2000; otherwise the next opportunity would lie way off in 2010 or 2014. Romania would benefit from an investment of $800–900mln, with a third of the total cost of $1.5bln potentially benefiting Sidex (Galați) for supplying pipes. Oil traffic could amount to 18mln.t for Romania and Serbia and 15mln.t for CEP. But there were other alternatives: Odessa-Gdańsk, Burgas-Macedonia-Durrës and the Burgas-Alexandroupolis bypass. Also the proposed 1,093km Baku-Tbilisi-Ceyhan (BTC) pipeline would completely outflank the Black Sea theatre. However the

Black Sea focus was sharpened by the opening of the upgraded $560mln Baku-Supse pipeline in 1999; providing an alternative to the costlier Baku-Novorossiysk link (prone to shutdown and vulnerable to damage in Chechnya and Dagestan). It seemed that its success might obviate the need for the Baku-Ceyhan route altogether and focus more attention on Romania (and its Balkan and Odessa-Gdańsk rivals). In 1999 Petrom issued its 'National Programme for the Construction of the Transport Corridor between Europe and Asia across Romania' while the Romania's National Development Programme for Infrastructures (NDPI) instigated feasibility studies for the Constanţa-Trieste pipeline by ENI (as noted above) via Hungary or Serbia (including upgrading of the Romanian crude transport system). American interest was demonstrated by $185,000 from the US Trade & Development Agency (USTDA) in 1999 to study the feasibility of rehabilitating and updating Constanţa oil terminal (following $650,000 from the same source to establish the feasibility of the Constanţa-Trieste pipeline. And believing that three to five pipelines would develop in association with Caspian oil, Raytheon Engineers & Constructors (an American oil and gas industry contractor) descended on Ploieşti. IFC allocated $200,000 for a secretariat to attract investment for a Constanţa-Pančevo-Omišalj pipeline (connecting 10 refineries) with links to Trieste and the Transalpine pipeline. Meanwhile USAID looked at the northerly route via Hungary at a time when the Kosovo problem was raising doubts over the link with Serbia.

Feasibility for the Constanţa-Trieste pipeline was agreed by US and Romanian experts in terms of implementation during 2000–2 with a capacity of 47mln.t/yr. A memorandum of understanding between Romania, Serbia and Croatia was drawn up in Brussels in 2000 backed up by a rising oil price. A pipeline forum on 'Romania at the Crossroads' brought agreement in October 2000 between Concordia Petroliera (Romania), Janaf (Croatia) and Jugopetrol (Serbia) to seek government support and an inter-governmental accord to help the search for finance. Concordia – an association including Oil Terminal Constanţa, Conpet Ploieşti, Petromidia Năvodari, Rafo Oneşti, Petrolexportimport and Argirom International – sought government guarantees (with an accord as quickly as possible after the Romanian elections) and stability in Belgrade. They were looking at a 400km Piteşti-Pančevo pipeline, costing $250mln for a 67mln.t annual throughout, to connect with the existing high-capacity Croatian pipeline link with Omišalj with pumping to start in autumn 2001. In 2001 a protocol was signed by the three countries in Belgrade on the creation of the Constanţa-Pančevo-Omišalj inter-state oil and gas transport system, encouraged by substantial new reserves along the Kazakhstan coast in 2000 and concern in Western Europe over declining North Sea reserves. Finance was missing at this point and a new protocol in 2002 between the three countries established a clearer legal framework and opened the prospect of loans to Petrom and

Petrotrans from several foreign banks and institutions. The 'middle way' between Russia and Iran was much favoured by USA politically – and seemed profitable thanks to price rises after September 2001. The proposal was also helped by the peaceful succession in Azerbaijan and the 'revolution of roses' in Georgia that brought a pro-US stance. After Kazakhstan events have moved on to Turkmenistan and Uzbekistan as part of a US penetration of Central Asia, with reduced importance for the Persian Gulf and the Iranian threat. However despite persistent delays there is a solid rationale for the project and an association agreement is ready for signing (2008) by Romania and her partners (Croatia, Italy and Serbia) at the time of writing. The project is expected to create 5,000 jobs of which 1,000 should be permanent. There is EU support, while Constanţa's role in oil transport is appreciated by SOCAR (Azerbaijan) who want storage capacity for 5.0mln.t oil at the city's oil terminal.

Threats of Competition include a possible Ukraine-Poland Odessa-Brody-Gdańsk link, built between Odessa and Brody in 2002 and initially used in reverse to take 9mln.t. oil/yr to Odessa's Yuzhniy refinery. The extension to Gdańsk was expected to start in 2006 and a new refinery is planned for Brody. Meanwhile a Bulgarian-Greek-Russian consortium was planning to complete the Burgas-Alexandroupolis pipeline in 2008 and Russia was discussing a continuation through Macedonia and Albania to an Adriatic crossing from Vlorë to Italy (for Western Europe). A grandiose Druzhba-Adria concept to link Kazakhstan with the Mediterranean via Ukraine, Belarus, Slovakia, Hungary and Croatia with a daily capacity of 100-300,000 barrels was however rejected by Croatia in 2005 (in its form at that time) through fears of damage to the Adriatic tourist industry. Most serious however was the threat from the BTC pipeline: designed in 2002, financed in 2003 (with \$4.0bln for a BP-led consortium from IFC, EBRD, national export credit agencies and 15 commercial banks) and due for completion during 2005–6. It is the largest export pipeline in the world (1.0mln barrels/day or 85mln.t/yr), undertaken because of US concerns over Russian and Iranian control: hence the Armenian route was rejected on the grounds of Russian influence while the Georgian separatist area of Ajaria is bypassed) – though this still leaves the hazards of corruption in Azerbaijan and Georgia, the war zone/earthquake faultline, engineering failures and mistakes over the choice of material to keep water out of the joints (which could lead to corrosion risks within the 40 year design timespan because the material cannot chemically stick to the pipes). The BTC system could always be extended eastwards to Aktau (Kazakhstan) to avoid tankers crossing the Caspian to Baku (Kaskagan).

Meanwhile Russia is poised to implement the 4,150km Siberian pipeline from Baikal to Pervoznaya near Vladivostock at a cost of \$15.5bln. Interest from China in a route leaving Russia at Skovorodino was trumped by Japan's offer of $7.0bln of assistance, plus more money to help Japanese companies prospect for oil along the pipeline route and ensure the maintenance of a daily the flow of 1.6mln barrels for Japan and for other markets (with 67bln barrels of current reserves in the area). But construction could take a decade and there are concerns over profitability as well as environment: since the 'tranquil bay' of Pervoznaya is used by the people of Vladivostock in summer and by the Amur leopard in winter. However a move to Vostochny, an industrial port beside Nakhodka, seems to have been ruled out. But this does not exhaust the potential. An Ankara meeting on Caspian and Black Sea oil and gas in 2005 underlined Romania's strategic position in relation to a pan-European oil pipeline as well as the Nabucco project for taking Caspian and Middle East gas to Europe (see below). A €1.9bln oil pipeline could now start in 2007 at the earliest and transport 112mln.t/yr. A feasibility study by Romania's consultant Hill International (UK) recommended an inter-government accord in 2005 with a commercial company to follow. Costs seem to vary widely between one very low estimate of €400mln and $1.0bln of finance agreed by Eximbank (USA), while the EU granted Romania €2.1mln for feasibility study of the best route. In 2006 agreement was reached between Romania, Serbia, Croatia, Slovenia and Italy for a 1,360km pipeline – connecting with existing pipelines to Austria and Italy – to carry 112mln.t/yr of crude (more than the 40–90mln.t predicted to yield $2.3–4.4bln for Romania in transit taxes over 20 years).

Gas

Deliveries from Russia are set to increase from 7.4bln.cu.m in 1996 to 14.0bln by 2010 thanks to the link opened in 1999 from Ukraine for Russian gas to northern Romania. The Romgaz/Gazprom association means that Russian gas can be imported without the need for an intermediary. Wintershall (Kassel, Germany) cooperated with Romgas and Transgas to build a $30mln transport system linking Romania and Ukraine starting work in 2005. The pipeline enters near Iaşi (thanks to a $20mln connection from Balţi in Moldova) and continues westwards to a methane gas distribution and processing station opened at Medieşu Aurit (Satu Mare). Connection of the Transgaz network with Central Europe through a $318mln investment during 2000–5 (including upgrading work and telecoms) has also produced a new $15bln cross-border link between Arad and Szeged with 1.5bln.cu.m capacity. But Romania is also involved in a tripartite j.v. with Gazprom and Howard Energy (USA) for a gas pipeline from Russia to Ukraine, Romania, Bulgaria and Turkey where Howard Energy are building eight thermal power stations. This involved Tranzgaz in a new line in 2001–2 across Romanian territory from Isaccea (on the Danube frontier with Ukraine) to Negru Vodă on the Bulgarian frontier to supplement the two existing transit pipes with an annual capacity of 14bln.cu.m annually. The project generated revenue through the use of tubes from Sidex (helping to pay some of their 95.4mln.lei electricity debts of 2001) as well as transit payments for a planned 20bln.cu.m of gas annually on completion, rising to 30bln by 2010 when supplies may reach Bulgaria, Greece, Macedonia and Turkey.

Diversification

Romania's gas imports – averaging 3.6mln.toe during 2000–3 (a quarter of total consumption) – have come from Russia. But some diversification was achieved by the LPG terminal on the Black Sea to supply gas into the distribution network to cover peak winter consumption and boost industrial efficiency; create an import-export balance for propane-butane needs in the petrochemical industry; and provide a liquefied gas buffer. The project was first discussed with the Americans in 1992 leading to a feasibility study 1997 and formation of the Romanian-American 'Black Sea LPG' j.v. involving the US Energy Transportation Group and three other American companies. Discussion with prospective partners led to 51 per cent US participation with a $160mln investment (plus Renel, Rompetrol and Romgaz for the rest) though Romania has the technical capacity to handle the project. The facility lies in the Constanţa free zone and needed Turkey's support in 1996 over gas ships passing through the Bosphorus. Annual initial storage is expected to rise from 0.6 to 1.0mln.t (but 0.1mln in the initial phase comprising a temporary facility in the form of a floating warehouse with an LPG-type ship quasi-permanently anchored). The project includes an LPG pipeline from Constanţa to Bucharest and propane units in Bucharest – Măgurele, 16 Februarie, Titan, Tunari and Vest – to mix propane with air for natural gas equivalent; with a pilot factory at Teleajen (Ploieşti). With the region's largest terminal open in 2000, Romania has become a warehouse, useful for the developing 'Silk Road' with scope for gas exports.

Nabucco Consortium. More speculatively, Transgaz National Natural Gas Company has been collaborating since 2002 with Turkey's BOTAS along with Bulgargaz (Bulgaria), Transgaz, Mol (Hungary) and ÖMV Erdgas (Austria) to research a gas pipeline from the Caspian that will extend to Austria with connections thence to France and Germany as well as Italy and Slovenia. The Nabucco Company Pipeline Study was set up in 2004 and in 2005 it was announced that the 2,841km pipeline (to transport 25bln.cu.m/yr) would be ready in 2010 at a cost of €5.0–6.0bln. There appears to be considerable political will, including EU and US support, while a European coordinator has been appointed. But the situation in 2008 is disappointing with no resolution to the funding problem which prevents selection of suppliers. The project could be assisted by Gaz de France (resisted by Turkey) as well as RWE (Germany), while Mol wants a political support organisation to provide 'clout' and harmonise political involvement. Romania and Hungary would also like progress with a complementary 'Sistemul de Transport al Noii Europe' (NETS) that would also supply the West Balkan states. But other projects arise through Ukraine's interest (with Turkmenistan) is a Caspian coast gas pipeline to reduce dependence on Russian supplies – which could also be part of a Ukrainian-German consortium bid to sell non-Russian gas to the EU – and such a 'White Stream' project could cross from Dobrogea to the Hungarian frontier. And while Romania entered into an agreement in 2005 with Russia regarding Gazprom-Romgaz cooperation – in extending Caspian routes from the Black Sea to the Mediterranean – Russia has other options. A 'North Stream' pipeline would pass well clear of Romania while an alternative 'South Stream' that Russia might implement in cooperation with ENI (Italy) might cross the Black Sea from Novorosiisk to Varna and transit Bulgaria and Serbia en route to Italy and Central Europe (though Romania would be welcome to participate if she desired). Nabucco is still 'on' for 2010–13, with current activity (2008) over pipeline capacity bids (dominated by equal shares for the partner states) but there appears to be a lack of political momentum.

Electricity

Romania has had little potential to export thermal power because in 1999 the export cost of power arising from foreign investment in updating thermal power stations was estimated at $50–200/MWh while the average price of Conel's domestic supplies was only $40 at the time. But with the expansion of nuclear capacity – and costs at Cernavodă of $15–20/MWh at the start of the millennium (before allowing for finance) Romania could become an important electricity exporter given adequate grid capacity. The situation has been complicated by the Comecon breakdown, compounded by difficult relations with Bulgaria where curtailment of nuclear power (due to EU pressure to close four Soviet-type reactors at Kozloduy) has brought resentment over Romania's export ambitions – expressed through demands for high transit payments – as well as a determination to create alternative nuclear power through its Belene project. Initially the only effective power links were with Greece and Serbia with the latter taking up to 1,000MW of capacity, but Phare showed interest in supporting an energy programme given Bucharest's key position for east-west connection. The eastern component may comprise a regional electricity market in the Balkans (by 2005) with a Balkan regional electricity exchange (subject to an agreed location!) suggested in 2002 for more stable and lower prices. Another component could well be an energy ring for the Black Sea or – in the event of continuing difficulties with Bulgaria which in any case has undersized cable – an underground cable to reach Greece and Turkey, notwithstanding the collateral required. After a memorandum of understanding reached in 2004 over a Romania-Turkey energy cable, a feasibility study was due in 2008 on the basis of 600MW capacity costing €400mln. It is now due for completion in 2012. It could be part of any wider Black Sea system or a hypothetical Mediterranean ring with African and Middle Eastern links eventually.

Further Export Options

Romania has also exported power to Moldova at preferential rates to meet energy crises. One emergency arose in 1998 when Ukraine cut 60 per cent of her power export to Moldova because an accord had not been signed and Romania helped out through the Oneşti station. A relaunch was reported in 2001 in the form of non-refundable aid arising out of power shortages due to drought, with government payments to Termoelectrica for delivery equivalent to 100MW capacity for three months in 2001. Deliveries were again noted in 2005 at low costs equivalent to charges on the Moldova home market. Exports of 1.3bln.kwh of electricity were made in 2001 in what was a second year of small exports mainly to Serbia. Surplus power also reached Greece (via Serbia and Macedonia) given the energy deficit in the region and there were exports to Albania in 2002 through a $46.5mln contract with the Swiss company Atel which handles Hidroelectrica's power exports. However there is great opportunity through Turkey's growing needs (plus its Middle Eastern and African connections) as well as European markets (especially Italy) that could well take hydropower (as well as nuclear) and conceivably even thermal power after rehabilitation has boosted efficiency. Western links are therefore being developed through Hungary – Arad-Sandorfalva and Oradea-Békéscsaba – which place Mintia power station near Deva in a particularly good position. National development planners proposed a 400kV connection with Hungary through Arad to boost capacity from 100 to 800MW – although an optimal connection avoiding any kind of disturbance actually requires four 400kV lines – and 'back to back' (ac/dc/ac) conversion at Isaccea: the interface of an eastern and (expanded) western European power system with the cooperation of Bayernwerk and Verbund.

At the time the two systems could not work concurrently – as with the Czech-German border facility operating until 1994 through former Comecon arrangements linking Poland with Hungary – and allow the possibility of Romania importing Russian electricity for re-export to Europe after connection to Europe after 2002–3 (albeit complicated by destruction of transit capacity on Ukrainian territory). However resynchronisation of the two zones finally allowed electricity exports from Ukraine to Romania in 2005 from the Burshtyn/Burshtya energy island (comprising parts of Lviv, Ivano Frankivsk and Transcarpathian regions where Zakhidenergo runs Burshtyn and Dobrotvir thermal plants with 600MW potential) which has a 400kV link from Mukačevo to Roşiorii de Vede. Ukraine now provides a link between a northern group (Hungary, Poland and Slovakia) and a southern group comprising Romania and her Balkan neighbours (Albania, Bulgaria, Greece, Macedonia and Serbia). Previously in 2002, Electrica gained ISO9001/94 certification for management quality in line with standards of the Union for the Coordination of the Transport of Electricity (UCTE: a body of electricity suppliers and distributors) and gained EBRD and EIB assistance to upgrade the high tension network: a great help for the developing partnerships in Romania and abroad.

ENERGY PRODUCTION AND PROSPECTING

As already noted, two crucial issues are the related challenges of using energy more efficiently and maximising domestic production. In 1995 Romania was consuming 2.5 times more energy per unit of GDP than the average European country. First, there were very high levels of power consumption in 'energy-eating branches': aluminium, steel, fertiliser and cement. Generating capacities for the metallurgical industries amounted to some 250MW each for Alro (Slatina) and Sidex (Galaţi), 130MW for Terom (Tulcea), 60–65MW each for COS (Târgovişte) and Siderurgica (Hunedoara) and 25–35MW each for Gavazzi Steel (Oţelu Roşu) and Industria Sârmei (Câmpia Turzii). But second, power was used inefficiently in factories while too many buildings lacked energy efficiency. Artificially low prices starved electricity generators and distributors of funds (needed for maintenance and upgrading of power stations based on obsolete technology) yet the resulting power failures were very costly in terms of interrupted production. Generators were also hit by falling industrial output but excess capacity was then increased as more output came from greenfield industrial projects: barely a third of the 21,000MW of installed capacity in use in the mid-1990s. Primary energy companies were very heavily in debt at the end of 1998: the ONLC was owed 1.3tln.lei and the Petroşani pitcoal company 150bln. In 1996 Romania enjoyed the benefit of a Phare 'clean coal project' for maintenance and operation of thermal energy plant, but at the start of the new millennium there was a looming generating gap with only 75 per cent of the 22.2gw capacity operational. As regards more efficient generation, $3.0bln is needed for the energy system during 2003–5 including $2.5bln for production alone. It will have to be found in the private sector, specifically the larger banks. The present energy strategy anticipated 4.5 per cent annual growth rate for 2001–5 peaking at 8.0 per cent during 2005–10, but with energy consumption growth growing by only 3.0 per cent. The key to a larger and cheaper power output may well lie with larger gas imports (rising from an estimated 12.5bln.cu.m in 2000 to 15.0bln in 2010).

Energy Efficiency

In connection with Phare, Romania launched an energy efficiency fund for key industries in 1997 with financial incentives to reduce energy intensity by 22 per cent by 2005. There was help for individual industries including investment by Pechiney (France) at Alro in 1998 to reduce energy consumption by 1,000Kw/t while increasing aluminium production by a tenth and also to control noxious gases. In 2000 a law seeking efficient use of energy required consumers using more than 200toe/yr to work out an energy balance sheet every two years; while consumers of more than 1,000t were to perform the exercise annually and formulate plans and feasible investments to reduce consumption. Administrators of state buildings larger than 1,500sq.m were to draw up an energy balance sheet every five years. Meanwhile consumers could benefit from financial assistance from a special fund for the development of the energy system offering credits with subsidised interest rates and customs tax concessions on imported equipment. Government continued the drive for efficiency and competitiveness after 2000. Of course rising energy prices could be seen as a spur to efficiency but most consumers – both enterprises and businesses – lacked the resources to make a positive response. Rather enterprise arrears tended to increase. Investment in efficient/clean technologies was still desperately needed but Green (1998, p.99) pointed out how "many industries within the region face a dilemma: they cannot afford to invest in energy efficient measures but without them they will find it increasingly difficult to survive and compete in the European market, particularly as energy costs increase". Meanwhile people tried to do without heat and light so that consumption fell through villages being typically plunged in darkness each evening, with lights switched off even in the commune office, police station, post office and town hall.

Government often found itself in a dilemma, appreciating the inevitability of energy price rises (given the real costs of imported energy and the EU agenda over realistic pricing) yet fearing the political consequences, especially when more expensive electricity, gas and petrol tended to spark a general round of price rises (often by a greater margin than could be justified by energy costs alone). Thus prime minister M.Isărescu tried hard but unsuccessfully to postpone price increases in the election year of 2000. However consumption levels in Romania (and the region) are low enough for efficiency savings to reduce energy consumption while permitting some improvement in the quality of life commensurate with a 'fair share' of global power based in population. Being relatively more sustainable than Western Europe (albeit by a dwindling margin) the region could leapfrog to a better model of dematerialised sustainable development rather than adopt the material intensive development path of Western Europe.

Coal

Romania's coal is generally poor in quality and expensive to produce. Despite high subsidies the price was still 25–30 per cent higher than imported coal in 1996. Imports were particularly necessary in metallurgy because of the high ash content of Romanian coal and the low technical standard of washing. Coking has been based entirely on imports since 1993 and there seems little chance of any change in this policy – hence the partial recovery of the steel industry has contributed to the expected growth in the import share of total coal consumption from 21.4 per cent in 1992 to 25.8 per cent in 2000. Meanwhile, restructuring of the coal sector began 1997. 'Substantial investment will be required to complete the closure of unprofitable mines and to mitigate social consequences and implications for regional economies' (Country Report 1998, p.35). Output fell after 1989 but then rose from 41.85 to 45.30mln.t during 1996–2000 (11.6 to 12.5 mln.toe of which 10.9 and 11.6 respectively were needed for electricity and heating). Power stations increased output from 25,100mln.kwh to 27,350 during 1996–2000, of which 21,010 and 23,018mln.kwh respectively was based on coal and 4,090 and 4,332 respectively on other resources. But having contracted for 27mln.t coal in 1998 Renel actually needed only 16mln (half of which was already in stock) because some consumers reduced their output or closed, while others became more efficient. With gas consumption increasing – accelerated by some large consumers (Alro, Carom Oneşti and Petrobrazi) who decided to build their own power stations – a reduction in coal output through closure of efficient mines seemed inevitable: from 24mln.t to 18mln.t for lignite (2000–2010) and 3.0 to 2.5mln.t for pitcoal. The future for coal became even bleaker as the uncertainty over Cernavodă Unit II nuclear power station was removed. Meanwhile, the Mining Law of 1998 provided a mechanism for closing mines and established a restructuring agency. Across the industry as a whole there were 20 mine closures at the end of 2000 and 44 in an advanced state of closure, leaving166 still to be dealt with. To the end of 2000 165bln.lei was spent on mine closures. The World Bank provided \$44.5mln – \$26.5mln to finance closures and the rest to ease the social impact – to moderate the sense of crisis in the coalfields where miners were producing low quality coal at prices above the cost of imports. Some small towns were particularly vulnerable like Anina (with 1,500 jobs in coal mining) poised 'on the brink of disappearance' in 1998 and finally closed after serious damage at the mine in 2006. Reorganisation has continued to be a drain on resources with further substantial funding required to continue the process through 2001–4 and beyond. Despite coal reserves of 1.46bln.t (lasting 48 years at the present rate of exploitation) there were reported debts of 25tln.lei in the industry when the new government was inaugurated in 2001, with a further 2.7tln needed for investment (0.3 in 2001 alone).

The Jiu Valley

This area has been greatly affected even though the downsizing in the industry provides an opportunity to convert some heating systems from lignite to hard coal. Overall the National Pitcoal Company (NPC) in Petroşani is quite uneconomic with costs as high as 3.3 times the value of production at the end of the 1990s and despite massive subsidies (the highest in the industry: 14.7mln.lei/year) there are still losses: production costs of $73.6/t (including transport) were way above the power station contracting price of $51.7 (19.4 and 13.4 respectively on the basis of g.cal) while South African coal could be delivered for 8.1. There were reductions in employment from 53.4th in 1989 to 42.0 in 1997 even before the mine closure programme ushered in more drastic redundancy ('disponibilizarea') that reduced employment to 18,200 at the end of 1999. NPC closed Câmpu lui Neag, Dâlja and Petrila Sud mines; balanced by modernisation at Valea cu Brazi in 1991 which meant that 70 men then produced the same amount of coal as the 3,000 at Aninoasa and the three mines subsequently closed! Modernisation with a $24mln ABN Amro bank credit also included a new preparation plant opened at Coroieşti (Vulcan) in 2003 (rationalising the processing of coal in the western part of the field, previously handled at Livezeni and Uricani as well as Coroieşti) and this unit now complements the facility at Petrila for the eastern sector. There has been some upgrading by the Japanese Itochu consortium (with Toshiba and Hitachi) using equipment from Kopex (Poland) to increase labour productivity – reducing production costs from $15 to $7.0/t – improve safety and achieve ecological benefits. NPC also aims to replace the exploitation of coal and waste rock through earth crumbling (used to an extent of 20–24 per cent) responsible for the serious accident at Vulcan when 14 miners were killed by a gas leak in 2001 (followed by another in 2002). Modernisation threatens jobs, it cannot seriously when finance is available, given the dangerous condition of the mines.

Limited Diversification. There has also been a decline in jobs in related machinery businesses e.g. at Umirom, Upsruem and Upsprom from over 3,000 to just 1,000; at Gerom International and Electroutil (now only 125 jobs); and the construction companies Consmin and Conpet (reduced to 628 jobs). The run-down of the industry is deeply resented by a workforce privileged under communism, especially with the rapid exhaustion of severance payments (which has increased poverty levels and contributed to an increase in crime). So in 1997 Hunedoara CC sought special legislation to encourage private enterprise through fiscal incentives – leading to the LFA programme with Valea Jiului among the first three areas to be declared in 1998. Even so diversification has been an extremely slow process, largely restricted to locally generated SMEs given the lack of foreign investment which is not unrelated to high salary expectations on the part of a workforce radicalised by the union incitement associated with the 'mineriada' syndrome. There have been attempts to privatise the mines. The commercial group '95 Petroşani' wanted to take over Paroşeni mine in 1999 and produce coal below the price of imports (with higher productivity) while improving the working conditions with greater priority for safety. In 1999 there was also a proposed takeover of mining and environmental work at Bărbăteni and Lupeni mines by the local Miniera company, with the trade union accommodation becoming a workers' club. Some stability has arisen through long-term contracts e.g. between NPC and Termoelectrica in 2000 for the supply of 3.2mln.t coal monthly for Mintia and Paroşeni power stations on the basis of an energy holding to overcome the problem of delayed payment for coal. And in 2002 the government awarded a Jiu Valley coalbed methane concession to Pannonian International (a subsidiary of Galaxy Energy Corporation) who have farmed out the business for evaluation to Falcon Oil & Gas. But the situation remains difficult with diversification limited, a high level of illness and continuing redundancy, with 13,000 more jobs to go in 2006.

Oltenia

The 'Lignit' company (ONLC) based in Târgu Jiu covers 80–85 per cent of the country's lignite production but with six per cent of production costs subsidised in order to survive: albeit a much better record than the small Ploieşti-based lignite company with costs 2.9 times the production value (and as much as five times at some individual mines). In 2001, both companies were owed money by generators and have debts in respect of mines in conservation, despite some payments for deliveries to state reserves. But the government was only able to find symbolic resources for investment (250mln.lei during 1997–2000) against massive subsidies of 1.9tln.lei, in the quest for a viable industry based on some 16 large mining complexes. Under the 1998 programme the company initially closed six unproductive mines with a further 11 to follow over two years. The company faced 28,000 redundancies (out of 80,000 in all mining) including the breakaway of 14 service companies. Unions accept that employment will not exceed 15,000 in 2010 (23,500 in 1998). But whereas there were no new jobs for miners made redundant in 1997 – when ONLC restructuring started with the curtailment of subsidies – the main mine restructuring programmes of 1998 were linked (as at Petroşani) with an LFA programme – and an Agency for the Development of Mining Areas – while the mining union also became involved in formulating projects. ONLC's strategy has been to shut down all underground mines and transfer workers to the quarries. This should achieve production costs of $7.5/t: competitive with imports after allowing for transport. There is even a chance for profitability – and foreign investment – especially if the main generators tied to lignite (the Craiova, Rovinari and Turceni complexes referred to below) remain stable over the next decade, notwithstanding the anticipated growth in generation based on gas as well as hydro and nuclear power. From

2000 the company has been demanding daily money transfers from Termoelectrica to avoid mounting debts but it seems that a permanent solution will lie with dedicated lignite workings that are detached from ONLC and become part of privatised electricity companies. However the company's initial strategy lay with rehabilitation at the opencast workings of Jilţ Sud, Lupoaia, Pinoasa, Roşia and Timişeni. This creates new working faces to help compensate for some of the lost production. Lupoaia has an annual production of 3.6mln.t but needs $21mln for new technology, linked to foreign credits in connection with a j.v. Production should then rise to 4mln.t. A similar strategy is intended at the other pits with a total production of 8.0mln.t, and the economics have been reviewed favourably in American circles to suggest possible exports to Greece and Turkey. The company also considered tendering for a lignite mine at Elbistan (Kazakhstan) to produce 15mln.t/yr (from a 3.5bln.t reserve 40m thick) where Mitsubishi and Siemens have built a 350MW power station.

Oil

Romania depends heavily on oil imports while domestic production fell slightly from 6.8mln.t in 1991 to 6.7 in 1995 and continued the downward trend to 6.2 in 2000 and 5.3 in 2005. Evidently the priority to maintain output at around 6.5mln.t (and ensure that problems over finance and technology should not be decisive) has not been sustainable, but there has been a major problem in the Black Sea during 2000–6 which has had a negative impact on production (as noted below) and in 2008 the potential for 7.0mln was quoted. Amoco implemented a $1.0bln programme in 20 Petrom oil and gas fields in 1997 in a bid to make them profitable, but decisions had to be made over small output fields that were barely profitable and Petrom closed some derricks with low production in the Videle field in Teleorman. Meanwhile 2,000t was being produced daily from fields in Argeş, Dâmboviţa and Prahova combined, though Dâmboviţa's output continued to fall – partly due to flooding with salted water – and financial losses were only partly offset by local methane sales. While there was a prospect of a new methane well at Vulcana-Pandele (Pucioasa), 50 unprofitable wells were closed by Petrom in Târgovişte. Meanwhile at Suplacu de Barcău (Bihor) in 1999 underground combustion and large scale steam injection (to extract heavy crude) seemed technically adequate for another decade: despite undertain profitability the system could not easily be stopped.

Technology Upgrade for Exploration and Well Management

This attracted €200mln of Petrom investment on the eve of privatisation to stabilise daily production at a level equivalent to 200,000 barrels commensurate with a 2004 production of 5.6mln.t of oil and 6.5bln.cu.m of gas (half the total gas output). Money came from a new bond issue in 2001 through ING Barings and ABN Amro (without government guarantee) to make existing fields profitable through re-equipment and updating, including new technologies for production of deposits in their final exploitation phase. Some new wells were opened in Dâmbovița; yielding an extra 333th.t from Moreni in 1999 (260 new wells) and 136th in 2000 (160, especially Brăgăreasa with 100t/day). Production was reported from the oilwell of Brăila Petrol (a Petrom subsidiary). Meanwhile, GTI Oil discovered a crude deposit at Pâncota (Arad) worth at least $1.0bln (when foreign companies could not make the business profitable) and now operates as an integrated oil company working from extraction to filling stations (including seven in the Timişoara area). Now the Pâncota find will make for tens of wells and 1,000 new jobs in the county. GTI will make offers to take over Romanian refineries and beside fuels it will give attention to the use of refinery gases: propylene and isobuthene may be processed at various installations: Archim (Arad), Carom (Oneşti) and Oltchim (Râmnicu Vâlcea) as well as the Arpechim, Petrobrazi and Petromidia refineries. In 1999 it announced a plan for a national distribution system with 250 stations (building seven per quarter); it also intended to sell liquefied gas to the population and offer consultancy on drilling, pipelines and refining.

Further Exploration on Land

It is assumed that resources up to 2,000m deep have been exploited to the tune of 80 per cent and the balance is difficult to detect. Most of the potential is lower down at 3,000–3,500m or more in geologically complex regions like the eastern Carpathians. Hence the need to involve foreign investors with adequate technology and financial resources (since $50–60mln is needed just for exploration). In 1992 Amoco and Shell leased areas with the potential for deposits inaccessible to Romania's current technology, but the contracts ended without success though both companies invested at least $50mln. Amoco drilled at the foot of the Carpathians 85kms northeast of Bucharest in the Lapoş VII bloc where the stake was shared with Arco (USA). In this geologically complex bloc Amoco drilled to hitherto untapped depths (a 'rank wildcat'). The company also set up 60 petrol stations in five years and (as already noted) negotiated with Petrom to upgrade 20 of its oil deposits while 15 oil and gas blocks were opened up to Amoco in 1996 (also Shell and the UK's Enterprise Oil) though evidently without result. Amoco became involved in the projected Bucharest North thermal power station and Petrom is reported as having raised the possibility in 1996 of a multimillion dollar contract for a field in southwestern Oltenia, although nothing seems to have transpired. Meanwhile Shell Romania Exploration spent $70mln on exploratory wells in a 6,000sq.km bloc near Cluj, sharing costs with Saudi Arabian Company Nimir Petroleum, with chances at this 'wildcat' put at 20 per cent (with gas thought more likely than oil).

Although the filling station and gas bottling businesses helped to balance disappointment in the prospecting field through the mid-1990s, both Shell and Amoco evidently found the fiscal incentives somewhat marginal: the tax system was ambiguous (with apparent liability to both royalties and excise duties) while the holiday of three years was considered poor by comparison with other countries, especially when five-six years would be needed to cover even a part of the expenditure with profit. The government also tended to display a certain ambivalence, according to Shell, as though it 'would rather have no slice of cake rather than share it with others'. They welcomed President Constantinescu's remarks about reforming the oil sector but did not become involved in any further exploration. Meanwhile Rompetrol began cooperation with Marine & Mercantile Securities (Ireland) in respect of exploration and development of Moineşti VI bloc in 1995. Dallas-based Toreador Resources Corporation was reportedly active in the Făureşti, Moineşti and Vipereşti blocks. And Europa Oil & Gas Holdings (a UK/European oil and gas exploration and production group) have been drilling at Bilca in the Brodina block and see their two wells as the core of a field development programme coming on stream in 2005, with further exploratory drilling at the same time. Seismic studies were reported in 2000 in the Pannonian Depression (Arad and Timişoara), Getic Depression (Piteşti and Târgu Jiu); Moesic Platform (Bucharest, Craiova and Uriziceni) and the Carpathian Depressions (Băicoi, Berca, Târgovişte and Vălenii de Munte). At present the picture is rather mixed because while some companies are giving up (e.g. UK-based Regal Petroleum at Bârlad) only nine of the 304 oil prospecting concessions are financed by integral Romanian capital and with rising oil prices raising the value of annual production to \$5.8bln there is an incentive for Romanian companies to compete more strongly for concessions in future.

Offshore Activity

This is now of prime importance (involving some 3.5mln.t/yr crude production) with respect to Black Sea Eocene deposits where exploration started in 1969 and where favourable conditions for hydrocarbon accumulation in the Black Sea were demonstrated in 1972. However exploration drilling requires high performance equipment and Romania had to cooperate with the West in order to produce the Gloria drilling rig, billed as a huge Romanian success (with the high cost kept secret), operating with the support of a supply base at Constanţa's berth 34. Activity by the Offshore Drilling Group and the Bucharest Drilling & Special Geological Works completed the first well in 1976 at 5,000m, followed by the first commercial oil deposit in 1979. Altogether there have been eight discoveries – six for crude and two for gas. A succession of mobile self-lifting offshore rigs came on stream for what became the Petromar company: Orizont 1980; Prometeu 1984; Atlas and Fortuna 1985, Jupiter 1987 and Saturn 1988. But since the revolution these rigs have been working in various parts of the world in connection with Petrom's global activities e.g. Fortuna and Orizont started offshore drilling in Turkey in 1994 and four years later they were updated in Dubai shipyards. As the only operator on the Black Sea continental shelf, Petromar handled the production from this area and became one of Petrom's 11 subsidiaries in 1998. In 1996 – when a total of 60 wells had been drilled – there were two producing wells responsible for 12 per cent of domestic crude (a third by the end of 1997) and one for natural gas in 1997. 1,500t of crude and 1.0mln.cu.m of gas are pumped daily by pipeline to the Petromar Midia terminal (opened in 1999) from a central complex 60kms offshore that separates the crude from gas and water. It includes two oil tanks, supply ships and tugs, floating crane and primary oil processing. Another seven sea platforms some 800kms off Constanţa are linked by a mini-fleet of 13 ships (1999). 80t/day goes from Midia to Petrom refineries with gas handed over to Romgaz.

Limited Success since 1989 involves one find in 1992 followed by a seven year wait for the important Pescarus discovery in 1999. Evidently the ship undertaking seismic survey work was scrapped in 1989 and work resumed only in 1994 using the services of the Western Atlas company (in collaboration with Elf Aquitaine): this revealed the potential of the Pescarus location in Petrom's Histria-XVIII bloc: close to the Lebada East and Lebada West deposits (already discovered) but much more substantial with a value of $2–4bln for an investment of $100mln. The Saturn offshore rig – the last of seven offshore rigs built in Galaţi for Petromar – started drilling in 1988 at the Pescarus location and made a discovery the following year that proved to be the largest since 1959. Petromar subsequently started pumping 350t of crude daily to the central platform, supplementing the 1,000t plus daily output from seven other continental shelf deposits – while natural gas is fed directly into the national distribution network. Exploration is also taking place in the Neptun-XIX bloc 250kms from the shore: an area of 10,000sq.kms on Romania's frontiers with Bulgaria, Turkey and Ukraine. Operations started in association with Total-Fina-Elf (France) in 1998 under a 30 year leasing deal: Petrom work in the western part at a depth below 100m while Elf contribute finance and high technology and also operate in the eastern part in 100–160m of water. By 2001 Conoco were also involved with an initial investment of $5.2mln (to 2002), possibly increasing to $40mln by 2005. Petromar also has an association with Enterprise Oil in respect of drilling in a Bulgarian block Bulgarevo Vest. However, a major factor affecting Romania's Black Sea oil production has been a trunk pipeline blockage between two platforms which affected crude delivery and salt water injection during 2000–6. The paraffin blockage was first tackled by replacing a section of the pipeline but this failed and it required 'hydraulic shock therapy' by Brenntag (Germany) to clean the pipe and remove the obstruction during 2004–6.

Gas

Production is again in decline, falling from 24.8mln.cu.m in 1991 to 16.3 in 2000 and 14.1 in 2005. Although some fields – like Denta/Moraviţa – offer local self-sufficiency, new supplies are needed. Romgaz has completed a €5.5mln programme to boost output from severely depleted fields by installing Thomasen compressor systems, while both Petrom and Romgaz have updated exploitation processes and improved gas transport by the SCADA computerised system. New exploration runs in parallel with the oil programme as an integrated hydrocarbon initiative and most of the successes on land have involved gas rather than oil. In 2000 19 new gas wells were opened (e.g. Turburea producing 20t/day of LPG) and 201 were rehabilitated. There was commissioning during 2002 of a 7.0bln.cu.m gasfield near Sighişoara, coinciding with the 200mln.cu.m underground storehouse near Târgu Mureş already referred to. As regards foreign companies, Shell drilled for gas in Transylvania in the 1990s beneath a salt layer at depths of 1,500m (beyond the capacity of Romgaz who were confined to shallower fields) and Amoco were also engaged, but without any positive results. Meanwhile Wintershall of Germany's BASF Group prospected in the Eastern Carpathians (south Transylvania) at various times in the 1990s and most recently in 2002 working with Romgaz in developing new gas reservoirs that could lead to a $200mln investment. Stirling Resources of Calgary (Canada) are drilling at Cetătuia, while a new field came on stream in 2005 (100,000cu.m/day) at Bilca-Frătăuţi in the Rădăuţi area of Suceava county where Romgaz were drilling in association with Falcon Oil & Gas Romania, Europa Oil & Gas (UK) and Millennium International (Switzerland). Falcon (with a major stake owned by Norfolk Capital Partners, impressed with Falcon's expertise in technical work and in negotiating projects with governments) have three wells that started feeding gas into the grid near Rădăuţi in 2005. And AIT Wireless (USA) have also been involved in bringing discovered gasfields into production. Aurelian Oil & Gas in partnership with Romgaz (Mediaş) are producing gas at Brodina (Suceava) while the Bega Group's 'Foraj Sonde' company are still hopeful of making discoveries in Vâlcea county in an area when Romgaz gas given up.

The Black Sea

This source could yield 3.0mln.cu.m/day for Romania and considerable progress has been sustained since hydrocarbon exploration was opened up to foreign companies in 1990 through production-sharing agreements. UK Enterprise Oil started operating in 1992 in Blocks XIII and XV (each 4,500sq.kms and shared to an extent of 35 per cent by Canadian Occidental and OGY Petroleum) on either side of Petrom's Lebada fields, with a five year licence and a 25 year production permit. A $25mln investment yielded gas within 2,000m to the extent of 490,000cu.m/day in 1995. Further gas reserves may be found at 2,500–3,000m or deeper, while research is being undertaken to see if natural gas can be obtained from salts on the Black Sea floor. Finally, reference should also be made to the Romanian Dafora drilling company, fully privatised in 1998. It was prominent historically in finding gas originally in Transylvania at Sărmăşel in 1909 and Copşa Mică in 1934. Although its current activities are diverse – building the Venus development in Mediaş and La Vinci in Sibiu (also hotels in Mediaş and Sighişoara) and operating tourist accommodation and catering/recreation facilities in the Mediaş area – it set up a gas company in Turkmenistan in 2004 to boost employment and turnover. Further potential in the Black Sea (for oil and gas) may emerge from arbitration around Insulă Şerpilor following a long-running dispute with Ukraine.

OIL REFINING

Romania's ten refineries have 34mln.t rated capacity – the highest for any country in the region – but the operational capacity is only 22mln and just 10.5mln of oil was actually processed in 2001 (with 12.0 estimated for 2002) due to falling domestic oil production and reduced demand in the petrochemical industry. The anomalies need to be resolved so that the required capacity can be fully modernised to create a more competitive industry complying with EU quality and environmental standards: a challenge which affects the Petrom refineries in particular. In 1996 the World Bank recommended that capacity be limited to 10mln.t by closing four refineries (two large units and two smaller ones) with imports of crude financed in balance with exports of petrol and diesel oil. It was recommended that updating should start with Arpechim (Piteşti-Bradu) and Petromidia (Năvodari), combined with drastic closure in the Ploieşti area involving Petrobrazi, Petrotel (Teleajen), Vega and Steaua Romană. This would assure updated capacity adequate to meet domestic consumption of 7–8mln.t while avoiding the high costs of $150mln required to resume operations at all refineries currently idle (notwithstanding their importance in yielding products vital for the Romanian economy).

Other feasibility studies at the time did not question the need for upgrading – to improve product quality, reduce power consumption and lower pollution (the latter requiring filters and exhaust stacks) – but wished to retain all five large refineries of Petrobrazi, Petrotel and Rafo (Oneşti) as well as Arpechim and Petromidia. There was also an argument that much of the spare capacity in oil refining and petrochemistry might be needed in connection with the westward flow of Caspian oil early in the new millennium. Against this however was the impending need for all refineries to meet higher European standards for automotive fuels: first the Euro Three standard (lead-free) by the end of 2004 (and for new car registrations in 2002) – at an estimated cost of some $200mln for each refinery – and then the jump to Euro Four fuel with reduced sulphur content. This was an issue unavoidable in the long run even though most oil companies said they would import Euro Three fuel initially. Another line of argument favoured a substantial refining capacity to supply a large and more efficient downstream industry based on a national petrochemical grouping – combining the relevant parts of Arpechim, Oltchim (Râmnicu Vâlcea) and Petromidia – strong enough to attract investment. Rompetrol expressed the view in 2003 that petrochemical plant was built on too small a scale in the communist period and was therefore unable to cope with the global competition.

Petrom at Arpechim and Petrobrazi

Petrom controls 40 per cent of the country's refining capacity through two large installations at Petrobrazi (Ploieşti) and Arpechim (Piteşti). Petrobrazi has two identical modules: the first dated 1961–72 using low-sulphur crude; and the second 1988–9 for imported crude (upgraded 1999 when capacity increased from 1.5 to 5.0mln.t/yr). Only the latter is operational with 5.1mln.t capacity (but it refined only 2.8mln.t of crude in 1998) and it uses domestic crude (though it could use imported). Its role is to export oil products and petrochemicals to help pay for imported crude. Meanwhile, the first module at Arpechim was finished in 1969 and the second in 1975, both with 3.5mln.t capacity for processing imported crude to yield fuel oil and engine oils as well as petrochemical raw materials for Oltchim: 639.5th.t of polyethylene, ethylene, acrylonitrile and propylene in 2000 (hence of the location here of Petrom's petrochemical company). Technological improvements were completed during 1999 on the one module being operated at the time (processing 2.4mln.t of crude in 1998), just in time to meet rising world market demand for diesel oil with low sulphur content (0.05 per cent compared with 0.20 per cent) and secure a premium of $30/t on the price: 24,000t exported by the end of the first quarter of 2000. Good progress was also made with engine oils to avoid dependence on imports: Super Two engine oil was launched in 1998 followed by Super Three in 2000; avoiding dependence on imports. It should also be noted that Petrom has an association contract with Ploieşti's Astra Romană for the processing of 50,000t/month to supply the Ministry of National Defence supply base at Floreşti (north of Ploieşti) and Petrom distribution depots in Arad, Cluj-Napoca and Târgu Jiu. It also produces certain industrial oils and diesel oil with a very low freezing point (a field in which Petrom was competing with Castrol, Shell and Texaco in 1999).

Much attention was given to upgrading in 2000 when a number of contracts were signed: with Universal Oil Products (USA) for work at the two refineries;

with Honeywell (Belgium) for the upstream section; and several other companies for downstream activities: Linde (Germany) for the bottling and marketing of nitrogen, oxygen and carbon dioxide from the Petrobrazi gas separation installation; AGA (Sweden) for bottling acetylene at the Petrobrazi factory; and Enron (USA) for the company's methane gas marketing and pipeline upgrading. The following year a deal was struck with Fisher Rosemount and Salzgitter Anlagenbau regarding automation and control systems at the two refineries as well as the Doljchim (Craiova) petrochemical plant. It was reported that Petrom had negotiated a syndicated credit of $62mln and $150mln Eurobond issue (without government guarantees) from EBRD and six other co-financing banks for the updating refineries (especially Arpechim) complementing enterprise funding. Decisions were also needed over ecological fuel. Petrobrazi supplied ecological fuel in 2000: Eurodiesel was exported in 2001 and the company was hoping that it might be able to produce jet fuel for NATO planes. But it faced the stark choice of investing heavily during 2003–5 to produce Euro Three fuel (Europremium and Eurodiesel) or risk losing market share. It decided in 2002 that by 2005 its refineries would produce exclusively at EU quality standards, with all its filling stations upgraded to supply both Europremium petrol from Petrobrazi and Eurodiesel from Arpechim. One consequence was Petrom's €42.7mln contract (partly covered by an EBRD loan) with a South Korean consortium in 2004 to extend the Petrobrazi upgrade with an alkylation plant for octane components required for Euro Three/Four fuels. Finally, Petrobrazi opened a new 45,000t/yr carbon black plant and a $46.5mln cogenerating plant with a capacity of 50MW and 220t/h of steam in 2001, the latter financed by Italian and South Korean credits and the company's own funds and installed by Hyundai Engineering & Construction (South Korea) with subcontractors from France, Germany, Italy and South Korea as well as Romania: Electroputere (Craiova) and ISPE and SAEM (Bucharest).

Lukoil at Petrotel

Lukoil bought the Petrotel refinery at Ploieşti-Teleajen (built in 1904 by Romano-Americană) in 1997–8 to process its own Siberian crude imported through Galaţi (having declined the options of taking Petromidia and Rafo) and launched a $283,000 modernisation programme with an $82mln IFC credit to achieve Euro Four norms and a greater output of lighter petroleum products (and also secure improvements in health, safety and energy efficiency). The company laid-off 1,900 of its 2,600 employees during the 18 month modernisation period and then offered 1,500 positions with re-commissioning in 2004 with its own hospital and power station. Lukoil have built an integrated petroleum business since acquiring the refinery, including a new filling station network costing $96mln that created 2,500 new jobs. 5,000 now work for the company of which 1,200 are at the refinery that also supplies 80 filling stations in Moldova and 26 others in Hungary where Lukoil have 5.0 per cent of the market. Prahova county was thus able to relaunch economic ties with Russia, while local firms were invited to join Lukoil in European ventures including 'big oil deals in the next century'. There are small holdings in oilfield engineering: Upetrom-1 Mai (Ploieşti) as well as Uztel and Sterom (Câmpina).

Rompetrol at Petromidia and Vega

It is also interesting to note the influence of Romanian companies in oil refining, thanks in no small measure to the political connections of certain native capitalists. Rompetrol, the company already referred to as being largely controlled by Liberal politician Dinu Patriciu, is integrated with the Petromidia and Vega refineries. Petromidia is located on the Black Sea coast near the town of Midia (20kms north of Constanţa) and was privatised in 2000. It was built during 1975–7 with a capacity of 3.5mln.t with modern technology to handle heavy Iranian crude. It subsequently gained immediate access to the Danube-Black Sea Canal and a 40km crude pipeline link with Constanţa but became vulnerable after 1989, despite some modernisation in the 1990s, given the command system of processing whatever crude the government could afford to bring in and working to an irrational pricing system requiring hard currency payments for crude and low prices on the domestic market. But deliveries recommenced on a barter basis (equivalent to the refined products) and there were reports of a $50mln capacity increase to 4.8mln.t during the early 1990s. But these arrangements became sporadic with the currency crisis making imports of crude increasingly difficult. There were huge debts and lay-offs but after lying in a moribund state, liquidation – proposed in 1997 – was narrowly avoided through two failed attempts at privatisation, the more promising of which was a $735mln deal with Akmaya (Turkey) the following year: $239mln for a 65 per cent stake, with $260mln to repay debts over 5–15 years and meet minimum environment standards plus $226mln for investment over five years.

Party Politics

While Akmaya were genuinely interested in updating the refinery the deal was undermined in 1999 by tensions between the main coalition parties forming the centre-right government and apparent moves to replace the Turkish company by another that would play a key role in the exploitation and trading of Caspian oil. At this juncture Patriciu's Liberal Party connections were of crucial importance given the ambitions of his Rompetrol Group (registered in Amsterdam): after purchasing almost 70 per cent of the shares from SOF for $50.5mln and taking over debts of $340mln owed to banks and state budget, Patriciu was able to raise the profile of the company from the level of the small service enterprise it had been in 1996. After acquiring the Vega refinery at Ploiesti in 1999 (following EMBO privatisation in 1994) he won the battle for Petromidia by auction in 2001 and $600mln debts were converted into bonds in 2003. The new owner agreed not to implement collective layoffs for at least five years but in fact extra staff were taken on besides the existing 3,500. The aim was to process 250,000t/month of mainly Ural-Caspian crude with 90 per cent of the products exported – mostly to Turkey but also Bulgaria and Serbia in 2000. But it was later claimed that supplies came equally from the Caspian and Iraq although the export bias to the Black Sea and Mediterranean could be retained if the home market – involving depots at Arad, Şimleu Silvaniei, Vatra Dornei and Zărneşti for a network of 50 filling stations plus 100 operating under franchise (28 per cent market share) is supplied from the company's Vega refinery where $22mln was invested in 2002 to modernise the bitumen plant. The company was soon to be favoured by grants totalling around $1.0mln from the US Trade & Development Agency for modernising the equipment for air and vacuum distilling, catalytic cracking, coking and hydration; with a big reduction in energy losses. There was also an increase in capacity by 20 per cent (to some 4.0mln.t of which 3.8 was reached at the end of 2003) and it was voted the best refinery in the CEE region in 2003 through its progress culminating in compliance with Euro Three petrol standards. €300mln was spent on modernising both refineries to EU standards for export to Western Europe; also diesel fuel enhancement ahead of the 2009 deadline requested by the EU.

A Successful Upgrade

Petromidia is now a sophisticated refinery with ISO9003 certification and high complexity indicators: there is a high degree of integration with a range of products produced internally. Following the upgrade, Rompetrol became the first producer to eliminate lead, with an entire range of products conforming to European standards: it was able to launch a new range of environment-friendly fuels in 2003 under the slogan 'Euro Standard at Romanian Prices'. It also campaigned against counterfeit fuel in the same year. After a $38mln investment, Rompetrol started production of Euro Five diesel in 2005 (complying with EU standards that will be compulsory in 2009) although more than half the output will be Euro Four. Petromidia's results in 2004 were good, with 3.3mln.t of crude processed and a $4mln registered profit (apparently the first in its history) thanks to the low price of Ural crude – although eight per cent of the crude is now from Romania's own offshore field in the Black Sea. Meanwhile, excellent refinery results contributed to the improved performance of Rompetrol as a whole. Although the local terminal is available for Petromidia as well as Petrom, further efficiency now arises through a new terminal seven kilometres offshore allowing ships of 25,000t to be received (compared with the 5,000t limit in Midia harbour). Capacity rose from 4.8–5.0mln.t in 2005 and investments reached some $200mln in 2007. However the company wishes to revive petrochemistry and this requires modernisation of the ethylene and polyethylene capacities which are now obsolete with 1980s technology and have not operated since 1996. Instead the company has been importing from TGR (Hungary) and a Lukoil subsidiary in Bulgaria. But work will now go ahead at Petromidia with know-how – and deliveries of ethylene – from Dow Chemicals in return for production (for Dow) of polymers amounting to 60–100,000t/yr. Vega meanwhile is an old refinery dating to 1904, with a 500,000t/yr capacity that was slated for liquidation in 1997 but purchased the following year by two Cyprus-based companies with the intention of reopening after environmental protection programmes. Patriciu however took over in 1999 and completed environmental improvements funded at Vega in 2001 over a lagoon responsible for soil and groundwater pollution. It is part of a major sludge problem (involving 1.0mln.t in various parts of Prahova) which can be broken down by the Flottweg system into water, petroleum (eventually usable as fuel) and solids. The refinery produces 'special boiling point' spirits, solvents, bitumen, heating oils and catalysts that include feedstocks for Petromidia.

The Rafo Connection

This generated a new dimension with rumours of a merger in 2004 between Rompetrol and Rafo, the ailing Moldavian refinery company with installations in Oneşti and Dărmăneşti, and a history of linkage (from the communist period) with the Oneşti synthetic rubber producer Carom: all part of a new chemical complex built at what was then the new town of Gh.Gheorghiu-Dej. The refinery proved difficult to restructure although there appeared to be potential for processing Russian crude in association with Petrom in 1999. It was eventually privatised in 2001 with 60 per cent shares sold by APMSH to Imperial Oil (Bacău) and Canyon Services (Portugal) and operations were resumed after a 2.5 year break. The most influential entrepreneur in the structure was C.Iacobov, a prominent figure in PSD. A web of business deals emerged including the Romanian-Moldovan j.v. Rafpet between Rafo and Onor Gas of Ungheni in 2001 – with Romanian state capital and private capital from Cyprus, Moldova and Russia – to promote Rafo products in Moldova and Eastern Europe. However the Rafo case became prominent during the 2004 election. By this time Balkan Petroleum was the principal owner and it was seeking both a merger with Carom (the nearby synthetic rubber producer) and a transfer of debts – 1.85bln.lei – to the state in return for shares (which would actually make the state the principal shareholder). Balkan Petroleum's interest gave prominence to the Romanian oil group VGB that owned 50 per cent of Balkan Petroleum, while another 25 per cent was owned by Central European Petroleum (previously Regal) – established by the well-connected foreign businessman Frank Timis (who claimed he sold his interest in 2004) – and the remaining 25 per cent was held by Acornline (UK).

In this way Rafo became part of the burgeoning industrial empire controlled by oligarchs close to the ruling party of the time who were suspected of gaining favours for fraudulent dealings through the debt for shares arrangement (beneficial to PSD through substantial cash contributions to party election funds); a matter later investigated as part of the anti-corruption drive of the Tăriceanu government. Although Alfa Oil of Switzerland expressed interest in taking over the government's shares (managed by the National Agency for Fiscal Administration) Rafo was sold for \$60mln to the Russian I.Goldovsky and the Bulgarian T.Batkov; oligarchs who operate discreetly on the Romanian oil and energy market. The refinery is now to be mothballed for a major upgrade during 2008–10. The Rompetrol angle is interesting because Patriciu claims that Tender and VGB 'blackmailed' him into the idea of merging Rompetrol and Rafo in order to save the latter – with pressure arising from the National Security Department's interest in the legality of Rompetrol's own 'bonds for debt' deal and the possibility of Rompetrol being investigated by the National Anti-Corruption Prosecutor's Office (a risk that would be averted with Patriciu's cooperation over the suggested merger). Patriciu claims that in his case the decision of the centre-right government (converting Petromidia's historic debts of \$320mln into shares) was unexceptional and represented a historic debt from before privatisation.

Bioethanol (Biodiesel) Refineries

An interesting new initiative is arising through the €47mln investment project by Martifer (Portugal) for a 100,000t/yr biodiesel plant opened in 2006 on a 10ha site at Lehliu Gara (Călăraşi county), processing rape from 150,000ha to secure the ecological fuel needed in connection with Romania's Kyoto obligations – increasing from 2.0 per cent of the fuel required in 2005 to 20 per cent in 2020, although despite doubling capacity after two years the Lehliu production will only produce 30 per cent of the biodiesel required in 2010. A further €25mln investment should enable the company to acquire 50,000ha of land which is the minimum needed to sustain plant, although the total area under rape and sunflowers could expand to 2.0mln.ha. Meanwhile a second project is in the pipeline by a Belgian firm for Ialomiţa county (also in the Bărăgan 'heartland' of sunflower production). There are a number of smaller projects: two in the Bărăgan by Expur (Urziceni) and Ultex (Ţăndărei); while Argus Constanţa plan a \$7–10mln investment for 20–30,000t/yr of biodiesel and Adrian Porumboiu's Racova Group will invest €18mln at Vaslui, using up to 40 per cent for their own needs while selling the rest (anticipating costs up to 40 per cent below the normal level). A Baia Mare taxi firm (Autoelite) is producing on a local basis. A €100mln investment in a biodiesel plant for Aţel involving

Sibiu County Council along with the local Dafora (Mediaş) company and MAN Ferrostal and Retter (Germany) was cancelled after biodiesel cost more expensive than diesel oil, but Mabio (Hungary) have a €150mln EU project for Dorohoi. Refining companies need to make provision and while Lukoil and Rompetrol plan their own units the rest will buy from others or import.

FILLING STATIONS

The expansion of roadside services has been one of the most conspicuous changes evident since 1989. In addition to a massive numerical increase in filling stations (eliminating delay and uncertainty) there has been a revolution in quality with many stations now providing a range of services e.g. the Livada station near Satu Mare has 16 pumps, a lorry park and a hotel). With the growth of informal open-air marketing – so characteristic of the country as a whole – some stations have now attracted substantial commercial activity. The base of the oil distribution system rests with Petrom as heir to the system in force in the communist period, with the filling stations gradually modernised e.g. note the innovation of natural gas supply (LPG-autogas) in 1999 for cars at half the petrol price, with filling stations supplying both the fuel and equipment for engine switch. The company became quite innovative with 24 hour opening and convenience shopping e.g. their complex at the Urziceni Crossroads (with important transit routes) comprising a new filling station with a shopping centre and mini-market in 1999. In 2002 Petrom had 450 stations but Rompetrol expanded rapidly to 86 stations early in 2005 plus 152 in partnership to secure 10 per cent market share; planned to increase to 15 per cent in 2006 with another 40 stations plus 100 more franchises; supported by the Petromidia refinery and a wholesaling network of depots in Braşov, Bucharest, Cluj-Napoca, Constanţa, Craiova, Deobeta-Turnu Severin, Oradea, Şimleu Silvaniei and Suceava. During 2005 Rompetrol opened stores, restaurants and internet points at 35 city stations starting in Timişoara. Expansion has also occurred abroad with the acquisition of the French Dyneff Group (as already noted) with 250 petrol stations (mostly franchised) in France and Spain, in addition to 32 units already in operating in Albania, Bulgaria, Georgia and Moldova.

Foreign Companies

These became more prominent and during the 1990s gradually exerted pressure on Petrom to update their facilities while closing others that were poorly equipped and located. Among the foreign businesses, reference may be made first to ÖMV which started independently before developing links first with

Rompetrol and now with Petrom. They planned expansion from 68 to 100 stations during 2005–8 for a tenth of the market, with €13mln on up to 10 new stations in 2005 alone, before the Petrom acquisition. ÖMW have also been prominent in the drive for green fuel with its ecological gas station in 2000 at Satu Mare. ÖMV also cooperated (with Lukoil, Mol, Petrom and Shell) in enabling Ploieşti to become the first county centre to sell only lead-free petrol and diesel with low sulphur content when the local authority contemplated a three-month ban (late in 2000) on the sale of all other fuels. And the company has joined with Agip, Mol and Shell in creating an independent Romanian Oil Association to promote the general interests and social reputation of the oil industry in Romania. Open to all oil companies with $5.0mln capital and 55 per cent private ownership, it has organised training to assimilate global best practices, promote safer environment-protection standards and encourage social programmes. Now that Petrom is under ÖMV ownership, a multi-facility Petrom V chain of 250 stations is envisaged by 2010 (178 new 'premium gas stations' are also to be provided in future). On the other hand 100 unprofitable units have been relinquished and on balance the company hopes to maintain a stable but profitable network of 550 stations ; while expanding to a total of some 250 in Bulgaria, Moldova and Serbia where a total €70mln has been invested (allowing for takeovers from ÖMV). Meanwhile Rompetrol has developed a network of 108 stations plus a partner network involving another 175 units. 70 'expres' stations were opened in 2007 but in 2008 the aim is to provide a better service with 200 new stations for rural areas which tend to be neglected although they account for 35 per cent of sales of oil products.

Shell, Lukoil and Mol

The other major foreign interests in 2002 were essentially Shell with 81 stations, Lukoil (Russia) 65, Mol (Hungary) 47 and Agip (Italy) 22. Shell made a big impact in the early years but development slowed down after the initial investment of $220mln although in 1996 they still contemplated 200 stations over 30 or more years. With no refinery in Romania, products have to be supplied from two refineries acquired in the Czech Republic in 2001. They invested in an aviation fuel depot (14,000sq.m facility) at Otopeni and provided funds for updating Petrobrazi refinery before selling their network in 2003–4, while retaining a major gas bottling business in competition with Linde (though this has also been disposed of – to Petrom). Companies from neighbouring countries are also active, with Lukoil growing explosively with investment of $150mln to expand from 19 stations in 2001 to 300 stations in mid-2005, with 60–70 more planned; while there is also activity in Hungary and Moldova coordinated in Romania. Mol started to open petrol stations in 1995 and nurtured the ambition of overtaking Shell who were initially in second place to Petrom. Their investment of $82mln to the end of 2001 placed the company in

Romania's top ten for FDI in 2002 with the intention of expanding to a network of 100–120 stations – opening 8–10 each year – with initial priority on the route from the Hungarian border near Oradea to Bucharest via Timişoara, Deva, Braşov and Ploieşti. However an ecological petrol station (including green spaces) was built in Baia Mare on land owned by the city hall and CFR in 1998.

Mol have been quite innovative with their own credit card system and the offer of the Euro Super Plus brand throughout the network in 2002. They then advanced rapidly during 2003–4 by acquiring Shell's 84 stations for €76mln: taking 25 in 2003 and 59 in 2004 and completing the assimilation with rebranding and reconstruction in 2005 to secure fourth place (with 133 stations) after Petrom, Rompetrol and Lukoil. Prista Oil (Bulgaria) has a tenth of the market for oil and lubricants and is also active in Hungary, Turkey and Ukraine. In addition, many of the 26 individual oilfields seemed poised to go into retailing in 1997, beginning with Arad Oilfield's stations at Vinga and Turnu. Reference should also be made to the Rafo (Oneşti) refinery that distributes fuel to 30 of its own stations (and 150 others), while aiming to invest €300mln in raising the total to 400 (backed by depots in Braşov, Cluj, Oneşti and Oradea with Bucharest, Craiova and Suceava to follow. They claim to have processed 3.30mln.t crude during October 2003–August 2005 since Balkan Petroleum took over and achieved a $1.31bln turnover. They will have to survive the pressures from government already reported in connection with fraud allegations but hope to avoid bankruptcy through a more cooperative approach by Bucharest. Finally it is expected that Socar (Azerbaijan) may well open a chain of filling stations as it enters the Romanian market to sell products from its Turkish plant. Finally, there is much counterfeit oil on the market – potentially damaging to vehicle engines – while the removal of guards from the national oil pipeline system in 2005 – because of money owed by the oil companies – has led to suspicions that some private independent stations are handling stolen petrol.

ELECTRICITY GENERATION

Capacity is huge but resources for for modernisation are desperately needed. Despite price rises Romanian power was once hailed as the cheapest in Europe after Ukraine; albeit with old equipment, an embarrassing history of debts to coal and hydrocarbon suppliers and dependence on credits to cover imported fuel (like the loan secured from 27 Romanian and foreign banks to pay for winter fuel in 2001). The industry needs $10.4bln of investment during 2003–15: $3.48bln for new thermal capacity; $1.89bln for nuclear (to finish Unit II of the Cernavodă station and implement Unit III) and $1.61bln for hydropower, plus $3.48bln for distribution and transport. More biomass and geothermal power is also envisaged. Production fell 64.3mln.Kwh in 1990 to a low of 50.7 in 1999 before rising to 53.9 in 2001, 56.6 in 2003 and 59.4 in 2005 (Table 7.2); still leaving a significant margin over consumption. In 2000, total capacity of some 22.0GW contrasted with an operational capacity of 16.0GW (allowing for rehabilitation in progress). Thermal capacity exceeds hydro by a ratio of roughly two to one, with 10 per cent for nuclear power; and within the thermal sector the ratio of coal-based to hydrocarbon base has changed dramatically from parity in 1997 to four to three in 1999 and five to three since 2000.

Naturally it makes good sense to maximise output of hydro and nuclear power so the thermal sector shows the greatest under-use: 13.9GW of installed power and 11.7GW of available capacity, but with normal usage not exceeding 3.8GW rising to a peak of only 4.5GW during the winter of 1999–2000. Clearly with new hydro and nuclear capacity in prospect some thermal plant can be dispensed with: 4.0GWwas suggested in 1999 and it was later planned that 2.9GW would close during 2000–5 (a total of 3.0GW since 1998), despite strong union hostility in the face of external pressure from the World Bank and IMF. Small power stations seemed the most vulnerable initially (e.g. Comăneşti, Doiceşti, Oradea and Ovidiu with capacities of 12–25MW) – even some of intermediate size (including Craiova-Işalniţa with 250MW and Paroşeni with 150MW) – during the years of negative growth at the end of the decade. But now that Termoelectrica has transferred many of its 51 thermal stations and heating units to local authorities or separate companies the focus has moved to some of the company's main power stations ahead of privatisation.

Thermal Power

The crucial issue has become one of efficiency in order to acquire larger coal stocks and sustain loans for rehabilitation as grid suppliers and/or local utilities providing heat or a combination of heat and power. Various financial models were investigated e.g. a Romanian-German joint holding to facilitate investment and Romanian export to the EU market followed Romania's affiliation into the European Organisation of Energy Carriers in 1999. In 2001 rehabilitation of heating stations was explored with KSB (Germany); also with Alstom for 300MW lignite-based generating groups as well as a j.v. with ABB Equity Venture in Timişoara. Power stations were grouped into four categories. First, ten stations with special importance for the grid including Brăila, Craiova (two stations), Luduş, Mintia (Deva), Rovinari and Turceni as well as Bucharest's Progresul, South and West stations. Second a large group of 21 other profitable stations: Arad, Bacău, Borzeşti, Braşov, Brazi, Galaţi, Midia, Năvodari, Oneşti, Oradea (two), Palas (Constanţa), Piteşti, Ploieşti (two), Reşiţa, Suceava, Timişoara and Zalău as well as the Bucharest stations of Grozăveşti and Titan.

Table 7.2: *Electricity Generation (Thermal/Nuclear and Hydro) 1985–2005*

Year	Capacity thMW			Output bln.kWh			Ditto mln.kWh/Kw			Fuels (percent)			
	All	Thml	Hydr	All	Thml	Hydr	All	Thml	Hydr	Coal*		Oil	Gas
1985	n.a.	n.a.	n.a.	71.82	59.92	11.90	n.a.	n.a.	n.a.	33.2	23.3	11.8	53.0
1986	n.a.	n.a.	n.a.	75.48	64.67	10.81	n.a.	n.a.	n.a.	30.9	22.7	16.4	50.1
1987	n..a	n.a.	n.a.	74.08	62.87	11.21	n.a.	n.a.	n.a.	32.9	24.1	15.8	48.8
1988	n.a.	n.a.	n.a.	75.32	61.70	13.62	n.a.	n.a.	n.a.	38.3	31.2	11.5	46.5
1989	n.a.	n.a.	n.a.	75.85	63.22	12.63	n.a.	n.a.	n.a.	38.6	31.7	13.5	45.7
1990	n.a.	n.a.	n.a.	64.31	53.33	10.98	n.a.	n.a.	n.a.	29.7	23.6	22.6	46.3
1991	n.a.	n.a.	n.a.	56.91	42.66	14.25	n.a.	n.a.	n.a.	32.0	25.2	14.9	51.9
1992	22.18	16.44	5.73	54.19	42.49	11.70	2.44	2.58	2.04	43.2	32.2	9.6	45.8
1993	22.26	16.39	5.87	55.48	42.71	12.77	2.49	2.61	2.17	44.7	34.3	12.1	42.1
1994	22.06	16.12	5.94	55.14	42.09	13.05	2.50	2.61	2.20	46.6	36.3	13.1	39.4
1995	22.28	16.26	6.01	59.27	42.57	16.69	2.66	2.62	2.78	48.4	36.0	13.1	37.5
1996	22.86	16.82	6.04	61.35	45.59	15.75	2.68	2.71	2.61	44.9	33.2	14.2	36.7
1997	22.84	16.77	6.07	57.15	39.64	17.51	2.50	2.36	2.88	42.5	31.1	16.7	25.4
1998	22.56	16.48	6.08	53.50	34.62	18.88	2.37	2.10	3.10	41.8	32.3	11.6	29.4
1999	22.24	16.15	6.08	50.71	32.42	18.29	2.28	2.01	3.01	45.3	34.1	11.4	26.0
2000	21.90	15.78	6.12	51.93	37.16	14.78	2.37	2.35	2.41	50.9	39.6	8.9	24.2
2001	20.86	14.74	6.12	53.87	38.94	14.92	2.58	2,64	2.44	50.6	37.7	13.5	20.7
2002	19.66	13.42	6.24	54.93	38.89	16.05	2.79	2.90	2.57	52.2	40.2	9.0	23.6
2003	19.37	13.12	6.25	56.64	43.39	13.26	2.92	3.31	2.12	53.8	43.5	8.4	25.8
2004	19.63	13.35	6.28	56.48	39.97	16.51	n.a.	n.a.	n.a.	53.7	44.1	5.4	26.2
2005	19.04	12.75	6.29	59.41	39.21	20.21	n.a.	n.a.	n.a.	55.9	45.1	4.6	24.5

Note: * two columns: the first for all coal (including lignite) and the second for lignite only

Source: Statistical Yearbooks: Table 16.10 and 16.11

In the third group were seven stations of essentially local importance that could be hived off: Calafat, Comăneşti, Doiceşti, Giurgiu, Gura Barza, Vaslui and Vulcan. And finally there were six worn-out stations retained only for standby purposes: Anina, Fântânele, Floreşti, Ianca, Ovidiu and Târgu Jiu.

The Role of Local Authorities

While privatisation was linked quite strongly with the first group of stations, the second and third groups were seen as more likely candidates for management by local authorities given the importance of cogeneration of power and heating that accounted for 40 per cent of Termoelectrica's capacity provision. Hence the restructuring carried out during 2001–2 among Termoelectrica's 41 stations, whereby single stations at Arad, Bacău, Borzeşti, Braşov, Doiceşti, Ploieşti and Reşiţa – and two each at Iaşi, Oradea, Piteşti, Suceava and Timişoara – were transferred to local authorities, while a subsidiary company or j.v. was set up in respect of installations at Brăila, Bucharest, Calafat, Comăneşti, Deva, Doiceşti, Galaţi, Giurgiu, Gura Barza, Midia, Vaslui and Zalău. Also 14 micro hydropower stations were transferred to Hidroelectrica in 2002. Meanwhile, Bucharest's determined action gave rise to a new 600MW Nord power station built by ABB Electroinvest-Amoco in the Pantelimon/Fundeni area of the city for heating hot water and electricity in 1997, after tenders had been submitted by ABB, Amoco and Siemens. The authority also examined the possibility of a private 500MW thermal power plant in Rahova to supply the south of the city. Pressure came from high electricity costs at Renel's Sud and Vest stations (through high fuel consumption) where modernisation was repeatedly postponed despite insufficient capacity to meet the city's needs). Sud and Vest were initially placed in Category One as important grid suppliers, but the logic of local management – especially given the heating functions – won the day and the result is a separate company – Electrocentrale Bucureşti – that now manages these two stations as well as Grozăveşti, Progresul and Titan (along with water filtration and evacuation and sewerage). The Radet heating company expects to increase efficiency by improvements at power stations especially Sud and Vest by 2005 based on an $1.0bln investment in upgrading by Termoelectrica. The programme includes several Termoelectrica stations comprising some 3,000MW of capacity crucial for the national grid and also of local importance through heating systems. In 2002 RCB credits were provided for rehabilitation of Constanţa Nord station and a new Oradea Sud 400Kv station: both important for inter-connection of Central European countries.

Improvements at Cogeneration Units

The first 50MW phase at Bacău South was completed 12 years after the start of construction in 1985 (four years later than planned), providing 600 new jobs and heating 7,000 apartments in a district where heating and hot water has been a problem. And Brăila-Chişcani station was completely re-equipped by Westinghouse in 1998 for eventual privatisation as an independent energy producer. But after restructuring municipalities were supported in their attempts to get credits from international banks for upgrading as deterioration of pipeline insulation makes for heavy losses. New capacities were already planned since 1997 at Arad (50MW), Bacău (100MW) and Timişoara (240MW) and some of the new independent energy companies – including Braşov, Bucharest, Cluj-Napoca and Târgovişte – have been boosting efficiency and cumulatively seeking $190mln of investment in over 200MW of new capacity in gas-fired stations to meet demand. In Sighetul Marmaţiei, the local heating company 'Accaterm' was taken by Swedish consortium ABB in 1999 for a $10mln refurbishment over two years (including individual household metering), with expectation of profit over 10 years. In 2000 Braşov entered into a PPPt with VEW (Dortmund) for a $50–100mln upgrading of the local coal-burning cogeneration plant (with 45MW and 60MW generators) for a 60–65 per cent increase in efficiency; also to install an extra 50MW of new gas-fired (or fuel oil) capacity to supply the city and district. VEW will also recycle 400,000t of garbage. At the same time, Oradea moved to upgrade thermal energy supplies using methane gas and geothermal water with metering of gas, hot water and heat for each consumer by Geisenwasser (Germany); while Petroşani gained Danish financial support for a heating company (separate from the operator of municipal services) to take advantage of LFA facilities and negotiate with Paroşeni power station over heat to Aninoasa, Petrila, Petroşani and Vulcan.

In 2001 Buzău and Paşcani negotiated Swiss help through a $4.0mln non-reimbursable loan for reconstruction of their heating systems, while Botoşani achieved a cost reduction of eight per cent (10bln.lei/yr) when the local Termica company installed a $1.2mln gas-fired Comotti cogenerating group, using a jet engine. In 2002 Constanţa Port and Eforie Nord signed a €4.9mln power station efficiency contract with ABB Calor Emag Schaltanlagen (Germany), while more significantly, government guaranteed a contract between the EIB and the Cluj Termoficare company to refurbish the heating system by upgrading Gheorgheni and Mănăştur heating plants with new boilers for natural gas and liquid fuel plus 12kms of new pipelines; also $50mln from the World Bank, a business consortium and some commercial banks to update the regional thermal power plant with a 25MW gas turbine and hot water boilers. And a further major improvement will see the integration of 12 formerly separate energy islands restricted to their own local heating plants, thanks to a consortium combining local energy management, the Romanian-German company Colonia and Rolls Royce (UK): each contributing $7.5mln (presumably on a PPPt basis). The small town of Huedin has rejected gas-based heating in favour of a PPPt with a Danish company to heat 600 local apartments using sawdust from the local 'Furnituri' and 'Vladeasa' factories. 65 per cent of the finance is coming from Denmark and 25 per cent from the industry ministry.

Finally in 2005, Rompetrol and Petromidia won the tender (76mln.lei for a 56.6 per cent stake) for a new Midia-Năvodari cogeneration power plant. There is clearly a good deal of work for foreign electrical companies. Thus ABB – with a new headquarters in Timişoara – have three companies in Romania dealing with electricity transmission and distribution, building technologies and financial services. The Remetrics company supplies electricity meters after ABB's successful competition with Siemens in the final stage of tendering for the Transelectrica tele-metering project for the Romanian wholesale electricity market in 2002. In system maintenance these companies (along with Alstom and Schneider) are working with Romanian firms such as Electroceramica, Electroputere and Eximprod Power Systems with an integrated IT system created in 2002–3. Finally, the predicament of small towns should be noted. Sulina in the Danube delta is poor now that not even the fishing makes a living and the cost of running solid/liquid fuel stoves is a heavy burden which might potentially be eased by a small power station; raising the possibility of groups of small towns getting together over viable projects. Much more needs to be done and so the National Regulatory Authority for Energy will assist energy producers to assimilate cogeneration technologies during the period 2009–22.

New Power Stations

Several have been built by large industrial complexes wishing to secure cheaper power not merely by negotiating directly with generators but by providing their own stations. Chimcomplex (Borzeşti) halved the cost of power by building its own 50MW gas-fired plant with an investment of $33mln and the help of the French company SIF: the first Romanian enterprise to be self-reliant. Any surplus will be marketed through the grid. The project of 1998 had implications for the existing Borzeşti power station which was already operating below capacity. Govora also became an independent power supplier in 1997 with a 200MW power station supplying Oltchim, the Govora soda works and local settlements including Râmnicu Vâlcea. Negotiated prices secured cost savings for consumers of rather more than 10 per cent while enabling the new station to work at full capacity (90MW at present) with any surplus to the grid. Finally a $100mln investment in cogeneration was made by Petrom at Petrobrazi in 2003 with two 26MW gas turbines – installed by Hyundai Engineering – to achieve heating 40 per cent cheaper and electricity 60 per cent cheaper than buying prices – also with scope to deliver surplus to the national energy system. As part of the 'dash for gas' the old Renel organisation set its sights on 2,000MW of new capacity in high-efficiency power stations using gas turbines and combined cycles to be built from 2006 (in the context of a 59–50 per cent reduction in the capacity share of thermal power this anticipated drastic plant closures). This thinking was extended through a link between Romgaz and Gazunie (The Netherlands) based on a joint project in 1998 for 11 gas-fired power stations to be supplied through the European gas pipeline system via the Szeged-Arad link (for 2.5bln.cu.m/yr of which 500mln.cu.m/yr would be earmarked for the new power stations). The latest plans for large power stations concern ArcelorMittal at Galaţi (700–1,000MW) which has attracted interest from Edison, Enel and Gaz de France; while E.On and Enel are looking at a similar project at Brăila. Coca-Cola are working with US Contour Global on two small thermal power plants (for the end of 2009) to cut carbon dioxide emissions and supply surplus power to the grid and Lukoil have a project at their Petrotel refinery. Schweighofer seek a 9MW cogeneration plant at their new Rădăuţi board factory while InterAgro have a similar plan for Zimnicea bioethanol plant.

Upgrading of Large Thermal Power Stations

In order to secure a longer term future for coal burning stations, this became a key issue under the national energy strategy for 2002–15. Anticipating liberalisation of the energy market and the ecological parameters required by the EU, the programme seeks extensive upgrading and 3,000MW of new coal-fired thermal capacity out of a total of 9,400MW overall (including the Cernavodă II nuclear project) planned for 2015, with generation costs kept within $3/Mwh. Rehabilitation was launched in 2002–3 with a $970mln programme seeking foreign assistance for 10 stations with a total capacity of 1,360MW: a total of four units at the three large Oltenian power stations (Craiova-Işalniţa, Rovinari and Turceni) at an estimated cost of $405mln; three in Bucharest: Grozăveşti, Sud and Vest ($180mln); as well as a total of seven units at the provincial co-generating stations of Borzeşti, Brăila, Doiceşti and Iernut ($205mln). 60 per cent of the investment was to come from foreign credits, with only $200mln of government guarantees. In addition a Finnish-German-Japanese consortium was engaged at Mintia (Deva) on a project worth €66mln in 2002 (for which some cooperation with Russia was envisaged). But much of the work has been done at two power stations in Oltenia: Rovinari and Turceni (which will cost a total of €3.7bln for technical upgrading, along with Craiova-Işalniţa). Rovinari (1,760MW) was inaugurated in 1968 with two 220MW units from Czechoslovakia that are now obsolete and are kept in conservation.

Expansion continued with four 330MW units from heavy engineering units (Vulcan/IMG) in Bucharest, one of which was added after the revolution as a $37mln self-funded investment. It is reported that three 330MW units are currently available although at times only one is actually operating. Turceni (2,310MW) opened in 1972 and a total of seven 330MW units were installed over the following 15 years, all by Vulcan/IMBG. But only four units are currently in operation, with higher costs than Rovinari because the lignite is transported over a greater distance (though both stations burn some fuel oil as well as lignite). Rehabilitation has been done by the German group Deutsche Babcock ABB under a PPPt deal valued at $600mln in respect of four units at Turceni alone. There are also projects by Itochu, Hitachi and Toshiba (financed by the Japanese Bank for International Cooperation) to reduce levels of sulphur dioxide at Turceni. Meanwhile restructuring of ONLC has integrated these two power stations and their lignite mines to enhance their attractiveness for privatisation (Turceni claims lignite productions costs 10 per cent below ONLC as a whole) and the same strategy has been adopted for Craiova-Işalniţa power station. Privatisation of all three stations was mooted for 2005 but without result to date. Meanwhile upgrading work is proceeding at Brazi Vest power station near Ploieşti under a €30mln agreement with Itochu (Japan) signed in 2003 involving the gas insulate system. The plan also envisages closure of 5.9GW of capacity (partly in anticipation of the Cernavodă II nuclear completion in 2007.

Hydropower

This is a major consideration given the country's potential and the low running costs, but high investment costs are a stumbling block which has (most recently) undermined the expectation that it would contribute 35 per cent of total power output in 2005 (compared with 27 per cent in the late 1990s) as a result of upgrading and new projects. The target was only just missed (33.0 per cent) and hydropower's share of power generated was slightly higher at 34.0 per cent due to heavy rainfall. But usually (e.g. 2001–4) the generation share falls below capacity share by some 2.0 per cent. The margin is even greater in years of serious drought like 2003 when river flow was 20–50 per cent below average: the total hydropower output of 13.2GWh was well below the norm of 17.3 with particularly large discrepancies for Buzău, Caransebeş and Haţeg (below 50%). Thermal plants had to work nearer to capacity (fortunately with some benefit from recent upgrading) although some coal- and hydrocarbon-fuelled plants had to restart production (including Borzeşti, Doiceşti and Iernut that the IMF had been recommending for closure). In that year hydro capacity was 32.3 per cent of the total but the share of power generated was only 23.4 per cent. It was also embarrassing that Hidroelectrica had to cut exports that had already been negotiated with foreign customers. However low water levels may also disrupt thermal power production because Rovinari faced problems in cooling in 2003 through the low water level of the Jiu river. In years of high rainfall the opposite situation arises: in summer 1998 both Turceni and Rovinari were virtually shut down because of heavy rain and a consequent increase in hydropower output.

Outline of Development

Capacity has developed throughout the twentieth century, although during the inter-war period the low cost of fuel oil meant that the high capital cost of really large hydropower schemes could not be justified. Nevertheless the capacity of individual projects has gradually increased, since the 1.0MW installed at Sinaia in 1898 (the largest at the time) was overtaken by Dobreşti's 16MW in 1930; eventually upstaged by Stejaru (Bicaz) with 210MW in 1960 and exceeded again in 1971 by the Iron Gates with 1,068MW on the Romanian side of the river (registering its highest output so far with 7.50mlnMWh in 1999). At present Hidroelectrica runs 350 plants and pumping stations at 126 separate sites with a capacity of 6.29GW and a 'normal' output of 17.3GWh already noted. Of the 12 area subsidiaries the greatest importance for capacity attaches to the Iron Gates (Porţile de Fier) with 1.40GW and Râmnicu Vâlcea with 1.18GW, followed by Bistriţa, Cluj, Curtea de Argeş, Haţeg, Sibiu and Slatina with 358–667MW and finally Buzău, Caransebeş, Sibiu and Târgu Jiu. However, due to variations in average capacity and the continuity of production, the Iron Gates has 0.9 percent of the stations but 22.2 per cent of the capacity and 37.9 per cent of the production, while Bistriţa, Cluj, Curtea de Argeş and Sibiu contribute 231 stations (66.0 per cent) but only 32.0 per cent of the capacity and 26.1 per cent of the production (Figure 7.1; Table 7.3)

Rehabilitation

This is a priority (as in the case of the thermal sector) since 40 per cent of the 300 generating units are 20–40 years old at the start of the millennium and Renel provided for this in 1997 through the j.v. with ABB-Energoreparaţii to upgrade plants being connected to the European network. The core of the programme consists of five projects: Iron Gates I at a cost of $188mln (plus the navigation sluices during 2002–9) to raise capacity for each of the six units from 175 to 194.4MW (a total increase of 116MW); and Iron Gates II, costing $125mln and delayed to 2003–16 with all ten units uprated from 27.0 to 31.5MW (an increase of 45MW). The work at the Iron Gates is in a special category because it requires cooperation between Romania and Serbia, based on conventions for upkeep and exploitation and agreement over rehabilitation with foreign contractors (although project details quoted relate only to the Romanian side). Work began at Iron Gates I actually during 1996–2000 on unit six, with unit five scheduled to follow. A contract was signed in 1998 for SwFr180mln for rehabilitation by Sulzer Hydro and Vatech Hydro (Austria) in collaboration with three Romanian firms: Electroconstrucţii, Hidroconstrucţia and UCM Reşiţa; and due for completion by 2006. However the deal was criticised for lack of tendering, in contrast to the situation in Serbia where refurbishment costs were much lower. Moreover the work reportedly went badly on account of many 'irregularities' involving a loss of $30mln in reduced electricity output. Meanwhile the contract for Iron Gates II was negotiated in 2001 with Vatech for rehabilitation from 2003 in collaboration with Electroputere, Energomontaj (Bucharest) and UCMR, with payment in electricity. Work is often long overdue: the original Soviet units at Iron Gates II (operational since 1984–6) were due for capital repairs after 80,000 hours although they have actually worked for 120,000 hours. But the $15mln annual loss at this station should be converted into a profit due with increased capacity (270–315MW) and reduced operating and maintenance costs by remote control working as one of Europe's most modern hydro stations, supplying a tenth of Romania's hydropower.

Another early candidate for rehabilitation was Lotru (Ciunget) power station costing £48mln during 2002–6 with capacity stable at 510MW (three 170MW units); the Olt valley below Slatina costing $110mln during 2002–10 with 20 units of 8–12MW raised to 13–14MW; and the 209MW Bistriţa (Stejaru-Bicaz) project costing $65mln during 2002–8 which will maintain two units at 50MW each and increase four smaller ones slightly from 26.8 to 27.5MW (total capacity 210MW). Râul Mare (2x167.5MW), Vidraru (4x55MW) on the Argeş, Marişelu (3x75MW) on the Someş in the Apuseni Mountains, and Galceag and Şugag (both 2x75MW) on the Sebeş are also candidates for a programme announced in 2001 and scheduled for completion in 2012 at a cost of some $0.6bln, largely from loans and only partially from Hidroelectrica's own sources. Sulzer Hydro will help with rehabilitation at Lotru (510MW) financed by a World Bank-approved €66mln guaranteed loan accepted by the government in 2004. The 2003 Athens meeting on SEE regional energy approved Lotru's integration into the EU system in 2005. All the projects are geared to a 30 year life cycle and should produce good results in terms of efficiency. Rehabilitation will embrace 54 groups (3,385MW) and secure an increase of 182MW. But the programme fell behind and only in 2007 were contracts expected for Galceag and Şugag as well as Marişelu and Stejaru.

New Projects

These continue despite many lapses after the revolution due to limited funding. There were capacity increases in 1997 (52.0MW and 94.0WGWh); 1998 (13.2/48.0); 1999 (1.3/6.0); 2000 (15.7/7.3); 2001 (4.6/8.2); 2002 (37.8/77.4), 2003 (33.0/n.a.) and 2005 (23.7/n.a. in five separate projects). It is not clear precisely where all these new capacities were secured apart from 2002, with an extra 27.5MW at Iron Gates II plus 16.8 at Cornetu (Olt valley) and 3.8 at Dragoslavele on the Dâmboviţa; while in 2003 there was 19.4MW extra at Iron Gates I, 10.0MW of pumping at Galceag and small capacities at Sălătrucu de Jos (0.8MW) and Trăisteni (1.2MW) in the Curtea de Argeş district. Under a project started in 1982 the Poiana Mărului barrage near Caransebeş was finished in 1999 and 55cu.m/sec now flows to Turnu Ruieni power station (140MW). However the increased capacity in that year is only recorded as 1.3MW (and 13.2 in 1998) so this power station must have opened earlier. Hidroelectrica also have plans for new capacity at Poiana Mărului (80MW) and Râul Alb (40MW), the first not commenced and the latter project suspended through lack

Table 7.3: *Hydroelectricity – Capacity and Privatisation*

Region	A	B	C	D	E	F	G	H
Centre	Sebeş	7	2.0	358.2	5.7	610	3.5	Mureş(Rastoliţa) $142; Olt(Hoghiz-Făgăraş)
	Sibiu(Olt)	34	9.7	147.1	2.3	383	2.2	$120, Olt(Cornetu) $150
North East	Bistriţa-Siret	81	23.1	667.2	10.6	1761	10.2	Bistriţa (Borca-Poiana Teiului) $45 Siret (Cosmeşti-Movileni) $85
North West	Cluj(Someş)	59	16.9	565.8	9.0	1096	6.3	Runcu-Firiza $14; Tisa (Săpânţa-Teceu) $116
South	C.de Argeş	67	19.1	635.9	10.1	1286	7.4	Argeş (Piteşti) $8
South East	Buzău	13	3.7	97.8	1.6	302	1.7	Buzău (Siriu-Surduc) $67
SouthWest	Iron Gates	3	0.9	1397.6	22.2	6561	38.0	Gilort (Novaci) $15; Jiu
	Rm.Vâlcea	26	7.4	1180.1	18.8	2751	16.0	Jiu(Valea Sadului-Vădeni) $106;
	Slatina(Olt)	8	2.3	379.0	6.0	889	5.1	Olt (Islaz) $100; Tismana $30
	Târgu Jiu	17	4.9	206.2	3.3	505	2.9	
West	Caransebeş	11	3.1	164.4	2.6	304	1.8	
	Haţeg (Râul Mare)	24	6.9	488.9	7.8	850	4.9	Bistra: Măru $12, Râul Alb $30, Zerveşti $1; Cerna-Belareca $28 Miniş (Poneasca) $1; Râul Mare-Retezat $36; Strei (Subcetate) $80
Total		350	100.0	6288.2	100.0	17298	100.0	

Notes: A Hidroelectrica Branch (Cluj includes Drăgan and Iad Valleys; Curtea de Argeş the Dâmboviţa; Râmnicu Vâlcea the Olt and Caransebeş the Bistriţa Mărului); B Number of Stations; C Ditto Percentages; D Capacity MW; E Ditto Percentages; F Normal Annual Output GWh; G Ditto Percentages; H Projects offered for completion by private enterprise in 2001–2 (river – with section where appropriate – and estimated cost in $mln)

Source: Hidroelectrica website and Romanian Business Journal 9 (2002) August 7–20 edition

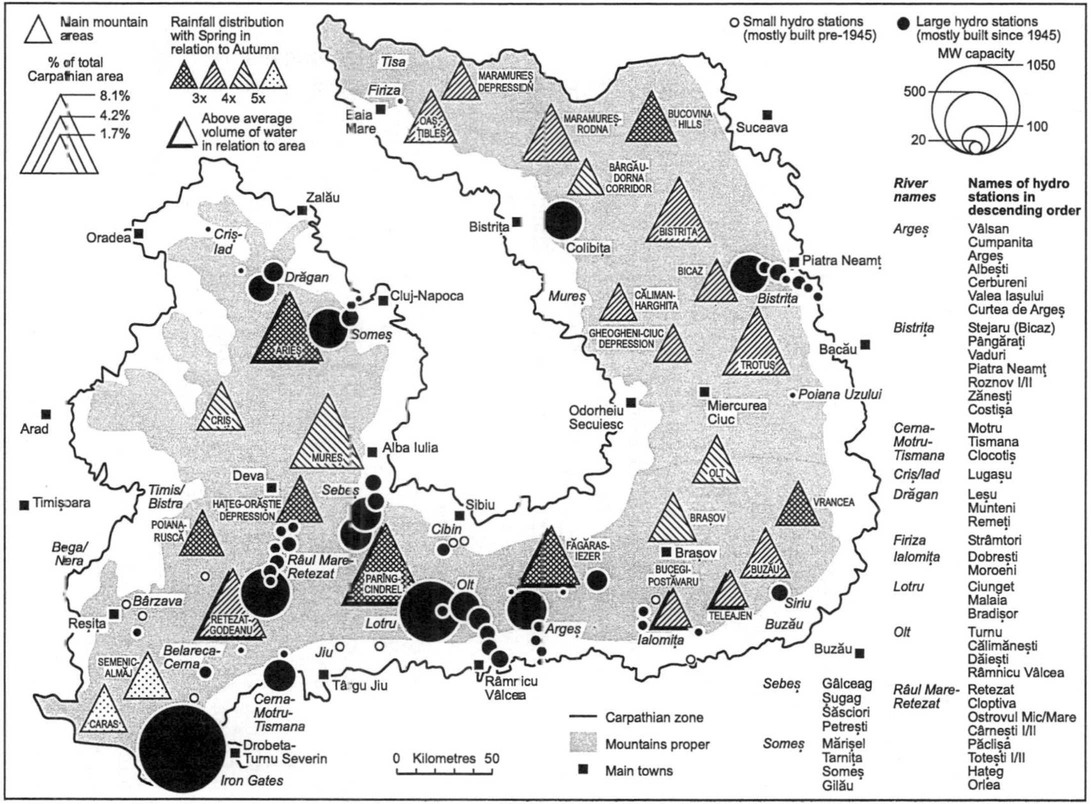

Figure 7.1 Hydroelectricity in the Romanian Carpathians
Source: Dragomirescu & Dragomirescu 1993; Hidroelectrica Bucharest

of funds. There was a reference in 2003 to a new project for the Livezeni-Bumbeşti sector of the Jiu with 65MW to be installed at Dumitra and Bumbeşti power stations. There is also some 800MW remaining on the Danube at Turnu Măgurele-Nikopol (which would involve cooperation with Bulgaria, and remains a commitment although work has not yet started), while a pumped storage project has been mooted for Tarniţa-Lăpuşeşti in the Someş catchment which is costed at 700mln. This is needed to complement the emerging nuclear complex at Cernavodă (see below) whose steady output needs adjusting to the daily pattern of sharply fluctuating demand.

The Olt Valley is still an important focus of interest despite the vast amount of work carried out under communism to create a chain of small stations, minimising disruption to settlements and infrastructure. The entire project involved 25 stations with a total capacity of 953MW. However the upper river in Covasna and Harghita was not considered while the middle section through the Făgăraş Depression was delayed with priority for Avrig station while Cornetu and Mândra (above Făgăraş) were delayed. Work eventually began at Cornetu through a j.v. with Tractel Engineering International (Belgium) negotiated in 1997 so that this station became operational in 2002; while lack of funds meant further postponement of the 27MW Mândra station, despite its importance for the supply of drinking and industrial water. Meanwhile south of Avrig, the three further stations of Lotrioara (Tălmaciu) Căineni and Racoviţa (with a total planned capacity of some 85MW) remain outstanding, partly because the idea of a single large dam at Căineni was eventually abandoned in favour of several smaller units. But since there are technical and strategic advantages in completing the Olt programme, Hidroelectrica now intend to overlook the normal economic tests of feasibility and complete a total of 105MW of capacity. Finally, close to the Danube, Vatech (Austria) was chosen to build the 28.8MW Islaz hep plant during 2003–7 – the first completely new hep project since 1989 – costing $125mln, with reversible turbines to (a) produce electricity from Olt water and (b) pump Danube water into an upstream reservoir that will allow the irrigation of 360,000ha. Feasibility surveys suggest it is potentially the most profitable of all the projects offered for leasing (see below) and it is central to the programme to complete the chain of six stations between Slatina and the Danube. Funding of $240mln (for the new station and upgrading of the others) has been secured under a regional development programme approved in 2002. At the same time, under an agreement of 2004 with Voith-Siemens, the five existing stations in this lowest chain below Slatina – Ipoteşti, Drăgăneşti, Frunzaru, Rusăneşti and Izbiceni, with a total capacity of 263MW (20 aggregates of 13.15MW) – will be modified for reversible operation linked with irrigation and navigation systems on this section.

Privatisation

Although the privatisation of Hidroelectrica is being seriously contemplated in 2008, there was some earlier interest in the model chosen by Bulgaria, operated in 1999 to start with the smaller stations (below 50MW) which proved successful because investors were able to build shops, hotels and restaurants beside the power stations. Bulgaria also envisaged mixed public-private companies for larger stations where private investors obtain a proportion of the shares: an approach that become better known in Romania as a result of an exchange of experience in 2003. However the only developments in Romania so far concern chains of micro hydropower plants (MHPPs) – all of them at least 20 years old and totalling 150 – so that modernisation can overcome the present high maintenance costs. A PPPt approach has been given up and in 2004 Hidroelectrica began to sell these stations by Dutch auction. By the end of 2007, 18 stations had been disposed of: three on the Oltenian Bistriţa (Tomşani) and five on the Gilort (Novaci) in a deal with ISPH (Romania); also five on the Topolog (Argeş) – at Suici/Sălătrucu – with Energy Holding; and another five on the Firiza (Maramureş) with ESPE (Italy). In 2008 Hidroelectrica announced the sale of another 69 very small power stations with an average capacity of around 1.0MW in the hope of raising a total of €120-160mln for use in refurbishing larger stations. Periodic auctions are held to deal with clusters of stations in particular areas.

Also, given the problems over raising capital for a number of projects attractive for electricity supply and improved water management, Hidroelectrica decided in 2002 to seek some $1.3bln of private capital to complete 21 schemes (with a total capacity of some 800MW) as part of the energy strategy for 2001–4 either by j.v. (with each party having rights according to equity capital contributed) or through the BOT (Build-Operate-Transfer) system (Table 7.3). Leasing along these lines was considered as a way of finishing several other projects that were 50–70 per cent complete in 1989 (as well as the important $100mln Islaz project on the Olt – already described – that has not even been started). Interest was attracted from around the world, including Marubeni and Itochu from Japan, while the US consulting company Harza Engineering (a leading world designer of hydropower equipment using Romanian engineers on projects in Asia and the Americas) made a feasibility study of the $32mln project to complete the Siriu-Surduc project on the Buzău by adding a further storage lake (175mln.cu.m volume with a 1.6mln.cu.m rock dam of 68m length) on the Bâsca Mare at Cireşu, with an 18km tunnel dropping 600m to the existing Nehoiaşu power station which is already working with water from the lake above the Siriu dam. Two Austrian companies (Vatech Hydro and Voith Siemens) were linked with work not only at Islaz but also Avrig, Răstoliţa, Săpânţa and Valea Sadului; while Italy's Enel were expected to submit six project applications (including Hoghiz and Răstoliţa), Neptun (Câmpina) was the favourite for the Bistriţa Râul Alb project and it was thought that the Fieni cement works would be interested in taking over a nearby hydropower plant. There was least interest in complex projects including dams, flood dykes, roads, houses and schools as well as power stations. Information is incomplete but it was announced that several schemes did not attract bids while contracts were awarded to Mecamidi (France), Enel (Italy) and Montizola (Czech Republic) as well as Neptun of Câmpina. Results have been rather disappointing overall although Enel have entered into a j.v. for Râul Mare-Retezat while Martizola hope to get finance from the banks to complete the 1.5MW Poneasca station (1.5MW) and Mecamidi are interested in the Cerna-Belareca, Firiza-Runcu, Gilort and Măru projects. The Romanian Romenergo company is in line for the Siriu-Surduc project but it is significant that another Romanian company (Neptun of Câmpina) has found the electricity price too low to justify financing work at Râul Alb. This appears to be a crucial problem facing further hydropower development. Meanwhile interest was still being shown in 2007–8 in the overhaul of small hydroplants for local supply e.g. Hobiţa and Teliuc in Hunedoara county (the latter for Hunedoara town). And there are also several projects in Sibiu county for brand new installations where €10mln of investment could generate power worth €2.0mln/yr. Two such units survive from the communist period at Gura Râului but a new concession (2008) provides for two more stations in this commune (on the Râul Mare upstream of Gâtul Berbecului costing €24mln by 2010 for 8.0MW of capacity), while three more are envisaged at Rasinari, two at Cristian and one at Balea Lac.

Other Sustainable Sources

Considerable progress has been made and Romania is aiming at getting 24 per cent of basic energy from renewables by 2020 (ahead of the European Commission target of one fifth) although at the start of the millennium there were only 9MW of renewable energy. There is a large potential for biomass and small hydropower units, with some geothermal energy in the Arad area. But there were experiments with wind power in the communist period e.g. at Curmatura Olteţului in the Lotru Mountains. No commercial establishment materialised at the time, but an aeolian park has been established in the Vrancea Mountains (involving Măgura Odobeştilor and elevated sites in Bârseşti, Corbiţa, Nereju and Străoane) after Vrancea county was selected for the implementation of a €100,000 'Wind Energy Potential' project across five European regions in 2002. In 1997 the possibility had been raised whereby aeolian generators with a total capacity of some 50MW might be placed within harbours; starting at Constanţa with 39 turbines on the north pier. And there was a further reference to this in 2001 with a proposal for a network of generators at Constanţa by ABB (Sweden) to meet the port's demand for power, with surplus energy delivered to the national grid. With a production value of $41/MWh the investment could be paid for in 20 years. There has been a recent surge in wind power with €50mln in 22 projects jumping to €1.5bln mainly as a result of a €1.0bln programme by the Polish investment fund Continental Wind Partners (now in the hands of the Czech company CEZ) for windfarms in Dobrogea at Fântânele de Vest (250MW) and Fântânele de Sud (85MW). Meanwhile Iberdrola (Spain) is to build 50 windfarms in Dobrogea (800 windmills with a total capacity of 1,600MW) costing up to €300mln; while another project by Martifer (Portugal) involves separate parks with a total capacity of 400MW by 2012 involving Dobrogea (where the Black Sea coastal area has the best potential) as well as Banat and Moldavia. Reference may also be made to a grant of €5.0mln in 2001–2 for co-financing biomass energy efficiency projects as part of Romania's negotiations for EU enlargement. This followed a cogeneration station burning industrial and domestic waste at a garbage dump in Târgovişte (with garbage collection reorganised to separate biodegradable waste from material required by the plant). In 1999 a Romanian-Danish j.v. was to operate the plant with finance from the local authorities (town and county), the EU and the Danish councils of Holstebro and Ringkobing, and income from sales to the grid. Electrica will now join with Warmbetreibe over a €400mln programme for 'several' biomass power stations of 200MW each. Finally an Austrian non-reimbursable government loan has financed the use of geothermal energy to heat some 600 dwellings in Călimăneşti during 2000–1. The project required water pipes from the northern part of the town and the installation of new boilers and heat exchangers; the hot water being unreliable and polluted at the time. The scheme involved local firms, 'Proiect Vâlcea' and Foradex (owners of the geothermal springs) as well as Austrian consultants.

THE NUCLEAR POWER OPTION: CERNAVODĂ

Nuclear power raises an acute dilemma, for against the benefit of reduced sulphur dioxide emissions and consumption of non-renewable resources there is great concern over safety (though more particularly over Soviet technology that is not really relevant to the Romanian project). Romania has a considerable fuel endowment but because much of the coal is low grade (with serious pollution hazards associated with the burning of lignite) while hydrocarbons are to be reserved for use in petrochemistry, a nuclear energy policy has been retained. The completion of the first 700MW unit at the Cernavodă nuclear power station in 1996 – the most up-to-date in the region – was a considerable morale booster, especially because the additional power was very helpful in dealing with winter shortages. The location is eminently logical: a small town beside the Danube – served by a main line railway and the electricity grid – in the centre of a large energy-deficient area (including Bucharest and Constanţa). And the nuclear option remains very important for Romania in meeting future demand for electricity. There is a substantial back-up available through factories to process nuclear fuel and produce the heavy water needed by the Candu system. But money was tight and in the early 1990s a balance had to be struck to control investment while progressing slowly to avoid irreparable damage to the country's capacity to build and commission further nuclear power stations.

Long delays have occurred since the 1960s when Romania's nuclear strategy was first envisaged. It was expected that with Soviet technology it would be possible to achieve 1,000MW of nuclear power by 1970 and 2,400 by 1980. However, it was only in 1970 that agreement was reached over a 440MW reactor and even this was abandoned in 1978 when cracks occurred in the foundations at the Cernavodă site (selected in 1977) as a result of earthquake damage later in the year. A switch was made to Canadian technology in 1977 and the following year the State Committee for Nuclear Energy signed a $680mln contract with Atomic Energy Company of Canada (AEC) for technical assistance over a single 700MW Candu (Canadian Deuterium Uranium) reactor. It is not clear how the change came to be made but it is known that the earthquake was responsible for reappraisals in several policies and the opportunity for a substantial Romanian input – given the nature of Candu technology then being adopted in Canada as well as Argentina and South Korea – would have had obvious attractions. Moreover the Candu system is extremely safe using natural uranium with heavy water as moderator: the core of the nuclear steam supply system is a large cylindrical vessel ('calandria') filled with cool low-pressure heavy water. The uranium is simple to use and easy to process into fuel assemblies, with refuelling during full power operation. Nevertheless, despite the domestic uranium supply (limiting any import of conventional fuel), there were substantial challenges of technology transfer over production methods for heavy water, nuclear fuel, nuclear components/ equipment and special materials for nuclear use; R&D for the building and operation e.g. the central control room at Cernavodă built by Automatica; a national authority for regulation and control; and the training of specialists.

The Canadian Export Development Corporation

On the basis of a 1.0bln Canadian dollar loan, work began at the site in 1979 for completion in 1984 (although both dates were soon put back by one year); and the project was extended to five reactors for completion by 1990, after Braşov and Bacău/Neamţ had been mentioned as separate nuclear power locations. A contract was signed with General Electric in 1981 for equipment (following blockages due to financial problems) and arrangements were made to obtain some natural uranium from Zambia under a j.v. that covered coal and nickel as well. The Halinga heavy water plant was built on the outskirts of Turnu Severin, a uranium processing facility was commissioned at Feldioara near Braşov in 1978 – on the basis of Soviet 1960s technology – to draw ore from several sources scattered across the Carpathians and a nuclear fuel factory built in Piteşti was eventually authorised to produce Candu fuel by AEC in 1994. National nuclear power capacity was set at 4,500MW in 1990, rising to 9,600 in 1995! However, hard currency resources created problems in obtaining essential equipment during the 1980s, although large numbers of workers were massed at the site. Repeated delays resulted in Canadian takeover of managerial responsibility after the revolution, with 1994 initially set as the revised target date for Unit I. The project was given top priority in a bid to overcome the perennial problem of winter power shortages. New arrangements were made with the foreign partners and finance was secured from foreign loans and large allocations from the austerity budget. In 1991 Renel signed a contract with the Canadian-Italian consortium involving AEC and Ansaldo for project management to secure completion of Unit 1 in mid-1996.

An Outstanding Economic Success for the First Phase of Transition

From early 1995 the first reactor was filled with heavy water (two thirds – 335t – from Canada), operation was authorised in May 1996 by the National Commission for Nuclear Activities Control and nuclear fuel was loaded at the end of that month with final testing and grid connection in June. Despite nominal power of 700MW, 706MW was reached in November and the station entered commercial exploitation by the Nuclearelectrica company at the beginning of December. The total cost was put at $2.2bln and the project has been judged a great success (producing a tenth of Romania's electricity) although after achieving record output in 2002, the drought crisis brought a halt in September 2003, pending the restoration of over two meters of water in the Danube (509GWh were lost but there were no interruptions to public power supply and no high-cost spot imports either). The servicing of foreign loans proved burdensome – on top of investment devaluation – raising the basic production cost from $14.5/MWh (compared with 27–28 for thermal plants) to as much as $50 according to some estimates. Financial problems in 1999 placed Nuclearelectrica's licence at risk due to a shortage of funds (136bln.lei needed) to operate during a one-month maintenance shutdown in a situation where the company was owed 1.5tln.lei by its sole customer Conel: eventually 5bln.lei per working day was extracted to cope with the crisis. In 2000 Nuclearelectrica was exempted from profits tax until 2010 and will invest profits in the project; while the payment of debts was deferred until 2006. And the energy law of 1999 enabled the company to sign contracts directly with consumers and pay Conel only for transport. A steady supply of uranium is needed: 100t uranium each year (whereas 1992 production was reported at 120t). Local impact was evident through a growth of population leading to a new high school with well-equipped laboratories and a new kindergarten for the children of plant employees.

Unit II

Political debate then moved on to consider the four additional units that were part of the Cernavodă plan to meet future demand for power but – despite public support (given the benefits of winter comfort) and the good prospects for electricity exports – finance is a great problem and foreign loans may be too expensive. Preliminary work on Unit II started in 1982 but progress was interrupted during 1990–5 when political support was limited to Unit I. But in 1996 – with the euphoria of Unit I completion – Unit II was seen as realisable in 2001 if finance could be arranged. Although the fuel was imported for Unit I, future needs would be met by the Piteşti facility. The DCR government was divided over the issue, given the depth of the depression arising from negative growth during 1997–9. There was initial support because the scheme had already consumed $600mln while $350mln more would be needed – with government guarantees – possibly from Canada, France, Germany or Italy. With Renel's close collaboration with AEC and Ansoldo already secure, the prospects of reduced energy dependence and reduced lignite consumption – plus the elimination of 'non-performing energy groups' – seemed attractive in the late 1990s. Proceeding further with the nuclear project would also make use of the experience gained in harnessing Western technology for Unit I and also exploit Romanian capacities in the domains of heavy water, nuclear fuel, research and design services, components and waste management – preserving 4,000 jobs. It would also help revive other Romanian enterprises and safeguard some 5,000 jobs with contractors and equipment suppliers (i.e. some 10,000 specialists were linked with the nuclear programme). And opportunities for work in nuclear technology would help to reduce the brain drain.

Protecting the Infrastructure

This became a major issue as people were laid off and plant dismantled e.g. the nuclear equipment factory of Independenta (Sibiu). Privatisation was not taking sufficient account of the strategic character of the nuclear domain: special conditions were advocated in the deal with Kvaerner (Norway) over the privatisation of FECNE (Bucharest) specialising in nuclear power plant equipment. The numerous companies relevant to the nuclear programme were grouped according to four levels of priority for state support through subsidy or conditioned privatisation (especially the first two) to maintain a strategic element of nuclear activity: 31 companies were involved in key sectors of strategic importance that should maintain their know-how, facilities and qualified staff; 38 companies were placed in a second echelon of particular economic importance for manufacturing; another 50 merited support by the state on account of benefits from real recovery and profitable operating opportunities; while 33 enterprises in the fourth echelon were unprofitable with the additional drawback of worn-out equipment (Anon 1998). It was also suggested that some savings could be made by 'a slight favouring' of the Romanian nuclear industry for components and materials that could be made at home; also priority use of Romanian experts in project management; and priority use of companies on site with expertise. But despite self-sufficiency over nuclear fuel and heavy water there was some concern during 2000 over the $700mln still needed – recalling the controversy over the Bell helicopter deal – as well as the cost-effectiveness of nuclear power (given the West European experience) and the question of safety. At the end of 2000 only 'strictly necessary work' was being done and at one stage the workforce was reportedly down to 500 Romanians and 12 foreigners, with only 20bln.lei/month allocated and a big injection necessary to avoid a conservation regime.

Government Uncertainty

There was much criticism of industry minister R.Berceanu for failing to give full support to Unit II (with downsizing of the Halinga plant already referred to) but the minister argued that demand for Unit II was not overwhelming – 9,000MW of total generating capacity was sufficient for a demand of 8,000MW in winter and 5,000MW in summer – and there could be no prospect for completing the full programme of five units in view of a worrying lack of expectation of rising energy demand after three years of recession. The opposing viewpoint emphasised the moderate cost of completion – very optimistically claimed to be equivalent to a classical energy unit of equivalent power – and the obsolescence of much thermal capacity, with low availability and a poor pollution record; also the country's limited and low quality primary energy resources and high import costs. Other points concerned the available infrastructure and expertise and the high cost of 'stopping and starting': delays would mean higher costs in the end through more demanding documentation and inefficient use of an infrastructure costing over $4.0bln, not to mention some unfinished enterprises: Zirom and Grantmetal (titanium and zirconium ingots and tubes) and Republica (stainless steel tubes). Specialists were being lost, some firms closed for lack of orders and research capacities underused. It was also argued that the heavy water was in hand: 500t would be needed of which 160t were ready; leaving a further 340t by 2003 at a rate of 128tpa (it would cost $340mln to purchase 340t abroad). In addition each unit uses 5.0tpa – hence 300t more needed for a 30 year lifespan.

The power would be available at a time when Chernobyl and Kozloduy would have closed their reactors and – with energy deficits in Greece and Turkey – there would be good prospects for energy exports to the region (all the more so with the end of war in the former Yugoslavia).

Support from Europe

The Country Report (1998, p.35) noted that 'the nuclear sector is considered a national priority and studies have shown that this is the least-cost option for fuel supply'. Hence a positive decision on funding was thought imminent. However a return to economic growth – marginally in 2000 and more substantially thereafter – changed the climate decisively. The project survived and it continued to be a priority of the new government in 2001. Even though international financial bodies were not keen to support nuclear projects, a loan agreement was reached in late-2002 to provide funds for AEC, Ansaldo, Alstom Power and other companies to proceed after years of virtual freeze. Ansaldo saw Cernavodă II as the most important realisation in the ECE energy sector and the best example of Western technical assistance to attain standards of nuclear safety in accordance with international norms. In 2002 another $680mln was needed: half from the Romanian and half from Canadian and Italian investors. In the light of growing energy consumption in 2001–2 there was an attempt at acceleration to achieve commissioning in 2005 (rather than 2006–7: ten years after Unit 1). The gap in costs was apparently increasing: $14/MWh at Cernavodă compared with $50–60 at thermal stations. There was also the possibility of halving the coal, oil and gas needed in power generation during 1997–2005, with reduced use of fossil fuels helping with the global warming problem. The current estimate is 2007, at a total cost of $777mln (with two units together generating 18 per cent of total output).

Units 111–V

Units III–IV were initially contemplated on a PPPt basis with Italy, South Korea and USA as possible sources of the €800mln needed for Unit III alone. Further capacity would meet Romania's entire energy consumption requirements and create massive export possibilities but the political climate of the late 1990s was not conducive to any government commitment. Mocanu (1998) argued that these units III and IV had already cost $400mln (over half of Unit II costs) and that excessive delay would see the technology obsolete and no longer licensed: new technology might take over such as the Advanced Boiling Water Reactor already in use in Japan by General Electric (USA) and Hitachi/Toshiba (Japan); not to mention the European Pressurised Reactor by Framatone and Siemens; or the Sizewell B PWR Reactor developed by cooperation between Westinghouse and Nuclear Electric. Mocanu went on to commend leasing as a way forward to preserve the Romanian nuclear industry and its experts: otherwise the unfinished complex would be fit only for agricultural purposes, a nuclear themepark or a grandiose art gallery. This formula found favour as a solution to the 'moral ageing' that would occur if there were delays until 2012–2020 when internal financing might be possible. As an alternative to international bidding, a Black Sea Power Ring – managed by an international company owned by signatories to the Black Sea Economic Cooperation Treaty – might generate $10bln over 10–15 years to finance the 2,000MW involved in Units III–V.

Continuing Government Interest

With the return of economic growth, the centre-left government swept into power in 2001 was able to support the nuclear lobby on the grounds of long-term increases in gas prices that would favour alternatives after 2010 with clean-technology lignite power stations as the only alternative to the nuclear option. They sought a PPPt to generate the €750mln needed for Cernavodă III to be built during 2006–12. It was stated in 2001 that the government would launch an international tender for Units III–V with joint exploitation for ten years before transfer to the state: i.e. the BOOT system of 'Build-Own-Operate-Transfer' favoured by the Canadians. Talks were held with Ansaldo and Enel (Italy), AEC (Canada), Hydro Nuclear & Power (South Korea) and LNM India-British Holdings. 12 letters of interest were negotiated, with financial and crediting conditions to be settled in the second quarter and a feasibility study. On this basis Unit III could be completed in 2011–2 (previously Units III–IV had been anticipated by 2015) at a total cost of $1.0bln. Units IV–V might now be expected for 2020. The most recent target for Unit III completion is 2011 with seven firms chosen for investment: Romania's own LNM Holdings and Assoc. Furnizorilor de Echipamante Nuclearelectrica, Enel and Ansaldo (Italy), AEC, Korea Hydro Nuclear & Power and Demir (Turkey). Bechtel are interested in building and Merril Lynch in financing ($700mln). Little was heard of the nuclear debate during 2005 and the views of the present centrist government were initially unclear, with Russia's Atomstroiexport expressing interest in producing reactors (assuming any change from Canadian HWR technology). However the intention is now to build Units III/IV (each with four 700MW generators) during 2008–14 with an investment of some €2.2bln with the help of a large consortium drawn from Belgium (Electrabel); Canada (AEC and Gabriel); Germany (E.On and RWE); Italy (Ansoldo and Enel); Luxemburg (Unit Investments); South Korea (KHNP); Spain (Iberdrola); Turkey (Yatirimlari and Dogus Holdings); and USA (AES) as well as Alro and Electrica from Romania. In 2008 it was expected that Nuclearelectrica would favour Enel, Iberdrola and RWE as well as CEZ (Czech Republic) and ArcelorMittal Romania, in anticipation of a 30 per cent nuclear contribution to power generated in 2015. There is also interest in

Cernavodă V and a search for a new location (for two to four units) which might be producing as early as 2020. In the communist period, as already noted, further nuclear development was envisaged close to the industrial regions of Braşov and Central Moldavia which were both energy deficit areas: the Olt valley near Făgăraş and the Bacău-Piatra Neamţ area (the Bistriţa-Siret confluence) were proposed locations and it will be interesting to see if they continue to attract attention, although the Mureş and Someş valleys could also be attractive. Cooperation with Areva (France) is also mooted using a new system in preference to Candu.

The Bulgarian Dimension

This provides a relevant footnote to Romania's nuclear ambitions. Downsizing at Kozloduy through the plans to close the four oldest reactors by 2006 appears to hand Romania a prime energy exporting opportunity. But this naturally creates resentment in Sofia, manifested by attempts to complicate Romania's access to the Turkish energy market through high transit charges. Now Bulgaria is seeking an energy surplus by reviving the Belene nuclear project of 1980 that was formally cancelled in 1991–2 at a time when foreign credits dried up. But the project was unblocked in 2002 (when the two oldest Kozloduy reactors were closed) and in 2003 a plan for two reactors was launched (six before), with encouragement coming from the EU's pro-nuclear energy commissioner on a visit in 2004. Subject to an appropriate choice of reactor there could be €300mln of EU finance to help with a total project cost of €2.0–4.0bln (although this does not allow for costs arising from spent fuel, decommissioning and any high level accidents). There is much opposition from ecological farmers in the area and also from the town of Svishtov which suffered over a hundred deaths in the 1977 earthquake and fears the consequences of a nuclear power station located in a seismic zone. But government appears heavily committed and is supporting Worley Parsons (UK) who carried out an EIA which critics find unsatisfactory because of inadequate public control over the appointment of contractors. And after scandals at Kozloduy there is concern of possible mafia involvement in a corporate carve up that could greatly increase costs. Nevertheless events are unfolding with bidding by Czech and Russian companies for the reactor contract.

Nuclear Support Facilities

Activity by the 'Uraniu' national company in Neamţ and Suceava will secure enough material to support all five units at Cernavodă in spite of the closure of uranium mining operations in Bihor (Băiţa) and Caraş-Severin (Ciudanoviţa and Lisava) where radioactivity remains a priority for Reşiţa Environmental Agency with European assistance for reclamation and more sophisticated monitoring beyond the capacity of equipment currently installed on the basis of 1970s norms. With regard to Neamţ, the possibility of reopening the Grintieş uranium mines has been raised because although the authorities are concerned about radiation, local people want to see more jobs for the young men in order to keep them at home instead of seeking work abroad. For processing, a new decantation pond has been provided since 1989 at Feldioara and much attention has been given to environmental protection. The final processing of nuclear fuel takes place at Piteşti Nuclear Fuel Factory to produce 5,000 Candu-type bundles/yr and with minor changes fuel for Unit II can be made: each 'bundle' – 21.5kg of powder – releases 1,115MWh (which in conventional terms would require 1,110t of pitcoal, or 2,220t brown coal, or 317t fuel oil, or 363,000cu.m natural gas). The Heavy Water Administration (Romag) now operates four modules (compared with the two installed just before the revolution in 1988–9) at its Halinga factory near Turnu Severin with a workforce of 2,400 in 1998 (see below). The output is 11kg/hour – 90t per module per year – and Romania is the third world producer after Canada and India. The total production of 130t by 1994 was insufficient for Unit I (and 335t of the 500t required was therefore imported) but the rate should be adequate in future even though the complex was designed on the basis of five modules.

Heavy Water

This is produced at Halinga (Turnu Severin) with 99.9 per cent purity: a very high standard that gives Romania scope for export (so much so that competitors after the revolution seemed keen to hamper recognition!). Exports of heavy water could help pay the Canadian loan as well as supplying all the requirements of the Cernavodă project. With a market price of $7,000–10,000/kg – many times the quoted production cost of $350–360/kg (since greater purity reduced the amount of uranium consumed) – there are customers in USA and South Korea now that the factory has returned what was lent by Canada. There is the possibility that Romania might supply equipment and components for Candu reactors built in developing countries; also training of staff with simulators and research institutes. Finally, weak, medium and strongly active waste is stored – respectively – in a special room; in special tanks with storage capacity for 30 years; and in concrete basins with capacity for 10 years which can be extended or switched to dry silos (1999). There is also a prospect of nuclear waste storage at Băiţa which is already operating for low and medium level waste. Indeed this facility could import waste from Austria, Germany and Hungary. 2004 saw the opening of the first spent fuel storage facility.

CONCLUSION

The chapter is entitled the energy complex to emphasise the range of issues that require continuing input from the state. Given a high level of import dependence (notwithstanding a history of petroleum exports) it has been a necessary but painful process to impose realistic energy costings after the communist years of symbolic prices for electricity as well as transport and raw materials; with additional pressure through the EU accession process. Of course domestic hydrocarbon resources remain (especially in the Black Sea) but the outlays on prospecting have to be balanced against other priorities: greater efficiency in the use of energy and in generating electricity, which raises a further issue of accepting higher installation costs for hydro and nuclear power as opposed thermal stations burning coal or hydrocarbon fuels. Romania has therefore struck a balance, including PPPt deals which spread the financial burden. Privatisation offers a way forward which has been successfully adopted with regard to electricity, gas and oil distribution but not, so far, for electricity generation apart from small hydro stations, although some power stations are locally managed and both domestic and foreign energy and manufacturing companies can build their own generators. A proposal that two of the three large Oltenian power stations (Rovinari and Turceni) should comprise one generating company along with Hidroelectrica has not found favour. Meanwhile good progress is being made with nuclear programme after the stagnation of the later communist years. Indeed the infrastructure provided at Cernavodă for a huge generating capacity may well be vindicated as an outstanding inspiration of the later communist period despite the extended timescale and the major reassessments. Complemented by the Tarnița pumped storage project it will meet the bulk of home demand. Meanwhile renewables are showing much promise – especially wind–powered generation – although here the constraint appears to be grid capacity with as much as 12GW of new capacity being contemplated by developers (not to mention the issue of alternative capacity when the windfarms are inactive): as it is, the grid system will need a €2.0bln overhaul by 2020 and further capacity for all the proijected wind-powered projects may not be possible. There is however a vision of substantial electricity exports with Romania gaining hub status in the Balkan-Black Sea region with the cable to Turkey (due in 2012) possibly acting as part of a new international grid system. This in turn could help offset the rising cost of imported fuels which are again fraught with problems regarding additional oil and gas pipeline capacity and the question of Russian influence over the Caspian region which is particularly high on the agenda after the 2008 invasion of Georgia.

8. Agriculture: The Political Imperative of Restitution

INTRODUCTION: THE SMALLHOLDING SYSTEM

Romania is well-endowed with agricultural land and the farming potential is very great, especially in the lowland areas of the east, south and west; while the Carpathian mountain arc remains heavily forested (Table 8.1). So it was highly significant politically that, despite the leisurely pace of privatisation in industry, there was an almost immediate transformation of the cooperative system of farming. Some historical background is important to appreciate the importance of peasant proprietorship so dramatically curtailed under communism. Until the late nineteenth century feudal arrangements sustained the peasantry while extracting services in full measure as the landlords exploited trade outlets for their grain surpluses. Abolition of serfdom in 1864 (soon after a similar reform in the Habsburg Empire) assured a nominally free peasantry a stake in the land, but their holdings were small and the only escape from 'minifundia' available to most families lay in contracts to work for the landlords as estate labourers and sharecroppers with generally declining returns as the owners were constrained by prevailing world wheat prices and their substantial household expenses in elegant town houses as their country properties were abandoned to Jewish agents under competitive tender. A revolt in 1907 highlighted the need for agrarian reform that was eventually achieved in 1921 in the context of the Greater Romanian state when the landlords were expropriated in favour of peasant proprietorship, while rural-urban migration was accelerated by the industrial programme. But the new equilibrium was always threatened by population growth and fiscal pressure, exacerbated by the high costs of protected industry expressed through a widening gap between the prices of farm equipment and household goods on the one hand and agricultural produce on the other. The wartime liaison with Germany gave a measure of stability through assured outlets for food (extending the security previously available through the Little Entente; offering a rewarding market for Romanian cattle in Czechoslovakia) and some further mechanisation and cooperation.

Table 8.1: *Land Use 1985–2005*

Year	A	B	C	D	E	F	G	H	I	J	K	L	M
1985	23.7	15.0	1.4	10.0	n.a.	293	n.a.	344	n.a.	2956	6.56	6.18	n.a.
1989	23.9	14.8	n..a	n.a.	n.a.	n.a.	n.a.	n.a.	n.a.	n.a.	6.68	6.25	n.a.
1990	23.9	14.8	n.a.	9.4	7.4	n.a.	n.a.	n.a.	n.a.	3216	6.68	6.25	1.01
1991	23.9	14.8	10.3	9.4	7.5	259	197	311	205	3197	6.68	6.25	1.01
1992	23.9	14.8	10.4	9.4	7.5	299	215	305	204	3202	6.68	6.25	1.02
1993	23.9	14.8	10.3	9.3	7.5	304	224	296	196	3203	6.68	6.25	1.02
1994	23,9	14.8	10.4	9.3	7.5	298	220	289	193	3205	6.68	6.25	1.02
1995	23.9	14,8	10.7	9.3	7.8	292	220	278	189	3211	6.68	6.24	1.02
1996	23.9	14.8	10.7	9.3	7.8	289	218	271	184	n.a.	6.68	6.24	1.02
1997	23.9	14.8	10.4	9.3	7.6	286	215	215	181	3089	6.68	6.24	1.02
1998	23.9	14.8	10.5	9.4	7.6	282	212	263	179	n.a.	6.47	6.23	1.03
1999	23.9	14.7	10.4	9.4	8.1	281	220	257	194	85*	6.69	6.23	1.02
2000	23.9	14.9	14.2	9.4	9.1	272	261	255	239	216*	6.46	6.22	1.02
2001	23.9	14.9	14.3	9.4	9.0	267	257	252	235	328*	6.61	6.23	1.02
2002	23.9	14.8	14.3	9.4	9.0	260	251	241	225	488*	6.66	6.24	1.03
2003	23.9	14.7	14.2	9.4	9.1	230	222	227	212	569*	6.75	6.22	1.04
2004	23.9	14.7	14.1	9.4	9.1	223	214	221	207	32.7#	6.78	6.22	1.04
2005	23.9	14.7	14.1	9.4	9.1	224	215	218	204	45.7#	6.74	6.23	1.05

Notes: A Total land area (mln.ha); B Agricultural area (mln.ha); C Ditto: private ownership; D Arable area (mln.ha); E Ditto: private ownership; F Vineyards (th.ha); G Ditto: private ownership; H Orchards (th.ha); I Ditto: private ownership; J Nominal irrigated area (th. ha) (* effective area only; # system administered by Administrația Națională pentru Îmbunătățiri Funciare only); K Woodland (mln.ha); L Ditto main forested area; M Land occupied by transport systems and buildings. **Source:** Statistical Yearbooks: Tables 14.1 and 14.2

The Communist Model

This was even more comprehensive through total state control of production balanced by accelerated industrialisation that systematically denuded the rural areas of their labour surpluses. It was coercive but also pragmatic; blatantly seizing the better land for the state farms ('Intreprinderi Agricole de Stat': IAS) organised efficiently on factory lines – with inputs of machinery, fertiliser and irrigation assured through successive Five Year Plans – to deliver fresh food and agricultural raw materials for urban markets and factories. But, following a regime of arbitrary quota impositions on private farmers, it also recognised the importance of making full use of the rural population, commensurate with state control, by cooperatives ('Cooperative Agricole de Producţie': CAP) under local political leadership that obliged peasants to contribute their land, livestock, equipment and labour. It was only in the early 1960s that this draconian exercise was deemed 'complete', thanks to propaganda backed by intimidation, but most of the sparsely-settled mountain terrain was left in private management subject to production plans and restrictions over amalgamation and the use of non-family labour. The cooperative members enjoyed a degree of freedom through the private plot, secured through 120 'labour-days' for the cooperative: a calculated incentive to 'work all hours' so that the cooperative effort would supply state warehouses while the plots would take care of peasant subsistence, including supplies to local free markets. From all points of view the system was pragmatic in the context of a totalitarian state seeking to maximise resources for industrialisation. Although highly destructive in the way that the old village elites were sacrificed in favour of opportunist party members and sympathisers, the model was eventually authenticated as a welfare system of a kind under which people could improve their houses and secure both piecework and pensions, while cash resources became more substantial when younger family members started commuting to work in the factories. Some villages were well-off thanks to cadastral anomalies that understated the area of land available and hence credited the relevant CAPs concerned with unusually high yields (Verdery 1994). A variant of this phenomenon enabled the peasants of Jina in Sibiu county to profit handsomely through the wool trade since large numbers of animals were sustained through transhumance systems to exploit distant winter grazings for which only token payments were made to the local CAPs. Yet there was constant pressure to work for modest returns and thinly-veiled intimidation (plus the looming threat of Ceauşescu's draconian rural planning project of 'sistematizare' including the promotion of some 550 key villages to urban status, with each centre coordinating agriculture across the surrounding communes through a single complex organisation in each district combining state and cooperative farms. Country people would often speak of a 'second serfdom' having lost their independence through communist expropriation.

RESTITUTION OF AGRICULTURAL LAND

This background is important for an understanding of agriculture since the revolution that was greeted with much euphoria in the countryside. FSN did not envisage radical change although Ceauşescu's resettlement programme was abandoned and all communities were left free to cultivate the enduring values of the Romanian village extolled in works published both within Romania and abroad (Iordache 1990). There was a surge in new house building and in structural repairs to old property lying outside the communist building perimeters. Reduced factory production and the consequent dismissal of commuters brought some improvement of village facilities through new bars and bakeries, while a surge of new church building arose from the relaxation of planning and the emergence of Uniate and Old Rite Orthodox congregations. But it was expected that the state farms would continue as before and that cooperatives might survive under more democratic management by combining the political imperative of privatisation with the economic rationale of large-scale production. Although the extremism of 'sistematizare' was abandoned, government was anxious that the institute concerned with cadastral matters (IGFCOT) should continue its work in planning optimum field and rotation systems to influence a new generation of cooperatives and associations.

The Salvation Front Strategy

This was shaped as events gained a momentum of their own and many cooperatives broke down as families unilaterally reclaimed their land, which became especially valuable with the breakdown of 'navetismul': commuting to work in the towns (von Hirschhausen 1998) coupled with the limited development of rural industry (Vincze 1999). The local authorities, even with some assistance from the police, were usually unable to prevent the 'de facto' collapse of the system in many areas, although in the lowlands the need for shared use of tools and machinery sustained some cooperatives into 1991, often with an increase in the number of workers to maximise employment for social reasons e.g. Arad. However the NSF had to come to terms with the near-universal desire to reclaim family land holdings from the former communist cooperatives and the government was astute enough to recognise the inevitability of land reform. Hence the carefully-crafted land law of 1991 ('Legea Fondului Funciar') allowing the allocation of land held by 3,588 former cooperatives and 132 associations of cooperative farms ('Asociație Economic Intercooperatistă'); also free distribution of animals (or the proceeds realised by their sale). Restitution holdings with a maximum size of 10ha (arable equivalent) would leave the vast majority of de facto restitutions on the right side of the law while allowing a large section of the peasantry to own land, at the very least through the symbolic 1.0ha plots (0.5ha in the case of families who were not members of cooperative farms). But with some 5.06mln potential claimants and only 9.11mln.ha available for distribution, it was obvious that the average holding would be below two hectares (although the situation varied regionally with the greatest pressure on land in the hilly Subcarpathian regions with a large rural population). Small plots promised to all rural dwellers could not be provided in 451 communes and only partially in 1,053 others (out of a total of 2,727) that put pressure on the state farms leading to many illegalities. Where plots were allocated the old cooperatives were weakened all the more, with frequent spontaneous liquidation that had to be officialised in 1991 (Otiman 1997). 10.3mln.ha out of a total of 14.8mln were in private ownership in 1991, rising to 14.2 in 2000 (Table 8.2)

Table 8.2: *Farm structure 1998*

Farms	Size Group	Pr/Cent	Area ha	Pr/Cent
3233,361	5.0ha or less	81.9	3992,641	37.9
424,033	5.1–10.0ha	10.7	2175.058	20.7
288,753	10.1–50.0ha	7.3	3015,407	28.6
503	50.1ha or	*	1341,967	12.8
3946.630	All	100.0	10525,073	100.0

Source: Râmniceanu 2004

Implementation

Ownership was validated temporarily by 'adeverințe de proprietate' whereas the full property titles ('titluri de proprietate') were often delayed with the unfortunate consequence that owners could not use their land as collateral. At the end of 1996 barely two-thirds of the 4.22mln new owners (67 per cent) had received titles, rising to 84.3 per cent at the end of 1999 and 92.6 per cent at the end of 2003 (86.9 per cent in terms of area: 8.78 out of 10.11mln.ha). Delay may be attributed to the passivity of local councils (especially when the mayor was not personally involved and there was a lack of staff continuity); as well as the complex cases that gave rise to disputes. Yet lack of proper documentation also held up land transactions and applications for farm subsidies when the DCR government came to power in 1997 and tried to develop the land market (to overcome restrictions on the sale and leasing of restituted land imposed in 1991) and include private farms in the agricultural support system. The small size of holdings remained a constraint – with land fragmentation a further obstacle to technological progress – while banks did not regard small farms as good business and even privately-owned SMEs found finance difficult.

Winners and Losers. Frequently the land returned to a particular family was identical to what had been forcibly taken a generation earlier i.e. the family farm was restored in its old place ('vechile amplasamente'), although this was not possible where old landmarks had disappeared and former farmland had been planted or built over. There were also difficulties for restitution in counties with a large number of state farms e.g. Brăila, Călăraşi, Giurgiu and Ialomiţa. Where it was not possible to satisfy all claims Verdery (1994) suggests that the chief losers in the competition were widows, urban dwellers (who could easily be deceived), immigrants and the poor. By contrast local politicians did relatively well along with civil servants (especially those concerned with implementing the land restitution law) and some elements of the old village elite who might receive more than 10ha (since the law specified 'arable equivalent'). Hence the changes of the 1990s created considerable upheaval and social tension in lowland villages, contributing to a lack of the ease and contentment ('veselie') idealising rural life in the past. But there was also a major cleavage between all categories of people who received land (including some with an urban background, lacking knowledge of or aptitude for agriculture) and others who had worked for a cooperative farm but who had no claim to a holding (beyond the basic half-hectare) because – like most Roma – they arrived during communism and now had to depend on neighbours for work to make a living.

Other Political Conceptions

Compared with the NSF who concentrated on small-scale restitution that continued to depend on the services of the machine stations (eventually privatised) the opposition DCR was prepared to contemplate larger holdings for former estate owners with the break-up of state farms if necessary. They also advocated provision of machinery for individual farms with easy terms for repayment over a long term; and training in western countries. But the DCR was vulnerable to NSF 'scare stories' about the danger of market forces leading to the expropriation of new smallholders (or alternatively of bankruptcy in the face of radical market reforms). So initially, the NSF and its successors were able to control the rural areas, almost solidly in Moldavia and Wallachia, as the key to their electoral successes when local democracy was constrained by the persistence of the old communist power structures (transformed into NSF networks) and the feeble penetration of opposition newspapers given the government's control of the media and the problems of newspaper distribution in rural areas. However after the DCR gained power in 1997 they eventually extended restitution (in 2000) when the maximum was raised to 50ha – also 10ha in the case of woodland where the initial allowance was limited to one hectare only – with eligibility restricted to those participating in the first wave. There were 863,300 applications involving 1.87mln.ha (0.62mln in excess of what was available): indeed only 11 counties could meet the demand. There were also 132,800 further claims for up to 10ha arable equivalent, involving a further 480,300ha; while 9,800 representatives of parishes, monasteries and convents – able to claim up to 5.0ha (10ha in the case of parishes) – sought a further 5,100ha. These claims could only be met from state farms and hence the so-called 'Lupu Law' catered for their dissolution as a precondition. Even so urgent measures had to be taken in 2003 to accelerate implementation.

LARGE FARM BUSINESSES

Agricultural Associations ('Asociații Agricole')

There was a powerful reaction against the communist cooperatives, resulting in the abandonment of many buildings (especially in the mountains). They were often sold-off for demolition and salvage of materials. Farmers were glad to regain their land and often wished to work independently. There was suspicion over elaborate models of cooperation, particularly over financial matters, and a lack of trust outside the narrow social circle of relatives and close neighbours. Even in the lowlands where shared use of machinery was a powerful incentive (with only one tractor per 74ha of arable on average), enough family members might be available (e.g. in relatively remote lowland villages where migration to urban employments had been restrained or substantially reduced after the revolution) to justify labour-intensive methods, along with animal power and limited hiring of machinery, to maximise output. Cooperation might also be frustrated by a lack of transparency in the operations of irrigation systems so that water appropriation rules were deliberately exploited by powerful people: hence the associations were not sustainable (Kideckel 1992, 1993).

Progress

Government tried to encourage associations working in liaison with the revamped Machine Tractor Stations ('Agromecs'), eventually privatised, or acquiring their own equipment to reduce costs and improve availability. Schrieder et al. (2000) distinguished between small private farms averaging 2.3ha; informal family associations with 132ha on average and farm associations with legal ('juridic') status through court order – often successors to the former cooperatives (and inheriting their buildings) – averaging 435ha. Compared with legally-constituted associations that involved high costs (and often incorporated elements of former communist cooperatives) family associations were based on simple verbal or written agreements with a minimum of 10 members who contributed land while retaining ownership rights.

Associations could be particularly useful for landowners living in towns and lacking experience of agriculture (overcoming high transaction and opportunity costs); also older people in the villages and those still commuting to non-agricultural work. Thus many members were not directly involved in agriculture but received a rent for their land (25–30 per cent of the gross profit in cash or kind): unlike conventional leasing operations when the rent is independent of profit, associations subtracted all costs and work on a profit basis. By contrast, households planning to farm privately had significantly more family members involved in farming (and more members in total) than households intending to join associations; they also tended to be younger (Meurs 1996, p.173). And in the lowlands there was often a split with family units as a buffer ('tampon') between the village core and the principal agricultural domain, following the tradition of 'bun de familia' expressed under communism through private plots.

Consolidation. In the early 1990s the situation was often confused with individuals rethinking their strategies and often changing from one association to another according to perceived differences in performance: there might well be several associations within a single village, with a tendency towards consolidation through bankruptcies. The system worked well as trust developed. Ianoş (1994a) suggests that the first people to join associations were those with the smallest holdings while those with larger units might join later after experiencing some difficulty working on their own. However associations initially sought to maximise employment, following the CAP mentality, and it took some time for management to adjust employment to financial performance at a time of falling national GDP and declining export opportunities. At Semlac in Arad county, Ianoş (1996) reports six organisations with membership drifting towards the three that secured the better results: especially '1 Decembrie', reconstituted on the former CAP structure, with a good fertiliser supply and technical capacity, including access to machinery precisely at the moment required. There was also a tendency for legal associations to swallow up smaller, informal organisations so that family associations (in Hunedoara county for example) declined from 380 to 14 during 1992 while legally constituted organisations increased from 15 to 45. But many individual farms survived and successful farmers could obtain more land by sharecropping if not by purchase.

Examples of Large-Scale Farming

In Sângătin village (Apoldu commune near Sibiu) progressive elements were able to reconstitute the substantial family farms run by descendants of people prominent before communism. Their activity reflects a 'civic consciousness that slowly and piecemeal creates trust-generating practices' (Stewart 1997, p.78). Often agronomists connected with the old cooperatives were responsible for the associations e.g. at Alexandria (Teleorman), Banloc (Timiş), Curtici (Arad),

Dobrosloveni (Olt), Măldăeni (Teleorman), Pecineaga (Constanţa) and Salonta (Bihor). The highly mechanised Curtici association near Arad embraced 2,500 landowners with 5,000ha. Meanwhile on Agrofarm at Feteşti (Călăraşi county) engineer Ştefan Poenaru employed 200 workers on the 7,000ha leased from 2,800 former members of the Borduşani, Coslugeni, Pietroiu and Stelnica cooperatives and the Jegălia vegetable association. With yields almost double the national average, good storage (with six modern cereal silos based on US technology) and a successful wheat export business landowners received 500–700kg of wheat for each hectare leased. Leasing also forms part of Adrian Porumboiu's 'Racova' organisation covering 40,000ha in the Vaslui area used for cereal, sunflowers and livestock farming. The business is highly mechanised with Landini tractors and combines and uses aerial spraying. There is an element of vertical integration through wheat storage (240,000t capacity, a quarter of which comes from his own production), food processing (bakeries and dairies in Suceava and Vaslui, plus a fodder factory in Bârlad and an oil mill in Vaslui) and retailing through a chain of 114 shops including a supermarket in Vaslui. Annual turnover was put at $100mln in 2005.

State Farms

The FSN government initially hoped to keep the state farms (IAS) intact and division into small units was resisted: those whose ancestors were expropriated gained shares in the appropriate farming company ('Societatea Comercială Agricole cu Capital de Stat') to prevent the shock of further fragmentation. However there was a division into animal and vegetable sections while state farm workers qualified for smallholdings of 0.25ha. But the DCR government was forced to make changes to deal with mounting losses and the 1997 Ciorbea reforms included state farm restructuring, particularly through privatisation (or liquidation) of pig and poultry breeding complexes during 1997–9. The matter was urgent because of falling livestock numbers and inadequate financial support. Of 2,890 companies, 1,003 were privatised during 1997–9 (34.7 per cent) while 162 were liquidated with 1,725 remaining. However, the process varied greatly between the different categories. Only 14 out of 517 commercial companies were privatised (0.3 per cent) while 17 were liquidated with 486 remaining; while on the other hand 43 of the 115 poultry ('Avicola') and pig ('Suin') farms – the top priority – were privatised (37.4 per cent) and 65 liquidated leaving only nine outstanding. The highest privatisation rate applied to 52 storage units e.g. for cereals (73.2 per cent of the total) with only five liquidated and 14 remaining); followed by 62.1 per cent in respect of 266 food industry units, with 25 liquidated and 137 remaining (Spiridion 2005). There were also 628 service providers privatised (35.7 per cent) with 50 liquidated and 1,081 remaining. The 2000 'Country Report' emphasised that few conventional state farms had been privatised, yet even so a number of transactions were being contested because of a lack of transparency. Other deals were running into trouble: in the case of Avicola Suceava, privatised in 1998 when Agricola Spera International took over, SOF indicated its intention to terminate the contract in 2000 because the company had not kept to its commitments, leading to heavy debts with serious social implications. Meanwhile, prolonged uncertainty over the future of the state farms inhibited investment in some of the most (potentially) productive areas.

Further Reform

In 1997 the Ciorbea government stated that land comprising IAS holdings and estates of the former National Agency for Agricultural Products would be given back to former owners while 100 state holdings (0.4mln.ha) would be restructured into small units. This could not be delivered until the breakthrough in 2000 that also opened the way for foreign capital to bid for state land (foreign ownership of land had been a taboo subject until that time). Even so the process was not completed and the matter passed to the PSD government of 2001–4 with the mood now firmly one of complying with EU norms. In 2002 the State Domain Agency, responsible for management of state land (and leasing to agricultural and forestry research institutes) had still to complete privatisation of some 320 state-owned farm companies (after 103 were dealt with in 2000 and 59 in 2001). This still left 506 state-owned farm companies in 2002, with 100 following in 2003. Further statistics then revealed a state agricultural area of 600–700,000ha at the end of 2003, following the private ownership recovery process (under laws of 1991 and 2000): less than a third of what the state farms used to operate. These lands were mostly being leased by competition in 2003: vineyards, orchards, hot houses/solariums, fisheries and rice plantations (Table 8.3). Presumably these included 80 units described in 1999 as being of strategic interest in terms of national food safety where the state would retain one per cent of the shares and a right of veto. 289 of 739 state farms were privatised in 2004.

Agribusiness has emerged from state farm leasing on top of the earlier restitution rounds. These are large-scale farms averaging 3,600ha – former state farms 'generally loss-making and heavily dependent on government subsidies' (Schrieder et al. 2000, p.1221). There are also some large Romanian businesses like 56,000ha Insula Mare a Brăilei farm leased to 'grain baron' and agricultural engineer Culiță Tărâță who also has logging interests in Neamț. Meanwhile the InterAgro company increased its land area – in the counties of Bacău, Ialomița, Prahova and Teleorman – from 3,300ha in 1996 to 46,200 in 2006; almost all of it leased or chartered rather than being owned by the company.

Table 8.3: *State agricultural land offered on concession in 2003 (units of over 400ha)*

Region	No	Th.ha	Largest estates (over 400ha)
Bucharest	3	1.6	Ciorogârla
Centre	18	17.1	Agnita, Albeşti, Axente Sever, Bazna, Catalina, Nocrich, Petreşti, Sighişoara, Slimnic, Zagăr
North East	25	10.5	Albeşti, Dângeni, Falciu, Laza, Mihai Eminescu, Rădăuţi, Suceava, Vaslui, Zorleni
North West	13	4.6	Bistriţa, Carei, Halmeu, Lazuri, Zalău
South	19	30.4	Blejeşti, Borcea, Borduşani, Mavrodin, Mircea Vodă, Olteniţa, Schela, Slobozia, Toporu, Traian
South East	46	50.4	Adamclisi, Băneasa, Boldovineşti, Cernavodă, Crucea, Deduleşti, Făgăraşu Nou, Focşani, Galaţi, Gropeni, Latinu, Mihail Kogălniceanu (Tulcea), Mircea Vodă, Ostrov, Pietreni, Rahman, Râmnicu Sărat, Săcele, Silistia, Smârdan (Galaţi), Smârdan (Tulcea), Stâlpu, Stăncuta, Stejaru, Târguşor, Tichileşti, Traian, Vultureni
South West	16	7.9	Brabova, Breasta, Calafat, Craiova, Goieşti, Moţăţei, Tâmna
West	18	7.4	Balinţ, Banloc, Berzovia, Buziaş, Cermei. Deta, Honorici, Ineu, Jamu Mare, Maşloc, Lipova, Păuliş
Total	158	129.9	

Source: Romanian Business Journal 10(2003) Aug 6–19

The bulk of this is used for cereals along with sunflowers and rape, but there are 600ha of tobacco and 380ha of orchards and vineyards as well as the Suinprod pig rearing complex and the cattle herd being built up at Interfarm. The new companies are investing in new equipment in line with European standards. Aaylex Grup are investing €26mln in Avicola Buzău with a large new farm (supplementing 10 in Buzău and one in Galaţi) to treble dead meat production to 30,000t. Another poultry company Transavia invested €15mln in 2007 to modernise their abattoir as well as the processing and distribution systems. The rise in fodder costs during 2007–8 is also forcing a process of concentration best seen in the policies of Transavia who bought Avicola (Braşov) in 2007, while Agricola (Bacău), the market leader for chicken, have acquired Lumina (Constanţa) at the start of a process to increase market share from 16 to 25 per cent. There is good potential for chicken in Romania with 17kg/pc annual consumption only 35 per cent of the EU level and although Agricola have lost fast-food contracts with Spring Time (who now have their own factory) and McDonalds (who have changed to a Polish supplier), they have 29 shops of their own and sell widely to supermarkets. They have also financed the modernizing of their abattoir by land deals arising from the relocation of farms to the outskirts of Bacău, making way for a Carrefour shopping development in one case. All this now compensates in some way for the labour-intensive operations of the communist period when, for example, 2–3,000 people worked for the Intreprinderea de Sere at 30 Decembrie (on the southern edge of Bucharest) which covered cattle, pig and poultry units and a fruit farm plus downstream activities involving conserves, drinks (Pepsi Cola licence), milk and salami, and a chain of 25 shops in the Bucharest-Giurgiu area.

Even before Romania's accession to the EU land could be bought by foreigners if they set up a company in Romania. There was much activity by Italian and Spanish interests in Banat – also by Italians, Greeks, Turks and others in Bărăgan and Dobrogea. During 1998–2004 acquisitions in Banat involved 108,000ha in Timiş county, 34,000 in Arad and 14,000 in Caraş-Severin; also 15,000ha in Constanţa. Foreign buyers are usually interested in the best land – in terms of soil, climate and infrastructure – which is available at relatively low prices and can generate good returns with the use of modern equipment, irrigation and refrigerated transport. Early Italian deals were struck in the Deta and Sânnicolau Mare areas following initial purchases of 150ha in Bârzava and Caradia communes. Emiliana have acquired 15,000ha in the Dudeştii Veche area of Timiş while Genagricola (part of the Italian Generali Group) farm 20,000ha in the Timişoara area and intends to acquire several thousand hectares for vineyards in Caraş-Severin. Riso Scotti have made a €30mln investment in the Bărăgan (the Giurgeni-Vlădeni area of Ialomiţa county) producing rice on an area that has expanded from 60ha of trials in 2004 to an estimated 10,000ha in 2007 (now extending into Brăila and Olt counties). Around 100 workers use state-of-the-art equipment for processing and wrapping. Meanwhile, Borcea Agro-Holding includes seven commercial companies in Călăraşi county that have attracted Canadian investment, while Spanish companies in Banat are interested in sunflowers and the oil extraction business, helped by cheap land and European programmes. Thus Bardeau Holdings based in Timişoara have 18,000ha of cereals, sunflowers and fodder peas as well as 14 livestock farms supported by a grain reception, mixed fodder factory and milk processing units. FirstFarms (Denmark) bought some 5,500ha of land (for €10mln) in the Bucharest, Sibiu and Timişoara areas during 2007–8 and expect to increase their holdings while prices remain attractive.

GOVERNMENT AGRICULTURAL ASSISTANCE

Despite restitution the state was not in a position to give peasant farmers much help over agricultural development. The fact that 35–40 per cent of people were living on agricultural revenues pointed to a mammoth bureaucratic exercise if any blanket assistance was contemplated, while any development measures for fundamentally non-viable holdings seemed not only expensive (in the context of scarce resources and huge commitments to loss-making state industries) but counterproductive given the minifundia syndrome that served as a rural welfare institution. On the other hand, inside the EU it would certainly not be possible to protect inefficient producers from imports and hence it was arguably crucial that some efficiency gains should be made before entry. Government also had to cope with the dilemma of farmer versus consumer since cheap imports were a curse to one but a blessing to the other. Concern over the destabilising effect of urban poverty made for government reluctance to tax imports while until 1997 a part of the bread supply was sold at subsidised prices. Thus until 1997 governments maintained a highly interventionist stance through controls over prices and external trade, while state farms were assisted by some free distribution of fertiliser which had a two-fold benefit in stimulating production and preventing a major collapse in the chemical industry. There was also help for state agricultural (and industrial) units through soft loans although these were insufficient to prevent run-down as already noted in the case of intensive stock rearing units.

But basically the neglect of rural areas evident under communism continued into the 1990s for although land restitution greatly increased the area of land in private hands beyond the 15 per cent level in 1989, there was delay in the issue of legal titles (one third of owners were still without them in 1997) and the development of a land market was frustrated. The state continued to control most of the infrastructure (inputs and marketing) while intervention to boost the food supply favoured only the state farms with an average of 19.2 per cent of budgetary expenditure during 1992–6 (Spiridion 2005). Indeed he suggests that the continued inefficiency of state-managed agriculture made life difficult in the towns and forced the poorer elements to return to countryside that scored a positive migration balance against the urban sector towards the end of the decade. But this overlooks the economic downturn that brought higher unemployment and the rise in temporary migration abroad (Sandu et al. 2000). The first regional development measures (1996) belatedly included support for agriculture in the Apuseni Mountains (with subsequent support from the International Foundation for Agricultural Development in 1999) as well as the Danube Delta and selected lowland counties with severe rural poverty. There was also a concern for mountain regions, giving rise to special initiatives over agricultural research, farming organisations and farm diversification, including draft legislation.

Policy from 1997

After 1996 the state sector was restructured, ultimately with land concessions to private businesses, while some farms were liquidated. Private farming continued to increase its share of total production during the late 1990s under the DCR government: from 86.4 per cent in 1994 to 89.5 in 1997 and 94.7 in 2000, but more strongly in the animal sector during the latter three years (84.9–88.2 per cent during 1994–7 to 98.0 per cent in 2000) than in the cropping sector with 87.4 per cent in 1994, 90.2 per cent in 1997 and 92.6 per cent in 2000. However, aid was reduced in 1997 but with a wider distribution so that all farmers became eligible. Input price controls were eliminated (along with others) and free distribution of fertiliser was phased out although – to ease the impact – vouchers were distributed direct to private producers to pay for inputs and services (fertilisers, seeds, plant protection, fuel and new machinery). The new scheme sought equity after previous governments had discriminated in favour of state farms. It eventually took various forms including an attempt to provide farmers with energy at concessionary prices e.g. coloured diesel fuel in 2000 to prevent misuse arising from abuse of the previous system of coupons to obtain concessionary fuel cost for ploughing for each hectare of tilled land (as well as coupons worth 50lei/ha for other inputs). Under the new scheme, government paid Petrom through promissory notes (also arrangements for electricity and gas used in farming and in fertiliser production). Farm commodity price controls were also removed – notably in connection with pigs and poultry, milk, wheat (including flour and bread, although a transitional wheat marketing scheme was put in place); while the customs regime was relaxed with all export bans, quotas and licences removed. Imported food products were encouraged to stimulate producers to lower costs and this thinking was reinforced by export incentives for cereals, poultry, dairy products, sunflower oil, frozen fruit and vegetables. To reconcile rural and urban interests the Ciorbea government experimented briefly with a National Agency for Agricultural Products (and later on the outgoing Năstase government launched a populist measure just before the 2004 elections by seeking to regulate free market farm product prices).

Agricultural Exports

These were much desired, especially geared to less-pretentious markets in CEE and Asia. By 2000 an export bonus was being paid at the rate of 35lei/t for cereals. Food imports were subject to tariffs, although these were largely standardised at 22 per cent in 1999, retaining the maximum ceiling at 45 per cent for the so-called sensitive products (meat and sugar products). The aim was to encourage a commercial approach and with this in mind government undertook to facilitate an efficient land market (from 1998): a more feasible option once the distribution of property titles had made further progress. However state farm land was not yet up for sale while most private owners either needed to work their own land or were making their own arrangements: either formally through associations or informally through sharecropping arrangements with trusted neighbours. These various initiatives were drawn together during 1997–8 into a more coherent strategy for Agricultural Sector Adjustment (ASA) – one of a series of World Bank Programmatic Adjustment Loans to support accelerated reform – that aimed at a stimulating framework for agriculture (prices, subsidies, commercial policies and taxes). There was also to be privatisation of state farms and food industry units, reform of the state cereal trading company Romcereal and legislation for cooperative systems, including a special regime for credit cooperatives (as distinct from consumption cooperatives) to strengthen their role in rural areas.

Consolidation of Small Farms

An abortive proposal in 1997 sought to draw more young people into farming through allocating 10ha arable free for five years to young experts in agriculture with exemption from taxes on agricultural income; with right to buy the land after five years. Housing plots were also proposed as part of this measure but the law was blocked in parliament. There has been discussion in government circles of a settlement programme whereby unemployed young people would be placed on smallholdings of three hectares, supported by a proportion of their former salary. The holdings would gradually increase in size while the financial support would be gradually withdrawn. But there was not enough land to justify such an approach. However it is now widely believed that intervention is necessary to encourage transfers to non-agricultural employment where marginal productivity is zero or near-zero and therefore help to address 'the vicious circle of subsistence farming' (Chirca & Teşliuc 1999, p.42). Hence the need for consolidation of subsistence farms ('restructurarea fermelor de semi-subzistenţa') and an improved quality of production. Agriculture could not continue indefinitely to employ 4.0mln people to produce just eight per cent of national value added (when the food industry needed only 170,000 to do the same). There was also powerful pressure from Europe to reduce the number of farms quite drastically by some 3.0mln. Consolidation would increase efficiency and provide a more viable basis for modernisation – with greater availability of irrigation, machinery, pesticides and fertilisers – to exploit the strengths that come from the natural conditions and the experience deriving from a farming tradition (currently compromised by poor infrastructure: mechanisation, investment and education as well as fragmentation and out-migration).

A Family Farm Concept was outlined by Ion-Tudor's (1996) model 20–40ha holdings with capital-intensive production technologies – facilitated by credit, land market, access to small farm technology and advisory system – and rural infrastructure, covering transport/ telecommunications, water/electricity, health/education (with scope for non-agricultural businesses to cope with the potential unemployment of 2.5mln people in 5–10 years). It also required better access to food processors with cheaper collection and easier monitoring of quality. The 'Country Report' (2000, p.44) thought it likely that private farming would expand because of: 'generational turnover in the countryside and the arrival of younger more individualistic people without memory of work under collectivised agriculture', along with economic stabilisation and increased profitability (assisted by the development of upstream and downstream markets. In 2003, agriculture minister Ilie Sârbu declared that the 'multifunctional family farm' was the only basis for a durable rural economy with the potential for efficiency: minimising production and transaction costs while associations might incur high transaction costs – due to collective decision making and inappropriate incentive structures – despite their superior productivity. But the process might well be slow because of poor markets for credit, land, inputs and production; unattractive trade prices and interest rates; and possible problems over exiting from associations through shared liabilities. However Romania has already established a high level of individual farming and evolution needs to combine small units rather than break down large ones. In order to encourage evolution the DCR government started pumping capital into peasant farming to the extent of 1.0–1.5 per cent of GDP, despite the difficult economic climate in difficult times (though this approach was discontinued in 2001 when budgetary funding for rural development fell below 1.0 per cent).

Demonstration Farms made a contribution. With the help of Dutch organisations (ETC Foundation and Agro Eco Consultancy) Phare launched a project at Cincşor (Voila commune near Făgăraş) starting in 1995: a mixed farm of 50ha producing vegetables and fodder. And Aveyron (France) started collaboration with farmers in Tulcea county through a pilot farm at Baia where five French families provide training. The Netherlands provided $1.5mln to set up and equip associations of primary producers in the Bucharest area for a maximum period of four years (1993–7): Dascălu, Dobroeşti, Domneşti, Nuci, Periş and Vidra; with Gruiu in prospect. Shareholding farmers will be responsible for management, re-investing a tenth of the profit while distributing the rest. The associations at Dascălu, Domneşti, Periş and Nuci will concentrate on milk (vegetables too at Nuci) and will acquire refrigerated tanks. Vidra will deal in vegetables and Dobroeşti fodder. Cooperation in milk processing could extend nationwide on the basis of a single network, but for the moment the Dutch have also moved on to Iaşi county where further multi-functional cooperatives are being set up, with help for institutions supporting private agriculture.

Other Potential Improvements

Light tractors and machines suitable for small farms could solve the problem of technology; while improved collection arrangements might cope with small surpluses, especially with better local processing capacities and the use of intermediaries to sell produce further afield and benefit from regional price differentials. Small meat packing businesses might help to create competition over the sale of livestock that was still dominated by the state at the turn of the millennium. Likewise there was scope for agricultural contracting and rural services with the possibility of private tractor hire to compete with the state's facilities (which have themselves been privatised). Farmers themselves might improve their capacity for processing with the acquisition of electrically-powered milling equipment to produce the feed necessary for enlarged herds. But the necessary restructuring could not occur spontaneously, even with the end to high inflation and improved systems of credit and marketing. Very modest land value increases (beyond the urban-rural fringe) were totally inadequate to stimulate the consolidation envisaged when a competitive land market was first energised in 1997 (Bohateret 1997; Toma 1997). Owners who sold needed security in exchange. Meanwhile a model based on 20–40ha family farms with capital-intensive production technologies could mean potential unemployment for 2.5mln people over five to ten years. A sudden consolidation would provoke a 'social explosion': the older people would need to retire with dignity in order to pave the way for young farmers to start new family farms stimulated by effective market competition and higher rural incomes.

Policy from 2000

Support to farmers changed annually according to emergency orders ('Ordonanţe de urgentă ale guvernului') and government decisions ('Hotarari de guvern'). In 2000 coupons for individual farmers were limited to a maximum of 0.35mln.lei; a 50lei/t bonus was paid for wheat sold for use by domestic bakeries; and there was a special subsidy for each liter of milk supplied to the domestic market. Farmers were also getting a 70 per cent subsidy for interest on credits for setting up cultures; while a quarter of the price of tractors and farm machines bought on the domestic market was paid for by the ministry (with an exemption year in credit execution and subsidised interest rate up to 75 per cent for a four year term covering the whole period of the credit). There was also free phyto-sanitary treatment for seed cultures, subsidised seeds up to 37 per cent and credits with subsidised interest for the purchase of bulls from reproduction centres. Farmers hoped that help would not be affected by the change of government, but the subsidised interest payments for new cultures were stopped; while the free phyto-sanitary treatment for seed cultures was halved – and the price doubled. On the other hand the new government undertook to restart export incentives for cereals, poultry, dairy products, sunflower oil, frozen fruit and vegetables (WTO agreements allowed subsidies for a limited list of farm products for which export contingents are allocated – for Romania oleaginous seeds, sugar, butter, beef, live animals, eggs and wine – if resources are available). Assistance over machinery was modified: 55 per cent of machinery costs with 80mln.lei allocated in 2001 (covering some 3,600 tractors and machines). An important innovation in 2006 was the payment of a subsidy of 0.7lei/l of fuel used for agricultural purposes. Romania is now getting substantial funding from the EU with special help in 2008 for milk, meat, vegetables, fruit and wine, although problems persist over absorbing all the funding available.

Commercial Farms

The widening of support was combined with the restriction of support to viable commercial farms. In 2000 livestock breeders had to organise into associations – with at least 50 milking cows – to get subsidies. The bias to large farms was also extended from subsidies to food processing contracts and Banca Agricolă loans. In 2001 (effective in 2002) government established a 'desirable' minimum size for commercial farms in order to improve the use of government subsidies and encourage consolidation of an estimated 47mln plots: for crops 110ha in the plains, 50ha in the hills and 20ha in the mountains; also for animals there was a target of 15 milking cows. Only 'agricultural exploitations' meeting these criteria would be able to access government agricultural support and subsidies (although small family farms missing out on subsidies are at least entitled to free business consultation through the advisory service). There was also an important switch in payments in 2002 from landowners to those actually working the qualifying holdings. In the past not only had payments often arrived too late for the intended purpose – and had often been wasted on drink as a result – but many went to city-based owners who often had no direct involvement with agricultural work. In that year there was direct support of 100lei for each cultivated hectare (but allowing half a hectare minimum for sugar beet or greenhouse vegetables) but subject to limits for each product. In 2003 4.4mln people owning up to 5.0ha of arable received 200lei per cultivated hectare and in 2005 a 15–18 per cent subsidy on diesel oil was announced ahead of the new ploughing season; with an intention to transfer other subsidies from crops to meat, based on deliveries to slaughter houses, with higher rates for chicken and pork. Financial aid for autumn sowing was announced at 175lei/ha for seeds, fertiliser and diesel oil. Of course specific Romanian agricultural support measures ended in 2007, apart from some direct market interventions but EU CAP funding is channelled to farmers by the Agricultural Payments & Intervention Agency (APIA). Subsidies are paid in June with Banca Agricolă and others providing interim loans supported by the Rural Credit Guarantee Fund. But the upgrading of agricultural information means that only 1.2mln farms will be eligible for EU CAP funds in future and the implications of denying help to 3.0mln others need urgent consideration. Meanwhile the issue of land taxes is highly sensitive and the matter was continually shelved until substantial increases were sanctioned in 2006, while the issue of social security contributions remained outstanding.

Assisting Land Transfers

The major decision taken in 2001 that only commercial farms would benefit from state support threatened to cast adrift millions of semi-subsistence farms in the run-up to EU accession (Davidova & Thompson 2003). The government now became concerned essentially with 169,300 such farms: 47,800 for arable, 30,300 for livestock and 91,000 for mixed farming (leaving some 200 for fish farming). 743 are over 1,000ha, of which 142 are larger than 5,000ha (Dumitru et al. 2004). But with this clear lead in favour of commercial farms, more active measures were advocated to encourage restructuring among small farms so that older farmers retire in order to provide small family holdings for younger farmers (Râmniceanu 2004). This approach was operationalised in detail by Manoleli et al. (2004) who proposed – over a period of five years – to take 2.0ha from each of 0.60mln farmers over 55 years of age in order to make 120,000ha available for consolidation into 10ha holdings for young farmers, with some 25,000ha re allocated each year (Table 8.4). The cost would arise largely through enhanced pension payments to the elderly and would gradually rise from €169.1mln in the first year and 846.5 in the fifth. The owners would need to be won over by careful persuasion bearing in mind that land is a 'symbol of freedom and independence' while poor market prices for land (away from the rural-urban fringe) encourage owners to hold on to their land even if they do not cultivate it. The plan was worked out on a regional basis to give more attention to communities in counties like Bacău and Botoşani where there are three to four people employed in agriculture per 10ha whereas at the other extreme in counties like Braşov and Prahova each person works 20–30ha on average. It has now been decided that in order to accelerate land consolidation, annuities will be paid for landowners aged over 62 who lease or sell land: the rates will be €50/yr for life for each hectare leased and €100/yr for each hectare sold, starting in the last quarter of 2005 or the first in 2006. The process may be accelerated by rising land values at the approach to EU accession (assisted by the removal of the heavy tax levied on changes in land use from agriculture – four times the purchase price); also by changes in taxation since the land tax which had remained quite nominal (despite all the health and education services

Table 8.4: *Calculations relating to the transfer of land to young farmers*

Region	A	B	C	D	E	F	G	H
Bucharest	1192.7	151.5	2226.5	269.4	9.1	2.2	0.4	4.4
Centre	1874.1	1512.4	2532.0	1053.3	106.0	29.4	5.9	58.8
North East	2373.8	1934.6	3674.4	2182.6	604.5	169.4	33.9	338.9
North West	2186.6	1769.0	2740.1	1339.9	258.7	70.9	14.2	141.9
South	2749.7	2348.2	3379.4	2037.8	342.5	111.1	22.2	222.2
South East	1836.7	1384.9	2848.2	1293.1	251.3	74.8	15.9	149.5
South West	1984.6	1720.6	2330.8	1193.4	295.9	103.6	20.7	207.3
West	1674.4	1337.8	1958.6	765.8	149.5	42.5	8.5	85.0
Total	15872.6	12158.4	21681.0	10135.3	2017.5	604.0	120.8	1208.0

Notes: A Total population 1948 (th); B Ditto rural population (th); C Total population 2002 (th); D Ditto rural population (th); E Rural population working in agriculture (th); F Ditto aged over 55 (th); G Young farmers to take over (th); H Land involved (th.ha)

Source: Manoleli et al. 2004

provided), rose sharply in 2006 across four accessibility zones and five quality grades. This resulted in variations between 30–60lei/ha. compared with the previous level of only 1.1lei. And in future the tax was to be payable to local authority budgets.

Rural Development Policy

The state eventually took a strong lead through a National Plan for Agriculture & Rural Development (NPARD) bringing together the ministries concerned with rural development, while multidisciplinary research on rural problems, triggered by the Phare-sponsored Rural Development Project (Guvernul României şi Comisia Europeană 1997), gave rise to a plan for an integrated and dynamic rural economy, based on the development of agriculture and agricultural services, along with the rationalisation of holdings on the basis of pluriactivity; improved living conditions and infrastructure; conservation of culture and patrimony through appropriate modernisation of villages; demographic reinvigoration with skills training and stimulation of business; and environmental protection through reafforestation, water management and more sustainable agriculture (Government of Romania & Ministry of Agriculture 1999). There were also plans for less-favoured areas, conceived in terms of selective subventions for disadvantaged segments of the rural and urban population. No regions were formally recognised as a basis for assistance (apart from the LFA programme of 1998 linked with mine closures, which did however include an agricultural component), but thinking nevertheless extended beyond the ad hoc projects of previous government, while the mountain focus was temporarily restricted to identify regions with either a defective infrastructure or heavy dependence on agricultural work. At the same time it was recognised that integrated rural development at the commune level would require enhanced human resources with entrepreneurial behaviour to generate activities consistent with environmental requirements (including veterinary and phyto-sanitary control) and the quality of the infrastructure which covers health and education services, water and sewerage as well as transport and telecommunications (including radio links for remote areas).

Agricultural Consultancy Services for Private Farmers

These were supported by the EU from 1996–7 and are certainly necessary in terms of diversification for it seems unlikely that Romania's medium- and long-term economic future lies with agriculture. Instead, long-term growth arguably depends on a somewhat reduced role for the rural economy balanced by a transfer of labour from rural to urban areas as public sector restructuring and a more favourable business environment further encourage the private sector contribution in services and manufacturing' (Mete 2003). Progress is now being

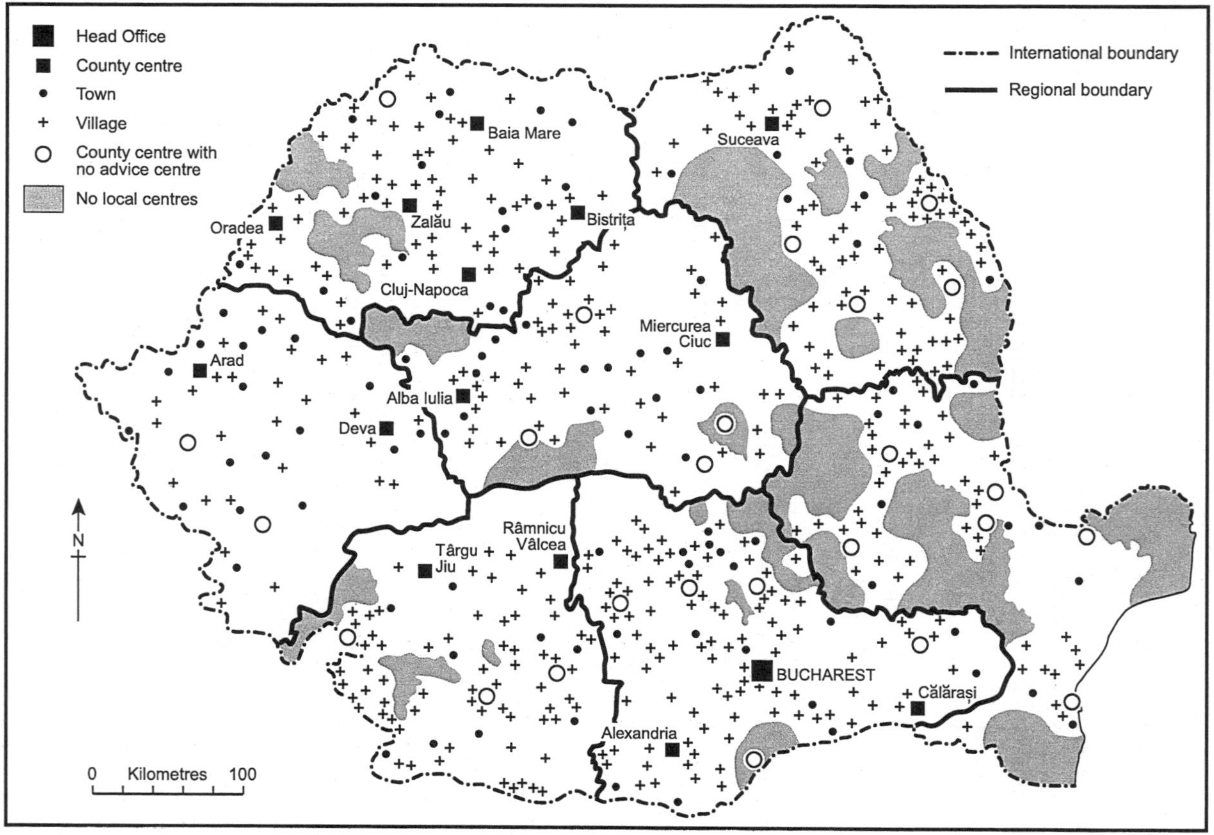

Figure 8.1 The National Agricultural Advisory Service Source: NAAC Bucharest

made in part through a network of some 540 advice centres (run by a National Agency for Agricultural Consultations: NAAC) to supply information on harvesting prospects and marketing; help plans for farm modernisation and the extension of pluriactivity into local industry and food processing; and provide limited credit to meet the costs of ploughing, seeds, chemicals and machinery. From 1998 NAAC operated initially in six pilot counties with 48 communal offices and there was a Phare training programme for agricultural extension in 100 villages in 16 counties. A national network of some 540 centres was in place in 2001 although there is no locally-based service in a number of areas which are presumably dependent on help from the central office in the relevant county (Figure 8.1). Encouraging enterprise is a necessary but complicated business (Sandu 1999) and the progress in SME development (mostly commerce and services) correlates primarily with urban centres (Ianoş 2000). But there are opportunities in agriculture, fishing and rural tourism to offset the problems of declining mining areas and polluted zones. 2004–5 saw the launch of a rural development programme in the North East (Bacău, Neamţ and Suceava), Central (Covasna, Harghita and Sibiu), South East (Buzău and Vrancea) plus Vâlcea in the South West. Each county had its 'Direcţia pentru Agricultura şi Dezvoltare Rurală' creating programmes for 2007–13 with finance from 'Fondul Internaţional de Dezvoltare Agricolă'.

Pluriactivity. NAAC also established contacts with similar agencies in Canada, Denmark, France, Germany and UK and there was scope for farmers to take training courses in these countries in 1999. It has also received 0.4mln.lei from the German AHT international company (needed for information brochures). Model farms alongside a complex information service are seen as the main propeller of rural development. Meanwhile international consultation with the UK produced an Agricultural Working Group (2004) with cooperation extending to a Writtle Agricultural College project for rural renaissance in accession states (including Romania) seeking a modern approach to rural business diversification and alternative land use for sustainable rural economies (including new enterprises appropriate to global warming). However there may still be an alternative to specialisation because pluriactivity is now appreciated as 'a consciously constructed nexus that allows on the one hand the continuation of farming and on the other hand makes for the reproduction of other economic activities that would be impossible if they had to be grounded on stable and full-time employment relations' (Van Der Ploeg and De Rooij 2000, p.46). There is scope for eco-farming given demand in the EU and also potential for rural tourism (given the country's biodiversity resources and a good range of locally-produced food); while 2.5mln.ha of degraded land – with 7.0mln.ha susceptible to erosion – provides opportunities in afforestation. Indeed, it is thought likely that in the EU member states pluriactivity will become more important, making heterogeneity intrinsic to rurality. ECE farms may not be become simply 'new hinterlands of Western European agribusiness' (ibid, p.52) and one response to poverty may lie in rural diversification and sustainable development.

SAPARD

NPARD and its associated initiatives were a crucial base for the EU's 2002–6 Special Accession Programme for Agriculture & Rural Development (SAPARD) providing focused pre-accession funding (as opposed to relatively diverse support provided by Phare) based on the work of an inter-ministerial committee that identified rural development as a priority for Romania's integration into European structures (Guvernul României 2000). SAPARD was to provide €153.2mln/yr of non-reimbursable funding over seven years, supplemented by a budget contribution of €50mln and private contributions to take the total to €300mln (for each project the private contribution must be 50–70 per cent, except in the case of non-revenue generating projects for communities). Although the amount actually absorbed was calculated at only €640mln during 2000–5, the investment helped Romania attain European standards over agricultural policy, food safety and environmental protection – also infrastructure and business development. Project evaluation began in 2002 and in 2003 grants were made in support of co-funded projects (facilitated by a credit guarantee scheme) in Category One seeking improved processing and marketing: involving new buildings; treatment and recycling; use of by-products; and monitoring and control systems. Funds were allocated to milk and dairy products (25 per cent); meat, meat products and eggs (23); vegetables, fruit and potatoes (17); cereals (13); wine (nine); fish (six); sugar (four) and oilseeds (three). So the bulk of the funding went to firms based in the towns. Meanwhile there was much funding under Category Two that covers rural infrastructure, with funding divided between roads, water and sewerage: reflecting the EU CAP emphasis on rural development through 'second pillar' measures. And with the necessary administrative capacity available, investment started in 2004 in Category Three covering agricultural holdings: equipment for modernisation of holdings (tractors, harvesters, irrigation); rehabilitation of orchards and vineyards (replacing old vines and hybrids by noble varieties on existing surfaces without increasing total area); modernising and extending buildings (with water, electricity and drainage); modernising greenhouses and installing new ones; acquiring pedigree stock and improving buildings e.g. milking halls. SAPARD also aided regional rural development programmes (already mentioned), with a positive impact on infrastructure and job creation despite 395 eligible infrastructure projects for which no finance was available.

On the whole the programme was effective in terms of enhanced competitiveness for rural areas as well as improved quality of life to help prevent depopulation, although there were problems of low absorption capacity, lack of knowledge and bureaucratic processing. Figure 8.2 maps the first few months of grant awards during August-December 2002 and shows a wide spatial distribution which made an early impact in the poorer, eastern half of the country (August-September, covered by Figure 8.2a) before all regions became fully active (Figure 8.2b); however some quite large areas of the Centre, North West and West did not attract grants during either period, especially Arad county in West region and Bistriţa-Năsăud in the North West; while much of the funding in Braşov and Sibiu counties (Centre region) went on food processing units: one in Sibiu city and another in the commune of Sercaia, east of Făgăraş. Table 8.5 deals with the overall programme until the end of 2005, showing an average investment of €109 per rural inhabitant (although much of the investment in food processing inevitably involved factories in the towns) and a reasonably equitable distribution across the regions. This is encouraging in the sense that no major areas are lacking in enterprise (since funding is awarded only for sound projects and not as an aid distribution). Thus in the North East, which is the poorest region, there was support for Agricola International's egg incubator and the Pescado fish processing unit in Bacău county; Adrian Poromboiu's 'Ulerom' enterprise in Vaslui county; and Mihai Popescu's automated pig-rearing unit at Coarnele Caprei in Iaşi county. Table 8.6 concentrates on food processing and the balance between modernisation and new projects (the latter strongest in meat processing and regionally in the South). From 2007 Romania is getting €881mln in direct payments, €732 for market measures and €2.42bln for second pillar, allocated through Agenţia de Plati pentru Dezvoltarea Rurală şi Pescuit to 1.5mln qualifying arable farms and 1.4mln livestock units.

INFRASTRUCTURE

Mechanisation

The communist MTSs were reprofiled as Agromecs and 450 (later 600) were slated for privatisation by the Ciorbea government, although there must have been some consolidation because it was later reported that 522 Agromecs were looking after some 4,000 mechanisation stations occupying 5,000ha of non-agricultural land. Privatisation was slow on account of gross over-valuation that pushed share costs out of line with potential profits: those who invested their vouchers in Agromecs were mainly employees wanting to keep their jobs. But in any case ageing fleets of heavy fuel-thirsty machines (many cannibalised to supply parts to keep the rest of the stock working) were not well adapted to the needs of private farmers and some new firms set up in competition. Moreover the Agromecs were hit by a big decline in mechanised

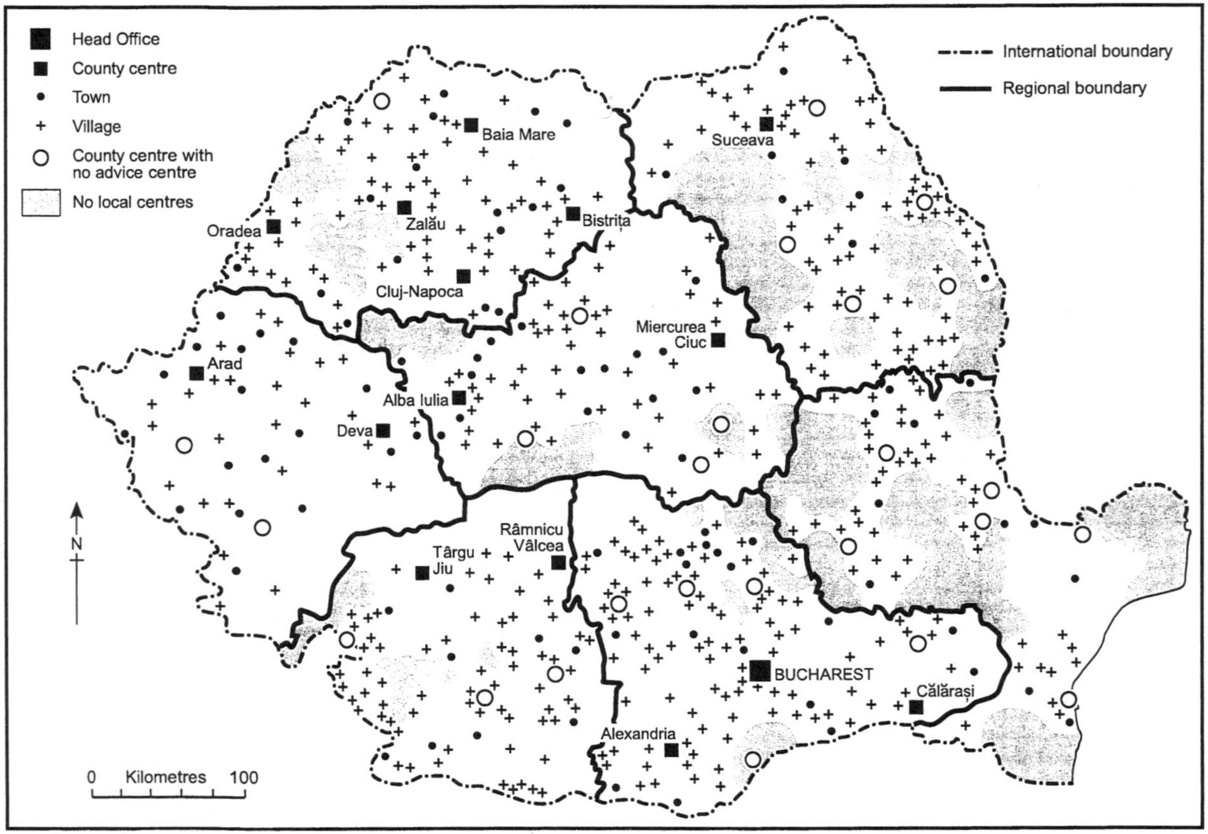

Figure 8.1 The National Agricultural Advisory Service Source: NAAC Bucharest

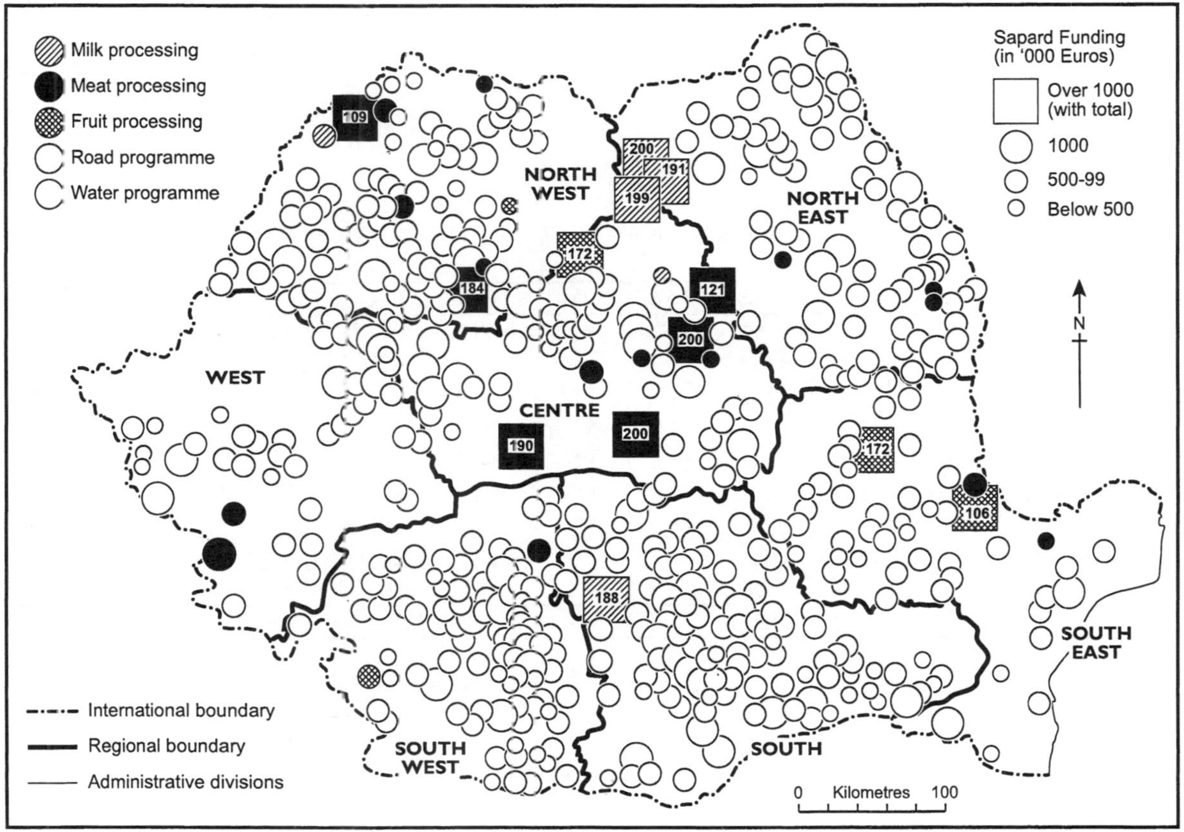

Figure 8.2b SAPARD Projects Approved during October-December 2002 Source: www.sapard.ro

Table 8.5: *SAPARD Projects 2002–2005*

Region	Farming		Processing		Tourism		Roads/Water		Total		
	No	€mln	No	€mln	No	€mln	No	€mln	No	€mln	€pc.
Bucharest	8	1.41	17	25.43			11	9.44	36	36.28	147
Centre	37	5.02	53	68.01	55	9.06	29	6.64	174	88.73	86
North East	100	11.89	41	42.25	36	5.80	203	172.13	380	232.07	105
North West	73	10.20	29	20.52	13	2.30	130	99.73	245	132.75	99
South	58	12.49	36	65.09	8	1.41	192	143.06	294	222.05	112
South East	67	13.06	41	60.82	16	2.44	119	87.94	243	164.26	128
South West	36	3.39	19	35.17	10	1.77	128	97.85	193	138.18	108
West	65	14.57	19	23.98	8	1.17	59	46.54	151	86.26	116
Total	444	72.03	255	341.27	146	23.95	871	663.33	1716	1100.58	109

Notes: Values relate to the total investment (€mln) and not merely the SAPARD contribution

Source: www.sapard.ro

Table 8.6: *SAPARD food processing projects 2002–5 with value in €mln (first line: all projects; second line new projects (NP), as opposed to modernisation of existing installations)*

Region	Dairy		Meat/Fish		Fruit/Veg.		Cereals		Total		
	No	Value	No	Value	No	Value	No	Value	No	Value	PerCent
Bucharest	1	2.00	9	14.15	2	2.32	5	6.96	17	25.43	
			4	8.88	1	1.13			5	10.01	39.5
Centre	15	19.31	24	36.31	12	8.96	2	3.43	53	68.01	
	4	6.52	4	9.98	7	3.63			15	20.13	29.6
North East	21	20.02	15	17.35	3	2.65	2	2.23	41	42.25	
	11	11.24	2	2.23	1	0.85			14	14.32	33.9
North West	11	3.90	12	10.80	3	1.69	3	4.13	29	20.52	
	4	1.63	4	4.40	1	1.47	1	2.71	10	10.21	49.7
South	7	10.57	20	42.53	8	8.01	1	3.98	36	65.09	
	1	2.06	11	28.32	4	4.12	1	3.98	17	39.48	59.1
South East	6	5.34	16	23.80	13	21.07	6	10.59	41	60.80	
	3	1.90	4	11.35	4	6.20			11	19.45	32.0
South West	3	2.39	8	23.74	5	7.72	3	1.32	19	35.17	
	1	0.35	3	17.07					4	7.33	49.5
West	3	4.52	7	9.54	2	1.71	7	8.21	19	23.98	
	2	4.34	1	2.00	1	0.99			4	7.33	30.6
Total	67	68.05	111	178.22	48	54.13	29	40.85	255	341.25	
	26	28.04	33	84.23	19	18.39	2	6.69	80	137.35	40.2
Per Cent NP		41.2		47.3		34.0		16.4		40.2	

Notes: Values relate to the total investment and not merely the SAPARD contribution. Percentages on both the bottom line and the far right column relate to the share of total investment in new projects.

Source: www.sapard.ro

agricultural work (only 60–70 per cent of the 1989 level in 1997), yet they could do little to stimulate most farmers since they had no financial resources to buy small machines. At the same time they were not allowed to lease land and farm on their own account.

Responses to Rising Prices

Farmers faced increasing real equipment costs since the cost of industrial products needed for agriculture increased 3,200 times during 1990–2001 compared with 1,200 times for farm produce. Put another way, a tractor cost the equivalent of 50t of wheat in 1990 but 92t in 2001 (while 1,000l of diesel fuel increased from 1.3 to 3.6t); alternatively 60–110t of maize (2.0–4.4); 25–59t of sunflowers (1.3–3.6); 167–690hl milk (4.2–27.3); 3.7–9.5t beef (0.09–0.38); 4.2–9.2t pork (0.11–0.36); or 5.0–10.2t of poultry meat (0.13–0.40). Domestic tractor sales fell from 17,000 in 1993 to just 1,000 in 1997; with a total fleet of 160,000 when 300–700,000 were notionally required in 1998. Even second-hand tractors were costing $5,000–8,000 in 1998 when the average monthly salary was below $150. The Braşov 'Tractorul' factory started leasing 6,000 tractors for agricultural use in 1998 while the machinery firm Semănătoarea (Bucharest) also set up a leasing company. By 2000 Tractorul were selling tractors with payment by installments in either cash or produce; they also set up a company to store and market cereals received through barter (with shareholders to represent the National Land Improvement Company and three other machinery and vehicle firms that were (presumably) involved in the scheme: Aro (Câmpulung), Hart (Miercurea Ciuc) and MAT (Craiova). Meanwhile Claas were becoming prominent in Romania through importers such as Agrocomerţ (Timişoara) and Agroservice (Constanţa) who went on to provide service systems including chains of shops selling spare parts; also a training and improvement centre. In Constanţa two people were given four to five days of free training for each harvester sold, with the MEGA204 model doing best. A dealer network also emerged for John Deere farm machinery with service and spares in Bucharest (Mogoşoaia), Brăila, Craiova and Timişoara.

American and Phare Projects. To try and break a vicious circle where mechanisation, as the key to greater efficiency, was blocked by the heavy risk of taking a bank loan at commercial rates, an attractive opportunity was presented by the US Case Corporation (a tractor and combine producer) and Valmost Industries (producing irrigation equipment) providing equipment through loans of up to $80mln (enough to benefit 150,000ha); working in partnership with the Land Planning Administration (designated by Ministry of Agriculture). The partners created 'Societatea Proiectului Agricol Român' (SPAR) to identify potential beneficiaries (i.e. farming associations and companies each working at least 500ha); supply the equipment in one of ten 'mechanisation packages' (including fertilisers and services); and sell produce (estimated at $750mln over five years) on the international market. Farmers could buy over five years with the state providing a guarantee and the project progressed gradually during 1996–8. The irrigation systems promised reduced water consumption by 40–60 per cent and the suppliers set up a distribution network for spare parts and training courses. US firms subsequently provided credits to help farmers acquire high-tech equipment (as well as seeds and pesticides) in the context of a $350mln World Bank loan for agricultural recovery. And 15 machine 'circles' (1,094 members and 10,945ha) emerged in Bistriţa-Năsăud, Braşov, Harghita and Mureş counties under a Phare programme managed by the Agro-Caritas.

Table 8.7: *Farm Machinery and Fertiliser 1985–2005*

Year	A	B	C	D	E	F	G	H	I	J
1999	184	54.1	102	50.4	49.1	1.7	n..a	n.a.	1.20	34.10
1986	185	54.0	119	52.5	52.9	2.5	n.a.	n.a.	1.29	38.96
1987	183	54.8	105	51.4	55.1	3.5	n.a.	n.a.	1.20	39.43
1988	165	n.a.	86.9	43.3	45.2	4.1	n.a.	n.a.	1.21	43.32
1989	151	n.a.	83.2	43.6	44.8	4.1	n.a.	n.a.	1.16	41.60
1990	127	74.4	73.2	35.8	35.8	4.9	5.6	46.3	1.10	24.79
1991	132	71.0	73.4	35.0	34.5	3.1	5.2	42.8	0.46	16.91
1992	146	63.7	80.7	37.0	34.5	2.9	5.2	42.7	0.42	15.79
1993	158	59.1	95.8	43.9	34.5	2.8	4.9	42.2	0.54	17.12
1994	161	57.9	103	47.7	35.6	2.7	4.4	42.7	0.48	16.94
1995	163	57.1	107	50.4	36.1	2.0	4.1	42.7	0.47	17.42
1996	165	56.5	114	51.6	35.9	1.8	3.6	41.3	0.43	17.87
1997	163	57.3	114	53.9	34.0	1.7	3.0	40.8	0.40	16.51
1998	164	56.7	121	55.7	31.5	1.6	2.7	38.8	0.38	15.84
1999	163	57.1	123	56.2	29.9	1.3	2.1	33.4	0.33	16.68
2000	160	58.6	123	57.7	26.8	1.3	1.6	29.7	0.34	15.81
2001	164	57.3	126	60.0	24.7	1.1	1.3	27.1	0.37	15.33
2002	169	55.5	131	62.1	24.2	1.1	1.1	26.4	0.33	15.75
2003	169	55.6	132	63.1	23.9	1.1	0.9	25.9	0.36	17.26
2004	171	54.8	136	65.3	24.7	n.a.	0.9	25.6	0.38	17.75
2005	173	54.5	137	66.7	25.1`	n.a.	0.7	25.8	0.46	16.32

Notes: A Tractors (th); B Hectares of arable per tractor; C Ploughs for tractors (th); D Mechanical seeders (th); E Combines for straw crops (th); F Combines for maize (th); G Combines for fodder (th); H Combines total (th); I Chemical fertiliser applied (th.t active substance); J Organic fertiliser applied (th.t)

Source: Statistical Yearbooks: Tables 14.1, 14.15 and 14.16

Foundation (Gheorgheni) in 1998. The 'circle' concept was born in Bavaria in 1958 to provide voluntary mutual help in production and marketing, through rational use of labour and machinery, and thereby avoid unprofitable investments for small farms. The situation is now somewhat improved. Owners in the Bărăgan hire engineers as drivers because the high wages are justified by the competence to keep the machines running. But there is only one tractor for each 90ha (20 in the EU) not to mention the 'structural deficit' through is wear and tear (for half the tractors were over eight years old at the start of the millennium). An emergency ordinance in 1999 provided subsidies for the purchase of tractors as well as harvesters and irrigation equipment with effect from July 2001. Overall the situation has improved with one tractor per 55.6h of arable compared with 74.4 in 1990 (Table 8.7).

Irrigation

Romania's continental climate makes irrigation essential for sustained high yields in the lowland areas in general, but especially the south and southeast. Irrigation schemes were installed under communism to treat 42.5th.ha in 1950, rising by the decade to reach 199.7 (1960), 731.3 (1970), 2,301.0 (1980) and 3,168.7 (1989). But the subsequent collapse of the farming system after 1989 (and its replacement by a much larger number of producers with different interests) meant that the facilities could not be maintained. The theft of pumping equipment and the illicit use of water by individual farmers (who refused to pay the taxes required to keep the stations in operation) became common. Administrative problems were complemented by technological defects (water shortages arising from high levels of evaporation from open canals), while the declining efficiency of water use gave rise to waterlogging and salinisation. At Mânăstirea (Călăraşi), irrigation management fell into disarray due to a lack of maintenance by the government (although the state remained in control of the infrastructure in spite of land restitution) or by local people. Farmers were cooperating but not at the scale required for a large irrigation system. There was a need to replace the state irrigation company – or municipality – by self-governing associations of water users (Lup 1997).

Complex Ramifications

Since it is crucial that irrigated cultures should be sown on ground that has been well-watered, the uncertainties encouraged land use changes. Hence restituted farms abandoned irrigation and planted wheat and barley instead of water-intensive crops like maize, rice and vegetables. Even specialist rice growers had to think about changing to cereals when the water supply became irregular. However the changing crop structure also reflected the instability of agricultural product prices: where water was available it might be stolen by small farmers (difficult to detect by water guards) and damage occurred to internal canal systems (the responsibility of municipalities) passing through privatised land. Lack of canal maintenance meant reduced supply and farmers requiring water had to draw on underground waters. Drilling wells and pumping water involved high costs while the cooler water caused stress to the plants. Meanwhile the environmental problems arising from irrigation had to be addressed: as water ran off the fields into ditches, these 'return flows' may carry dissolved salts as well as nutrients and pesticides. Unless wells are deep, there will be increased salinisation (deposition of harmful salts around the roots of crops, preventing crops from absorbing water and nutrients) in irrigation water; thereby reducing yields and damaging soils to the extent that crops might no longer be grown. Also, waterlogging prevents roots from penetrating the soil and cuts off essential nutrients, while water pollution complicates drinking water supply in dry areas.

World Bank Support

This was part of a major programme of $116mln for rural development including agricultural services, biodiversity management and forestry. It allowed a start to the transfer of irrigation management to user groups in 1997, but only four of the 60 pilot groups were still functioning in 2000 due to weaknesses in local property regimes and governance structures (i.e. weak monitoring and haphazard enforcement of penalties for violations). Only in a few cases were charismatic local leaders able to overcome the general atmosphere of distrust to motivate cooperative efforts. Meanwhile agriculture was suffering from low rainfall, aggravated by absence of policy on irrigation and agricultural risk insurance. The severe drought problems of 2002 ('a third year of drought') correlated with USAID help over the use of water ($3.8mln for 2002–5) and a World Bank programme of overhaul making use of small portable systems (Tambur Mini, Midi and Maxi) that can be operated manually or with light tractors. The help was channelled through a National Land Improvement Company (NLIC) aiming at 1.5mln ha of irrigated land by the end of 2003 – double the area of 0.75mln.ha actually irrigated in 2002 – including restoration over 80,000ha in that year. A ten year programme for rehabilitation and updating of irrigation worth a total of $636mln was intended to update 45 irrigation systems over 1.36mln.ha. But the initial work planned in 2003 was geared to just 150–170,000ha: benefiting 40,000 farming/association member families and including four pilot schemes – each of 1,000ha – to demonstrate technical aspects. Initial finance to NLIC amounted to $103mln: $80mln from the World Bank, with repayment over 17 years (the major part of an investment of $116mln in rural activities including agricultural services, biodiversity management and forestry), $20.7mln from the state budget and $2.3mln from local water consumer associations.

Wider Conceptions

Water endusers' associations will lay the basis for privatisation of irrigation systems as management is transferred to them from NLIC, which initially conducted a $0.65mln pilot project (financed by a non-repayable loan of $250,000 from the Japanese government, through the World Bank) to consolidate associations of irrigation water users, while setting up new associations, granting technical assistance and training staff. Some flood protection work and treatment of soil erosion is intended as well as rehabilitation: indeed NLIC is being turned into a land reclamation agency (including drainage and anti-erosion work) going well beyond the restoration of irrigation systems. Meanwhile, investment by American companies like Lemna is complemented by equipment producers in Romania. In 2002 Grup Romet of Buzău began to produce parts for Nebraska irrigation systems made in partnership with Lindsay-Europe (USA) – a world leader in manufacturing centre pivot and lateral-move irrigation systems – and Rolland France, European leader in the field of sprinkler irrigation systems. Grup Romet think that Nebraska systems are perfectly adaptable to Romanian agriculture to fight the effects of drought on the Bărăgan (especially since the government subsidises 70 per cent of the price of equipment). The Ceres farming company at Slobozia seek efficient crop production for maize and sunflowers (based on 4,000ha of irrigation) in addition to cattle breeding and dairying in order to pay-off loans and generate income for investment in machinery and irrigation equipment. However in 2006 only 60,000ha were covered by some 50,000 irrigation contracts while the maximum arable area that could be irrigated was estimated at 1.50mln.ha of which only 0.86mln was in a good state (for although the 2004 law requires peasants to create irrigation associations many of the systems transferred to associations – 1.18mln.ha – have been degraded by the theft and resale of aluminium pipes). Possibly because of warnings of a dry year 125,000 irrigation contracts were signed by mid-January 2007.

Fertiliser

There was a sharp fall in use after 1989 and the trend continued slowly thereafter – with a similar experience with pesticides – while reduced use of certified seed in favour of self-produced seed helped to depress yields. Fertiliser use is now increasing again with 461,000t (active substance) in 2005 after only 342,000t in 2000 (Table 8.6). The fertiliser industry (privatised by 1998) was not in a good situation in view of out-dated technologies aggravated by high energy consumption and pollution problems (especially for nitric and sulphuric acid) and falling world prices that further reduced competitiveness. There was an initial subsidy for state farms covering 80 per cent of fertiliser costs but as support was reduced after 1992 (and subsidies were replaced by vouchers covering input costs in general after 1996) consumption fell sharply from 602,000t in 1992 to 383,200 in 1994, forcing the closure of units at Arad (fertiliser) and Curtea de Argeş (bioprotein). Most of the fertiliser was used by state farms and associations with contracts with state distribution agencies. Oltchim (Râmnicu Vâlcea) found a novel solution to falling demand for pesticides by setting up a food and agriculture division which acquired substantial local assets including poultry and pig farms as well as fodder and canning factories. In this way pesticides were paid for through cereals (processed at the fodder plant to supply the livestock units) as well as vegetables and fruit destined for the canning factory. Finally, fresh animal and vegetable products, along with canned goods, generated cash in the shops: not the perfect strategy for a sophisticated chemical complex but one that helped to overcome the financial blockage that was a serious problem in the 1990s. In 1998 Oltchim was also maintaining a supply of fertiliser to the 'Insula Mare', lying within the Danube south of Brăila, linked with Bursagrirom (Brăila) growing and marketing cereals. But after limited recovery in production the less-efficient firms were hard-hit by a further surge in natural gas prices in 2006.

Marketing

Although some state companies continued to operate e.g. Fructexport began sending tomato juice to Heinz in the UK for making ketchup, the market economy required a much more diverse and efficient organisation that was very slow to emerge. In many cases producers had to make their own arrangements. Thus Braşov-based Codlea Greenhouses (the biggest horticultural company in Romania, producing vegetables, flowers and ornamental trees and shrubs) invested $1.4mln and won contracts to export vegetables to Austria, the Czech Republic, Germany and Switzerland in 2001 after output had previously supplied the domestic market only. Meanwhile the Seromgal (Galaţi) greenhouse complex developed their own chain of 20 local shops (selling fresh fruit and vegetables as well as canned goods) in addition to exports to Austria, the Czech Republic and Moldova. In 1995 EBRD announced an investment programme to support the cereal trade of the Danube-Black Sea region. Bulgaria, Hungary and Romania would benefit from a total investment of $600mln, with $250mln for Romania to go on infrastructure including telecommunications and harbour equipment. Storage difficulties at Constanţa-Agigea resulted in a new $25mln computerised 100,000t capacity warehouse for wheat and maize (18,000t daily) opened in 1998 in the port's free zone with access to 33,000dwt ships – increasing capacity from the previous level of 33,000t (6,000t daily). This encouraged transit, which in 1995 amounted to 442,000t from Hungary – diverted from Rijeka – and Ukraine (but could also involve Bulgaria, Moldova and Serbia by virtue of the Danube river and the Danube-Black Sea Canal). During 2000 work began at Constanţa on a soya and technical cultures plant; after the local Comcereal had started (in 1999) to manage a silo network taking crops from farmers for possible export with IT monitoring for moisture and temperature.

Bucharest Wholesale Market

This provided new facilities for vegetables, fruit and flowers in a 14ha covered complex on a 30ha site at Berceni in the south of the city, depending on rapid transport and good infrastructure covering banking, catering and parking. It was based on a $31mln investment, supported by a credit from EBRD and a German contribution of $3.5mln, and was conceived to replace an old unhygienic regime (where producers were under pressure from speculators and middlemen) with European standards of sorting and packaging for fruit, vegetables and flowers; bringing together producers (among whom the project originated) with wholesale traders and service providers on the same site to maintain a steady supply throughout the year. The venture developed during the late 1990s with the aim of reaching full capacity by 2000 with a throughput of 550,000t/yr. The complex stores bananas until ripe (and handles other imported produce), but it depends primarily on a network of collecting, sorting and packing centres: including Brezoaiele (Dâmboviţa), Ciolpani (Ilfov), Cuza Vodă (Călăraşi), Giurgiu (Giurgiu), Mihaeşti (Argeş), Moviliţa (Ialomiţa) and Vidra (Ilfov) while ultimately the supply area should also include Olt, Prahova and Teleorman counties as well. In the case of the Moviliţa centre, which was set up in 1997 with the creation of 20 jobs, the basis lay (as with the other centres) with the local farmers' association whose 36 members secured high yields through use of selected seed and fertiliser, with assistance to meet the requirements of modern technologies. They saved time previously spent doing their own marketing and secured higher returns through larger volumes and better market information.

Organisation of Suppliers. In the case of Cuza Vodă the Horticola enterprise takes some 12,000t of produce from seven other enterprises based at Călărasi, Grădiştea, Independenţa and Mircea Vodă. The Brezoaiele centre opened in 1998 in an established area of early potato production (also apples, broccoli, cabbage, salad onions and strawberries). Italian equipment replaced manual sorting. The local association grew rapidly from the original 10 in 1997 to over a hundred, drawn from surrounding areas including Băleni, Cândeşti, Petreşti, Poiana, Slobozia Moară and Voineşti. Farmers receive seeds, fertiliser and technical assistance to help them achieve consistent output and standards. There are good prospects for ecofarming in the basis of local associations like the professional association started in the central villages of Cândeşti commune that became a model to be emulated: it has 300 members across the Dâmbovita fruit-growing region (and beyond) and links with Voineşti research station and the national association of fruit growers as well as local agricultural advisors (Mihai 2001). Meanwhile at the downstream end four Bucharest street markets were modernised (Obor, Matache, Mureş and Rahova) and over the longer term a trademark for Romanian fruit and vegetables is anticipated. The Bucharest project received technical assistance from the Ministry of Economics & Technology as part of a project for a national wholesale trade system with Phare support in 1995 for six other wholesale markets outside Bucharest – Arad, Medgidia and Râmnicu Sărat for fruit and vegetables; Gura Humorului and Sângeorgiu de Mureş for livestock; and Slobozia for cereals – in order to update distribution and marketing (with modern information), expand agricultural services and accelerate regional economic growth. Progress was also maintained with German money to modernise wholesale and produce markets in Cluj-Napoca and Timişoara in 2002 (especially for fruit and vegetables in the latter).

Rural Finance and Business

All forms of business have to come to terms with the inadequacies of rural infrastructure evident in most areas away from the urban fringes. The problems relate to education (calling for better information and consultancy services) and organisation (cooperation and professional support) as well as investment including credits and subventions. There is a considerable literature on the need to improve finance for both farming and rural diversification first raised by Hare & Davis (1997) with subsequent contributions by Heidhues et al. (1998), Davis & Gaburci (1999) and Heidhues & Schrieder (2000). In 1998 the World Bank highlighted rural finance as a crucial issue and in the following year $16.5mln was allotted under an agreement signed in Rome for the improvement and stabilisation of the economic environment and the promotion of food sector activities and rural development services in general. Subsequent research confirmed that 'rural regions can be restructured effectively only if the domestic financial market provides at least basic financial services to the private agricultural and non-farm sector to enable it to acquire working capital and finance investments' (Schrieder et al. 2000, p.1217) i.e. inputs as well as incentives, institutions and infrastructure (involving rural extension and training as well as land market development, with uncertainties over ownership removed) to help sustain rural innovation and initiative. The situation was improved by the privatisation of Banca Agricolă in favour of Raiffeisen (Austria). In addition, Popov & Lubieniechi (2001, p.v) recommended commune development plans aided by business development support and more organisations (women's groups and business/farming clubs to help with marketing and training); also 'partnerships among groups of communes with common problems where these can be addressed more effectively at a larger scale than the individual commune'. There has to be a rediscovery of identity and all areas need encouragement to help themselves. National programmes for SMEs have been extended through private projects e.g. during 1999–2002, the Centre for Economic Development (a member of the Soros Open Network) successfully implemented micro-credits granted in 36 rural areas in Călăraşi, Dâmbovita, Iaşi and Prahova, part of a total portfolio of 1,800 such credits worth $0.9mln altogether. The focus rests on agriculture (procurement of seeds, fertilisers and fuel) but also handcraft workshops and services e.g. rural tourism.

Rural Credit

This is essential and the financial sector needs to find a way of supplying retail and micro-finance services profitably because most rural clients seek only small transactions. However, 'there is credible empirical evidence that the necessary conditions exist in Romania for rural bank branches to operate profitably by allocating retail credit and collecting deposits and for NGOs to allocate micro-loans in a sustainable manner' (Chaves et al. 2001, p.87). Agricultural insurance has considerable potential, although little use is made of it and in the livestock sector it is almost non-existent. 1.39mln.ha of cropland were insured in 1996 (90 per cent by Agras: a company owned by Vienna Insurance that specialises in agricultural insurances) but only 0.21mln.ha in 2000. In 2002 there was thought of compulsory insurance in respect of land rented from Agency of State Domains to provide a guarantee and also to stimulate the insurance market. But there is a ministry scheme for subsidised premiums in respect of compensation for natural disasters with specific insurance companies authorised to issue qualifying contracts to farmers in 2003–4: Agras, Allianz, Ardaf, Asiban, Asirom, Astra, Generali, Provitas and Tiriac (fewer than the previous year since Asitrans, Atlassib, AGI Romania, Interamerican, Omniasig and Unita were removed from the list). Since then Agras has been closed because of falling business, although there was speculation that the 2007 drought might boost the market to €25–30mln in 2008. However at the end of 2008 farm insurance was reported at only a quarter of the European level, although one company (Faţa Asigurari) is set to establish a nationwide chain of offices which should improve accessibility. Another consideration is mandatory home insurance that comes into effect in 2009. This will be problematic in rural areas prone to landslides and may have a bearing on the viability of some remote hamlets in Subcarpathian areas (particularly in Buzău and Vrancea counties) that are vulnerable to the hazards of landslides and mudflows. Such settlements were earmarked for evacuation under Ceauşescu's infamous 'sistematizare' programme of settlement consolidation and it would be ironic if the realities of modernisation were now to revive some of the trauma temporarily relieved by the 1989 revolution. A related issue is vehicular access since roads are extremely difficult to maintain: flood damage in Vrancea in 2005 was only tackled in 2008 with EU support for the local authority's two-year plan.

CONCLUSION

Although Romania's future may not lie primarily with agriculture, the fact that much rural labour will transfer to other sectors over the coming years should not obscure the fact that the country has a splendid basis for farming through soil and climatic characteristics that justify investment. However, while the state has removed itself from the cares of day to day farming activity, its pragmatic actions have produced a highly-polarised profile. Much of the old state sector has been concessioned for large-scale production, while an effective land market now opens the possibility for local agents to consolidate worthwhile perimeters of interest to foreign-owned agribusiness. The top 50 agricultural landowners – includeing a number of foreign companies as well as Romanian nationals like Ioan Neculae (InterAgro) and Adrian Porumboiu (Racova Group) – own four per cent of Romania's 9.4mln.ha of arable: 7,500ha each on average This is quite a small share but the value of land is now appreciating quite rapidly. Risiing prices for agricultural commodities (wheat sold for €250/t in 2008) have helped to push the price of arable land to €1,500/ha encouraging many small owners to sell. So, for example, the Italian company Riso Scotti is now half-way towards its target of a 4,000ha estate for growing rice at Gighera (Dolj),

Meanwhile, for political reasons the minifundia tradition was also reasserted after 1989. This may be regretted in terms of efficiency, but communism settled for a partial revolution through cooperative farming linked with family plots so that the rural community remained largely intact with only the former landowners removed. And despite the economic advantages of retaining an element of cooperation, the early transition years of rapid deindustrialisation gave intensively-worked small farms an important subsistence value (while the viability of state farms was being undermined by price controls imposed in the interest of urban consumers). But there is now considerable support for the smaller farms. Although only 30 per cent of Romania's farms had reached the EU standard in 2008, SAPARD has helped family farms to modernise and meet EU quality standards and there are also domestic investment programmes coming on stream: some of them national in scope like the 760mln.lei 'Farmers Programme' handled by leading banks, while others are more local like the 'Agro Capital' offered by the Credit Europe Bank in the southeast. Strategies may also be found for small farms presently unable to absorb funds, for rural Romanians continue to find a way forward even though their destination may remain uncertain. With cultural change very much the order of the day, even in the more traditional northern districts of Maramureş and Oaş, authenticity becomes a matter for some debate now that architectural norms and household practices are being everywhere transformed by the European wage levels of migrant workers.

Postscript

As EU accession has effectively brought transition to an end, there can be no doubt about the momentous nature of this event that hardly seemed possible in the early 1990s: indeed for some it was hardly even desired at that time and even after the formal application for membership and the commencement of annual reports of progress towards accession, the list of failures and shortcomings seemed monumental. The end of the centre-right coalition, decisively and predictably rejected in the elections at the end of 2000 – and of the Constantinescu presidency (a particularly abject surrender given the refusal of the incumbent even to stand for re-election) seemed to spell doom to any prospect of early membership. The electorate was radicalised by three years of negative growth that the stronger performance of 2000 (when the National Bank governor Mugur Isărescu was brought to the helm) did no more than arrest rather than reverse. Romania came so close to choosing the maverick nationalist Vadim Tudor that the right was forced to turn out in the second round to ensure that Iliescu would prevail. Yet against all the odds (including Iliescu's long-standing prejudices) the reality that transpired – after the discredited outgoing government had completed the basic reforms and laid the foundations for a future in Europe – offered the PSD enough opportunities in further European aid, FDI and privatisation to keep the party faithful on side: certainly the younger and more acquisitive faction for whom premier Năstase was a role model. And of course in fairness to Romania, since so-called 'European' statistics frequently covered only EU states and candidates for accession, poor transition performances rarely highlighted the 'other Romanian state' – Moldova – where reform has been far more difficult to sustain. With one in three families now having at least one member abroad (usually in Russia – since travel is cheap and there is minimal risk of being sent back) there are few enterprising people left at home in what has become a 'country cottage' where government is now afraid to liberalise the economy and has even reversed some privatisation measures.

So Romania's wagon ('căruță') continued to roll westwards even though some foreign academics liked to calculate how many decades it would take for Romania to reach the salary and productivity levels of Western Europe – and advocated 'plain speaking' to Bucharest concerning the facts of life following the apparent 'failure' of the centre-right reform programme. But then Brussels played derogation politics and allowed that not quite everything needed to be perfect for accession to proceed as timetabled. Rather than continually deny entry to a country making a 'bona fide' application, more assistance (through ISPA and SAPARD) became appropriate to accelerate convergence. And in Bucharest where the left had previously been enraged by any privatisation 'soft option' for a foreign buyer, it now became acceptable to sell the country's patrimony for a single dollar where substantial investment was promised. Thus, if the late 1990s were a 'nightmare' for Romania the new millennium has been the reverse with greater stability in the region and a readiness by investors to take Romania more seriously, as well as greater pragmatism in both Brussels and Bucharest. Poverty is being eased by more generous social security but more significantly by rising employment and easier travel across Europe so that the young unemployed have found their 'El Dorado' in Italy or Spain. Whereas before there had been rejection (1997) there has now been admission to both NATO (2004) and the EU (2007). Not everything in the garden is perfect because after the success of a completed IMF agreement in 2001 (the first in 25 years). Romania once again had to break-off negotiations through unreasonable pressure over economic policy. And certainly wage rises and soaring imports can only aggravate the current account deficit and make the Romanian workforce less competitive (a problem underlined by the inflow of capital and the appreciating leu that increases the cost of exports until some softening occurred in 2008.

Of course accession is not a panacea for all Romania's modernisation problems and the future will hardly turn out to be mere 'history' as the saying goes. There are much larger injections of European money, partly through the cohesion funding that a decade ago was supporting the weaker regions of Western Europe. But while competing with Bulgaria for the distinction of being the EU's poorest country will certainly help maintain the flow of FDI, it is less clear to what extent this benefit will be offset with reduced competitiveness compared with Russia, Ukraine and above all China; not to mention probable reductions of employment in sectors where substantial productivity gains will be needed. Regional variations are still very significant with foreign investment heavily polarised on Bucharest and the western regions. There must surely be more effort – partly through the investment in the Eurocorridors – to ensure that the sort of entrepreneurship evident in Banat (where thousands of Italians are running successful small businesses in clothing and footwear) can be spatially extended eastwards by the next generation of Romanian businessmen. While Romania is now considered a developed country, according to UNCTAD 'World Investment Report' – despite GDP pc only 40 per cent of the EU average – it is still possible for Oltenia and Moldavia to be regarded as relatively unknown areas of the country (in terms of foreign investment) where few two halls have the expertise to negotiate in such matters.

Bibliography

Agenţia Naţională pentru Dezvoltare Regională (ANDR) 2000a, Planul national de dezvoltare 2000-2002 (Bucharest: ANDR).

Agenţia Naţională pentru Dezvoltare Regională 2000b, Dezvoltarea pentru aderare (Bucharest: ANDR).

Allen, J. 1996, 'The experience of the ROM-UN Centre in Romania': J.Levitski ed., Small business in transition economies: promoting enterprise in Central and Eastern Europe and the Former Soviet Union (London: Intermediate Technology Publishers) 123-34.

Anon 1998, 'Romania's nuclear programme should continue', Romanian Business Journal 5(51-52), 8-9.

Bacon, W. 2004, 'Economic reform': H.F.Carey ed., Romania since 1989: politics economics and society (Lanham, Md.: Lexington Books) 373-90.

Bălănescu, S., V.Achim & A.Ciolte 2002, Istoria conducerii mineritului a metalurgiei neferoase şi preţioase din nord-vestul României: organizare coordonare coordonare dezvoltare (Baia Mare: Editura Gutinul).

Bălteanu, D. & M.Şerban 2006, 'Umweltsituation': T.Kahl, M.Metzeltin & M. R.Ungureanu eds., Rumänien (Vienna: Lit Verlag) 131-50.

Beck, S. 1991a, 'What brought Romanians to revolt?' Critique of Anthropology 11(1), 59-71.

Beck, S. 1991b, 'Toward a civil society: the struggle over University Square in Bucharest, Romania: June 1990', Socialism & Democracy 13, 135-54.

Beck, S. 1993, 'The struggle for space and the development of civil society in Romania: June 1990' H.G. de Soto & D.G. Anderson eds., The curtain rises: rethinking culture ideology and the state in Eastern Europe (Atlantic Highlands, New Jersey: Humanities Press) 232-65.

Benedek, J. 2006, 'Raumplanung und Regionalentwicklung': T.Kahl, M.Metzeltin & M-R.Ungureanu eds., Rumänien (Vienna: Lit Verlag) 105-30.

Ben-Ner, A. & J.M.Montias 1994, 'Economic systems reforms and privatization in Romania': S. Estrin ed., Privatization in Central & Eastern Europe (London: Longman) 279-310.

Berberoglu, B. 2003, 'Transnational capital and the impact of privatisation and market-oriented reforms on East European agriculture: focus on Romania in transition 1989-2000', International Review of Sociology 13, 273-303.

Berry, D. 2004, The Romanian mass media and cultural development (Aldershot: Ashgate).

Blujdea, V., I.V.Abrudan & C.Pahontu 2003, 'Scenariul de acumulare a stocului de carbon in cadrul unui proiect de impadurire a terenurilor degradate in Romania', Revista Pădurilor 118(2), 1-4.

Bohateret, V. 1997, 'The forming of the organized land market: case study - county of Iasi': D.Gavrilescu ed., Agricultural restructuring and rural transition in Romania (Bucharest: Agro International) 97-107.

Boia, L. 2001, Romania: borderland of Europe (London: Reaktion).

Borcoş, A. & A.Vîrdol 2002, 'Aspecte metodologice privind ierarhizarea zonelor miniere defavorizate din România', Revista Geografică 7, 178-83.

Braghină, C. & L.Dumitrache 1997, 'Changes in the socio-professional structure of Romania's population in the transition period': D. Light & D. Dumbraveanu-Andone eds., Anglo-Romanian geographies: proceedings of the second Liverpool-Bucharest Geography Colloquium (Liverpool: Liverpool Hope Press) 77-88.

Brewer, P.A., M.G.Macklin, D.Bălteanu et al. 2002, 'Sediment and water quality in Maramureş county following the January and March 2000 tailings dam failures', Proceedings of the Romanian Academy: B Chemistry Life Sciences & Geosciences 4(1), 41-8.

Brewer, P.A., M.G.Macklin, D.Bălteanu et al. 2003, 'The tailings dam failures in Maramureş county and their transboundary impacts on the river systems': W. Leal Filho & I.Butorina eds., Approaches to handling environmental problems in the mining and metallurgical regions (Dordrecht: Kluwer) 73-83.

Bush, L.S. 2004, 'Trade unions and labor relations': H.F.Carey ed., Romania since 1989: politics economics and society (Lanham, Md.: Lexington Books) 419-38.

Carey, H.F. 2004, 'Conclusion: ambiguous democratization?': H.F.Carey ed., Romania since 1989: politics economics and society (Lanham, Md.: Lexington Books) 553-618.

Carey, H.F. & C.Eisterhold 2004, 'Introduction': H.F.Carey ed., Romania since 1989: politics economics and society (Lanham, Md.: Lexington Books) 1-26.

Cartwright, A. 2000, 'State law and the recognition of property in rural Romania', Max Planck Institute for Social Anthropology Working Paper 10.

Celac, S. 1998, 'Romania: a pivotal country along the Europe to Asia business route': G. Erdeli & D. Dumbrăveanu eds., Romanian-British Geographical Exchanges: Proceedings of the Third Romanian-British Colloquium (Bucharest: Corint) 13-18.

Chaves, R.A., S.Sanchez, S.Schor et al. 2001, Financial markets credit constraints and investment in rural Romania (Washington DC: World Bank).

Chirca, C. & E.D.Teşliuc 1999, From rural poverty to rural development (Bucharest: World Bank).

Cioacă, A. & M.Dinu 1998, 'Restructuring lignite mining in Romania and its environmental effects', Revue Roumaine de Géografie 42, 135-48.

Ciupagea, C. 2002a, 'Romania' and 'Economic functions of informal activities in Romania': R.Neef & M.Stănculescu eds., The social impact of informal economies in Eastern Europe (Aldershot: Ashgate) 113-18; 188-212.

Ciupagea, C. 2002b, 'Romania': R.Neef & M.Stanculescu eds., The social economy of informal economies in Eastern Europe (Aldershot: Ashgate) 113-19.

Coleman, D.Y. 2004, Romania: 2004 country review (Houston Tcountry Watch).

Comisia Naţională pentru Prevenirea şi Combaterea Sărăciei/Programul Naţiunilor Unite pentru Dezvoltare 1998, Proiectul de Prevenirie şi Combatere a Sărăciei: strategia naţională - recomandări şi soluţii alternative (Bucharest: CNPCS)

Constantin, D-L., V.Vasile, D.Preda & C.Nicolescu 2004, 'Migration phenomenon from the perspective of Romania's accession to the EU', Romanian Journal of European Affairs 4(4), 15-35.

Crăciun, O. 1997, 'Modernizarea reţelei de telecomunicaţii a SNCFR', Revista CFR 84(4), 3-10.

Craiutu, A. 1999, 'Light at the end of the tunnel: Romania 1989-1998':G.Pridham ed., Experimenting with democracy: regional change in the Balkans (London: Routledge) 169-94.

Craiutu, A. 2004, 'Romania: the difficult apprenticeship of liberty 1989-2004', Woodrow Wilson International Center for Scholars: EES News, September-October 5-9.

Creţan, R., L.Guran-Nica, D.Platon & D.Turnock 2005, 'Foreign direct investment and social risk in Romania: progress in less-favoured areas': D.Turnock ed., Foreign direct investment and regional development in East Central Europe and the Former Soviet Union (Aldershot: Ashgate) 305-48.

Croucher, R. 1998, Economic development and trade unions in a transitional context: the Romanian case (London: Pluto Press, Labour & Society International Discussion Paper).

Dăianu, D. 1994, 'The changing mix of disequilibria during transition: a Romanian background', IMF Working Paper 94/73.

Dăianu, D. 2001, 'Balkan reconstruction: Romania', South East European & Black Sea Studies 1, 203-18.

Dăianu, D. 2002, 'Romania and the European Union': T.Straubhaar, F-P.Vadean & A.G.W von Czege eds., Romania on the path to the EU: labour markets migration and minorities (Hamburg: Europa-Kolleg Hamburg, Institute for Integration Research Discussion Paper 1/2002) 93-108.

Dăianu, D. 2004, 'Fiscal and monetary policies': H.F.Carey ed., Romania since 1989: politics economics and society (Lanham, Md.: Lexington Books)

391–418.

Dăianu, D., L.Albu, L.Croitoru, C.Tarhoacă & C.Ivan-Ungureanu 2001, The underground economy in Romania (Bucharest: Cerope).

Dăianu, D., L.Voinea, B.Pauna et al. 2001b, Winners or losers in the process of European integration: a look at Romania (Bucharest: Romanian Centre for Economic Policy).

Davidova, S. & K.J.Thompson 2003, Romanian agriculture and transition to the EU (Lanham, Md.: Lexington Books).

Davis, J.R. & A.Gaburci 1999, 'Rural finance and private farming in Romania', Europe-Asia Studies 51, 843-69.

Denekas, D.G. & M.S.Khan 1991, The Romanian economic reform program (Washington DC: IMF Occasional Paper 89).

Dinescu, A. 1995, 'Parametrii de performanţă ce se impun în transporturi combinat european', Revista CFR 82(4), 38-9.

Dincescu, V. 1996, 'Dezvoltarea reţelei de mare viteza în zona europenă de sud-est: lucrările grupei UIC', Revista CFR 83(3-4), 9-11.

Dinu, D. 1996, 'Strategia dezvoltării materialului rulant motor şi remorcat de mare viteză la SNCFR', Revista CFR 83(3-4), 7-9.

Dinu, D. 1997, 'Modificări ale mediului produse sub influenţa acrtivităţilor umane: câteva cazuri de Subcarpaţii Vâlcii', Analele Universităţii din Timişoara: Geografie 7, 129-38.

Dobrescu, E. 2000, Macromodels of the Romanian transition economy (Bucharest: Editura Expert).

Dragomirescu, S. & S.Dragomirescu 1993, 'Hydro-Electricity in the Romanian Carpathians', GeoJournal 29, 31-40.

Dumbrăveanu-Andone, D. & L.Dumitrache 1997, 'Romania: a gateway to Europe': D.Light & D.Dumbraveanu-Andone eds., Anglo-Romanian geographies: proceedings of the second Liverpool-Bucharest Geography Colloquium (Liverpool: Liverpool Hope Press) 89-98.

Dumitrache, L. & I.Armas 1998, 'The health state of the Romanian population during the transition period', GeoJournal 44, 151-60.

Dumitrache, L. & I.Armas 2000, 'Health and health care in post-communist Romania': D.Light & D.Phinnemore eds., Post-communist Romania: geographical perspectives (Liverpool: Liverpool Hope Press) 75-88.

Dumitru, M., D.Diminescu & V.Lazea 2004, Dezvoltarea rurală şi reforma agriculturii româneşti (Bucharest: Centrul Român de Politici Economic).

Duran, R. 2000, 'Romanian state-society relations: better understanding democratization?' Slovo: An International Journal of Russian Eurasian Central & East European Affairs Special Issue 1-30.

Estrin, S., M.Dimitrov & X.Richet 1998, 'State enterprise restructuring in Bulgaria, Albania and Romania', Economic Analysis 1, 239-55.

Eurostat 2004, Regions: Statistical Yearbook 2004 (Luxembourg: Office of the

Official Publications of the European Communities).

Eyal, J. 1993, 'Romania': S.Whitefield ed., The new institutional architecture of Eastern Europe (New York: St.Martin's Press) 121-42.

Featherstone, K. & G. Kazamias 2001, Europeanization and the southern periphery (London: Frank Cass).

Floricel, G. 1994, 'Lina de feribot Constanţa-Samsun: o linie de transport bimodal asteapta de 50 de ani', Revista CFR 81(3), 31-4.

Freyberg-Inan, A. 2002, 'Which way to progress?: impact of international organizations in Romania': R.H.Linden ed., Norms and nannies: the impact of international organizations on the Central and East European states (Oxford: Rowman & Littlefield) 129-64.

Gabanyi, A.U. 2004, 'The new business élite: from nomenklatura to oligarchy': H.F.Carey ed., Romania since 1989: politics economics and society (Lanham, Md.: Lexington Books) 353-72.

Gallagher, T. 1995, Romania after Ceauşescu: the politics of intolerance (Edinburgh: Edinburgh University Press).

Gallagher, T. 2005, Theft of a nation: Romania since communism (London: Hurst).

Gallager, T. & K.Hudson 1996, 'Romania after Ceauşescu', Europe-Asia Studies 48, 668-91.

Gardó, S. 2006, 'Rumänien:Wirtschaft in Transformation': T.Kahl, M.Metzeltin & M-R.Ungureanu eds., Rumänien (Vienna: Lit Verlag) 655-92.Gatti, R. 2003, Poverty and growth in Romania 1995-2002 (Bucharest: World Bank).

Gavrilescu, D. 1994, 'Agricultural reform in Romania: between market priority and the strategies for food security': J.F.M.Swinnen ed., Policy and institutional reform in Central Europe (Aldershot: Avebury) 169-209.

Gherănescu, N. 1996, 'The integrated advisory service for private business in Romania': J.Levitski ed., Small business in transition economies: promoting enterprise in Central and Eastern Europe and the Former Soviet Union (London: Intermediate Technology Publishers) 135-44.

Gilberg, T. 1990, Nationalism and communism in Romania: the rise and fall of Ceauşescu's personal dictatorship (Boulder, Col.: Westview).

Government of Romania Ministry of Agriculture 1999, Rural development in Romania (Bucharest: EU Phare).

Green, J. 1998, Energy and the environment in the EU: training documents for NGOs in accession countries (Brussels: Friends of the Earth Europe).

Grigoraş, V. 2001, 'Strategii de mobilitate în Sâncrai-Hunedoara', Sociologie Românească 3, 232-9.

Gross, P. 2004, 'Media in the first post-communist decade': H.F.Carey ed., Romania since 1989: politics, economics and society (Lanham, Md.: Lexington Books) 195-214.

Groza, O. 1991-2, 'Paşcani – oraş industrial: trei ani de tranziţie consideraţii de geografie umană', Lucrările Seminarului Dimitrie Cantemir 11-12, 189-204.

Groza, O. 1994, 'Paşcani – ville industrielle en Roumanie: années de transition'. L'Espace Géographique 23, 329-41.

Groza, O. & I.Muntele 1998, 'L'efficacité du reseau ferroviaire et l'accessibilité teritoriale en Roumanie', Revue Roumaine de Géographie 42, 15-28.

Guran-Nica, L. 2002, Investiţii străine directe: dezvoltarea sistemului de asezări din România (Bucharest: Editura Tehnica).

Guvernul Romaniei 2000, SAPARD: planul de dezvoltare rurală al României - evaluare ex-ante (Bucharest: Guvernul României).

Hall, R.A. 2004, 'Political culture in post-Ceauşescu Romania': H.F.Carey ed., Romania since 1989: politics, economics and society (Lanham, Md.: Lexington Books) 215-25.

Hare, P. & J.R.Davis 1997, 'Reforming the systems of rural finance provision in Romania: some options for privatisation and change', Quarterly Journal of International Agriculture 36, 213-35.

Heidhues, F., J.R.Davis & G.Schrieder 1998, 'Agricultural transformation and implications for designing financial policies in Romania', European Review of Agricultural Economics 25, 351-72.

Heidhues, F. & G.Schrieder eds. 2000, Romania: rural finance in transition economies (Frankfurt: Peter Lang).

Heller, W. 1997, Migration und sozioökonomische Transformation in Südosturopa (Munich: Südosteuropa-Studien 59).

Heller, W. 2002, 'Spatial development of the economy amd spatial mobility in post-socialist Romania': T.Straubhaar, F-P.Vadean & A.G.W von Czege eds., Romania on the path to the EU: labour markets migration and minorities (Hamburg: Europa-Kolleg Hamburg, Institute for Integration Research Discussion Paper 1/2002) 45-64.

Heller, W. 2006, 'Demographie Migration und räumliche Entwicklung': T.Kahl, M.Metzeltin & M-R.Ungureanu eds., Rumänien (Vienna: Lit Verlag) 39-62.

Heller, W. & I.Ianoş 2004, 'Spatial patterns of economy and migration in post-socialist Romania', Europa Regional 12(1), 4-12.

Hillinger, N. & D.Turnock 2001, The historical geography and post-communist restructuring of the Reşiţa Industrial Complex (Leicester: University of Leicester Department of Geography Occasional Paper 42).

Hillinger, N., M.Olaru & D.Turnock 2001, 'The role of industrial archaeology in conservation: the Reşiţa area in the Romanian Carpathians', GeoJournal 55, 607-30.

Hirschhausen, B. von 1998, 'The collapse of 'navetismul' and the redefinition of town-country relations in Romania: the example of Arad county': W. Heller ed. 1998, Romania: migration socio-economic transformation and perspectives of regional development (Munchen: Sudosteuropa-Gesellschaft, Sudosteuropa Studien 62) 257-70.

Hoffman, O. 1992, 'Problemele protecţiei sociale în procesul tranziţiei în România', Sociologie Românească 3(3), 263-72.

Holban, H. 1991, 'Pagini din istoria industriei româneşti: Uzinele Malaxa', Magazin Istoric 25(5), 33-6; (6), 85-8; (7), 38-41.

Hutanu, L. 1997, 'Extinderea spre est a reţelei trans-Europene de mare viteză şi preocupările SNCFR', Revista CFR 84(2), 3-9.

Iacob, G. 1994, 'Regiunea metalurgică Baia Mare: continuitate diversitate şi implicare în mediul inconjurător': P.Urdea ed., The First Regional Geography Conference: geographical researches in the Carpathian-Danube space (Timisoara: Universitatea de Vest din Timisoara, Deparamentul de Geografie) 269-74.

Iacob, G. 1995, 'Activităţile minieră din estul Munţilor Maramureşului şi implicaţiile acestora asupra mediului', Studii si Cercetări: Geografie 42, 73-9.

Iacob, I. 2001, 'Infrastructures and integration', Romanian Business Journal 7(10), 12-3.

Iancu, A. 2000, 'Some problems of the strategy for development and integration into the EU', Romanian Business Journal 7(9), 6.

Ianoş, I. 1994a, 'The Romanian village advances towards a new state of equilibrium': D.Turnock ed., Rural change in Romania (Leicester: University of Leicester Department of Geography Occasional Paper 33) 12-8.

Ianoş, I. 1994b, 'On the "central place" functions of rural settlements in Romania', Revue Roumaine de Géographie 38, 49-57.

Ianoş, I. 1996, 'The changing Romanian village: the case of Semlac in Arad County, Romania', GeoJournal 38, 175-9.

Ianoş, I. 2000, 'Potenţiel economiei al teritoriului şi dezvoltarea sectorului autreprenorial în România', Terra 30(2), 64-70.

Ianoş, I. 2001, 'Economic transition and urban industrial employment in post-communist Romania': D. Light & D.Phinnemore eds., Post-communist Romania: coming to terms with transition (Basingstoke: Palgrave) 191-206.

Ianoş, I. L.Dobraca 1995, 'Housing resources in Romania's towns: geographical disparities', Revue Roumaine de Géographie 39, 13-20.

Ianoş, I. & L.Nica-Guran 1997, 'Geographical considerations on recent international migration in Romania': W. Heller ed., Migration und sozio-ökonomische Transformation in Sudosturopa (Munich: Sudosteuropa Gesellschaft) 185-92.

Ianoş, I. & C.Tălângă 1994, Oraşul şi sistem urban românesc în condiţiile economiei de piaţă (Bucharest: Institutul de Geografie).

Ielenicz, M. 1998, 'Salt massifs and their touristical usage': G.Erdeli &

D.Dumbrăveanu eds., Romanian-British geographical exchanges: proceedings of the Third Romanian-British Colloquium (Bucharest: Corint) 89-93.

Ilie, S. 2002, 'Formal and informal incomes of Romanian households': R.Neef & M.Stănculescu eds., The social impact of informal economies in Eastern Europe (Aldershot: Ashgate) 169-87.

Ingham, H. & M.Ingham 2002, EU expansion to the East (Cheltenham: Edward Elgar).

Institutul pentru Ştiinţe şi Reforma Socială Program PNUD Economic empowerment of rural women in Romania 1998, Raport privind evaluarea comunităţilor rurale din Judeţul Buzău (Bucharest: ISRS).

Ionete, C. & V. Dinculescu eds. 2000, National human development report: Romania 1999 (Bucharest: Romanian Academy for the United Nations Development Project).

Ion-Tudor, C. 1996, 'Rural development: a step towards prosperity', Romanian Business Journal 3(21), 6.

Iordache, G. 1990, 'Le rôle des communautés villageoises dans la vie spirituelle des Roumains': P.H.Stahl ed., Études Roumains et Aroumaines (Paris: P.H.Stahl) 69-73.

Iordache, C. & B.Trencsenyi 2003, 'The question of national identity in Romanian studies 1990-2000', East European Politics & Societies 17, 415-53.

Ipatiov, F. 1996, 'Influenţa poluarii industriale asupra starii de sanitate populaţiei în oraşul Baia Mare', Studia Universitatis Babes-Bolyai: Seria Geographia 41, 175-82.

Isărescu, M. 1992, 'The prognoses for economic recovery': D.N.Nelson ed., Romania after tyranny (Boulder, Col: Westview) 149-66.

Istratescu, C., A.Sereny & G.Parnuta 2001, 'Forest products annual market review 2000-2001: Romania's forest products markets', FAO Timber Bulletin 54(3), 21-32.

Jackson, M.R. 1995, 'Political incredibility and bureaucratic transition in Romania': J.P.Hardt & R.F.Kaufman eds., East Central European countries in transition (Armonk, N.Y.: M.E.Sharpe) 552-78.

Jackson, M.R. 1997, 'Political economy of agricultural reform in Romania': J.F.M.Swinnen ed., Political economy of agrarian reform in Central & Eastern Europe (Aldershot: Ashgate) 283-320.

Jolly, A. & N.Kettanek eds. 1999, Doing business in Romania (London: Kogan Page).

Kideckel, D.A. 1992, 'Peasants and authority in the new Romania': D.N.Nelson ed., Romania after tyranny (Boulder, Col.: Westview) 67-81.

Kideckel, D.A. 1993, 'Once again the land: decollectivization and social conflict in rural Romania': H.G. de Soto & D.G. Anderson eds., The curtain rises: rethinking culture ideology and the state in Eastern Europe (Atlantic Highlands, New Jersey: Humanities Press) 62-75.

Kideckel, D.A. 2002, 'The unmaking of an ECE working class': C.M.Hann ed., Post-socialism: ideals ideologies and practices in Eurasia (London: Routledge) 114-32.

Kideckel, D.A. 2004, 'Minders and wives in Romania's Jiu Valley: perspectives on post-socialist class gender and social change', Identities: Global Studies in Culture and Power 11, 39-63.

Kideckel, D.A., B.E.Botea, R.Nahorniac & V.Soflan 2000, 'A new "cult of labor": stress and crisis among Romanian workers', Sociologie Românească 2(1), 142-61.

King, C. 2003, 'The European question in Romania and Moldova': A.Lieven & D.Trenin eds., Ambivalent neighbours: the EU NATO and the price of membership (Washington, DC: Carnegie Endowment for International Peace) 269-94.

Kligman, G. 1990, 'Reclaiming the public: a reflection on creating civil society in Romania', East European Politics & Societies 4, 393-438.

Kramer, J.M. 1999, 'Energy and environment in Eastern Europe', Problems of Post-Communism 46(6), 213-38.

Light, D. & D.Andone 1996, 'The changing geography of Romanian tourism', Geography 81, 193-203.

Light, D. & D.Dumbrăveanu-Andone 1997, 'Heritage and national identity: exploring the relationship in Romania', International Journal of Heritage Studies 3(1), 28-44.

Light, D. & D.Dumbrăveanu 1999, 'Romanian tourism in the post-communist period', Annals of Tourism Research 26, 898-927.

Lup, A. 1997, Irigaţiile în agricultura României (Bucharest: Editura Agris).

Luxmoore, J. 1997, 'A review of religious life in Albania, Bulgaria, Romania, Hungary, Slovakia, Czech Republic and Poland', Religion States & Society 25(1), 89-101.

Macklin, M.G., P.A.Brewer, D.Bălteanu et al. 2003, 'The long term fate and environmental significance of contaminant metals released by the January and March 2000 mining tailings dam failure in Maramureş county', Applied Geochemistry 18, 241-57.

Manoleli, D.G., V.Câmpeanu, D.Giurca & L. Chivu 2004, Pre-accession impact study: setting the development priorities for Romanian agriculture and the rural sector: the impact of the new Common Agricultural Policy reform (Bucharest: European Institute of Romania).

Marga, A. 1993, 'Cultural and political trends in Romania before and after 1989', East European Politics & Societies 7, 14-32.

Matei, E. 2003, 'Consideraţii asupra stresul peceput de populaţia din Municipiul Bucureşti', Comunicări de Geografie 7, 239-42.

Mete, C. 2003, Labour force participation: unemployment and the poor (Bucharest: World Bank).

Mete, C., N.Burnett, E.Teşliuc et al. 2003, Romania: poverty assessment (Bucharest: World Bank Report 26169-RO).

Meurs, M. 1996, 'The persistence of collectivism: responses to land restitution in Romania': D.R.Hall & D.Danta eds., Reconstructing the Balkans: a geography of the new Southeast Europe (Chichester: Wiley) 169-77.

Miroiu, M. & L.Popescu 2004, 'Post-totalitarian pre-feminism': H.F.Carey ed., Romania since 1989: politics economics and society (Lanham, Md.: Lexington Books) 297-314.

Mocanu, D. & N.Mares 2005, 'The Romanian labour market: towards a European labour market?' South East European Review of Labour & Social Affairs 8(1), 123-36.

Mocanu, H. 1998, 'Leasing units 3-5 of Cernavodă: a possible financing solution of Unit 2', Romanian Buisness Journal 5(10), 6.

Muică, N., D.Turnock & V.Urucu 2000, 'Coping strategies in rural areas of the Buzău Subcarpathians', GeoJournal 50, 157-72.

Mungiu, A. 1996, 'Intellectuals as political actors in Eastern Europe: the Romanian case', East European Politics and Societies 10, 333-64.

Nica-Guran, L. 1998, 'Daewoo Automobile Romania: economic geographical impact of a big foreign investment in Romania', Revue Roumaine de Géographie 42, 149-59.

Niculescu, N.G. & D.Adumitracesei 2001, Romania on the way to European integration (Bucharest: Editura Economica).

Otiman, P.L. 1997, Dezvoltarea rurală în Romania (Timişoara: Editura Agroprint).

Pais, A. 1997, 'Tourism: an industry that might be very profitable for Romanians', Romanian Business Journal 4(6), 16.

Pălăseanu, M. 2000, Studies of heavy metal contamination in soils from Baia Mare city (Tampa, Florida: University of South Florida, Department of Environmental Science & Policy, Master's Thesis).

Papadimitriou, D. 2002, Negotiating the New Europe: the European Union and Eastern Europe (Aldershot: Ashgate).

Papuc, M. 2004, 'Reshaping the Romanian consumers' behavior through EU regional social and cohesion policy', Romanian Journal of Economic Affairs 4(3) 49-56.

Parnuta, E. & I.Machedon 2000, 'Forest and environmental legislation in Romania', Anon ed., Challenges in implementing forest and environmental legislation in European countries with economies in transition (Zurich: ETH) 69-77.

Pavel, S. 2001, 'Nivelul de trai în România: o abordare conceptuală', Geographica Timisiensis 10, 95-100.

Phillips, D. 1998, 'Health environment and development: issues in developing and transitional countries', GeoJournal 44, 97-102.

Plop, L. 1999, 'Marketing and promotion in Romanian tourism', Romanian Business Journal 6(39), 12-3.

Pop-Eleches, G. 1999, 'Separated at birth or separated by birth?: the communist successor parties in Romania and Hungary', East European Politics & Societies 13, 117-47.

Popa-Bota, H. & I.Uiga 1999, 'The migratory movement of the population from Maramureş Depression': V.Surd ed., Rural space and regional development (Cluj-Napoca: Editura Studia) 266-72.

Popescu, C.R. 1993, 'Geographical considerations on the Romanian industrial small and medium-sized industries', Revue Roumaine de Géographie 37, 13–21.

Popescu, C.R. 1995, 'Industria rurală: caracteristici şi perspective', Geographica Timisensis 4, 159-65.

Popescu, C.R. 2000, Industria României în secolul XX: analiza geografică (Bucharest: Editura Oscar Print).

Popescu, C.R. 2006, 'Spatial structures of the Romanian economy': T.Kahl, M.Metzeltin & M-R.Ungureanu eds., Rumänien (Vienna: Lit Verlag) 89-104.

Popoiu, P., G.Stoica & D.Işfănoni eds. 2004, Roşia Montan: studiu etnologic (Bucharest: DAIM Seria Anthropos Alburnus Maior).

Popescu, C.R., S.Negut, I.Roznovietchi et al. 2003, Zonele miniere defavorizate din România: abordare geografică (Bucharest: Editura ASE).

Popov, S. & S.Lubieniechi 2001, Opportunities and constraints for rural development in Romania (Aberdeen: Scottish Agricultural College).

Pralong, S. 2004, 'NGOs and the development of civil society': H.F.Carey ed., Romania since 1989: politics economics and society (Lanham, Md.: Lexington Books) 229-46.

Ramboll Group 1966, Regional disparities in Romania 1990-1994 (Bucharest: Ramboll Consultancy Group).

Ramboll Consultancy Group 1997, Profiles of the Romanian development regions (Bucharest: RCG for Phare Programme, Regional Development Policy).

Ramet, S.P. 2004, 'Church and state in Romania before and after 1989': H.F.Carey ed., Romania since 1989: politics economics and society (Lanham, Md.: Lexington Books) 275-95.

Râmniceanu, I. 2004, Probleme structurale de agriculturii româneşti în perspectiva aderarii la UE (Bucharest: Institutul European din România).

Roper, S.D. 1998, 'From opposition to government coalition: unity and fragmentation within the Democratic Convention of Romania', East European Quarterly 31, 519-42.

Roper, S.D. 2004, 'Parliamentary development': H.F.Carey ed., Romania since 1989: politics, economics and society (Lanham, Md.: Lexington Books) 159-77.

Rusu, B. 2001, 'Small- and medium-sized enterprises and total quality management: experiences in post-communist Romania': D.Light & D.Phinnemore eds., Post-communist Romania: coming to terms with transition (Basingstoke: Palgrave) 224-42.

Sandu, D. 1999, 'Dezvoltarea şi sărăcie în satele României', Sociologie Românească 10, 117-38.

Sandu, D., M.Stănculescu & M.Şerban 2000, Social assessment for rural development projects: social needs and actions in Romanian villages (Bucharest: World Bank).

Sarris, A.H. & D.Gavrilescu 1997, 'Restructuring of farms and agricultural systems in Romania': J.F.M. Swinnen, A.Buckwell & E.Mathijs eds., Agricultural privatization, land reform and farm restructuring in Central & Eastern Europe (Aldershot: Ashgate) 217-26.

Sauleanu, D. & D.Parlea 1997, 'Restructurarea în industrie mineră: disponibiliizarea forţei de munca în bazinul carbonifer al Vaii Jiului', Revista Romană de Sociologie 8, 505-18.

Schrieder, G.R., J.Münz & R.Jehle 2000, 'Rural regional development in transition economies: the case of Romania' Europe-Asia Studies 52, 1213-35.

Sellin, F. 2004, 'Democratization in the shadows: post-communist patrimonialism': H.F.Carey ed., Romania since 1989: politics economics and society (Lanham, Md.: Lexington Books) 117-36.

Shafir, M. 2001, 'The Greater Romania Party and the 2000 elections in Romania: how obvious is the obvious?' Romanian Journal of Society & Politics 1(2), 91-126.

Shen, R. 1997, The restructuring of Romania's economy: a paradigm of flexibility and adaptability (Westport, Conn.: Praeger).

Siani-Davis, P. 2005, The Romanian revolution of December 1989 (Ithaca, N.Y.: Cornell University Press).

Smith, A. 1996, 'Problems of the transition to a market economy in Romania Bulgaria and Albania: why has the transition proved to be so difficult?' I.Jeffries ed., Problems of economic and political transformation in the Balkans (London: Pinter) 111-30.

Snyder, T. & M. Vachudova 1997, 'Are transitions transitory: the types of political change in Eastern Europe since 1989', East European Politics & Societies 10, 1-35.

Spiridion, M. 2005, 'Rural development and agricultural policy in the context of negotiating the European acquis', Romanian Journal of European Affairs 5(1), 93-111.

Stan, L. 1997, 'Romanian privatization program catches up with the east': L.Stan ed., Romania in transition (Aldershot: Dartmouth) 127-62.

Stewart, M. 1997, '"We should build a statue to Ceauşescu here": the trauma of decollectivisation in two Romanian villages': S. Bridger & F. Pine eds., Surviving post-socialism: local strategies and regional responses in Eastern Europe & the Former Soviet Union (London: Routledge) 66-79.

Stocchiero, A. 2002, 'Migration flows and SME internationalisation between Romania and the Italian Veneto Region': T.Straubhaar, F-P.Vadean & A.G.W. von Czege eds., Romania on the path to the EU: labour markets migration and minorities (Hamburg: Europa-Kolleg Hamburg, Institute for Integration Research Discussion Paper 1/2002) 33-43.

Stoica, C.A. 2004, 'From good communists to even better capitalists?: entrepreneurial pathways in post-socialist Romania', East European Politics & Societies 18, 236-77.

Teşliuc, C., L.Pop & F.Panduru 2003, Poverty in Romania: profile and trends during 1995-2002 (Bucharest: World Bank).

Tismaneanu, V. 1993, 'The quasi revolution and discontents: emerging political pluralism in post-Ceauşescu Romania', East European Politics & Societies 7, 30948.

Tismaneanu, V. 1997, 'Romanian exceptionalism?: democracy ethnocracy and uncertain pluralism in post-Ceauşescu Romania': K.Dawisha & B.Parrott eds., Politics power and the struggle for democracy in South East Europe (Cambridge: Cambridge University Press) 403-51.

Tismaneanu, V. & D. Pavel 1994, 'Romania's mystical revolutionaries: the generation of Angst and adventure revisited', East European Politics & Societies 8, 402-38.

Toma, C. 1997, 'The conversion of the peasant's farm into a competition farm: a case study (Ţigăneşti, Teleorman)': D. Gavrilescu ed., Agricultural restructuring and rural transition in Romania (Bucharest: Agro International) 72-95.

Turnock, D. 2001, 'Regional inequalities and regional development in post-communist Romania': D.Light & D.Phinnemore eds., Post-communist Romania: coming to terms with transition (Basingstoke: Palgrave) 150-74.

Turnock, D. 2002, 'Romania: contemporary geopolitical perspectives': A.H.Dawson & R.Fawn eds., The changing geopolitics of Eastern Europe (London: Frank Cass) 119-40.

Turnock, D. 2003, 'Romania's railways under transition: reorganisation rehabilitation and regional development' Promet Traffic-Traffico: Scientific Technical Journal for Traffic Theory & Practice 15(4), 241-69.

Turnock, D. 2007, Aspects of independent Romania's economic history with particular reference to transition for EU accession (Aldershot: Ashgate).

United Nations Development Programme 1998, Poverty in transition (New

York: UNDP).

Van Frasum, Y.G., U.Gehmann & J.Gross 1994, 'Market economy and economic reform in Romania: macroeconomic and microeconomic perspectives', Europe-Asia Studies 46, 735-56.

Van Der Ploeg, J. & S.De Rooij 2000, 'Agriculture in Central & Eastern Europe: industrialization or repeasantization?': D.Brown & A.Bandlerova eds., Rural development in Central & Eastern Europe (Nitra: Slovak Agricultural University) 45-53.

Vasi, B. 2004, 'The first of the working class: the social movements of the Jiu Valley miners in post-socialist Romania', East European Politics & Societies 18(1), 132-57.

Verdery, K. 1994, 'The elasticity of land: problems of property restitution in Romania', Slavic Review 53, 1071-1109.

Verdery, K. 1998, 'Property and power in Transylvania's decollectivisation': C.M.Hann ed., Property relations: renewing the anthropological tradition (Cambridge: Cambridge University Press) 160-80.

Verdery, K. 2002, 'Seeing like a mayor or how officials obstructed Romanian land restitution', Ethnography 3, 5-33.

Vincze, M. 1999, 'The rural employment as a factor of the rural development in Romania': V. Surd ed., Rural space and regional development (Cluj-Napoca: Editura Studia) 1899-6.

Weiner, R. 2001, 'Romania the IMF and economic reform since 1996', Problems of Post-Communism 48(1), 39-47.

Young, S. 2001, Romanian regional economic development 1945-1995 (Nottingham: Nottingham Trent University Ph.D. thesis).

Zinnes, C.F. 2004, 'The environment in transition': H.F.Carey ed., Romania since 1989: politics economics and society (Lanham, Md.: Lexington Books) 439-57.

Index